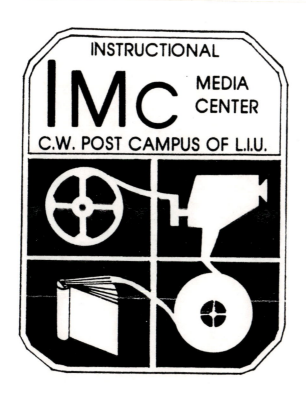

SECOND EDITION

EFFECTIVE TEACHING IN ELEMENTARY SOCIAL STUDIES

Tom V. Savage
California State University, Fullerton

David G. Armstrong
Texas A & M University

Macmillan Publishing Company
New York

Maxwell Macmillan Canada
Toronto

Maxwell Macmillan International
New York Oxford Singapore Sydney

Cover Illustration: Mark McDevitt
Editor: Robert Miller
Production Editor: Stephen C. Robb
Art Coordinator: Peter A. Robison
Cover Designer: Robert Vega
Production Buyer: Patricia A. Tonneman

This book was set in Caledonia by Carlisle Communications, Ltd. and was printed and bound by R. R. Donnelley & Sons Company. The cover was printed by Lehigh Press, Inc.

Macmillan Publishing Company
866 Third Avenue
New York, NY 10022

Macmillan Publishing Company is part of the
Maxwell Communications Group of Companies.

Maxwell Macmillan Canada, Inc.
1200 Eglinton Avenue East, Suite 200
Don Mills, Ontario M3C 3N1

Library of Congress Cataloging-in-Publication Data

Savage, Tom V.
    Effective teaching in elementary social studies / Tom V. Savage, David G. Armstrong. — 2nd ed.
        p.   cm.
    Includes bibliographical references and index.
    ISBN 0-02-406411-4
    1. Social sciences — Study and teaching (Elementary) — United States.   I. Armstrong, David G.   II. Title.
    LB1584.S34   1992
    372.83′044 — dc20   91–22396
                                                                                    CIP

Printing: 1 2 3 4 5 6 7 8 9   Year: 2 3 4 5

PHOTO CREDITS

PREFACE

The conclusion of World War II ended the bad old days and heralded an era of peace and prosperity. Then came the Cold War of the 1950s; social turmoil and the Vietnam war in the 1960s; Watergate, energy crises, and economic disarray in the 1970s; a conservative backlash, economic rebirth, festering social ills, and perception of moral decay during the 1980s. The 1990s arrived with the astounding collapse of the Soviet Union and the Eastern Bloc, the unexpected reunification of Germany, China's democracy movement crushed, war in the Persian Gulf, and still more economic uncertainty. All the while, technology bounds ahead, and we struggle to stay aware of events and their impact on us. We reel toward the third millennium knowing only one thing for certain: More surprises are in store for us.

Many adults feel they no longer understand the world. Rapidly changing realities perplex children even more. The challenge of the social studies is to help children cope with change. Making it possible for teachers to do this is a particularly great national interest. New state and national elementary social studies guidelines testify to a demand for excellence in this part of the elementary program.

New guidelines by no means assure quality social studies instruction. Difficulties for teachers remain. Among the problems are how to motivate learners, how to select content from diverse sources, how to plan and deliver effective lessons, how to deal with values issues, how to organize learners into effective kinds of instructional groups, how to address important multicultural and sex-equity issues, how to infuse new technologies into instructional programs, and how to assess what pupils have learned. This text prepares teachers for the challenges represented by these important "how to's."

Effective Teaching in Elementary Social Studies has been used success-fully in undergraduate and graduate courses. It is designed for use in ele-mentary social studies methods classes, in advanced curriculum classes, as a basis for inservice work with elementary social studies teachers, and as a personal reference work for elementary social studies teachers.

The second edition features much new content. This includes:

- up-to-date information about elementary social studies curricula
- expanded treatment that now includes grades 7 and 8 as well as grades K through 6
- a new chapter on teaching thinking skills
- material on "cooperative learning" and other important group learning techniques
- a new chapter on law-focused education
- a new chapter on global education
- updated material on the important issue of classroom management in social studies classrooms
- a new chapter on multiethnic and sex equity education
- a new chapter on environmental and energy education
- expanded material on tying general reading and writing activities to the social studies program
- more than 60 practical lessons that are ready for classroom use (For read-ers' convenience, a separate section of the table of contents pinpoints the location of each of these lessons.)

Each chapter of the second edition of *Effective Teaching in Elementary Social Studies* includes:

- *Objectives* to help focus attention on key chapter content
- *Pretests* to allow readers to engage in a self-test before reading
- *Introductions* to provide a meaningful context for the content that follows
- *Special features* including (1) "boxes" that pose questions and challenge readers to think about issues and (2) other activities and information to enrich understanding
- *Key Ideas in Summary* to pull together and reinforce important chapter content
- *Questions* to prompt recall of specific information and additional thought about issues. (Higher-order questions are included.)
- *Activities* that suggest options for follow-up work to provide for enriched understanding
- *Supplemental Reading* to identify titles of articles and books for follow-up research and inquiry
- *References* to direct readers to sources used in the preparation of the chapter

Continuing the pattern begun with the previous edition of *Effective Teaching in Elementary Social Studies*, an **Instructor's Guide** has been prepared. It has been completely revised for the second edition and includes:

- overviews of the chapter content
- alternative ideas for course sequencing
- suggested activities
- a collection of questions suitable for quizzes and tests, with accompanying keys

Content has been organized to allow for flexible use. Some people may wish to use material in the order in which it is introduced. Others may elect to follow quite a different pattern. To accommodate either approach, information in individual chapters stands alone. Users are not compelled to follow a prescribed sequence to ensure comprehension.

Four major categories have been used to suggest the general flavor of information in related chapters. The first four chapters, under the heading "Contexts for the Social Studies," set the stage. They focus on the structure of the social studies program, characteristics of learners, sources of information for lessons, and general approaches to planning.

The second category, "Fundamental Approaches to Instruction," features chapters that respond to specific types of planning. These chapters present innovative approaches for teaching concepts and generalizations, organizing pupils into productive learning groups, providing for development of thinking skills, and recognizing the roles that values play in arriving at conclusions.

The third category, "A Selection of Themes," highlights four critical kinds of social studies lessons. These are (1) law-related lessons, (2) global education lessons, (3) multiethnic and sex-equity lessons, and (4) environmental and energy lessons.

The final category, "Supporting, Managing, Assessing," provides practical information about infusing the new technologies and important map and globe skills into many kinds of social studies lessons. One chapter features practical guidelines for using social studies lessons to reinforce general reading and writing skills. Many good social studies lessons require pupils to move and talk. This raises classroom-control issues. One chapter in this section suggests ways to ensure compatibility between the demands of a good social studies lesson and the need to keep some order in the classroom. The final chapter explores alternative ways to assess what pupils have learned.

Effective Teaching in Elementary Social Studies, Second Edition is a practical book. It goes beyond telling "what" should be done. The emphasis is on "how to do it." Content builds on years of experience of successful elementary social studies teachers. Try the ideas. They work.

Let's conclude with recognition of those patient and tolerant people who assisted in the development of *Effective Teaching in Elementary Social Studies, Second Edition*. We would especially like to thank Jay A. Monson of Utah State University and C. Alan Riedesel of the State University of New York at Buffalo for their insightful reviews of the manuscript. Our wives also deserve special commendation for their assistance and tolerance while we worked on this revision.

T. V. S.
D. G. A.

CONTENTS

PART I **CONTEXTS FOR THE SOCIAL STUDIES** 1

CHAPTER 1 **AN INTRODUCTION TO THE SOCIAL STUDIES** 3

Pretest 4 / Introduction 4 / The Motivation Problem 5 / Purposes of the Social Studies 6 / Components of Citizenship Education, History and Social Science Education, and Problem-Solving Education 10 / The Social Studies Curriculum in Grades K through 8 16 / Relating Basic Social Studies Purposes to Subject Matter Covered at Each Grade Level 22 / Key Ideas in Summary 25 / Posttest 26 / Questions 26 / Extending Understanding and Skill 27 / References 28 / Supplemental Reading 28

CHAPTER 2 **THE CONTENT SOURCES: HISTORY, GEOGRAPHY, AND ECONOMICS** 29

Pretest 30 / Introduction 30 / The Structure of Knowledge 32 / History 34 / Geography 41 / Economics 48 / Key Ideas in Summary 55 / Posttest 56 / Questions 56 / Extending Understanding and Skill 57 / References 58 / Supplemental Reading 58

CHAPTER 3   **THE CONTENT SOURCES: POLITICAL SCIENCE, SOCIOLOGY, ANTHROPOLOGY, AND PSYCHOLOGY**   **59**

Pretest   60 / Introduction   60 / Political Science   60 / Sociology 66 / Anthropology   71 / Psychology   78 / Key Ideas in Summary 82 / Posttest   83 / Questions   83 / Extending Understanding and Skill   84 / References   84 / Supplemental Reading   84

CHAPTER 4   **PLANNING FOR INSTRUCTION**   **85**

Pretest   86 / Introduction   86 / Aims, Goals, and Instructional Objectives   87 / Information Needed in Making Instructional Planning Decisions   99 / Using Planning Information   102 / Unit Plans   103 / Lesson Plans   108 / Key Ideas in Summary 112 / Posttest   114 / Questions   115 / Extending Understanding and Skill   115 / References   116 / Supplemental Reading   116

PART II   **FUNDAMENTAL APPROACHES TO INSTRUCTION**   **117**

CHAPTER 5   **CONCEPTS, GENERALIZATIONS, AND INDIVIDUALIZED LEARNING**   **119**

Pretest   120 / Introduction   120 / Teaching Concepts and Generalizations   120 / Individualized Learning: Basic Features 128 / Individualized Learning: Some Instructional Approaches 130 / Key Ideas in Summary   137 / Posttest 139 / Questions   139 / Extending Understanding and Skill 140 / References   141 / Supplemental Reading   141

CHAPTER 6   **GROUP LEARNING**   **143**

Pretest   144 / Introduction   144 / Basic Group Types 146 / Preparing Pupils to Work in Groups   149 / Three Popular Group Techniques: Classroom Debate, Role Playing, and Simulation   154 / Cooperative Learning Techniques   160 / Key Ideas in Summary   164 / Posttest   165 / Questions   165 / Extending Understanding and Skill   166 / References   167 / Supplemental Reading   168

CHAPTER 7   **THINKING-SKILLS INSTRUCTION**   **169**

Pretest 170 / Introduction 170 / Teaching Children to Monitor Their Thinking 171 / Inquiry Approaches 175 / Creative Thinking 181 / Critical Thinking 182 / Problem Solving 183 / Decision Making 186 / Key Ideas in Summary 189 / Posttest 191 / Questions 191 / Extending Understanding and Skill 192 / References 192 / Supplemental Reading 193

CHAPTER 8   **DEVELOPING PROSOCIAL BEHAVIOR**   **195**

Pretest 196 / Introduction 196 / Values, Morality, and Prosocial Behavior 197 / Approaches for Dealing with Values, Morality, and Prosocial Behavior in the Classroom 200 / Key Ideas in Summary 222 / Posttest 223 / Questions 224 / Extending Understanding and Skill 224 / References 225 / Supplemental Reading 225

PART III   A SELECTION OF THEMES   **227**

CHAPTER 9   **LAW-RELATED EDUCATION**   **229**

Pretest 230 / Introduction 230 / What Is Law-Related Education? 231 / Goals of Law-Related Education 231 / Law-Related Education Topics 232 / Sources of Information 235 / Classroom Approaches to Law-Related Education 237 / Community Resources 246 / Key Ideas in Summary 247 / Posttest 249 / Questions 249 / Extending Understanding and Skill 250 / References 250 / Supplemental Reading 250

CHAPTER 10   **GLOBAL EDUCATION**   **253**

Pretest 254 / Introduction 255 / What Is Global Education? 256 / Global Education: Issues 257 / Organizing Global Education Learning Experiences 258 / Key Ideas in Summary 267 / Posttest 268 / Questions 269 / Extending Understanding and Skill 269 / References 270 / Supplemental Reading 271

CHAPTER 11 MULTICULTURAL AND SEX-EQUITY EDUCATION 273

Pretest 274 / Introduction 274 / The Several Faces of Multicultural Education 277 / Sex-Equity Education: Its Purposes 278 / Basic Goals of Multicultural and Sex-Equity Education 279 / Monitoring Classroom Procedures 282 / Classroom Approaches to Multicultural and Sex-Equity Studies 284 / Sources of Information 292 / Key Ideas in Summary 294 / Posttest 295 / Questions 295 / Extending Understanding and Skill 296 / References 297 / Supplemental Reading 297

CHAPTER 12 ENVIRONMENTAL AND ENERGY EDUCATION 299

Pretest 300 / Introduction 300 / Pressing Environmental and Energy Challenges 301 / Classroom Approaches to Building Environmental and Energy Awareness 307 / Key Ideas in Summary 315 / Posttest 316 / Questions 317 / Extending Understanding and Skill 317 / References 318 / Supplemental Reading 319

PART IV SUPPORTING, MANAGING, ASSESSING 321

CHAPTER 13 COMPUTERS AND TECHNOLOGY 323

Pretest 324 / Introduction 324 / Computers in the Schools 324 / Computers in Elementary Social Studies Classrooms 328 / Videocassettes 336 / Optical Discs 337 / Key Ideas in Summary 338 / Posttest 339 / Questions 340 / Extending Understanding and Skill 341 / References 341 / Supplemental Reading 342

CHAPTER 14 UNDERSTANDING MAP AND GLOBE SKILLS 343

Pretest 344 / Introduction 344 / Globes 346 / Maps 350 / Basic Map and Globe Skills 354 / Teaching All of the Skills at Each Grade Level 364 / Key Ideas in Summary 366 / Posttest 367 / Questions 367 / Extending Understanding and Skill 368 / References 368 / Supplemental Reading 369

CHAPTER 15 **READING, WRITING, AND SOCIAL STUDIES LESSONS** **371**

Pretest 372 / Introduction 372 / Developing Reading Study Skills 372 / Readability Issues 385 / Working with the Parts of the Textbook 395 / Integrating Writing into Social Studies Lessons 401 / Key Ideas in Summary 406 / Posttest 407 / Questions 407 / Extending Understanding and Skill 408 / References 409 / Supplemental Reading 409

CHAPTER 16 **MANAGING THE SOCIAL STUDIES CLASSROOM** **411**

Pretest 412 / Introduction 412 / Dimensions of Classroom Management 413 / Responding to Incidents of Misbehavior 422 / Key Ideas in Summary 436 / Posttest 437 / Questions 437 / Extending Understanding and Skill 438 / References 439 / Supplemental Reading 439

CHAPTER 17 **EVALUATING LEARNING** **441**

Pretest 442 / Introduction 442 / Informal Evaluation 444 / Recordkeeping and Informal Evaluation 451 / Formal Evaluation 454 / Using Evaluation Results to Improve Instruction 467 / Key Ideas in Summary 468 / Posttest 469 / Questions 470 / Extending Understanding and Skill 470 / References 471 / Supplemental Reading 471

Subject Index **473**

Name Index **481**

LESSON IDEAS

Developing Inquiry Skills: What the Visitor Wore   35

Evaluating Eyewitness Information: Yesterday on the Playground   35

Resolving Conflicting Accounts of Events   36

Location   43

Regions   44

Migration   45

Environmental Perception   46

Making Choices   50

Economic Systems   52

Resource Utilization   53

Rule Making   62

Conflict Resolution   64

Cooperation   67

Roles   69

Norms and Sanctions   70

Learning from an Artifact   75

Invention and Toolmaking   77

Understanding Perception   79

Observing Human Behavior   81

The Changing Community   127

Where in the World Are You?   133

Primary Sources   134

The Division of Labor   136

Goods and Services   136

Local History   136

Working in Groups: Two-by-Two's   150

Working Together: Inside-Outside   151

Buzz Session: Moving to America   152

Role Playing: How Can Needs Be Met?   156

Jigsaw: South America   160

Finding Distances   171

The Unhappy Tale of the Mongoose   173

Inquiry Lesson: Maps and Globes   176

Nations of Latin America   178

Weather Patterns   183

Decision Making: Electing School Officers   186

What Would You Do with Your Time?   201

Open-Ended Sentences   202

Values-Situation Role Playing: Self-Understanding   204

Values-Situation Role Playing: Using Content from History   206

Self-Understanding: Worry About the Future   214

Appreciating Decisions Made by Others   217

A Case Study: Police Search   239

A Case Study: Hurt on the Job 240

Intercultural Emphasis: Hide and Seek 263

The Parking Lot Survey 264

Where Clothing Is Manufactured 265

Where Do Different Dog Breeds Come From? 266

What Does a National Anthem Tell Us about People? 285

How Do Legends Help Us Understand People? 286

What Jobs Can a Woman Have? 288

Moving Westward 290

Contents of the Wastebasket 307

The Dreaded Litter Creature 309

Biodegradable Litter 310

Pollution 312

Electric Appliance Survey 313

Making Energy-Collage Posters 314

Learning about Map Symbols 357

Learning about Relative Location 361

Using Visual Frameworks: Spanish Colonizers and the Caribbean 377

CONTEXTS FOR
THE SOCIAL STUDIES

1

AN INTRODUCTION
TO THE SOCIAL STUDIES

This chapter provides information to help the reader:

1. describe some issues related to motivation and the elementary social studies program,

2. identify some major purposes of the social studies component of the elementary school program,

3. describe important components of citizenship education, history and social science education, and problem-solving education,

4. point out grades K–8 scope and sequence patterns for the social studies, and

5. suggest ways to relate basic social studies purposes to the subject matter covered at each grade level.

PRETEST

Answer each of the following true/false questions.

1. Though people who live in widely separated parts of the world differ in many ways, they also share some common concerns.
2. Pupils in elementary school typically rate their interest in social studies as "very high."
3. One widely acknowledged purpose of social studies programs is to develop good citizens.
4. In typical elementary social studies programs, pupils study the United States in grade five.
5. It is desirable to devote some attention at each grade level to lessons focusing on (a) citizenship education, (b) history and social science education, and (c) problem-solving education.

INTRODUCTION

Differences among the world's peoples are remarkable, but perhaps even more striking are the many similarities in their basic concerns. For example, history records that human beings have always tried to discover some meaning in their lives. Religions and philosophies developed in widely separated settings have sought to provide answers to the fundamental "Why am I here?" and "What does my life mean?" questions (Table 1–1).

Throughout the world, and throughout history, people have chosen to band together to solve problems of security and survival. This drive to gather has also prompted a need for rules and regulations governing social life. Though types of government vary enormously from place to place, human beings everywhere have developed them to provide for collective safety and order.

All people have had to come to terms with their physical environments. In the American Middle West people thrive on the lush prairies. In remote reaches of the Sahara other people have learned to live under conditions of perpetual drought. Throughout the world's inhabited land areas, people have learned to use their local environments. Responses to the need to adapt to local conditions have been as diverse as the range of the earth's peoples and physical settings.

The elementary social studies program challenges learners to investigate the infinite variety of humans and their ways of interacting with their environment. It celebrates their successes and tries to learn from their failures. Learning in the social studies challenges each individual to find his or her own sense of identity and to understand the responsibilities and rights of citizenship. These purposes make social studies a basic and important elementary school subject.

TABLE 1–1
Common human dilemmas and social studies focus questions.

Dilemmas	Selected Focus Questions
Stability vs. change	How do we preserve what is "good" in society while adapting to meet changing conditions?
Reaction to differences	How can we live in harmony with people who are different? How can we avoid irrational prejudice?
Providing for wants	How can we organize ourselves for economic production? What should be produced? How should production be distributed?
Individual freedom vs. social control	How can we reconcile individual freedom with other needs (security, for example) that require collective action? What is the proper relationship between the individual and his or her government?
Population problems	What can be done to reduce the rates of population growth where they are too high? What places need fewer people? What accounts for the differences?
Environmental issues	How can we use the resources of the earth wisely? How do we assure that future generations will enjoy a quality of life at least equal to our own?
Technological changes	How do we prepare to deal with accelerating rates of change? What should the responses be to challenges resulting from innovations that bring people from very different cultural traditions into closer contact?

THE MOTIVATION PROBLEM

Despite the importance of the social studies, many surveys have found that the subject ranks close to the bottom of the list of subjects elementary learners find interesting (McGowan, Sutton, and Smith 1990). Much of this reputation, we believe, results not from the content of the subject, but rather from how it is taught.

Elementary school learners are concerned about themselves and about other people. Consider how eager they are to share information about their personal experiences and the experiences of members of their families. Good elementary social studies lessons build on children's personal and family interests to extend their concerns to other peoples and places.

Instruction that helps pupils to make these connections places heavy demands on teachers. They cannot simply assign learners to master content on certain textbook pages. Neither will long-winded lectures get the job done. Elementary school children must be provided with opportunities to engage the social studies directly. They must be able to *do* something with the content. Lessons must have an immediate and personal relevance. (Even older elementary pupils will not accept the argument that "you should read this now, because it will help you when you get to high school and college.")

BOX 1–1   Motivation and the Elementary Social Studies Program.

**Think
About
This**

Try to recall your own elementary social studies classes. Then answer these questions:

1. What are your most vivid memories?
2. What topics did you study? How did you react to these topics? Why do you think you felt as you did about them?
3. What methods were used to teach social studies content? How did you react to these methods? Would you have preferred to do something else? If so, what and why?
4. How important for you personally did you find social studies content? If you did not much care for your social studies lessons, how could they have been improved?
5. What are some of your own ideas about how a social studies teacher might go about interesting children in the subject?

Successful social studies teachers are sincerely interested in the content of the social studies program. Elementary school pupils are more perceptive than beginning teachers sometimes suppose them to be. They are quick to spot a teacher who is simply "going through the motions" of teaching social studies, mathematics, science, or any other part of the curriculum. Conversely, these children easily identify the teacher who has a personal enthusiasm for the content he or she is teaching. This kind of enthusiasm is contagious. It is a mighty force for stimulating learners' interest.

PURPOSES OF THE SOCIAL STUDIES

The leading national association of social studies education professionals is the National Council for the Social Studies. Recently this organization's Task Force on Scope and Sequence (1989) made this statement about the role of the social studies:

> Social studies education has a specific mandate in regard to citizenship education. *That mandate is to provide every American school child and adolescent with the opportunity to learn the knowledge, the abilities, and the beliefs and values needed for competent participation in social, political, and economic life.* . . . Most of all, social studies should prepare young people to put into practice what they learn in school as they fulfill their obligations as citizens, deciding and acting responsibly when confronted by personal and social issues and problems. (p. 377) [Italics are those of the task force.]

From this statement we can infer that one important objective of the social studies program is the promotion of "citizenship." Few individuals dispute the importance of citizenship education in the social studies program.

A sense of adventure and exploring the unknown are important ingredients in social studies programs.

Evidence mounts that an emphasis on citizenship is particularly critical at the present time. Recent statistics about the civic consciousness of adult Americans are not encouraging (Taylor 1990). The Bureau of the Census was dismayed to find that, during the 1990 census, fewer than two-thirds of the households returned their census forms. In recent elections nearly two-thirds of the electorate have failed to vote. For every five dollars in federal taxes that are owed, one dollar in tax liability is being evaded. It is estimated that the difference between what is owed and what is paid in taxes to the federal government will soon exceed $100 billion annually.

"Education for citizenship" implies three things. First, it suggests a need for learners to commit to core American values such as democratic decision making. Second, it suggests a program that encourages learners to subject present practices to critique (Leming 1989). Finally, it suggests a hope that young people will emerge from schools with a predisposition to become actively involved in public affairs.

In support of the need to view citizenship broadly, Sanford Horwitt, a director of a citizenship education project, has commented, "Young people have an impoverished notion of citizenship. . . . Basically, they think it's not breaking the law, and that's all" (Taylor 1990, 7). The social studies program seeks to counter this "impoverished" notion. The National Council for the Social Studies Task Force on Scope and Sequence (1989) has written:

> Most of all, social studies should prepare young people to put into practice what they learn in school as they fulfill their obligations as citizens, deciding and acting responsibly when confronted by personal and social issues and problems. (p. 377)

Our system is based on a set of values and ideals that include freedom, justice, informed decision making, responsibility, equality, and the freedom to dissent. These assumptions support efforts to help learners grow to maturity as psychologically secure individuals who are willing to participate actively in our democratic decision-making process.

The importance of citizenship education is reflected in the definition of "social studies education" developed by the National Council for the Social Studies Task Force on Scope and Sequence (1989):

> *Social studies education is a basic component of the K–12 curriculum that (1) derives its goals from the nature of citizenship in a democratic society that is closely linked to other nations and peoples of the world; (2) draws its content primarily from history, the social sciences, and, in some respects, from the humanities and science; (3) is taught in ways that reflect an awareness of the personal, social, and cultural experiences and developmental levels of learners; and (4) facilitates the transfer of what is learned in school to the out-of-school lives of students.* (p. 377)

This definition adds dimensions to the social studies that complement the purpose of citizenship education. The definition makes reference to the content of the social studies. This emphasis of the social studies program might be termed "history and social science education."

History, the social sciences, and the humanities have all developed some methods of investigation and some understandings that enrich individuals' lives and increase their capacities for exercising their responsibilities as good citizens. Effective citizenship rests on a solid knowledge base.

Though we have chosen to call the academic-content dimension of the social studies "history and social science education," the content of this part of the social studies program is not limited to history and the social sciences. Any component of any subject that deals with the social aspect of human behavior is appropriate content for the social studies program. This lets the educator include information

Social studies instruction should help pupils investigate enduring social issues and problems such as war and peace.

drawn from a wide variety of subjects, even such "nonsocial" disciplines as engineering and the hard sciences.

Educators who are organizing information in the history and social science component of the elementary social studies program seek knowledge that can help young people understand their world. Information about person-to-person and person-to-environment interactions that is derived from a variety of sources helps to guide instructional planning. The important thing is not that learners study a subject labeled "history" or "geography," but that they learn significant ideas about human beings.

Citizens of democratic societies need effective thinking tools. Adult members of such societies are called upon to respond to pressing problems. Decisions they make influence their own lives as well as those of other members of the community, state, and nation. Hence, *problem-solving education* is an important component of the elementary social studies program. This important dimension helps pupils develop techniques to address problems. (Specific treatment of some tested problem-solving approaches is provided in Chapter 7, "Thinking Skills Instruction.")

COMPONENTS OF CITIZENSHIP EDUCATION, HISTORY AND SOCIAL SCIENCE EDUCATION, AND PROBLEM-SOLVING EDUCATION

For each broad social studies purpose there are three subareas that need to be identified. These are (1) knowledge, (2) skills, and (3) values. (See Figure 1–1.)

The Components of Citizenship Education

Knowledge.   Young people should be exposed to knowledge related to the American heritage, the Constitution, the Bill of Rights, political processes followed at the local, state, and national levels, and other basic information an educated adult citizen is expected to know.

Skills.   Elementary school pupils need to be taught the processes associated with decision making in this country. They need to learn how to negotiate and compromise, to express views, and to work productively with others.

The social studies purposes matrix illustrates the major components of a comprehensive elementary social studies program. Each cell of the matrix indicates an important emphasis. All of these components should be addressed somewhere during the total elementary social studies program. However, not necessarily all of them will be addressed during a given year. Also, conditions in individual places will result in various degrees of emphasis being accorded to each component in the matrix.

	Citizenship Education	History and Social Science Education	Problem-Solving Education
Knowledge			
Skills			
Values			

FIGURE 1–1
A social studies purposes matrix.

Values. Citizens make decisions based not just on information alone. They also consider social and personal values. Certainly learners need to be exposed to the values associated with democratic decision making and with others that undergird the operation of local, state, and national governments in the United States.

Table 1–2 illustrates how citizenship education outcomes develop common themes from grade level to grade level.

TABLE 1–2
Some examples of citizenship outcomes by grade level.

The social studies program attempts to build on basic themes in each grade level. Treatment becomes more sophisticated as pupils progress through school. Note these examples.

Citizenship Education: Knowledge

				Grade Levels					
Basic Theme: Regulations and the Individual	K	1	2	3	4	5	6	7	8
State the classroom rules.	X								
Explain the need for community rules.		X							
Identify those who make rules in the local community.			X						
Identify an individual's responsibility to the community and state.				X					
Identify the basic functions of local state governments.					X				
Explain the basic rights and responsibilities of United States' citizens.						X			
Point out that both written and unwritten rules shape people's behavior in all world societies.							X		
Describe differences in the role of the "good citizen" as defined by different world cultures.								X	
Point out how the concept of "good citizen" has evolved over time in the United States.									X

Citizenship Education: Skills

				Grade Levels					
Basic Theme: Developing Group Membership Skills	K	1	2	3	4	5	6	7	8
Engage in fair play.	X								
Work cooperatively in a group.		X							
Cope with the group-individual conflict.			X						
Assist in establishing group goals.				X					
Decide how state citizens should work together to solve a problem.					X				
Simulate citizen actions to influence the decisions of the U.S. government.						X			
React as a group to problems that are worldwide in their scope.							X		
Take action to stay well informed about political and social problems affecting people in other nations.								X	
Express opinions in a public setting about major issues facing the United States.									X

TABLE 1−2
Continued

Basic Theme: Acceptance of the Roles of Group	K	1	2	3	4	5	6	7	8
Citizenship Education: Values									
				Grade Levels					
Respect others.	X								
Accept the leadership of others.		X							
Volunteer for leadership roles.			X						
Accept the rights of others.				X					
Defend the importance of the rights of others.					X				
Accept the idea that people depend on one another to satisfy their needs.						X			
Commit to the idea that majorities rule, but that minorities have their rights, too.							X		
Accept the diversity of values represented in cultures throughout the world.								X	
Accept the idea that people of good will can interpret a common set of information and arrive at varying conclusions because of differences in their values.									X

The Components of History and Social Science Education

Knowledge.   The academic disciplines including history and the social sciences include many powerful insights that are related to human behavior. These need to be taught as part of the elementary school social studies program.

Skills.   Elementary social studies programs emphasize skills used by academic content specialists in gathering and assessing the importance of information. General information about how the scientific method can be used to verify and modify hypotheses is often included.

Values.   There are certain values implicit in how academic content specialists gather and process information. For example, there is a predisposition to prize knowledge based on data more highly than knowledge based on simple intuition or feeling. Learners in the elementary program need to be exposed to this value orientation.
    See Table 1−3 for an illustration of how social studies education outcomes can be tied to themes selected from each grade in the K−8 sequence.

The Components of Problem-Solving Education

Knowledge.   Young people need to learn basic information about how rational decisions are made. Steps in identifying problems and applying relevant information are important concerns of this part of the social studies program. Additionally,

TABLE 1–3

Some examples of history and social science education outcomes by grade level.

As is the case with citizenship education, the social studies program attempts to build on basic themes related to social science education at each grade level. Pupils deal with these themes in a more sophisticated manner at each successive grade level. Note these examples.

History and Social Science Education: Knowledge

	Grade Levels								
Basic Theme: Economic Interdependence	K	1	2	3	4	5	6	7	8
Identify how different people help us to meet our needs.	X								
State how people with different jobs in the family contribute to helping the family as a whole.		X							
Describe how people in the community depend on one another to supply goods and services.			X						
Point out how the work of people in one community contributes to the well-being of people in other communities.				X					
Explain the economic ties between the pupil's state and the other parts of the United States.					X				
Describe the interdependence among the regions of the United States.						X			
Explain how the United States and other nations of the world are economically interdependent.							X		
Describe several unique characteristics of the economies of selected nations of the world.								X	
Point out key events in history that helped shape the present economic interpendence of regions of the United States.									X

History and Social Science Education: Skills

	Grade Levels								
Basic Theme: Finding Places on Maps and Globes	K	1	2	3	4	5	6	7	8
Find things on a drawing of the classroom.	X								
Find things on a simple map of the school and the immediate neighborhood.		X							
Use a very simple coordinate system to find things on a simple map.			X						
Use a grid system to find things on a map of the community.				X					
Use latitude and longitude to locate places in the state on a globe.					X				
Use latitude and longitude to determine the locations of places in the United States.						X			
Use latitude and longitude to find places throughout the world using maps and globes.							X		
Use lines of latitude and the international date line to determine the correct date and correct time in selected world cities.								X	
Locate selected cities in the United States when given their coordinates of longitude and latitude and point out their relative location to a given place.									X

TABLE 1-3
Continued

History and Social Science Education: Values

Basic Theme: Tolerance of Diversity	Grade Levels								
	K	1	2	3	4	5	6	7	8
Allow others to express ideas.	X								
Listen attentively to the ideas of others.		X							
Demonstrate respect for the ideas of others.			X						
Support the view that the community profits from a diversity of opinions.				X					
Accept the idea that a diversity of opinions within the state makes it a better place in which to live.					X				
Commit to the view that a diversity of views make the United States a good place in which to live.						X			
Respect the rights of people in other parts of the world to hold opinions that differ from those of most Americans.							X		
Accept that people in other parts of the world may change their views over time much as people in the United States do.								X	
Encourage a sharing of views on controversial U.S. policy issues that supports the right of people holding the widest possible range of opinion to be heard.									X

pupils need to master techniques associated with organization and evaluation of data, and the formulation and testing of hypotheses.

Skills.   Development of problem-solving abilities is promoted when pupils have opportunities to make decisions about real issues. In the lower elementary grades, problem-solving skills are developed as learners work with problems of personal and family importance. As pupils mature, they are provided experiences focusing on a broader range of social and civic problems.

Because many problems in a democratic society require collective decision making, part of the social studies skill-development program in the area of problem solving involves helping pupils to work productively in groups. Pupils are provided opportunities to engage in the kind of give-and-take discussion that characterizes group decision making.

Values.   Instruction in this general area attempts to develop pupils' appreciation for problem-solving decisions that are based on rational thinking. It is hoped that they will come to prize decisions that rest on evidence and logic and to resist jumping to conclusions as a result of unexamined assumptions or restrictive biases. Development of a commitment to tolerance for diverse views is another purpose of this area of the social studies program.

See Table 1-4 for an illustration of how problem-solving education outcomes develop common themes from grade level to grade level.

TABLE 1–4
Some examples of problem-solving education outcomes by grade level.

The elementary social studies program attempts to develop pupils' problem-solving skills as much as it seeks to promote citizenship education and social science education outcomes. Pupils learn to deal with common problem-solving themes in a more sophisticated manner at each successive grade level. Note these examples.

Problem-Solving Education: Knowledge

					Grade Levels				
Basic Theme: Making Decisions	K	1	2	3	4	5	6	7	8
Explain how a choice is made.	X								
State the specific steps used in solving a problem.		X							
Identify the problems faced by people in the neighborhood.			X						
Point out the problems that need to be solved by members of the community.				X					
Explain the kinds of information that people would need to solve a problem facing citizens of the state.					X				
Identify the criteria to be used in making a decision about a problem facing citizens of the United States.						X			
Describe how people in different parts of the world use different kinds of logic to arrive at conclusions.							X		
Contrast ways of problem solving in other countries with those favored in the United States.								X	
Describe problem-solving techniques used by historical figures to respond to dilemmas that the United States faced in the past.									X

Problem-Solving Education: Skills

					Grade Levels				
Basic Theme: Applying the Decision-Making Techniques	K	1	2	3	4	5	6	7	8
Recognize that a problem exists.	X								
Propose a general plan of action for solving a problem.		X							
Suggest alternative solutions to a problem.			X						
Arrange data into categories that will be useful in solving a problem.				X					
Distinguish between fact and opinion when considering data to be used in solving a problem.					X				
State and test several hypotheses when seeking a solution to a problem.						X			
Compare and contrast viewpoints of several individuals who have proposed alternative solutions to a complex problem.							X		
Distinguish between problem-solving techniques used by representatives from two or more foreign countries in responding to a common international problem.								X	
Apply tested problem-solving techniques to suggest tentative solutions to present and past problems of the United States.									X

TABLE 1–4
Continued

Problem-Solving Education: Values

Basic Theme: Commitment to Rational Decision Making	Grade Levels								
	K	1	2	3	4	5	6	7	8
Accept the need to think about a personal problem before taking action.	X								
Commit to a pattern of socially acceptable disagreement when conflicts with others arise.		X							
Accept the need for compromise when working with others to solve problems.			X						
Demonstrate a willingness to follow through on a planned course of action once a decision has been made about how a problem should be solved.				X					
Commit to studying all the relevant aspects of a problem before making a decision.					X				
Accept as legitimate the questions about why a particular response to a problem has been selected.						X			
Commit to the view that decisions based on evidence are to be preferred over those based on unsupported opinion.							X		
Analyze alternative solutions to pressing international problems and commit to one or more that seem clearly based on evidence and acceptable values priorities.								X	
Defend selection of a policy alternative that is designed to respond to an important problem facing the United States in terms of the supporting evidence and of the values priorities reflected in the policy.									X

The major purposes of citizenship education, history and social science education, and problem-solving education and the subcategories under each comprise the comprehensive elementary social studies program. Well-balanced programs should provide *some* experiences directed toward each of these components. However, it is unlikely that each of the areas will receive equal attention at each grade level. In a particular grade, several areas might play primary roles with the others playing less important parts. Some school districts will have priorities favoring an emphasis on certain program elements. Those designated as "high-priority" areas will receive more attention than others.

THE SOCIAL STUDIES
CURRICULUM IN GRADES K THROUGH 8

Traditionally, the elementary school social studies program was organized around the idea of "expanding horizons." In this pattern, learners first encountered topics that were familiar to them in their daily lives. For example, in the primary grades, programs focused on families, schools, neighborhoods, and local communities. In the middle and upper grades, topics expanded to include emphases on the state, nation, and the world. This basic sequence, with some important local variations, continues even now.

Children today are much more aware of patterns of life beyond their own communities than were children who grew up before the television age. From their earliest years, television brings images into their homes of patterns of living that may be quite different from their own. Films, too, expose young people to different places and cultures. Information young people glean from their exposure to the media and the growing interdependence of the world's peoples have influenced the organization of the school social studies program.

Today, children do not simply study their own schools, families, communities, and neighborhoods. They are encouraged also to compare and contrast these familiar patterns of living with those of other lands. As the National Council for the Social Studies Task Force on Scope and Sequence reported, "Social studies programs have a responsibility to prepare young people to identify, understand, and work to solve the problems that face our increasingly diverse nation and interdependent world" (1989, 377).

The past decade has witnessed attempts to identify a scope and sequence for the social studies program that would enjoy broad national support. The National Council for the Social Studies commissioned the Task Force on Scope and Sequence to review different proposals and make recommendations, which were presented in the group's final report (pp. 380–82). The task force identified a common set of course titles for grades K through eight. Recognizing that different

BOX 1–2   **Alternative Sequences for Grades 6, 7, and 8**

The National Council for the Social Studies Task Force on Scope and Sequence (1989) identified these three alternative sequences for grades six, seven, and eight:

Alternative   Grade 6: People and Cultures: Representative World Regions
One   Grade 7: A Changing View of Many Nations: A Global View
Grade 8: Building a Strong and Free Nation: The United States

Alternative   Grade 6: European Cultures with their Extension into the Western Hemisphere
Two   Grade 7: A Changing World of Many Nations: A Global View
Grade 8: Economics and Law-Related Studies (one semester of each)

Alternative   Grade 6: Land and People of Latin America
Three   Grade 7: People and Cultures: Representative World Regions
Grade 8: Interdisciplinary Study of the Local Region

Think   1. What advantages and disadvantages do you see for each option? Which do you
About   prefer? Why?
This   2. Which of these options represents the "best" fit with the social studies program in
grades K through five? Why do you think so?

---

course patterns are in place for grades six, seven, and eight, three alternative sequences were identified for these grade levels. These sequences are outlined in Box 1–2.

The pattern suggested by the task force fits the present program in many schools quite well, especially in grades K through five. There tends to be somewhat more local variation in grades six, seven, and eight (though United States history of some kind continues to be widely taught at grade eight). The subsections that follow introduce examples of content taught in each grade of the basic grades K–8 sequence presented in the NCSS Task Force report.

Kindergarten: Awareness of Self in a Social Setting

The purpose of social studies instruction in kindergarten can be summed up in one word: *socialization*. These young children learn about themselves and about expected patterns of behavior in home and school settings. They are encouraged to master rules governing social relationships.

Grade 1: The Individual in Primary and Social Groups: Understanding School and Family Life

In grade one, socialization experiences begun in kindergarten continue. Certain basic social studies concepts are introduced. For example, the NCSS Task Force

(p. 380) suggests that different categories of school personnel be used to introduce the idea of "division of labor" and that varying places of residence serve as a vehicle to introduce the concepts "urban" and "rural."

Grade 2: Meeting Basic Needs in
Nearby Social Groups: The Neighborhood

Using the learner's neighborhood as a context, the second-grade program introduces the study of communication, transportation, production, consumption, and goods and services. These topics often are introduced in lessons that feature content about how people in neighborhoods and local social groups in other countries go about meeting their needs.

Grade 3: Sharing Earth Space with Others: The Community

The social studies program in grade three emphasizes the learner's local community. There is an emphasis on the interdependence of cities and communities in the state, nation, and world. Lessons focus on issues such as change and growth in communities, governments of communities, history of communities, and locations of communities.

Grade 4: Human Life in Varied Environments: The Region

At this grade level, learners are introduced to the concept of "region." Often there is an in-depth study of the home state as an example of a region. World geographic regions are introduced, and lessons afford opportunities to compare and contrast them with characteristics of the home state and with one another.

Grade 5: People of the Americas:
The United States and Its Close Neighbors

The title of this course, particularly as it pertains to the "close neighbors" of the United States, reflects more of a hope of the NCSS Task Force than an accurate image of present practices. Most present grade-five programs are heavily oriented to the study of the history and geography of the United States. Often coverage of Canada and Latin America receives sparse attention. It is hoped that, increasingly, fifth-grade programs will deal with the United States as a country of the Western Hemisphere and that more attention will be paid to the history and geography of both Canada and Mexico.

Grade 6: Peoples and Cultures: Representative World Regions

The focus of instruction in grade six is on representative people and cultures of both Latin America and the Eastern Hemisphere. Learners are encouraged to become familiar with important cultural contributions of people from these areas of the world. Interdependence among nations is a common theme. A persistent problem at grade six has been a tendency for some teachers to cover too many topics without developing any in depth. Better programs focus on sample nations or subregions and provide a variety of lessons about these areas. This arrangement produces more substantive learning outcomes than a more general, "cover everything" approach.

Alternative emphases at grade six include (1) "European Cultures with their Extension into the Western Hemisphere," and (2) "Land and People of Latin America."

Grade 7: A Changing World of Many Nations: A Global View

The content of the grade-seven program often ties closely to that in grade six. (There are important local variations. For example, in some places a state history course is taught in grade seven.) The major intent is to increase learners' awareness of the world, particularly the world outside the Western Hemisphere. Physical geography and place location receive heavy emphases. Historical information

Social studies should help pupils apply what they are learning to contemporary issues. Newspapers are excellent teaching tools for this purpose.

TABLE 1–5
Focus questions by grade level.

Kindergarten: Awareness of Self in a Social Setting			
Focus Questions	Citizenship	History and Social Science	Problem Solving
What is our national flag like? Our state flag?	X		
What are our classroom rules? Our school rules? Why do we have rules?	X		
What are the names of our community, state, and nation?	X		
What are the basic directions (up, down, right, left)?		X	
What are the basic time concepts (minutes, hours, days)?		X	
What do the basic symbols and signs mean (road signs, and so on)?		X	
How do we make choices?			X
How do we know when a problem exists?			X
What kind of class rules do we need?			X

Grade 1: The Individual in Primary Social Groups: Understanding School and Family Life			
Focus Questions	Citizenship	History and Social Science	Solving
Why do communities need rules?	X		
How can we work cooperatively in groups?	X		
What are some of our patriotic customs?	X		
How do different family members contribute to the family as a whole?		X	
How is the calendar divided into days, months, and years?		X	
How can a simple map of the classroom and school be made?		X	
What specific steps should be taken in solving a problem?			X
What kinds of problems do family members face?			X
How do family members work together to solve problems?			X

about selected areas is provided to give learners insights pertaining to changes over time. Distinctions are drawn between nations of the developed and developing world.

An alternative emphasis at grade seven is "People and Cultures: Representative World Regions." This emphasis is favored in places where the grade-six program has been restricted to a study of Latin America.

Grade 8: Building a Strong and Free Nation: The United States

The primary objective of the eighth-grade program is to introduce students to the economic and social history of the United States. Political history receives less

TABLE 1–5
Continued

Grade 2: Meeting Basic Needs in Nearby Social Groups: The Neighborhood

Focus Questions	Citizenship	History and Social Science	Problem Solving
How are rules made for people in the neighborhood?	X		
What happens when people break rules?	X		
What are fair rules like?	X		
How can time lines be used to depict a sequence?		X	
What important kinds of transportation and communication are there?		X	
How does the local environment change with the seasons?		X	
What kinds of problems do neighborhoods face?			X
How can groups work to solve problems?			X
What categories of information are needed to solve a problem?			X

Grade 3: Sharing Earth Space with Others: The Community

Focus Questions	Citizenship	History and Social Science	Problem Solving
What is a person's responsibility to the community?	X		
What are the basic functions of local government?	X		
Who enforces laws in the community?	X		
How does the work of people in one community help people in other communities?		X	
What are the contributions of various ethnic and culture groups to the community?		X	
What kinds of maps display information about the community?		X	
What are some problems that the community must face?			X
What are some causes of the events in the community?			X
How can information best be arranged for problem solving?			X

emphasis. The idea is to engender interest in our country's history by focusing on lives of people, especially ordinary people. Instruction also emphasizes the role of the United States in world affairs and mutual dependency among nations.

Alternative emphases at grade eight include (a) "Economics and Law-Related Studies" (one semester of each), and (b) "Interdisciplinary Studies of the Local Region."

RELATING BASIC SOCIAL STUDIES PURPOSES TO SUBJECT MATTER COVERED AT EACH GRADE LEVEL

In planning for instruction at each grade level, it is easy to lose sight of the three basic purposes of the social studies program in grades K through eight: (1) citi-

Grade 4: Human Life in Varied Environments: The Region

Focus Questions	Citizenship	History and Social Science	Problem Solving
What are the basic functions of state government?	X		
How do groups help governments to make decisions?	X		
How can a person develop group leadership skills?	X		
What economic ties are there between the state and other parts of the United States?		X	
How have people of the state used their environment in different ways at different times?		X	
How do landforms influence climate?		X	
What kinds of information do people need to arrive at solutions to problems facing the state?			X
How can a person tell the difference between statements of fact and of opinion?			X
What might be the consequences of different approaches to solving a problem facing the state?			X

Grade 5: People of the Americas: The United States and Its Close Neighbors

Focus Questions	Citizenship	History and Social Science	Problem Solving
What are the basic rights and responsibilities of citizens?	X		
What are the major political parties? What are their symbols?	X		
What qualities do people seek in national leaders?	X		
How are regions of the United States interdependent?		X	
What were the major historical events in the development of the United States?		X	
How do innovations change the economy of the United States?		X	
What criteria should United States' citizens apply as they attempt to solve problems facing the country?		X	
How can hypotheses about complex problems be developed and tested?			X
What role do personal values play in decisions people make?			X

zenship education, (2) history and social science education, and (3) problem-solving education. At each grade level, teachers need to consider how much instruction will be related to each of these major purposes.

Once a general decision is made regarding the relative emphases to be placed on citizenship education, history and social science education, and problem-solving education, it is useful for the teacher to identify some focus questions that will guide instruction. Cross-referencing questions to the major social studies purposes can assure that each purpose receives at least some attention in the instructional program at each grade level. Table 1–5 lists sample focus questions for each grade level.

Questions included in Table 1–5 are simply examples of those that might be developed. Note that this example features the same number of questions for each

TABLE 1–5
Continued

Grade 6: People and Cultures: Representative World Regions

Focus Questions	Citizenship	History and Social Science	Problem Solving
What unwritten rules shape citizens' behavior?	X		
What rights should minorities have in a democratic society?	X		
What are the expected relationships between the citizens of the United States and the citizens of other nations?	X		
How are the United States and other nations of the world interdependent?		X	
How are the climates in various parts of the world explained?		X	
What contrasts are there between the government of the United States and the governments of selected nondemocratic nations?		X	
What differences are there between the kinds of logic used by individuals in different parts of the world to solve problems?			X
How can cultural perspectives be recognized in a statement of position on a world problem?			X
Why do some problems have neither right nor wrong answers?			X

Grade 7: A Changing View of Many Nations: A Global View

Focus Questions	Citizenship	History and Social Science	Problem Solving
How are "good citizens" defined in different countries?	X		
Do all countries view "democratic decision making" similarly?	X		
How do countries differ in terms of percentages of citizens who choose to vote in elections?	X		
What geographic advantages and disadvantages characterize selected countries of the world?		X	
How do patterns of historical development of selected countries compare with our own?		X	
What variables are associated with "high status" and "low status" in selected countries of the world?		X	
How is the relative logical strength of an argument determined?			X
How can situations arising from conflicts about values that are prized by selected world cultures best be resolved?			X
Do all problems have solutions?			X

BOX 1–3   Deciding about Your Own Social Studies Program

Think About This   Identify a grade level at which you might like to teach. Brainstorm to identify some content that might be taught at this level. Next, write down what you know about learners of this age. Then, considering the major purpose areas of citizenship education, history and social science education, and problem-solving education, decide what you might include in your program at this grade level.

Grade 8: Building a Strong and Free Nation: The United States

Focus Questions	Citizenship	History and Social Science	Problem Solving
What is the definition of a "good citizen"?	X		
Should people be fined if they fail to vote?	X		
What might happen if, over time, people become less and less interested in politics?	X		
Are there revolutionaries today?		X	
What is special about our economic system?		X	
What is the role of interest groups in the American political process?		X	
Why are some problems more difficult to resolve than others?			X
What roles do American values play in how decisions are made in this country?			X
How can problems be solved in ways that protect rights of minorities?			X

social studies purpose. In reality, planning probably will result in an unequal number of questions for each major purpose. Think about the issue of focus questions as you do the activity described in Box 1–3.

KEY IDEAS IN SUMMARY

1. Though people in different parts of the world vary from one another in many ways, they also share certain common characteristics. For example, people everywhere have pondered reasons for their own existence, have gathered together in communities protected by governmental authorities, and have made adaptations to local environmental conditions.

2. There is broad agreement that citizenship education is an important purpose of the social studies program. Other key purposes include those related to history and social science education and problem-solving education.

3. There is evidence today that levels of citizen participation are decreasing. This may result in some dangerous long-term consequences for our country. This situation underscores the importance of citizenship development as a focus of the social studies program.

4. Citizenship education, history and social science education, and problem-solving education each have associated (a) knowledge components, (b) skills components, and (c) values components.

5. The National Council for the Social Studies Task Force on Scope and Sequence provided these recommendations for content focus in grades K through eight: (a) Kindergarten: Awareness of Self in a Social Setting; (b) Grade one: The Individual in Primary Social Groups: Understanding School and Family Life; (c) Grade two: Meeting Basic Needs in Nearby Social Groups: The Neighbor-

hood; (d) Grade three: Sharing Earth Space with Others: The Community; (e) Grade four: Human Life in Varied Environments: The Region; (f) Grade five: People of the Americas: The United States and Its Close Neighbors; (g) Grade six: People and Cultures: Representative World Regions; (h) Grade seven: A Changing View of Many Nations: A Global View; and (i) Grade eight: Building a Strong and Free Nation: The United States.

6. It is important for educators to devote some attention to citizenship education, history and social science education, and problem-solving education at each grade level. However, depending on specific pupil characteristics, it is probable that degrees of emphasis on each will vary from grade level to grade level and across individual classrooms at the same grade level.

POSTTEST

Answer each of the following true/false questions.

1. It is hoped that, as a result of the emphasis on citizenship education in the social studies, young people will develop a desire to become actively involved in public affairs.

2. Learners in kindergarten and the first grade cannot be expected to know much about the world other than what they have encountered personally in their lives with their families.

3. There is more agreement about what content should be taught in grades one, two, and three than about what content should be taught in grades six, seven, and eight.

4. Development of pupils' problem-solving abilities is an important purpose of the social studies program.

5. According to the report of the National Council for the Social Studies Task Force on Scope and Sequence, both Mexico and Canada should receive attention in the grade-five social studies program.

QUESTIONS

1. What are some concerns that seem to be common to people throughout the world?

2. What are some major purposes of the social studies program?

3. What are some likely causes of the lack of enthusiasm some pupils have for the social studies?

4. What does the National Council for the Social Studies Task Force on Scope and Sequence recommend as the content focus for the social studies in each grade, kindergarten through eight?

5. What might a teacher do to assure that each major social studies purpose is addressed in his or her program?

6. Why do you think social studies is so unpopular with many elementary school learners? What are some specific things you might do to remedy this situation?

7. A large majority of social studies education experts feel that development of patterns of "good citizenship" should be an important objective of the school social studies program. Others suggest that development of citizenship is what the *entire* school program is about. Consequently, they question the wisdom of placing so much emphasis on citizenship education in the social studies. What are your own feelings about the importance of citizenship education in the elementary social studies program?

8. Some people believe that the elementary school social studies program is as important as the reading program and the mathematics program. Do you agree? What led you to adopt your position?

9. Is it really appropriate for younger elementary children, those in grades K through two, to be involved in problem-solving lessons? Why, or why not?

10. Is there a danger that exposing elementary school pupils to values prized by people in other lands will make them less likely to commit to core American values? Why, or why not?

EXTENDING UNDERSTANDING AND SKILL

Activities

1. Choose a curriculum guide for the grade level of your choice. Evaluate the guide using the Social Studies Purposes Matrix illustrated in Figure 1.1. To what extent are citizenship, history and social science education, personal education, and decision-making included in the guide? Under each of these categories, what is the relative attention given to knowledge, skills, and values?

2. Choose a topic taught at a grade level that interests you. Write a short paper in which you include at least one example of how each of the major purposes of the social studies might be included in lessons related to this topic.

3. Interview the person in charge of the social studies program for a local school district. (Depending on the size of the district, the person might hold a title such as "Director of Social Studies," "Coordinator of Social Studies," "Social Studies Curriculum Director," "Director of Elementary Education," or "Curriculum Director.") Your instructor may be able to suggest the name of a likely contact person. Ask this individual to tell you the major social studies content for each grade from kindergarten through grade eight. Compare this arrangement with the scope and sequence recommended by the National Council for the Social Studies Task Force on Scope and Sequence. Prepare an oral report in which you comment on similarities and differences.

4. Prepare a complete list of focus questions to guide social studies instruction at a grade level of your choosing. Your course instructor will critique your list.

5. Interview several children who are in a grade level you would like to teach. Ask them about their likes and dislikes regarding social studies. Summarize their comments in a short paper. Make particular note of those things they like. Suggest how you might build on their ideas to make your own social studies program more appealing to your pupils.

REFERENCES

LEMING, J. S. "The Two Cultures of Social Studies Education." *Social Education* (October 1989), pp. 404–408.

McGOWAN, T. M., A. M. SUTTON, AND P. G. SMITH. "Instructional Elements Influencing Student Attitudes Toward Social Studies." *Theory and Research in Social Education* (Winter 1990), pp. 37–52.

NATIONAL COUNCIL FOR THE SOCIAL STUDIES TASK FORCE ON SCOPE AND SEQUENCE. "In Search of a Scope and Sequence for Social Studies: Report of the National Council for the Social Studies Task Force on Scope and Sequence." *Social Education* (October 1989), pp. 376–85. [Report revised 1 July 1990.]

TAYLOR, P. "A National Morale Problem—Americans Feel Increasingly Estranged from Their Government." *The Washington Post National Weekly Edition* (14 April–20 May 1990), pp. 6–7.

SUPPLEMENTAL READING

BARR, R. D., J. L. BARTH, AND S. S. SHERMIS. *Defining the Social Studies.* Bulletin 51. Arlington, VA: National Council for the Social Studies, 1977.

HARTOONIAN, H. M., AND M. A. LAUGHLIN. "Designing a Social Studies Scope and Sequence for the 21st Century." *Social Education* (October 1989), pp. 388–98.

KNIEP, W. M. "Social Studies within a Global Education." *Social Education* (October 1989), pp. 385, 399–403.

McFARLAND, M. A. "Questions and Priorities for Improving Social Studies Instruction." *Social Education* (February 1984), pp. 117–20.

PARKER, W. C. "Participatory Citizenship: Civics in the Strong Sense." *Social Education* (October 1989), pp. 353–54.

THE CONTENT SOURCES: HISTORY, GEOGRAPHY, AND ECONOMICS

This chapter provides information to help the reader:

1. identify relationships among facts, concepts, and generalizations,

2. describe some special perspectives of history, geography, and economics,

3. point out the relationship between (a) history, geography, and economics and (b) the elementary social studies program,

4. identify selected concepts and generalizations from history, geography, and economics that can be incorporated in an elementary social studies program, and

5. develop social studies lessons that draw content from history, geography, and economics.

PRETEST

Answer each of the following true/false questions.

1. Individual facts have broader explanatory powers than individual generalizations.
2. Concepts are useful because they help people to organize large quantities of information under a common label.
3. As they study history, it is desirable for pupils to learn how to ask good questions and to rethink interpretations of historians.
4. The concept "region" as used in geography always refers to physical characteristics of a given portion of the earth's surface.
5. Authorities generally agree that the only emphasis of economics in the elementary social studies program should be "personal economics."

INTRODUCTION

Elementary social studies programs have multiple purposes. Among these are development of pupils' sensitivity to pressing social problems, fostering learners' personal development, and familiarizing learners with perspectives of certain fields of disciplined knowledge. Much content related to this last purpose is drawn from history, geography, and economics.

History, geography, and economics provide useful frameworks for looking at the world. Specialists in these fields have identified concepts and discovered generalizations that explain complex phenomena. Insights from these disciplines play an important role in the elementary social studies program. They help learners to better comprehend social problems and to grow in terms of their own self-understanding (Figure 2–1).

History, geography, economics, and the other social sciences are by no means the only content sources elementary social studies teachers use in planning lessons. For example, some lessons draw heavily on content from literature, art, music, the physical sciences, and philosophy. Information from these sources provides keen insights into certain aspects of the human condition. Nevertheless, it is probably fair to say that more elementary social studies content is drawn from history and from the social and behavioral sciences of geography, economics, political science, sociology, anthropology, and psychology. (See Chapter 3 for information about contributions of political science, sociology, anthropology, and psychology to the elementary social studies program.)

When information is drawn from history and the social sciences, it sometimes comes exclusively from one discipline (for example, from history or geography

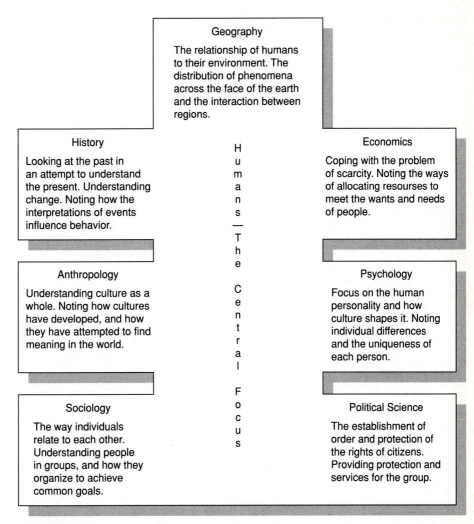

Geography

The relationship of humans to their environment. The distribution of phenomena across the face of the earth and the interaction between regions.

History

Looking at the past in an attempt to understand the present. Understanding change. Noting how the interpretations of events influence behavior.

Economics

Coping with the problem of scarcity. Noting the ways of allocating resourses to meet the wants and needs of people.

Anthropology

Understanding culture as a whole. Noting how cultures have developed, and how they have attempted to find meaning in the world.

Psychology

Focus on the human personality and how culture shapes it. Noting individual differences and the uniqueness of each person.

Humans — The Central Focus

Sociology

The way individuals relate to each other. Understanding people in groups, and how they organize to achieve common goals.

Political Science

The establishment of order and protection of the rights of citizens. Providing protection and services for the group.

FIGURE 2–1
The relationship of the academic disciplines to the study of human behavior.

only). Other content is interdisciplinary in nature, deriving from a combination of history and one or more social sciences.

As a beginning point for understanding how information from other academic disciplines can be used in the social studies program, a background in the basic structure of knowledge is essential. A grasp of this information and of information related to the special perspectives of history and each social science discipline provides a basis for building sound discipline-based lessons.

THE STRUCTURE OF KNOWLEDGE

Teachers need a way to make sense of the tremendous amount of information associated with history and the social sciences. Some kinds of content associated with each of these subjects are more important than others. The structure of knowledge approach, derived from the work of such important learning theorists and social studies specialists as Jerome Bruner (1960) and Hilda Taba (1962), provides a way to scale kinds of content in terms of their importance.

The structure of knowledge approach presumes that a given element of content becomes more important as it increases its potential to provide information that applies to diverse situations. The more all-encompassing elements are assigned a higher priority than the elements that deal with restricted bits of information.

There are three major content types in the structure of knowledge. From the narrowest (and least important) to the broadest (and most important) these are (1) facts, (2) concepts, and (3) generalizations. Figure 2–2 shows the relationships among these content types.

Facts

Facts have limited explanatory power. They refer to specific circumstances and have little transfer value. Here are some examples of social studies facts:

- Lincoln was born in 1809.
- Mountains cover between 10 and 15 percent of New Mexico.
- Wyoming has fewer people than Colorado.
- Austin is the capital of Texas.
- Mexico City has a larger population than New York City.

Because there are so many facts about every subject, it is never possible to teach them all. A selection must be made. Facts that are specifically related to the next two content types in the structure of knowledge—concepts and generalizations—should be selected. These facts broaden pupils' appreciation of

FIGURE 2–2
The structure of knowledge.

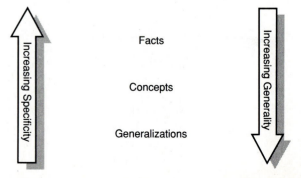

Increasing Specificity

Facts

Concepts

Generalizations

Increasing Generality

the meaning of concepts and heighten their grasp of the explanatory power of generalizations.

Concepts

Concepts are labels that help us make sense of large quantities of information. For example, the concept "automobile" helps tie together ideas about makes and models, thoughts about production line manufacturing, and other details as well. Concepts are powerful organizers. Unlike facts, which are limited to specific situations, concepts are broad enough to apply to many sets of conditions. Here are some examples of social studies concepts:

- Monsoon wind
- Latitude
- Folkway
- Inflation
- Self-determination

Concepts have assigned meanings. Their meanings depend on their definitions. The defining characteristics of concepts are called *attributes*. For example, the concept "triangle" is defined by these attributes: (1) it is a two-dimensional figure that is (2) enclosed by no more and no fewer than three straight lines.

In the social studies, few important concepts are as easily defined as "triangle." Concepts such as "democracy," "culture," "socialization," and so forth have many defining attributes. The complexity of these concepts presents a challenge for teachers as they develop lessons designed to help pupils master them. Pupil understanding of important concepts is a necessary prerequisite to their understanding of even more sophisticated content embedded in generalizations.

Generalizations

Generalizations are statements of relationship among concepts. The "truth" of a generalization is determined by reference to evidence. Some generalizations that we accept today may have to be modified in the future in light of new evidence. Generalizations concisely summarize a great deal of information. This feature makes them attractive to planners of social studies programs. Here are some examples of social studies generalizations:

- Opinions that originate in an earlier period persist to be influential in a later period.
- The more demands a natural environment places on people for physical survival, the less attention people pay to supernatural phenomena.
- As a society becomes increasingly educated and industrialized, its birthrate declines. (Berelson and Steiner 1967)

Note some of the concepts that are included in the last generalization: "society," "educated society," "industrialized society," and "birthrate." Pupils need to understand these concepts before they can grasp the significance of the generalization. There are specialized concepts and generalizations associated with individual academic disciplines. In this chapter, examples of concepts and generalizations related to history, geography, and economics will be introduced.

HISTORY

History is important in the elementary social studies program. Interpretations of historical events influence how people see themselves and others. People generalize from their impressions of past events. Teachers have an obligation to help pupils avoid misinterpretations. Sound lesson planning requires careful attention to central questions, concepts, and generalizations associated with history (Figure 2–3).

The following are examples of central questions, concepts, and generalizations that are important to historians. They are useful to elementary social studies teachers when they make decisions about what to include in lessons related to history.

Central Questions (a selection)

What are the values and biases of the writer?

What parts of the account are fact? What parts are fiction?

What kind of language is used to describe an event or a person? How does this language influence the view of the reader?

Where did the writer get his or her information?

Where else might we get information about these events?

What do others say about what happened?

Concepts (a selection)

Change, innovation, multiple causation, interpretation, movement, primary sources, secondary sources, era, period, epoch, century, A.D., B.C., season, year, calendar, medieval, ancient, modern, prehistoric, validity, time, chronology.

Generalizations (a selection)

Continuous change is universal and inevitable.

The rate of change within a society varies with such factors as the values of the society, the amount of pluralism in the society, and the extent of the society's contacts with other cultures.

Events of the past influence events of the present.

The history of a society provides guidelines for understanding thought and action in a society's present-day affairs.

The history of a nation influences the culture, traditions, beliefs, attitudes, and patterns of living of its people.

FIGURE 2–3

Central questions, concepts, and generalizations associated with history.

In its broadest sense, history encompasses everything that has happened in the past. No professional historian can hope to deal with more than a fraction of the total human experience. It is always necessary to make choices about what is included and what is excluded. The historian's decisions reflect personal values. For example, a historical account written by someone who sees the class struggle as the dominant theme in human affairs will look different from an account written by someone else who sees technological change as the dominant theme.

History-Related Classroom Activities

Because history reflects the perspectives of those who write it, its study calls on learners to go beyond simple recall of provided information. Pupils need to be taught to rethink historians' arguments, ask questions about historians' interpretations of fact, and suggest alternative explanations of events (Gagnon 1989). This suggests that elementary school social studies programs should actively involve pupils in the processes of historical inquiry (Bradley Commission on History in Schools 1988). Some examples designed to familiarize learners with these processes follow.

LESSON
• IDEA •

Developing Inquiry Skills: What the Visitor Wore
Grade Level: K–4. *Objective:* Learners can state how different people view the same event differently. *Suggested Procedure:* Make arrangements for the principal to make a brief visit to your classroom. When the principal leaves, ask members of the class to answer questions such as these:

1. What was the principal wearing?
2. What side of the desk did the principal stand on?
3. Who spoke first, the principal or the teacher?
4. About how long was the principal in the room?

Other questions might be asked as well. Questions in this simple exercise are designed to lead into a discussion about how people who are present at the same event do not always remember it in the same way. With an older group of learners, the teacher can move the discussion toward a consideration of the historian's use of eyewitness accounts of events. How reliable are they? How might a historian decide to believe in a case where accounts of eyewitnesses vary?

LESSON
• IDEA •

Evaluating Eyewitness Information: Yesterday on the Playground
Grade Level: 3–6. *Objectives:* Learners can (1) write an eyewitness account of an event, (2) identify why historical accounts of events may differ, and (3) state the problems historians face when writing about an event. *Suggested Procedure:* The teacher asks class members to write a description of the recess period on the playground. This might be done individually or by pupils working together. When everyone finishes, the teacher reads the accounts to the class. Alternatively, pu-

pils' work can be posted and class members invited to read all of the accounts. When everyone in the class has become familiar with each account, the teacher leads a discussion.

During this discussion, the teacher makes a tally mark on the chalk board each time a given event is mentioned. Members of the class can be asked to speculate why some events were mentioned by large numbers of people while others were noted only by a few. The individual accounts can be compared in terms of what they say about the sequence of observed events. Accounts can also be analyzed in terms of what they say about specific locations on the playground where reported events took place.

At the end of the discussion, the teacher uses an overhead transparency and works with the class as they collectively attempt to write an "official history" of what went on during the recess. This culminating activity can help pupils understand some problems that historians face as they work with primary evidence. It should also underscore the importance of working with multiple information sources.

LESSON · IDEA ·

Resolving Conflicting Accounts of Events

Grade Level: 5–6. *Objectives:* Learners can (1) identify bias in historical accounts and (2) state the importance of identifying bias in things they read. To help learners recognize different perspectives, sometimes it is useful to provide them with several short accounts of an event written from the viewpoints of individuals with widely differing opinions. *Suggested Procedure:* Have class members read the following accounts.

Event: The Burning of Washington in the War of 1812   Account 1: Victorious troops of the crown swarmed into Washington. With huzzahs all around, torches were passed. Officers led their men on a block by block campaign to torch the rebel capital. Officers of the general staff report that this action may soon break the back of the American resistance. There is talk that before the year is out these rebel colonies will be rightfully returned to the crown. American resistance is said to be crumbling. Loyal subjects of the king are said to be waiting in Canada for the signal to return south and re-establish the colonial governments. (Report filed by a correspondent of the *London Gazette.*)

Account 2: The British barbarian showed his true colors today. Consistent with the pattern of 25 years ago when American rights were trampled into the ground, the undisciplined British troops took on Washington today with unprincipled savagery. With little regard for the safety of women and children, they went on a rampage that resulted in the burning of most of the buildings in Washington. American troops are rallying. Spirits of the soldiers have never been higher. All look forward to taking a revenge that will forever free this continent from the British. (Report filed by a correspondent of the *New York Review.*)

After pupils read these accounts, the teacher conducts a debriefing discussion. This discussion might include questions such as these:

1. How are the accounts similar?
2. What are the differences in the two accounts?
3. How might you explain any differences?

Time and Chronology

History requires familiarity with many time concepts. These include seconds, minutes, hours, years, decades, and centuries. Many young children, particularly those in the early primary grades, have very distorted ideas about time. It is not uncommon for some of them to believe their parents rode dinosaurs to school.

Misunderstandings about the rate of change are often associated with confusion about time concepts. For example, some pupils may believe that all modern conveniences have been developed within their own lifetimes. They may answer "yes" to a question such as "Is it true that 15 years ago there were no street lights?"

To help pupils gain an improved understanding of time and change, a timeline chart is helpful. Such a chart might include information about (1) birth dates of members of the class, (2) birth dates of parents and grandparents of class members, and (3) dates when specific items were invented. An example of a timeline chart that has been constructed in this way is provided in Table 2–1.

The timeline chart helps to personalize human events. Historical happenings become more interesting to pupils because they are introduced in a context that includes birth dates of relatives. Information on the chart may lead pupils to ask questions of relatives who were alive when certain events took place (World War II, for example).

How Historians Judge the Truth

Professional historians use special techniques to help them determine what is "true." Good history is not simply a matter of the writer's personal opinion. It rests on the careful consideration of evidence. As appropriate to their age, grade level, and sophistication, elementary pupils should be introduced to the idea that his-

Learning about famous Americans can help pupils develop an understanding of change and continuity in history.

TABLE 2–1

Example of a timeline chart showing birthdates of pupils, pupils' parents and grandparents, and dates of selected inventions.*

	1905	1915	1925	1935	1945	1955	1965	1980	Birthdays of class members, their parents, and their grandparents
Grandfathers (father's side)	Jones	*Grandfathers (father's side)* Adams, Cole, Finn, Barnes	*Grandfathers (father's side)* Daly, Estes, Howe, Isles		*Fathers* Adams, Cole, Daly, Finn, Howe	*Fathers* Barnes, Estes, Isles, Jones		*Our Class* Adams, Barnes, Cole, Daly, Estes, Finn, Howe, Isles, Jones and so on	
Grandfathers (mother's side)	Barnes	*Grandfathers (mother's side)* Adams, Cole, Jones	*Grandfathers (mother's side)* Daly, Estes, Finn, Howe, Isles		*Mothers* Adams, Daly, Howe	*Mothers* Barnes, Cole, Estes, Finn, Isles, Jones			
Grandmothers (father's side)		*Grandmothers (father's side)* Cole, Finn, Howe, Jones	*Grandmothers (father's side)* Adams, Barnes, Daly, Estes, Isles						
Grandmothers (mother's side)		*Grandmothers (mother's side)* Adams, Cole, Jones	*Grandmothers (mother's side)* Daly, Estes, Finn, Howe, Isles						

Inventions	1914	1924	1934	1944	1954	1964	1974	1989
Electric vacuum cleaner 1907	Automatic toaster 1918	Television 1927; electric razor, 1931	Parking meter 1935	Long-playing records 1948	Laser 1958			
Kinds of schools								
Games children played								
Wars								
Clothes people wore								

* *Using the Timeline Chart:* Each column represents ten years of time. Note, for example, the first column begins with the year 1905 and ends with the year 1914. Information in this column relates to events occurring during the time period 1905–1914. Labels on the right below the information about birthdays of children, parents, and grandparents will vary in terms of the content being emphasized. The idea here is to provide youngsters with a way to tie phenomena in the past to people with whom they can identify. For example, if a youngster notes that his or her grandmother was alive in the 1930s, she might be someone he or she could ask about what people wore then. Many teachers have found that use of this type of a timeline chart can provide youngsters with a good feel for historical sequence. The timeline chart is a very flexible teaching tool that the teacher can easily modify for use in a number of lessons drawing on content from history.

39

torians consider (1) external validity and (2) internal validity when they attempt to establish whether something is true.

External Validity

External validity has to do with the issue of authenticity. Suppose a historian found a document that was supposed to have been written in England in the year 1610. The historian might arrange for chemical analyses of the paper and ink to establish whether the document's paper and ink represented types available in 1610. The words used in the material might be compared to words used in other documents known to be written around the year 1610. While doing this, the historian tries to find any words in the mystery document that were inconsistent with what might logically have been expected in a document of this date. The kind of detective work associated with external validity is used to unmask forgeries.

Internal Validity

Internal validity seeks to determine the accuracy of the information contained in a historical record. For example, it would be possible for a document that really was produced in 1610 to contain inaccurate statements. In the search for internal validity, the historian must consider whether the person who allegedly wrote the material was really capable of doing so. For example, did he or she have an education that would allow for the use of the kinds of sentences and words found in the document? Did the author of the document have an interest in writing the truth, or was there some reason for the writer to deliberately distort some, or even all, of the information?

In the search for internal validity and external validity, the historian is looking for explanations that go beyond the obvious. This search is part of the excitement of the historian's craft. History then is not just a matter of collecting and writing down information about the past. It is rather a question of disciplined thought about the past.

A Selection of Information Sources

The National Council for History Education

During the latter half of the 1980s, concerns about the quality of history instruction in the school prompted the formation of the Bradley Commission on History in Schools. Bradley Commission members included leading historians, history education specialists, and public school educators with interests in history. Many symposia, conferences, and curriculum projects were supported by the Bradley Commission.

In 1988, the Bradley Commission on History in Schools (1988) issued curriculum guidelines that have been widely discussed by individuals interested in improving the quality of history in both elementary and secondary schools. The Bradley Commission initiated publication of a monthly newsletter, *History Mat-*

ters, which often features information of interest to elementary teachers who are concerned about history.

In 1990, the Bradley Commission on History in Schools changed its name to the National Council for History Education. The organization continues to publish *History Matters* and provides other important services to educators who wish to improve the quality of history instruction in the schools. For membership information, write to: National Council for History Education, 26915 Westwood Road, Suite A-2, Westlake, OH 44145.

The National Council for the Social Studies

The National Council for the Social Studies (NCSS) is the largest national organization of educators interested in social studies education. For many years, NCSS has published *Social Education*. The "Elementary Education" section often features articles with guidelines for introducing content from history to elementary school learners. A subscription to *Social Education* is included in the basic annual NCSS membership fee.

Recently, NCSS began publishing another journal specifically for elementary school teachers, *Social Studies and the Young Learner.* For subscription information, and for other information about services provided by the NCSS, write to: National Council for the Social Studies, 3501 Newark Street N.W., Washington, DC 20016.

The Social Studies

The Social Studies is a professional journal for both elementary and secondary level social studies teachers. Articles frequently suggest innovative ways to treat historical content in the elementary school classrooms. (Ideas for other kinds of elementary social studies lessons also frequently appear in this journal.) For subscription information, write to: *The Social Studies,* Heldref Publications, 4000 Albemarle Street NW, Washington, DC 20016.

GEOGRAPHY

Geography is the study of patterns of spatial distributions and of interactions across space. *Guidelines for Geographic Education: Elementary and Secondary Schools* (Natoli et al. 1984), a joint publication of the Association of American Geographers and the National Council for Geographic Education, identifies five major themes of geography. These are (1) location, (2) place, (3) human-environment interactions (4) movement, and (5) regions.

Location

Lessons with this orientation focus on absolute location and relative location. *Absolute location* refers to a precise place on the earth's surface. *Relative location* refers to a place in terms of its relationship to other places. Studies of relative location help young people understand the important concept of interdependence.

Place

Each place on the earth's surface has unique characteristics. These distinguish it from all other places. Lessons with this emphasis focus on basic physical characteristics of the land and on cultural characteristics of people in different places.

Human-Environment Interactions

Human beings modify physical landscapes. Specific changes that occur may result because of cultural, economic, social, political, and technological characteristics of individual human populations. Lessons with this emphasis are designed to promote an appreciation of the kinds of human-environment interactions that occur and of their consequences.

Geography explores the relationship between people and their environment in all parts of the world.

Movement

Studies of movement focus on interactions between and among places. Lessons may emphasize patterns of movement of people, resources, and ideas. They often also promote an understanding of the impact varying levels of technological development can have on movement patterns. Studies of movement emphasize the interconnectedness of people who live in different places across the surface of the earth.

Regions

A region is an area that assumes a particular identity because it contains phenomena that share certain common characteristics. Regions are not restricted to landscape types. For example, some regions are so designated because the people who live there speak a common language or because they have chosen a common form of government. Regions provide convenient units of analysis for studying the world.

Geography lessons play an important part in the elementary social studies program. Some examples of geography-related activities are introduced in the subsection that follows. In planning learning experiences, teachers consider some central questions, concepts, and generalizations associated with geography. Some examples of these are provided in Figure 2–4.

Geography-Related Classroom Activities

LESSON
▪ IDEA ▪

Location
Grade Level: K–3. *Objective:* Learners can improve their understanding of "absolute location" and "relative location." *Suggested Procedures:*

1. Ask pupils where the busiest entrance to the school is located. Conduct a discussion to help them understand why this entrance is busier than others.
2. Ask members of the class to explain where the principal's office is. If they don't know, tell them.
3. Next, ask the class whether the principal's office or the custodian's office is closer to the busiest entrance. (In most buildings, the principal's office will be closer.)
4. Ask members of the class to suggest reasons that might explain why the principal's office is closer than the custodian's to the main entrance. (They may need help in understanding that the principal and his staff often have parents, central office administrators, and other people coming to see them. The custodian, on the other hand, tends to have fewer visitors during the day. For this reason, it is not important for the custodian's office to be as close as the principal's office to the main entrance.) Follow up with other simple examples that also illustrate the concept of relative location.

The following are examples of central questions, concepts, and generalizations that geographers consider important. They provide guidance to elementary teachers as they plan lessons related to geography.

Central Questions (a selection)

Where are things located? Why are they there?

What patterns are reflected in the groupings of things?

How are these patterns explained?

How can things be arranged to create a "region?"

How do people influence the environment? How does the environment influence people?

What causes changes in the patterns of distribution over time?

How do these changes affect how people live?

Concepts (a selection)

Environment, landform, climate, weather, latitude, longitude, elevation, spatial distribution, density, diffusion, interaction, spatial association, area differentiation, location, relative location, site, region, land use, urbanization, central place, accessibility, Equator, North Pole, South Pole, density, natural resource, settlement pattern, region, migration, rotation, revolution (of the earth)

Generalizations (a selection)

Human use of the environment is influenced by cultural values, economic wants, level of technology, and environmental perception.

Each culture views the physical environment in a special way, prizing particular aspects of it that may be different from those prized by other cultures.

Humans and the environment interact; the physical environment influences human activity, and humans influence the environment.

The character of a place is not constant; it reflects the place's past, present use, and future prospects.

Successive or continuing occupancy by groups of people and natural processes go together to give places their individual distinctiveness.

More change occurs near the boundaries of regions than in the interiors of regions.

The location of a place in relation to other places helps to explain its pattern of development.

The accessibility, the relative location, and the political character of a place influence the quantity and type of its interactions with other places.

FIGURE 2–4
Central questions, concepts, and generalizations associated with geography.

LESSON ▪ IDEA ▪

Regions

Grade Level: K–4. *Objectives:* Learners can (1) identify criteria for establishing a region and (2) draw the boundaries of a region.

A given region contains phenomena that share certain common characteristics. Because one or more characteristics are chosen when a region is being defined does not mean that other kinds of things are absent from the region. This is a point of some confusion among young pupils. For example, they may mistakenly conclude that there are vast fields of corn in the "corn belt," but no cities. In teaching about regions, it is important to point out that though certain distinctive features may make a given region unique, this region may share different characteristics with other regions.

Suggested Procedures: Regions should not be thought of as vast expanses of territory on the earth's surface. A region can be very limited in physical extent. For example, there are regions of activity in a room, in a building, or on a playground. To help pupils understand this point, encourage them to look around the school playground and, with the help of the teacher, prepare a simple map. Have pupils identify and list regions of the playground, and draw boundaries around them on the map. Sample regions include the following (categories can be altered to fit features of a playground at an individual school):

1. The baseball-playing region
2. The soccer region
3. The upper-grades region
4. The lower-grades region
5. The swings region
6. The running-and-general-playing region
7. The no-running region
8. The lining-up-to-go-inside region

Followup questions can probe learners' reasons for establishing boundaries for the regions they identify. The teacher might ask whether these boundary lines are permanent. Under what conditions might they change? Comments here can lead into a more general discussion of the nature of regional boundaries. Some possibilities for consideration might include city-limits boundaries, county boundaries, state boundaries, national boundaries, as well as boundaries of nonpolitical regions of various kinds.

LESSON
• IDEA •

Migration

Grade Level: 4–6. *Objectives:* Learners can (1) locate places on a map, (2) identify movement patterns, and (3) state reasons for movement from one place to another.

People, goods, and services move from place to place. An understanding of the nature of migration can help pupils grasp the nature of the linkages that tie places together. The following activity focuses on the issue of migration as a reflection of interactions among places.

Suggested Procedures:

1. As a homework assignment, ask pupils to identify the places of birth of their parents and grandparents. Ask them to bring in a list of all the different places their parents and grandparents have lived.
2. When learners have brought this information to school, give them an opportunity to work with a large, wall-sized United States map and a large, wall-sized world map. Their task is to identify and label the locations of

birthplaces and former and present residences of the parents and grandparents. (Bright colored circles with "sticky" backs, available from office supply stores, work well as labels to mark locations on the maps. Obtain labels in three separate colors. Use one color for birthplaces, a second color for places where parents and/or grandparents used to live, and a third color to indicate places where parents and grandparents live now.) After all pupils have put their labels on the maps, hang the maps on the wall so everyone in the class can see them.

3. A followup discussion focuses on such questions as:
    a. How many different states are represented?
    b. How many different countries are identified?
    c. Are there patterns of movement (east to west, north to south, rural to urban, and so forth) that seem to be indicated? (The teacher will need to help pupils see these patterns.)
    d. How can we explain these movements? (The teacher might help pupils think about wars, economic opportunities, and so forth. The need for teacher help will vary with the sophistication of the pupils.)

A modification of this activity requires pupils to interview their parents and grandparents about their reasons for moving. Results of these interviews can be shared and can form a basis for a discussion of migration.

LESSON
▪ IDEA ▪

Environmental Perception

Grade Level: K–3. *Objective:* Learners can state the influence of past experiences on their ideas and perceptions.

Geographers interested in environmental perception believe that human behavior is not adequately explained by the world "as it is." Rather, behavior results from what people "believe" the world to be.

Personal experiences help shape how people view the world. For example, surveys of people who live in different parts of the United States have revealed great variations in opinions about the location of the "best" place to live. Misperceptions of distance are common among people who are unfamiliar with an area. Longtime residents of the Northeast United States often underestimate the distance separating the far-off West Coast cities of Los Angeles and San Francisco. West Coast residents experience a similar difficulty in sorting out distance relationships between pairs of cities such as Washington and New York or New York and Boston. Only Texans seem to know that El Paso is closer to San Diego than to Houston.

Suggested Procedures: Social studies lessons can be developed that help learners recognize how their personal experiences shape their perceptions of the world. A lesson many teachers have used requires learners to imagine that they have been asked to design the "perfect" park. The exercise begins with questions and concludes with a debriefing session.

1. What kinds of things should be put in the park? (Teacher writes responses on the chalkboard.)

2. Where did your ideas come from? Did you see something on a trip or on some other occasion that helped you to decide on something? If so, what was it, and where did you see it?
3. The teacher conducts a debriefing discussion to help pupils understand that their own past experiences have influenced many of their choices about what to put in the park. This discussion can be broadened to include other areas. (Why do some people prefer certain makes of cars and not others? Has past experience shaped their preferences? Why do some people prefer to take vacations in the city, while others like to go to the mountains?)

These activities are very brief examples of what can be done with geography-related content. Content drawn from geography can serve as the basis for highly motivating lessons. Additionally, these lessons can develop pupils' higher-level thinking skills. Geography has much more to offer to learners than the deadly, outdated, memorization-of-state-capitals requirement.

"Is this your job, or is it your hobby?"

A Selection of Information Sources

National Council for Geographic Education

The leading national professional organization for educators interested in geography is the National Council for Geographic Education (NCGE). NCGE publishes the excellent *Journal of Geography.* A subscription is included as part of the annual membership fee. Many issues feature articles about imaginative approaches to introducing geographic content to elementary school pupils. For information, write to: National Council for Geographic Education, NCGE Central Office, Indiana University of Pennsylvania, Indiana, PA 15705.

Joint Committee on Geographic Education

Members of the Joint Committee on Geographic Education were drawn from two professional groups whose members have long been interested in improving the quality of geographic instruction in the schools. These two groups are the National Council for Geographic Education and the Association of American Geographers.

The Joint Committee's *Guidelines for Geographic Education* (1984) provides suggestions regarding what kinds of geographic content should be taught at various grade levels. Elementary school recommendations provide guidelines for grades (1) kindergarten through two, (2) three and four, and (3) five and six. Many libraries have copies of the *Guidelines.* Copies are also available through the National Council for Geographic Education.

Geographic Alliance Network

The National Geographic Society has become very much interested in revitalizing the quality of geographic education in the schools. To this end, the Society has sponsored the formation of more than forty state-based Geographic Alliances. Alliances draw additional support from state governments and from private sources.

A Geographic Alliance joins together professional geographers and classroom teachers. Each alliance is led by a coordinator who helps to organize activities and provide information about state activities. Alliances sponsor summer geographic education institutes, put on one- and two-day workshops, and support the development of high-quality instructional materials. Many activities and programs of Geographic Alliances are directed toward elementary teachers.

For information about the Geographic Alliance Network write to: Geographic Education Program, National Geographic Society, Washington, DC 20036.

ECONOMICS

Scarcity is the fundamental concern of economics. People's wants often exceed the resources available to satisfy them. Hence, decisions must be made regarding how limited resources are to be allocated and about which wants are to be satisfied.

Economics is the study of approaches to making decisions in response to the universal scarcity problem.

Traditionally, many elementary economics lessons focused on consumer economics and personal economics. Consumer economics sought to teach learners how to become alert and careful buyers. Personal economics focused on skills such as personal budgeting, management of savings accounts, and (for older learners) balancing checkbooks.

Today's more comprehensive economics programs go beyond consumer economics and personal economics. Increasingly, there are attempts to provide learners with a basic understanding of the operation of the entire American economic system. Hence, many economics-based lessons today emphasize economic systems in general and the American economic system in particular.

Content from economics often can be introduced in lessons that draw much of their information from other subjects. For example, in history lessons, the economic motivations of settlers can be included. Lessons focusing on decisions of businesses to locate in particular places can combine information from economics and geography. Problems governments face in allocating tax revenues can draw on content from both economics and political science.

Categories of Economic Systems

All economic systems try to accommodate these important social goals:

1. Economic growth
2. Economic efficiency
3. Security
4. Stability
5. Equity
6. Freedom

As economic systems attempt to respond to the scarcity problem, they also attempt to attend to each of these goals. Individual goals never receive equal emphasis in a given economic system. Economics lessons help pupils appreciate that different economic systems have established different priorities. For example, some place more emphasis on the goal of economic security than the goal of economic freedom.

As they are taught to think about how different economic systems respond to the six basic social goals, children in the middle and upper grades are introduced to three basic economic system types: (1) traditional economies, (2) command economies, and (3) market economies.

Traditional economies respond to the problem of scarcity by following long-standing patterns or customs. Such systems are found most frequently in technologically underdeveloped societies.

Command economies allocate scarce resources by following a master plan. The plan is devised and enforced by a strong central government. Until quite recently, many countries in Eastern Europe had command economies. This form has been declining in popularity.

Market economies allocate resources in a decentralized way. There is no master plan. Governments play a relatively minor role. Resources are devoted to the production of those goods and services that individual consumers wish to buy. The United States and many Western European nations have long had market systems.

Market systems are becoming increasingly popular throughout the world. Because of this trend, social studies programs now pay particular attention to helping pupils understand how they operate. Lessons may focus on such market system characteristics as the following (Allen and Armstrong 1978):

1. Private property
2. Economic freedom
3. Incentives
4. Decentralized decision making
5. Special and somewhat limited role for government

When they plan economics-related lessons, teachers refer to central questions, concepts, and generalizations associated with the discipline. Some examples of these are shown in Figure 2–5.

Economics-Related Classroom Activities

The following are examples of activities that can help pupils master ideas associated with economics.

LESSON
▪ IDEA ▪

Making Choices

Grade Level: K–3. *Objectives:* Learners can (1) identify choices they have to make and (2) explain how choosing one thing eliminates another that could have been chosen.

Scarcity requires people everywhere to make choices. This primary-level activity is designed to help young elementary school pupils develop an appreciation of the scarcity problem.

Suggested Procedures:

1. The teacher says, "Pretend I am Santa Claus. I want to know what to get you. I want to know five things you want. Draw me a picture of your five things."
2. The teacher collects the drawings. The drawings are used as a focus for the rest of the exercise. The teacher says, "All right, I have Sarah's list here. Now Sarah, pretend that I'm still Santa, but I've lost your list. To make up for it, I'm going to give you a nice crisp five-dollar bill for Christmas. But there's a catch. I am going to say that each item on your list costs two dollars. This means you'll be able to buy only two things. That will take four dollars. You'll still have a dollar for your piggy bank. Now, tell me what you'll buy."
3. The teacher concludes with a discussion focusing on questions such as:
   a. Why couldn't Sarah buy everything she wanted?

The following are examples of central questions, concepts, and generalizations associated with economics. They provide guidelines for elementary teachers interested in planning economics-related lessons.

Central Questions (a selection)

How have different societies coped with the problem of scarcity?

How can resources be allocated responsibly and fairly?

What is the proper role of government in regulating an economy?

Does the economic system provide an equality of opportunity?

Is the economic system stable, or is it characterized by uneven growth, high levels of unemployment, and high levels of inflation?

What is the overall quality of life provided by the economic system?

Concepts (a selection)

Scarcity, resources, cost, opportunity cost, private property, land, labor, capital, public property, specialization, goods, market, traditional economy, command economy, market economy, services, interdependence, consumer, producer, price, competition, supply, demand, incentives, division of labor

Generalization (a selection)

The wants of people are unlimited whereas the resources to meet those wants are scarce; hence, individuals and societies must make decisions as to which wants will be met.

Allocating scarce resources can be done in a variety of ways.

Different nations have taken different approaches to solving the problem of economic scarcity.

Unequal distribution of resources and population makes trade a necessary ingredient of economic well-being.

Specialization and division of labor promote the efficiency of an economic system.

The economic development of a nation is related to the availability of resources and investment capital and the quality of the labor force.

The government plays an important role in the economic development of every society, but its role varies from place to place.

FIGURE 2–5
Central questions, concepts, and generalizations associated with economics.

    b. Sarah, how did you feel when you had to choose?

    c. What did you give up that you would most like to have had? Do you think other people sometimes have this problem? (This is a very brief introduction to "opportunity cost," an important idea in economics. When a decision to use a scarce resource in one way has been made there is an "opportunity cost": this decision means the resource cannot be used in another way.)

    d. Do people ever have enough money to buy everything they want? (This question should lead to the idea that human wants expand more rapidly than the resources needed to satisfy them. The incomes of people expand more slowly than their wants.)

LESSON
▪ *IDEA* ▪

Economic Systems

Grade Level: 5–6. *Objective:* Learners can identify features of traditional, command, and market economies. The following materials are needed:

1. Three large cards respectively captioned (a) traditional economy, (b) command economy, and (c) market economy.
2. A variety of small items (puzzles, marbles, and so forth) of interest to young children. There should be enough so that each child will have at least one small item.

Understanding basic economic concepts such as the market and trade helps pupils understand market economies.

Suggested Procedures:

1. Whole Group Activity
   a. Ask pupils who are the eldest children in their families to stand. Tell others that these individuals will receive all of the wealth (all of the small items). Others in the class will receive nothing. Ask pupils to guess which kind of an economic system would be most likely to give all of the resources to the eldest children (traditional). Discuss children's feelings and the general features of a traditional economic system.
   b. Announce that you are the "government." Arbitrarily identify two or three pupils who will receive most of the items of wealth. Select a few other pupils who will receive one or two items. Give pupils no choice as to which items they will receive. Select a final group who will receive no items at all. Ask learners to identify the kind of an economic system that might result in this kind of a distribution of wealth (command). Discuss children's feelings and the general features of a command economy.
   c. This leaves the market system. Show the card with this label to the class. Ask pupils to guess about the features of this system. Accept all ideas.
2. Interaction Activity
   a. Give each pupil one item. Then give members of the class an opportunity to trade with one another. Explain that they do not have to trade if they want to keep what they have.
   b. During a debriefing session, ask class members what happened. Emphasize features of a market system. Point out that both the freedom to sell (or trade) and the freedom not to sell (or trade) are features of a market economy.

**LESSON
▪ IDEA ▪**

Resource Utilization

Grade Level: 4–6. *Objectives:* Learners can (1) list different resources, (2) identify different categories of resources, and (3) identify potential uses of different types of resources.

The term *resources* is much used in economics. It is a concept that elementary pupils find difficult to grasp. Part of the difficulty is that many kinds of things qualify as resources.

In general, economics identify three basic categories of resources: (1) natural resources; (2) capital resources; and, (3) human resources. *Natural resources* include phenomena occurring in nature that can be used to meet human needs. Good agricultural land, coal, petroleum, and forests are examples of natural resources. *Capital resources* are resources that are used to create additional production or wealth. Computers and machinery are examples of capital resources. *Human resources* refer to the talents of people. The production of wealth demands people who understand what must be done and how to do it. For example, a firm specializing in highway surveys must have trained engineers; these engineers are among the firm's human resources.

Suggested Procedures: To assist pupils in thinking about each of the three basic kinds of resources, teachers can provide them with a blank chart similar to the following. Choose a business or economic activity that is familiar to members of the class. For example, a construction activity close to the school might suggest the appropriateness of a construction company as a focus for the lesson:

Ace Construction Company Resource Needs

Natural resources	Capital resources	Human resources
Petroleum	Cranes	Engineers
Water	Trucks	Steelworkers
Wood products	Backhoes	Bricklayers
Metal products	Tractors	Electricians

It is useful to have pupils fill out similar charts on several different kinds of businesses. To make this easer, various firms might be assigned to separate groups of pupils. Once information is gathered, the teacher can conduct a discussion focusing on such questions as these:

1. Where does the business get the resources it needs?
2. What types of human resources are needed? Do different companies have different human-resource needs?
3. Who decides how the resources will be used?

A Selection of Information Sources

Joint Council on Economic Education

The Joint Council on Economic Education is dedicated to the improvement of economics-related instruction in the nation's schools. It is an independent, nonprofit, nonpartisan organization. The Joint Council has produced many practical materials for elementary social studies classes. For information, write to: Joint Council on Economic Education, 1212 Avenue of the Americas, New York, NY 10036.

National Center for Economic Education for Children

The National Center for Economic Education for Children is particularly concerned with the improvement of economic understanding among the nation's elementary school learners. It publishes a quarterly journal called *The Elementary Economist*. Each issue includes practical teaching suggestions for the elementary grades. Information about the Center's activities can be obtained by writing to: National Center for Economic Education for Children, Lesley College, 35 Mellen Street, Cambridge, MA 02138.

Other Sources

Many economics education centers exist around the country. Most of them are located on college and university campuses. These centers are dedicated to improvement of the nation's economic literacy. Many of them have materials suitable for use in elementary classrooms. It is also common for economic education centers to offer in-service programs for classroom teachers.

Chambers of commerce, unions, private organizations, and other private and public organizations produce economics-related materials. Some of these tend to reflect narrow points of view, and teachers need to select with care to assure that pupils receive a program of instruction that reflects an appropriate balance of competing perspectives.

KEY IDEAS IN SUMMARY

1. When they build lessons drawing content from history, geography, economics, and other content sources, teachers must decide what elements of content to emphasize. Many of them find that reference to the "structure of knowledge" helps them to do this. The structure of knowledge organizes information into the broad categories of (a) facts, (b) concepts, and (c) generalizations.

2. Lessons focusing on history have several purposes. One of these is to give pupils a sense of their own place in time. Additionally, these lessons promote the development of important analytical thinking skills.

3. Historians, as they attempt to determine the "truth" are concerned about both external validity and internal validity. Procedures used to determine external validity are concerned with establishing the likelihood that a document or other historic artifact could have been produced at the time it was alleged to be produced. Internal validity studies seek to determine the accuracy of the information found in the source material.

4. Geography focuses on spatial patterns. Guidelines produced jointly by the Association of American Geographers and the National Council for Geographic Education have identified five key geographic themes. These are (a) location, (b) place, (c) human-environment interactions, (d) movement, and (e) regions.

5. The National Geographic Society has been encouraging the development of Geographic Alliances in each state. These are coalitions of professors of geography and classroom teachers interested in geography. The Geographic Alliances sponsor summer programs, one- and two-day workshops, and geographic education-related materials development.

6. Economics lessons focus on scarcity and human reactions to this universal problem. Often pupils are introduced to responses made by (a) traditional economies, (b) command economies, and (c) market economies. At the elementary level, pupils are helped to appreciate that they live in a world characterized by unlimited wants and limited resources with which to respond to them.

POSTTEST

Answer each of the following true/false questions.

1. History, geography, and economics are the only sources of content for the elementary social studies program.
2. A generalization tends to summarize more content than a fact.
3. Among other things, geographers study regions.
4. In general, the income of people tends to rise faster than the growth of their wants.
5. "Scarcity" is a key concept in economics.

QUESTIONS

1. What are some of the purposes of lessons that draw content from history?
2. What are the characteristics of facts, concepts, and generalizations?
3. What are geography's five themes?
4. What are some sources of information that teachers can use in providing instruction drawing content from history, geography, and economics?
5. What do economists study?
6. State legislatures have required elementary teachers to provide instruction on state and national history because such content is thought to contribute to the development of citizenship. Do you agree that there is a connection between the study of this kind of content and citizenship? Why, or why not?
7. Would the elementary social studies program be stronger if all content were drawn from one discipline—for example, history? What would be strengths and weaknesses of a policy decision to do this? If it were done, should the focus discipline be history, geography, economics, or some other discipline? Why do you think so?
8. What, if anything, might be lost if content from history, geography, and economics were removed entirely from the elementary social studies program?
9. Many economic issues are "pocketbook related." This means that biases of individual groups often come into play when these issues are raised. Some people argue that these biases are too sophisticated for elementary school learners to understand. They recommend that instruction related to economics be delayed until the secondary school grades, when learners are more mature. How do you react to this idea?

10. Some people remember little about the geographic instruction they received in school other than the "pain" they felt when asked to memorize names of the capitals of the states. How might you talk to a parent with this kind of recollection? Specifically, what could you say about the kinds of things happening in elementary geography lessons today? What might you say regarding geography's potential for developing pupils' higher-level thinking skills?

EXTENDING UNDERSTANDING AND SKILL

Activities

1. Review several issues of *History Matters*. Share some arguments included in this publication regarding the role of history in the elementary curriculum with others in your class. For information about receiving *History Matters*, write to: National Council for History Education, 26915 Westwood Road, Suite A-2, Westlake, OH 44145.

2. Read about the "six vital themes" of history on pages 10–11 of the Bradley Commission on History in Schools' publication, *Building a History Curriculum: Guidelines for Teaching History* (available from the National Council for History Education and in many school libraries). Then, read about the five "fundamental themes" in pages 3–8 of *Guidelines for Geographic Education: Elementary and Secondary Schools*, a joint publication of the National Council for Geographic Education and the Association of American Geographers (available from the National Council for Geographic Education and in many libraries). What similarities and differences do you note between the "vital themes" of history and the "fundamental themes" of geography? Share your observations with your instructor.

3. Review several elementary school social studies textbooks. Select two or three written for a grade level you would like to teach. Determine the approximate percentage of content in each selected from history, geography, and economics. Prepare a graph illustrating rough percentages. Share this information with others in your class.

4. Select four or five key concepts from history, geography, and economics. Begin building resource files to support instruction related to each concept. Include photographs, illustrations, newspaper stories, and journal articles that might help you teach these concepts to elementary school pupils. Your course instructor will critique your files.

5. Interview two or three teachers who teach a grade level that interests you. Ask them to comment on some specific difficulties children have in grasping content related to history, geography and economics. Ask them to suggest techniques they use to overcome these problems. Share this information in an oral report to your class.

REFERENCES

ALLEN, J., AND D. ARMSTRONG. *Hallmarks of a Free Enterprise System.* College Station, TX: Center for Education and Research in Free Enterprise, Texas A&M University, 1978.

BERELSON, B., AND G. STEINER. *Human Behavior: An Inventory of Scientific Findings.* New York: Harcourt Brace Jovanovich, 1967.

BRADLEY COMMISSION ON HISTORY IN SCHOOLS. *Building a History Curriculum: Guidelines for Teaching History.* Westlake, OH: The Bradley Commission on History in Schools, 1988.

BRUNER, J. *The Process of Education.* Cambridge, MA: Harvard University Press, 1960.

GAGNON, P. *Democracy's Half-Told Story: What American History Textbooks Should Add.* Washington, DC: American Federation of Teachers, 1989.

NATOLI, S. J., R. G. BOEHM, J. B. KRACHT, D. A. LANEGRAN, J. J. MONK, AND R. W. MORRILL. *Guidelines for Geographic Education: Elementary and Secondary Schools.* Washington, DC: Association of American Geographers and National Council for Geographic Education, 1984.

TABA, H. *Curriculum Development: Theory and Practice.* New York: Harcourt, Brace and World, 1989.

SUPPLEMENTAL READING

CURRICULUM TASK FORCE OF THE NATIONAL COMMISSION ON SOCIAL STUDIES IN THE SCHOOLS. *Charting a Course: Social Studies for the 21st Century.* Washington, DC: National Commission on Social Studies in the Schools, November 1989.

JENNESS, D. *Making Sense of the Social Studies.* New York: Macmillan, 1990.

MAY, E. R. "The Dangerous Usefulness of History." In B. R. Gifford, ed., *History in the Schools: What Shall We Teach?* New York: Macmillan, 1988, pp. 227–35.

3

CONTENT SOURCES: POLITICAL SCIENCE, SOCIOLOGY, ANTHROPOLOGY, AND PSYCHOLOGY

This chapter provides information to help the reader:

1. identify the relationships among the social science disciplines of political science, sociology, anthropology, and psychology, and the curriculum of elementary social studies,

2. describe the special perspectives of each discipline in studying human action and behavior,

3. identify central questions, concepts, and generalizations from each discipline, and

4. develop social studies lessons that draw content from each social science discipline.

PRETEST

Answer each of the following true/false questions.

1. Including political science in the curriculum is of recent origin.
2. Power is one of the basic political science concepts appropriate for inclusion in the elementary curriculum.
3. Sociology helps individuals understand the nature of membership in the total human community.
4. Content from sociology is best delayed until the upper grades.
5. Anthropology helps bridge the gap between biology and the social sciences.
6. The focus of psychological content in the elementary curriculum tends to be on the understanding of one's own development and the development of positive self-esteem.

INTRODUCTION

Elementary social studies programs attempt to achieve multiple purposes. Among these are helping pupils to understand their social environment and develop sensitivity to social issues and problems. Pupils need a broad understanding of the social science disciplines to develop these skills. Social science perspectives and generalizations are powerful tools for understanding human complexities, tools that help us as we attempt to solve our enduring problems.

Teachers need to remember that the reason for including these disciplines in the curriculum is not to make pupils into "miniature social scientists," but to draw on social science perspectives to help students understand themselves and their world. The following sections provide a brief overview of selected social science disciplines and present sample activities that draw on their content.

POLITICAL SCIENCE

Elementary social studies have long included content from political science. In the past this content was labeled "civics" or "government." Civics, or government, in the social studies program was narrowly focused on ways to "Americanize" the children of immigrants, to inculcate them with the political values and perspectives of the United States government. Educators believed that teaching students about the Constitution, the Bill of Rights, how bills become laws, how our government is organized, and other related facts would result in individuals who would participate politically and who were committed to democratic government.

However, the outcome of this indoctrination was not always anticipated. For example, a state legislator once remarked that the social studies had obviously failed because so many individuals were lacking in patriotism, as evidenced by their willingness to criticize the government and actively demonstrate against United States involvement in Vietnam.

In recent years interest in ideals of citizenship has been stimulated by concern over what appears to be voter apathy and citizen disenchantment with government. There have been renewed efforts to include political science content in the social studies curriculum. Recent approaches have attempted to focus on basic concepts and principles of government so that students can begin to understand how different types of government function and how they affect those who live under them. Some concepts that have been used to organize political science content are law, authority, power, freedom, conflict, equality, citizenship, and justice.

Studying these concepts and how they function in different contexts helps students understand such ideas as how political systems operate and why conflicts

Political science components help pupils learn how to bring about change such as these people are attempting by signing petitions to save the harp seals.

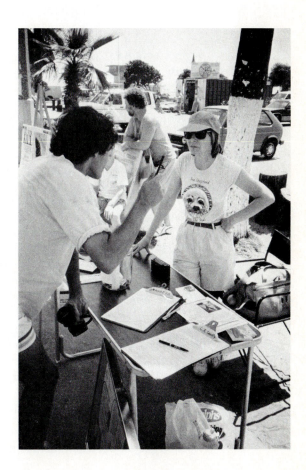

between groups and nations occur. Educators often develop these concepts by introducing several basic themes:

Government and Governmental Processes.   This theme emphasizes how decisions are made and how widely held values become formalized as laws. It also focuses on how leaders are selected and how authority is distributed.

Comparative Political Systems.   This theme emphasizes the ways people at various times and various places have organized governments. Content emphasizes the ways of allocating power. It also focuses on how different governments strike a balance between providing for efficient decision making and, at the same time, responding to the concerns and rights of individual citizens.

Political Theory.   This theme deals with the issue of how people *ought* to be governed to preserve the rights of individuals and to assure the continuation of the society as a whole. Concepts such as "justice," "equality," and "freedom" are associated with this emphasis.

Sample Activities

Figure 3–1 contains central questions, concepts, and generalizations around which activities can be developed. Samples of activities that can be used to focus on political science content follow. Additional activities related to political science are found in Chapter 9, "Law-Related Education."

LESSON
▪ IDEA ▪

Rule Making.   Grade Level: K–2. *Objectives:* Learners can identify reasons for and advantages/disadvantages of rules. Learners can also become familiar with making decisions about controversial issues. *Suggested Procedures*: The selected focus issue must be interesting to the pupils. Consider this example:

Teacher: Our student council has two ideas about our playground. We need to talk about these ideas. As you know, several people have been hurt on the swings.

The first idea is to allow only fourth, fifth, and sixth graders to use the swings, unless a teacher is present. If a teacher is there, then it would be all right for first, second, and third graders to swing.

The second idea is to require everybody who swings to attend a ten-minute lesson on swing safety. This would be taught on the playground by a teacher. No one would *have* to take this lesson, but everybody who wanted to swing would have to go. After each lesson, the teacher would give a button to those who attended. People will have to wear these buttons before they can get on the swings. The buttons will tell teachers on the playground that these people have had the swing safety lesson.

Let's begin by thinking about the first idea:

(a) What do you like about this idea?
(b) What do you think the people who thought about this idea liked about it?

The following are examples of central questions, concepts, and generalizations that are important to political scientists. They are useful to elementary social studies teachers when they make decisions about what to include in lessons related to political science.

Central Questions (a selection)

Who decides the rules or laws?
Are the rules or laws accepted by the people that are governed?
What difference does it make who decides the rules or laws?
What values are reflected in the laws?
Who enforces the laws?
How much impact do the citizens have on the decisions made by the government?
What are the alternative ways that people have established for making political decisions?
What is the decision-making process in different governmental systems?
How does the system change?
What happens if the system does not change in the direction that the people desire?

Concepts (a selection)

Power, decision making, Constitution, law making, due process, justice, freedom, citizenship, state, nation, public services, equal protection, rights, responsibilities, civil liberty, separation of powers, conflict resolution, legal system, common law.

Generalizations (a selection)

Every society establishes an authority structure that makes decisions and enforces social regulations on members of the society.
A stable government facilitates the social and economic growth of a nation.
Some consent of the governed is required in all governments, and without it a government will eventually collapse.
The government acts to help resolve conflicts when individuals and groups have competing goals and values.
In order for a system of government to survive it must have the ability to change as values and circumstances change.
A democratic society depends on the presence of educated and informed citizens who have a willingness to compromise and a respect for the rights of minorities and the loyal opposition.

FIGURE 3–1
Central questions, concepts, and generalizations associated with political science.

    (c) Why do you think they want to restrict swing use to fourth, fifth, and sixth graders?
    (d) What do you think the real purpose of this idea is?

(These are simply examples of the questions that might be asked. The idea is to help pupils recognize the specifics associated with a given position, the assumptions undergirding a given position [older pupils are less likely to get hurt than younger pupils], and the values underlying a position [health and safety are valued higher than the right of everybody to use the swings].)

Now let's think about the second idea:

(Follow here with the same kinds of questions introduced during the discussion of the first idea.)

Let's think about both ideas together:

(a) Which idea is the better one?
(b) Why do you think so?
(c) If the idea you like is adopted, what can you do to see the new rule is carried out?
(d) What if the other idea is adopted? Will you have to obey it?
(e) Do other people have to accept things that they might not like but that have been favored by a majority?

(Follow again with similar questions.)

This discussion might conclude with the students deciding what they might do to influence the decision of the student council. Pupils can be helped to understand that group action can influence political decisions.

LESSON
• IDEA •

Conflict Resolution.   Grade Level: 4–6. Objectives: Learners can identify (1) steps that can be used in resolving a conflict and (2) the potential role of government in conflict resolution.

One function of government is to resolve conflicts among citizens. These conflicts often arise because individuals have different ideas about what is important. Government acts as a referee that brings conflicting ideas together, sets forth rules as to how to resolve these conflicts, and specifies how these resolutions should be enforced. Mock government exercises focusing, as appropriate, on a city council, a state legislature, the United States Congress, or the United Nations can help pupils become more familiar with the conflict-resolution function of government.

Suggested Procedures: The following lesson is an example of how a mock government experience can be organized.

Introduction: The teacher summarizes for the class a newspaper report concerning a decision to build a new park. The account describes a city council meeting at which several citizens protested a decision to build the new park near their homes. These citizens contended that the park would lower the value of their homes because of the increased noise and trash that would result.

Other park protestors contended that the proposed site was too expensive. They felt that the city would be better off selling the property to a firm wanting to build a new shopping center.

Another group of people supported the idea of building the park. They pointed out that the children of the community needed a place to play. They disputed the contention that the park would reduce the value of nearby homes. They also insisted that in the long run the new playground would be of more benefit to the city than the money from the sale of the land.

After the teacher discusses this basic information with the class, the lesson develops through the following steps:

1. *Defining the issue.* At this stage, the teacher leads a class discussion focusing on the issue at question. Special attention is paid to identifying the specific goals of the contending groups.
2. *Organizing the mock council.* Members of the class are divided into three groups. One group will represent the home owners opposed to the park because of a fear that their homes' values will drop. One group will represent the people who think that the city would benefit more from the money that could be had from selling the land. One group will represent the people who think that the park is needed to provide play space for the community's children.

BOX 3-1   **What Should Be Taught?**

Two parents were overheard arguing about what should be taught in the elementary school about government.

Parent 1

I'm really tired hearing about how we need to teach our children about every type of political system in the world. Our children don't know about our own system and how it works. They are uninformed about their responsibilities as American citizens. Elementary youngsters are too immature to understand all this abstract information about other governments. In addition, many of these teachers use the study of other governments to criticize our own government and way of life. This creates a lack of patriotism and loyalty—inexcusable behavior because it is our government that is paying the salary of those teachers. It is time we quit wasting time teaching the virtues of other governments and instead, spend classroom time teaching children the advantages of democracy in America.

Parent 2

I agree that our children need to know about their responsibilities as American citizens. I disagree that this is best accomplished by excluding study of other governments. We live in a global community, and future citizens need to know how people govern themselves in different parts of the world. In addition, it is time we faced up to the fact that our government is not perfect. Our government does some things that are wrong, and children should learn about them. If studying the truth means less *unthinking* allegiance to America, that's all right. It's time our children realized that we can learn how to solve some of our pressing problems by looking at how others are solving them.

Think
About
This

1. What do you see as the strongest part of parent 1's argument?
2. What do you see as the strongest part of parent 2's argument?
3. How would you respond to these two parents?
4. How does a teacher decide to allocate the time devoted to teaching about our responsibilities as citizens and about other governments? Is there enough time to do both?

3. *Establishing the council meeting rules.* Rules are needed to govern how council members will be called on, how long each will be permitted to speak, and how other matters will be handled. The teacher and the class can discuss these matters and make decisions together.

4. *Presenting positions.* The council meeting begins. The members of each group present their case.

5. *Identifying criteria and identifying alternatives.* At this stage of the exercise, the teacher leads a discussion designed to help pupils identify criteria that they will apply in deciding whether their decision is "good" and in identifying possible alternative decisions.

6. *Making the decision.* Members of the class, acting as a city council, make a decision about the location-of-the-park issue. The issue is decided by a majority vote.

7. *Debriefing.* The teacher leads a debriefing discussion, including a review of the entire decision-making process. The class examines the decision itself, decides why this particular decision was reached and the other possible alternatives were rejected; and explores other relevant matters.

SOCIOLOGY

People everywhere live in groups. Each individual belongs to several different groups beginning with the family and including social organizations, ethnic groups, political parties, and religious organizations. Sociologists study groups— why they form, how they are organized, how they influence the behavior and the values of their members. They study the formation of norms and values, how these are passed from one generation to the next, and how they change over time. Sociology is an important area of study, as evidenced by growing public interest in changes in family composition and the roles of family members, concern about increasing gang warfare in American cities, and awareness of prejudice, racism, and discrimination among various groups within society.

Topics with a sociological flavor are introduced early in the elementary curriculum when pupils begin studying about families. They may investigate roles and relationships between family members and examine family structures in other cultures. This study is extended in the primary grades when pupils begin studying about their local community and how its residents live and work together. Several basic themes can be used to highlight the concepts studied in sociology:

Institutions.   Sociologists look at the institutions a society creates to influence its members, such as the family, the school, the government, and the military.

Voluntary Groups.   This theme includes the study of groups that are less permanent than institutions, including political parties, special interest groups, clubs, and gangs.

Sociology helps pupils understand the contributions of different groups to society.

Stratified Groups.   Membership in some groups in society is open only to those who have command of certain social resources such as wealth, power, and prestige. Sociologists are interested in how the members of these groups are identified and how they exercise power, and in the impact these groups have on the rest of society.

Relationships within and among Groups.   Because different groups have different goals, norms, values, and levels of power, conflicts often arise among them. An important thrust of sociology is to discover how these conflicts arise and how they are resolved. Predicting and preventing conflict can be seen as an important contribution of sociology.

Sample Activities
Figure 3–2 introduces selected questions, concepts, and generalizations that can be used to develop classroom activities. Examples of elementary social studies activities that draw content from sociology follow.

LESSON
▪ IDEA ▪

Cooperation: *Grade Level*: 4–6. *Objectives:* Learners can state the advantages of working with others to solve problems.
    Many teachers use lessons derived from sociology to build youngsters' skills in working in groups. Some teachers have found useful a simple exercise designed to

The following are examples of central questions, concepts, and generalizations that are important to sociologists. They are useful to elementary social studies teachers when they make decisions about what to include in lessons related to sociology.

Central Questions (a selection)

How do individuals learn what is appropriate and what is inappropriate behavior in society?

How are the roles and the values of society changing?

Who are the individuals that are ascribed high status in society?

How do the groups that we belong to influence our actions?

What are the people in society trying to achieve?

What are the basic social institutions of society?

How do individuals in society show their disapproval of unacceptable social behavior?

What are the forces that are facilitating change and what are the forces that are hindering change in society?

What are the various levels of social class in society?

Concepts (a selection)

Roles, values, sanctions, norms, customs, traditions, beliefs, social institutions, socialization, social stratification, social class, status, primary groups, secondary groups, minority groups, ethnic groups, social change, group interaction, conflict, cooperation, assimilation, accommodation, competition

Generalizations (a selection)

The family is the basic social unit in most societies and the source of some of the most fundamental learning.

Social classes have existed in every society, although the basis of class distinction has varied.

Every society develops a system of roles, norms, values, and sanctions that guides the behavior of individuals within the society.

The norms and the values of society change over time; things that were considered radical in one generation may be accepted in another.

People in groups may behave differently than individuals.

All societies develop institutions that condition people to accept core social values.

The satisfaction of social needs is a strong motivating force in individual behavior.

Status and prestige are relative to the values held by the social group. Behavior that is rewarded in one group may be discouraged in another.

FIGURE 3–2
Central questions, concepts, and generalizations associated with sociology.

help pupils see that collective, cooperative thought rather than individual thought on a problem often results in better, more comprehensive answers.

Suggested Procedures:

1. The teacher poses this problem to the members of the class:
   You are a member of an army in the old days of knights in armor. Your general selects you to take a message back to headquarters. You leap on your horse and ride off.

After some hours, you see headquarters. But there is a big problem. Headquarters lies on the other side of a river that is too wide and too deep for the horse or you to swim.

How will you get your message to headquarters? This is how I want you to let me know what you would do. I'm going to give you three minutes to write down every idea you have. Write as quickly as you can. Stop when I say "Stop."

2. The teacher asks each youngster to count the number of solutions he or she developed.

3. The teacher asks youngsters, one at a time, to identify each solution. The teacher writes each solution on the chalkboard. When a solution is mentioned by more than one pupil, a tally mark is made. At the end of the exercise, the teacher counts up the total number of different solutions. ("I see we came up with 32 different ways to get the message delivered. Good thinking!")

4. The teacher says:

Now I have a different problem for you. Listen carefully. You are fishing off an ocean cliff. You are using an expensive new fishing rod and reel that your father gave you for Christmas. The water you are fishing in is 30 feet deep. You do not know how to swim. There is no one with you. Suddenly, you drop your rod and reel. It falls to the bottom of the sea.

How many ways can you think of to get your rod and reel back? This is how I want you to think about this problem. When I say "Go," I want everybody in the class to start thinking about this problem. We won't write answers this time. Instead, I am going to call on you one at a time to give me your ideas. Listen carefully to what others say, then tell me what you think. Let's start with you, Bobby. I'll write your ideas on the chalkboard. (The exercise proceeds. At the conclusion the teacher says, "That's everybody. Now let's see, we have 48 separate solutions. Very good.")

5. The teacher conducts a debriefing discussion.
   (a) Why do you think we came up with more solutions to the second problem?
   (b) How did you feel about working alone on the first problem?
   (c) How did you feel about working as a group on the second problem?
   (d) Do you think we can learn from others who are thinking about the same problems we are thinking about?

(Similar questions follow. This exercise is not foolproof, but in a surprisingly high number of cases, collective thinking will produce more solutions and more imaginative solutions than isolated thinking. This is consistent with findings of sociological research.)

LESSON • IDEA •   *Roles. Grade Level*: 1–3. *Objectives*: Learners can state the similarities and differences of the roles of men and women and how those roles are changing.

All individuals in society learn roles. Often youngsters think that the roles they have learned for themselves are the natural roles for everyone. When they come into contact with individuals who have a different understanding of roles, conflict may result. The following activity is designed to help youngsters understand the variety of roles that men and women have in society.

Suggested Procedures:

1. As a homework assignment, have the class find as many pictures as they can of men and women performing different tasks.
2. When all the pictures have been gathered, have the class separate them into different groups showing a variety of tasks. Each picture should be labeled with a title that is appropriate for the task that is pictured. Each group can be made into a chart.
3. Divide the chalkboard into two sections, one section labeled Men and the other Women. Under each section list the variety of tasks that the class found the men and women performing.
4. Compare the two lists. Ask the class: "What similarities and differences did we find? How do you account for the similarities and differences? Where do people learn their ideas about appropriate tasks for men and women?" Are these ideas changing?

*LESSON
▪ IDEA ▪*

Norms and Sanctions.   Use the following focus questions to stimulate a discussion of norms and sanctions. List student responses on the chalkboard so that they can be compared.

1. What are some of the things that parents expect of you at home?
2. What are some of the things that are expected of people in your neighborhood?
3. What are some of the things that are expected on the playground?
4. After listing and discussing the above, the teacher might tell the pupils that these expected behaviors are called *norms*. Students might discuss how norms vary from family to family and neighborhood to neighborhood. They might also discuss how norms in one place, at home, are different than norms at another, on the playground.
5. When you do not behave at home as your parents expect you to, what do they do to show you that they do not approve?
6. How do people in the neighborhood show that they do not approve of unexpected behavior?
7. How do people on the playground show that they do not approve?
8. A discussion can follow the responses in order to point out to the youngsters the variety of *sanctions* that are used by individuals in society and how those sanctions influence our behavior.

Sociologically based lessons, similar to lessons drawing content from other disciplines, should take advantage of youngsters' backgrounds and interests. This does not necessarily mean that all lessons must center on the school or the local community. Today's youngsters watch a great deal of television, see films, and have access to other information that tells them there is a world beyond the one they confront directly every day. Lessons derived from sociology and other similar

---

BOX 3–2   **Is Sociology Un-American?**

A school board recently received a letter from a concerned citizen. Part of this letter is printed below.

> I take *strong* exception to the decision of the district to include content from sociology in the elementary social studies. For one thing, sociology is a weak, weak academic discipline. Some refer to it as "pap"; others have referred to it in even less elegant terms. My concern, though, is that it is dangerous.
>
> Sociology places too much emphasis on the group. It downplays the actions of individuals. It ridicules free choice. Sociology claims that we are all helpless victims of our social environments. This is nonsense.
>
> Our country was built by strong leaders who refused to knuckle under to the values of the common person. This is the kind of person our world so desperately needs today. Sociology makes fun of such people. I regard the content as standing in direct contradiction to our nation's values. Let's keep such un-American content out of our schools.

Think   1. How do you assess the logic of the letter writer?
About   2. How do you think the school board will respond?
This   3. What is your personal reaction to the position expressed in the letter?
                   4. Suppose that you decided to write a letter defending sociology as being consistent with core American values. What would you say?

---

sources often involve youngsters in comparing and contrasting the patterns of life near-to-home with those elsewhere. These lessons seek to help pupils better understand the nature of their membership in the total human community. (See Box 3–2.)

ANTHROPOLOGY

Anthropology is the study of the history of human culture. It examines the various ways in which people interpret and assign meaning to their social and physical world. Lessons in anthropology help pupils understand that the members of each culture tend to be *ethnocentric*, that is, they believe that their interpretation of the world around them is the most "natural" and "logical" one.

Anthropology content has long been a part of the elementary school curriculum. Such topics as the study of native Americans, Africans, and early civilizations draw heavily on anthropological content. When taught from an anthropological perspective, these and similar topics provide pupils with significant insight about what it means to be human and help them develop an appreciation of the world's diverse cultures and peoples. Recent educational theory emphasizes multicultural education. Anthropological concepts and generalizations can be invaluable to a

"No, Jason, I did *not* ride a dinosaur to school when I was your age."

teacher who is designing such education experiences. Several basic themes can be developed through the study of content associated with anthropology:

Archaeology and Prehistory.   This area of anthropology tries to reconstruct the nature of human existence before written history. Archaeologists study artifacts and try to find ways to make those artifacts tell their story. This aspect of anthropology is interesting to even the very young child, and the social studies teacher will find that students are easily motivated to study it.

Human Evolution.   Anthropology is concerned with the development of the human species, bridging the gap between the biological and social sciences. Anthropologists are interested in how humans have developed and changed throughout their existence. Although this topic is somewhat controversial and some teachers are hesitant to confront the issue of evolution, pupils are interested in stories of early peoples and how they might be similar or different from themselves.

Culture.   This concept is central to the study of anthropology. *Culture* is defined as the constellation of values, beliefs, and institutions that is unique to a given group of people. It is important that pupils learn that these elements all seem natural to the members of the culture. For example, a primary research method of cultural anthropologists is that of the "participant observer." The anthropologist tries to become a part of a culture so as to observe it as a participant. The anthropologist can then identify the ways the members of the culture view the world and integrate their cultural and physical environments. This idea can apply to the elementary classroom. The teacher may have pupils role play and act out the way they believe individuals in another culture relate to each other and try to solve the common problems of human existence. Comparing another culture with

Understanding cultures and cultural change is a major thrust of anthropology.

our own provides insights into our own society and behavior that pupils might not otherwise discover.

Cultural Change.   This theme is of great interest. Cultures throughout the world today are changing rapidly. Studies of how others have coped with such rapid cultural change can provide important insights into the process in our own culture and may suggest ways to respond so as to preserve chosen cultural elements. Studying people who lived long ago or far away becomes more interesting and meaningful when such study is used to learn ways to handle current problems of international affairs, rapid change, and social upheaval.

Sample Activities

It is important that teachers foster respect for other cultures and do not exaggerate unfamiliar customs so that pupils feel they are merely studying about "funny people." There are many possibilities for building culturally sensitive anthropo-logically oriented lessons that are interesting for elementary-level pupils. For example, many objects exist around the average home that are no longer used and are somewhat mysterious to children. Using these as a stimulus can help pupils learn how to obtain meaning by observing and questioning. Stamps and coins available from a variety of places often identify cultural features and values that can be used to stimulate social studies discussions. Travel books and photographs from such magazines as *National Geographic* are also good sources for discussion material.

Children's Literature as a Resource.   Children's literature has become a rich source of anthropology-related teaching material. Numerous excellent books at a variety of reading levels may be used to study and understand other cultures and groups. For example, *Ashanti to Zulu: African Traditions* by Margaret Musgrove offers short descriptions of customs and legends from different African tribes and provides insight into these cultures. *Annie and the Old One* by Miska Miles is a story about Navajo culture and beliefs that helps readers clearly understand the relationships among different customs and beliefs. At a more mature reading level, *Dogsong* by Gary Paulsen deals with Eskimo beliefs and customs, and tells how a young boy grows to adulthood in that culture.

Many cultural traditions have been passed down through the oral tradition of *storytelling.* Teachers may use the storytelling technique to discuss with pupils not only the ideas and values in a story but also the ways in which such stories can be used to communicate beliefs and values over many generations. Pupils can also learn their favorite stories and tell them to the class.

The social studies teacher may also find it useful to construct literature-based *data retrieval charts.* These are charts that organize assigned readings according to concepts that the teacher wishes to teach the class. For example, the teacher may construct a chart showing how characters in different stories face the issue of change, which would then be the focus of a discussion on how pupils feel about and cope with change. The following is an example of such a chart.

Book	Character	Feelings	Result
Annie and the Old One	Annie	Tried to stop change	Felt guilty
	Grandmother	Accepted change	Taught Annie an important lesson

Once a data retrieval chart has been completed the teacher could then ask such questions as: Why did Annie dislike change? What changes do you dislike? What did Annie try to do to stop change? Did it work? Can we stop change? How did Annie learn to accept change? How did she feel when she learned how to accept change? How can we learn to accept change?

From the story and discussion pupils can both learn about another culture and learn how to cope with change in their lives. While they will discover that change is inevitable, they may also realize that there is continuity. They can then begin to look for elements of change and continuity in their own environment.

Figure 3–3 lists selected questions, concepts, and generalizations that can be used to develop other lesson ideas. Further sample lessons follow.

LESSON • IDEA •

Learning from an Artifact. *Grade Level:* 4–6. *Objectives:* Learners can (1) make at least one statement about a culture based on an investigation of an artifact and (2) learn how wrong conclusions can be drawn when investigating an artifact. *Suggested Procedure:* The teacher poses the following scenario.

I want you to imagine that we live thousands of years in the future. We live on another planet. We have come to earth and have found only ruins. We want to know how the people lived, and we begin digging in some promising place for clues. After a lot of hard work, somebody finds a jar. It is full of nickels. We don't find anything else. It is our task to find out as much as we can about this culture by looking at the nickel. What might we be able to say?

(The teacher provides each youngster with a nickel to look at. Youngsters provide ideas. The teacher provides hints to keep youngsters thinking.)

Some possible ideas that might emerge include:

(a) These people must have been fairly technically advanced. They refined ores into metal; they were able to cut a perfect circle.
(b) They might have been bilingual. There are two languages on the coin, English and Latin.
(c) One of the Latin phrases, *E pluribus unum* ("one from many" in English) is confusing. Does it mean that this place had many parts, or does it mean this place was a part of something even larger?
(d) There is a male figure on the coin. He might have been a hero, a leader, or a representation of a god of some kind.
(e) These people prized liberty as a value.
(f) These people were also religious. The words "In God We Trust" are on the coin.

The following are examples of central questions, concepts, and generalizations that are important to anthropologists. They are useful to elementary teachers when they make decisions about what to include in lessons related to anthropology.

Central Questions (a selection)

What is human about human beings, and how did they get those qualities?
What are the common characteristics of different cultures?
How do the religious beliefs of the culture influence the other parts of the culture?
How does the culture change to accommodate different ideas and beliefs?
What does the language tell us about the culture?
How does the language influence cultural and environmental perception?
How do individuals achieve adult status in the culture?
What is valued in the culture?
How are wealth and status measured in the culture?
How are information and tradition passed on from one generation to another?

Concepts (a selection)

Culture, cultural change, cultural borrowing, cultural lag, adaptation, diffusion, religion, ritual, tradition, nuclear family, extended family, race, technology, artifact, innate behavior, learned behavior

Generalizations (a selection)

Every society has formed its own system of beliefs, knowledge, values, and traditions that may be called its culture.

Societies around the world have common needs, but they have created different cultural systems to meet these needs.

The art, music, architecture, food, clothing, and customs of a people produce a national identity and reveal the values of a culture.

Increased contact between the people from different cultures results in increased cultural change.

FIGURE 3–3
Central questions, concepts, and generalizations associated with anthropology.

(g) There is a large number on each nickel. But this number is not the same on each coin. There are, for example, coins marked 1979, 1980, 1982, 1984, and 1987. This suggests a measure of time. What might have been the starting point for this counting?

(h) There is a building on the back. These people must have been skillful architects. It might have been an important building. It seems to have its own name, Monticello. This seems to be a word from a third language, Italian. What might it mean? (The teacher might take time to explain that Monticello was Thomas Jefferson's home and that the name means "little mountain." The house sits atop a small mountain in Virginia.)

(i) The words "five cents" indicate that this coin was worth five units of some denomination. The word "cents" means hundredths. This coin was worth five hundredths of something larger. What might that thing have been?

(j) The words "United States of America" might indicate a place name.

(k) The man on the front of the coin has his hair in a pigtail. Is this what was the style in the 1970s and 1980s?

This exercise can generate a surprising volume of information. It can also help youngsters understand that we often have incomplete information when we study other cultures, particularly cultures from the distant past. Hence, we cannot be absolutely sure that all guesses about what life was like are completely accurate.

LESSON
▪ *IDEA* ▪

Invention and Toolmaking. Grade Level 4–6. *Objectives*: Learners can (1) create a tool from limited resources, (2) identify the difficulties in creating something new, (3) appreciate the importance of invention, and (4) predict changes that might occur in a culture as the result of invention and innovation. *Suggested Procedures*:

1. Give each pupil several objects (ice cream sticks and string work well). Then ask the students to invent a tool.

2. Compare and discuss some of the tools that were invented. Ask the class to identify what they had to think about as they underwent the process of invention.

3. Choose one or two of the inventions, and have the class predict the changes that might occur as a result of the invention. An alternative activity would be to provide the class with a hypothetical invention and have them predict the consequences. One activity that works well is to have the class predict the changes that would occur if a pill that took care of all of our food needs for a day at a time were invented.

4. Map an invention. Choose a common object and begin to map the prerequisites that led to the invention, and the consequences of the invention on society. For example, the clock is an invention that is familiar to students and that can be mapped. To perform the mapping, place the word "Clock" in a box near the center of a sheet of paper. On the left-hand side of the page, list the need that the invention met and other inventions that were needed before it could be created. On the right-hand side of the page, list the changes that the invention brought about. If the level of sophistication of the class allows, the items on both side of the paper can be connected, using lines to illustrate relationships between the items on the lists.

Modern technologies draw the peoples of the world closer together. Today's youngsters will come into more direct contact than any previous generations with other peoples of the world. Lessons drawing content from anthropology can help them understand and work with individuals from widely differing cultural backgrounds. (See Box 3–3.)

BOX 3–3   Is Content from Anthropology Too Confusing?

A parent recently made the following comments to a school principal.

> I want you to understand that I'm not complaining, but I do have some concerns about the social studies program I would like you to know about.
>
> When I was in school, I remember reading nice stories about early American settlers. It seems to me that some of the information the youngsters are getting now is focusing on some pretty strange groups. My daughter's class seems to be studying some Northwest Coast Indians. As I understand it, people in this group gained status by giving away as many of their possessions as possible. Apparently the idea was for them to become as poor as possible, as fast as possible.
>
> Personally, I find this very interesting. However, I question whether it's content that is appropriate for elementary school children. We parents work hard to get our children to take good care of their things and to value their personal property. I think the information they are getting about the attitudes of these Northwest Coast Indians may confuse our young people at the very time we are trying to get them to accept the way we do things here.

Think About This

1. Suppose you were the teacher of the class in which information about the Northwest Coast Indians had been introduced. If the principal asked you to explain the purpose of this content, how would you respond?
2. How do you feel about the parent's concern that school content should support the development of the values parents are trying to develop at home?
3. Do you personally see any danger in introducing children to the special perspectives of other world cultures?

PSYCHOLOGY

Few topics spark more interest than the idea of the *self*. We are interested in many aspects of the self, such as why we think and feel the way we do, how we are alike or different from others, why some people seem to be smarter than we are, how we can learn to be smarter, how we can be happier, and how we can understand the forces that influence our behavior. Evidence of this interest is easily found in the popularity of radio talk shows, newspaper columns, and the many current books with psychological topics. Unfortunately, few teachers have considered these concerns to be a legitimate component of the social studies curriculum. Psychology focuses on understanding ourselves and the behavior of those around us and certainly must be a part of any curriculum that seeks to helps students understand their social world.

As a discipline, psychology has far-ranging concerns. Most lessons that include content from psychology focus on pupils' self-concept and sense of self-acceptance. Many of these lessons are now included in programs that focus on drug and alcohol abuse. It has been recognized that such programs must help individuals develop a positive self-image and learn how to cope with life's pressure and stress.

Although including psychological content in programs aimed at preventing drug abuse is welcome and necessary, opportunities for including such content in other social studies programs are frequently overlooked. It is important to understand human behavior if one is to understand history and the social sciences. If we know our own hopes, fears, aspirations, and motivations we then have a foundation for thinking about these same elements in other, different people. This helps the social studies become meaningful for pupils. Understanding what motivates people to do different things can, for example, help pupils understand why explorers are willing to take risks by venturing to unknown lands.

One advantage to including psychological perspectives in the social studies curriculum is that pupils already have experienced many feelings and have observed others in their social world. As a consequence, they have formed some hypotheses about why individuals behave the way they do. Teachers can use these understandings as motivation to study about others.

Sample Activities
Figure 3–4 lists selected questions, concepts, and generalizations on which lessons may be based. The issues youngsters must face as they mature during their elementary school years can also provide a useful framework for planning psychology-oriented lessons. Some of these issues include the following:

1. How do I please my parents?
2. How can I get along with my brothers and sisters?
3. How do I deal with people who want me to do something wrong?
4. How do I handle verbal abuse from others?
5. What is my responsibility toward others who are being picked on?
6. How will I ever be able to do the complicated work I will be expected to do when I move to a new grade next year?
7. Why can I not (hit the ball as well, read as fast, print as clearly, etc.) as some other classmates?
8. How can I survive on the bus with all those big kids?

**LESSON
• IDEA •**

Understanding Perception.   Individuals' values and previous experiences influence how they perceive reality. The following exercise combines art and social studies into a lesson designed to help pupils appreciate the importance of individual perception.

Grade Level: K–3. *Objective*: Learners can state why different people might view the same thing differently. *Suggested Procedures*:

1. Pupils are given pieces of construction paper folded in the middle. They are asked to unfold the paper. A small drop of paint is dropped near the middle of each page along the fold line. Then pupils refold the paper and press it together. This will produce a symmetrical image as the paint spreads on both sides of the fold line.

The following are examples of central questions, concepts, and generalizations that are important to psychologists. They are useful to elementary teachers when they make decisions about what to include in lessons related to psychology.

Central Questions (a selection)

In what ways are all people alike, and in what ways are they different?
Why do people who observe the same event have different explanations of the event?
Why do people behave as they do?
Why do some people feel capable and others feel inadequate?
How do we use our different senses to learn?
What influences the way people develop and grow?
What are the basic needs of all people?
How do different people meet these basic needs in different ways?
How can people help each other meet their needs?

Concepts (a selection)

Learning, self-concept, individual differences, personal needs, personality, acceptance, security, leadership, aggression, fear, achievement, habits, motives, perception, uniqueness

Generalizations (a selection)

All individuals share some common needs, yet have individual differences.
Heredity and environment both play a part in shaping the unique personality of individuals.
Human behavior is influenced much more than the behavior of other species by learned patterns.
Individual perceptions of events is influenced by a variety of factors, including values, motives, and expectations.
All individuals have the needs to achieve, to belong, to be accepted, and to achieve freedom from fear.
Humans are social beings who seek to establish positive relationships with others.

FIGURE 3–4
Central questions, concepts, and generalizations associated with psychology.

2. When the paint dries, post some of the prints. Ask individual members of the class to describe the objects they see in the "paintings." (Typically, different people will see different kinds of things.)
3. The teacher asks the class why everybody did not see the same things. The teacher might ask questions such as these:
   (a) What did you see?
   (b) Did something you have seen before help you to "see" something in the paintings?
   (c) Do you think that what others might have seen before might have something to do with what they "saw" in the paintings?
4. The teacher extends the discussion to other events. He or she might ask such questions as these:

(a) What does this tell us about how different people might interpret something they see on the playground?

(b) Would it be helpful to know something about a person's past experience before we listened to what he or she had to say about something he or she had seen?

LESSON
• *IDEA* •

Observing Human Behavior.   Psychologists observe individuals and study their reactions to different situations. Elementary social studies lessons can help to sharpen pupils' own observational behaviors. The following activity illustrates how this might be done.

Grade Level: 4–6. *Objectives*: Learners can (1) collect data through observation and (2) identify patterns and form conclusions from data. *Suggested Procedures*:

1. *Gathering data.* Have the class divide into teams to collect data by observing individuals in different settings. For example, one team might be asked to observe pupils on the playground. Another team might observe the younger children, and another the older children. Instruct them to note who played together or alone, how individuals cooperated with each other, where pupils played, and any other aspects deemed significant. Other observation areas might include the school cafeteria and the principal's office. The teams should be provided with a form they can use as they observe and record the data.

The following is an example of a form a teacher might provide for this activity.

Observation Record

Place of observation:

Time of observation:

People who are observed:

Observation sequence:

Time   **Behavior observed**

_____   _____

_____   _____

2. *Interpreting data.* After the information has been entered on the form, have the members of each observation team look for patterns. They should try to answer such questions as these:

(a) Who were the individuals who were together?

(b) How many people were alone?

(c) How was the behavior of the people in groups different from that of the people who were alone?

(d) How and why were the behaviors of people observed different from one another?

(e) What special features of the place you observed contributed to what the people did there?

3. *Class discussion.* The teacher leads a discussion that focuses on all the information that has been gathered. Focus questions might include these:

(a) Were people of different ages observed doing different things?

(b) Did people in similar groups do similar kinds of things? If so, how do groups influence what people do?

(c) What motivated people to behave as they did?

(d) How do people learn what kind of behavior is appropriate for a given place?

Psychologists know that human beings tend to follow certain patterns of development as they mature. Younger children have not yet developed these patterns, and many of them do not realize that such patterns exist. For example, many pupils think that no other young people experience the kinds of problems they face. Lessons that help elementary pupils realize that "they are not alone" can go a long way toward smoothing their maturational development. Psychology offers a fertile source of content material for instructional activities of this kind (see Figure 3.4).

KEY IDEAS IN SUMMARY

1. Political science topics have long been a part of the social studies curriculum. Such content was formerly labeled "civics" and educators' intent was to "Americanize" individuals by convincing them of the virtues of the American political system. Current emphases go beyond this narrow focus to help pupils learn such key concepts as power, authority, freedom, and justice, and about alternative political systems.

2. Sociology is concerned with the behavior of individuals in groups. Lessons with sociological content should help pupils learn about the influence of groups on their behavior, about group processes, and about why some groups change and adapt while others disappear.

3. Anthropology focuses on the central concept of culture and on how different social groups view the world. Lessons drawing on anthropological content can help pupils learn about different cultures and how these cultures respond to basic human concerns.

4. Psychology focuses on why individuals behave the way they do. Because of its personal application, psychology content is usually very interesting and motivating to pupils.

5. Lessons selected for study from all of the social science disciplines should begin with attention to topics and issues that are of interest and concern to the pupils.

POSTTEST

Answer each of the following true/false questions.

1. Political science content should focus mainly on what is required for effective citizenship.
2. There are few places where sociological content can be included in the elementary school program.
3. Topics such as the study of Native Americans may easily involve anthropological concepts.
4. The topic of prehistory is too abstract and is not interesting to the elementary pupil.
5. Elements of psychology included in the elementary curriculum should primarily focus on the development of self-esteem.

QUESTIONS

1. What basic political science concepts should be included in the elementary curriculum?
2. Why should sociological content be included in the social studies curriculum?
3. What are some of the topics in the elementary curriculum that might include content drawn from anthropology?
4. How might the concept of cultural change be taught to pupils?
5. How might psychology content be used to motivate students to study about others?
6. How would you respond to individuals who argue that political science lessons should inculcate individuals with the virtues of democracy and the "American way?"
7. One sociological topic that could be included in the elementary curriculum is the influence of religious groups in American history. How would you approach that topic? Do you think it is an appropriate topic for discussion?
8. How would you defend the inclusion of anthropological content in the social studies curriculum?
9. Where are some of the places content from psychology might be included in the curriculm?
10. Do you think that content from the various social science disciplines should be taught separately or should it be integrated? Why?

EXTENDING UNDERSTANDING AND SKILL

1. Write a short paper on good citizenship. Identify what your definition of this implies for the objectives and methods used in teaching citizenship to elementary pupils. Compare your statements with those of others.

2. Review several social studies textbooks written for a grade level that interests you. Approximately what percentage of the content of the book is related to political science, sociology, anthropology, and psychology? Prepare a chart showing your analysis that includes examples from the book.

3. Select four or five key concepts from political science, sociology, anthropology, and psychology. Build a resource file to support instruction related to each concept. Include photographs, illustrations, newspaper stories, artifacts and objects, and charts that might help you teach these concepts to elementary school pupils.

4. Identify a selection of children's literature that could be used to teach social studies content. Describe each book and the social science concepts that might be taught using the book. Develop a complete plan for using one of the books in the classroom.

5. Interview several experienced teachers of a grade level that interests you. Ask them to describe the self-concept problems pupils in this grade tend to have. Ask them to discuss instructional approaches that could be used to develop pupils' sense of self-worth.

REFERENCES

Barr, R., J. Barth, and S. Shermis. *Defining the Social Studies*. Bulletin 51. Washington, D.C.: National Council for the Social Studies, 1977.

Dynneson, T. "An Anthropological Approach to Learning and Teaching: Eleven Propositions." *Social Education* (September/October 1984), pp. 410, 416–18.

Gross, R., and T. Dynneson. *What Should We be Teaching in the Social Studies?* Bloomington, IN: Phi Delta Kappa Fastback Series, no. 199, 1983.

Jarolimek, J. "Curriculum Trends: Social Studies." *Educational Leadership* (November 1983), p. 78.

Johnson, E. "Framework and Philosophy for an Integrated Curriculum." *The Social Studies* (January/February 1981), pp. 4–7.

SUPPLEMENTAL READING

Abraham, K. "Political Thinking in the Elementary Years: An Empirical Study." *Elementary School Journal* (November 1983), pp. 221–31.

Baldwin, D. "The Thinking Strand in Social Studies." *Educational Leadership* (September 1984), pp. 79–80.

Miller, S., and M. Brand. "Music of Other Cultures in the Classroom." *The Social Studies* (March/April 1983), pp. 62–64.

4

PLANNING FOR INSTRUCTION

This chapter provides information to help the reader:

1. identify relationships among aims, goals, and objectives,
2. describe types of information that are used in planning for instruction,
3. plan objectives that vary in type and sophistication,
4. point out elements included in an instructional unit,
5. state the purposes of daily lesson planning, and
6. develop formats both for instructional unit plans and for lesson plans.

PRETEST

Answer each of the following true/false questions.

1. Because there is so much unpredictability in teaching, teachers should not spend much time planning.

2. Aims are broad statements of direction or purpose that are of limited use in a teacher's everyday planning.

3. Instructional objectives focus on what pupils are expected to be able to do as a result of their exposure to a lesson.

4. Goals for a given grade are usually determined by the school district; hence, teachers have little need to know their own pupils as they plan their lessons.

5. Often, the academic program for a school year is divided into different instructional units.

INTRODUCTION

An observer who watches a skilled professional teacher at work might be forgiven for commenting, "Teaching is easy. Everything flows so smoothly." Appearance fails to mirror reality: Good teaching is hard work.

Similar to professionals in other fields, teachers spend much time preparing for their workday. The careful planning behind a smooth, coherent classroom presentation often is invisible to an observer. During the planning process, among other things, the teacher establishes priorities for instruction, considers alternative teaching approaches, identifies needed learning materials, considers organizational issues, and makes decisions related to pupil and program evaluation. Without careful preparation, the orderly flow of instruction of the skilled teacher simply would not happen. Therefore, developing competence in planning is a high priority for people preparing for careers in the classroom.

Teaching is basically a decision-making process. During a typical day, teachers are called upon to make a wide range of choices. Clark and Peterson (1986) cite research that reveals that, on average, teachers make decisions about how to structure learning experiences once every two minutes. In addition to making choices about organizing and presenting content, teachers make decisions related to unanticipated events, deportment of learners, and paperwork management. Clearly, the teacher leads a busy and complex professional life.

Doyle (1986) points out that classrooms are places characterized by multidimensionality, simultaneity, immediacy, and publicness. These characteristics produce a pressure-filled work environment for teachers. Careful planning helps teachers to reduce some of the unpredictability of the classroom setting. As they plan, teachers consider (a) the nature of their pupils, (b) the nature of the content

---

---

to be taught, (c) alternative teaching approaches, (d) alternative learning materials, (e) ways to sequence learning experiences, and (f) implications of basic principles of learning and teaching.

AIMS, GOALS, AND INSTRUCTIONAL OBJECTIVES

The planning process begins with identifying a direction or purpose. Instructional planning that lacks direction will result in disorganized teaching behaviors that lead to confused, unmotivated, and inattentive learners.

Borich (1992) identifies three dimensions of direction or purpose that are particularly useful for teachers. These are (a) aims, (b) goals, and (c) instructional objectives. There are relationships among the three dimensions, and each has its own important characteristics.

Aims

Aims are broad statements of direction. They establish a general sense of direction for school programs. For example, the public often gives voice to the general aim that all students who graduate from high school will be good citizens. Aims provide a general planning context for teachers. They suggest what society in general and the local community in particular expect from the schools.

Often, schools are assessed by media pundits and by the general citizenry in terms of how well they respond to widely accepted aims. Among common social studies aims are the following:

- Every person should be informed about important social and political issues.
- All people should know their rights and responsibilities as citizens of a democracy.

Because they are general in nature, aims do not provide concrete guidelines for teachers to use as they decide what to include in daily lesson plans. The first step in making aims more useful for instructional planning is to break them down into more specific goals.

Goals

Goals are more narrow and tightly focused than aims. They spell out specific directions for a given subject or grade level. For example, goals for a third-grade social studies program indicate the particular role social studies is to play at this grade level in contributing to the general aims of the school. In reference to a general aim related to "producing good citizens," goals can be generated for the third-grade program in response to this question: "What should pupils learn in third-grade social studies that contributes to the development of citizenship?"

Goals most often are established at the school district level. They may be identified by school boards, curriculum committees, or even textbook-selection committees. Goals are often found in such documents as curriculum guides. In some states, goals are established at the state level. Where this is done, the state produces collections of goals under such titles as "The Social Studies Framework" or "Essential Elements for the Social Studies."

Goals help teachers to understand the expectations that the school district (and, in some cases, the state) has for them. Goals for the social studies program that relate to the general aims of schooling introduced earlier would include:

- Pupils are aware of current issues facing society.
- Learners grasp the basic outline of the historical development of the United States.
- Pupils are aware of rules that govern their behavior.

Goals provide teachers with a sense of direction for their programs. They suggest what the year's instruction should be about. But goals do not particularly help teachers grapple with decisions about what to teach on Monday, how to teach it, and what to do to assess learning. To get at these purposes, an additional element of specificity, instructional objectives, must be introduced into the process of establishing direction.

Instructional Objectives

Instructional objectives state in specific terms what pupils will be able to do as a consequence of their exposure to instruction. Additionally, they include criteria

---

---

the teacher can use to determine how well learners have mastered content. The following are examples of instructional objectives that relate to the aforementioned aims and goals:

- Each pupil will correctly label each of the original thirteen colonies when given a blank outline map of the United States.
- Each will match correctly at least 80 percent of the articles from the Bill of Rights with their descriptions on a matching test.

Beginning teachers may have difficulty writing good instructional objectives, sometimes confusing them with goals or with learning activities. For example, an inexperienced teacher might state that the objective for a lesson is for pupils to "discuss the Bill of Rights." Discussion is the process to be used to promote learning, not the outcome of learning. A properly formatted instructional objective clearly states what pupils will do to demonstrate that they have learned.

Several formats for instructional objectives have been developed. One that is widely used is the *ABCD* approach.

The ABCD Approach

According to the *ABCD* approach, a complete instructional objective has four components. These are *A, Audience; B, Behavior; C, Condition;* and *D, Degree.*

Audience.   The *A* component of the objective identifies the person or persons to whom the instruction is directed. This might be the entire class, a small group, or an individual. When they plan lessons, teachers examine this component to determine whether pupils have the necessary prerequisites to accomplish the objective. In addition, specifying the audience identifies which learners are expected to master the objective. Examples of the *A* component follow:

All fifth grade pupils completing the westward-movement unit will . . .
Zelda Zike will . . .
All individuals who choose the learning center activities on Lewis and Clark will . . .

"I know you're great on motivation, but can you plan?"

Behavior. The *B* component defines the behavior that pupils will be expected to demonstrate. Note that the emphasis is on pupils' behavior, not on the teacher's.

It is important to describe behaviors with verbs that indicate clearly observable actions. Verbs such as "know," "appreciate," and "understand" are not precise enough to use in instructional objectives. The teacher must decide what pupils must *do* to indicate what they "know," "appreciate," or "understand." Verbs indicating these more precise behaviors are used in instructional objectives. Examples of the *B* component follow:

. . . trace the route of the Lewis and Clark expedition . . .
. . . describe the sequence of events leading to the adoption of the Bill of Rights . . .
. . . list the steps followed in passing a bill into law . . .
. . . draw a picture of a covered wagon . . .

Conditions. The *C* component describes the conditions under which pupils will be expected to demonstrate the behavior. The conditions component might specify whether pupils will be able to use other resources, such as books or notes; whether they will need to demonstrate the behavior individually or in a group; and whether there will be a time limit for performing the task. The conditions component may specify whether the behavior will be measured on a test, through creation of some kind of a "learning product," or in some other way. Examples of the *C* component follow:

. . . on a multiple-choice test . . .
. . . using notes gathered from several sources . . .
. . . while working with a group of pupils . . .
. . . by creating a model of a colonial town . . .

Degree. The concern of the *D* component is with proficiency, with how well pupils must perform the behavior described in the instructional objective. One criterion teachers often apply is that of repeated successful performance. A single correct response is not a valid indicator that an objective has been learned. One success might be the result of chance. Teachers must consider what kind of pupil responses are required for them to have confidence that pupils have learned. In preparing the degree component, teachers often specify the minimum number of correct answers needed on test items pertaining to the objective, the number of things to be included in a learning project, or the number of inferences pupils should make when confronted with an unresolved situation. Examples of the *D* component follow:

. . . will respond correctly to eight of ten test items that relate to the journey of
     Lewis and Clark.
. . . will make three inferences about a place from a climatic map.
. . .will state at least one probable consequence of that choice.
. . .will identify at least one value held by the individual making the choice.

Putting It All Together. The *A*, *B*, *C*, and *D* components typically are arranged in an order that gives the statement of objective its clearest logical flow. Though the order of their occurrence is not fixed, it is critical that each of the four elements be included. (The component examples in the preceding sections do not relate to each other. Following are two examples of *complete* instructional objectives. The *A*, *B*, *C*, and *D* components have been indicated.)

"A"   "B"
Each pupil in the first grade will cite the names of the days of the week and
               "D"   "C"
the months of the year with no errors orally as requested by the teacher.

"A"   "B"
<u>Each fifth grader will</u> <u>identify proper examples of</u> countries, counties, and
                    "C"   "D"
<u>continents</u> <u>by responding correctly on a true/false test</u> <u>to at least fifteen</u>

<u>of twenty items.</u>

Instructional Objectives and Domains of Learning

The intended kind of learning must be considered when instructional objectives are written. The three major domains of learning are: (1) the cognitive domain; (2) the affective domain; and, (3) the psychomotor domain.

Cognitive Domain. The cognitive domain is concerned with intellectual learning. An example of a cognitive domain activity is having primary pupils learn the days of the week and the months of the year.

In the 1950s, Benjamin Bloom and several colleagues set out to develop a scheme to identify the subordinate categories of the cognitive domain. The result was the classic educational document, *Taxonomy of Educational Objectives: Handbook I: The Cognitive Domain* (Bloom, 1956). This document, generally referred to as Bloom's *Taxonomy,* describes six levels of cognitive thinking. These levels, presented in Figure 4–1, range from relatively simple mental tasks to extraordinarily difficult and sophisticated thought processes.

As the expected levels of learning grow more complex (as they proceed along the taxonomy from "knowledge" to "evaluation"), more time is required to prepare pupils. It takes longer to teach evaluation-level thinking than application-level thinking. Similarly, application-level thinking requires more instructional development than knowledge-level thinking.

These time requirements make it essential for teachers to think seriously about cognitive levels as they develop instructional objectives. Some teachers find it useful to lay out this information in a *table of specifications* like the one depicted in Box 4–3.

The table of specifications allows teachers to quickly determine the cognitive level of each instructional objective. Focus topics of the objectives that require high-level pupil thinking will need more instructional time. Teachers can use this information as they organize lessons with these objectives.

Affective Domain. The affective domain includes values and attitudes. Social studies teachers often are interested in raising pupils' interest in topics associated with history and the social sciences. They also wish to help elementary school children to commit to widely held American values such as respect for the individual and tolerance of diversity.

Instructional objectives in the affective domain also concern pupils' attitudes and values. Krathwohl and others (1956) developed a hierarchy of affective domain thinking. Raths, Harmin, and Simon (1966) did useful additional work on the

Knowledge

This lowest level of the taxonomy refers to the recall of specific elements of previously learned information. A pupil at this level will be asked to do little beyond naming or describing something.

Objective: Each pupil will correctly name the five days of the week orally when asked to do so by the teacher.

Comprehension

This level implies an ability to simultaneously recall several pieces of previously learned information. The pupil should also be able to arrange the elements in a proper order or sequence. He or she should also be capable of changing the form of the original information.

Objective: Each fifth grader will recognize the steps a bill goes through to become a law and what happens at each step by responding correctly to twelve of fifteen true/false questions related to these issues.

Application

Application-level thinking requires that information learned in one context be used in a different and unfamiliar setting. Pupils are called upon to "do something" with the content they have learned previously.

Objective: Each pupil will use the scale on the globe as a basis for determining the correct point-to-point distances between at least four of five given pairs of cities.

Analysis

Analysis calls on pupils to describe the characteristics of something by comparing and contrasting its individual parts. Analysis requires them to look at the separate but related fragments of a whole and describe the general characteristics of the whole.

Objective: Each sixth grader will describe the characteristics of an assigned nation in Asia. Assessment will take the form of an essay. Each essay must make specific references to this nation's (1) religious practices, (2) form of government, (3) industrial and agricultural development, and (4) people and their racial and ethnic makeup.

Synthesis

Synthesis-level thinking calls on pupils to look at isolated pieces of information and to create brand new information (at least information that is new to them) from these pieces. Often, creative thinking is involved in synthesis thinking.

Objective: On an essay, each pupil will predict the probable climatic consequences for California if all the mountains in the state suddenly disappeared. Each response must include specific references to the (1) rainfall patterns, (2) wind patterns, and (3) temperature patterns.

Evaluation

Thinking at the level of evaluation requires pupils to make judgments in light of specified criteria. The "specified criteria" provision is important. Without these criteria, attempts to elicit evaluation-level thinking may produce little more than exchanges of unsupported personal opinion.

Objective: Each sixth grader, on an oral examination, will critique one of the proposals for a new federal "flat tax." Specific references must be made to (1) fairness, (2) satisfactory ability to raise needed money, and (3) ease of administration. Furthermore, each pupil must explain clearly what he or she means by "fairness," "satisfactory ability to raise money," and "ease of administration."

FIGURE 4–1
Levels of the cognitive domain and examples of objectives written at each level.

BOX 4–3   **Table of Specifications for a Cognitive Domain Instructional Objective.**

		Knowledge	Comprehension	Application	Analysis	Synthesis	Evaluation
				Cognitive Level			
	1	X	X	X			
Instructional	2	X					
Objective	3	X	X	X	X		
Number	4	X					
	5	X	X				

The terminal X (farthest to the right) indicates the cognitive level of each instructional objective. Note that the first objective is at the level of application, the second objective is at the level of knowledge, and so forth. The Xs to the left of the terminal X imply that pupils are expected to be able to function at all of these levels when they finish the unit of instruction. For the first objective, pupils need to be able to function at the knowledge, comprehension, and application levels; for the second objective, pupils need to be able to function at only the knowledge level; and so forth.

**Think
About
This**

1. Which of these objectives would probably require the most instructional time? Why?
2. Which of these objectives would probably require the least instructional time? Why?
3. Which objectives would probably require you to gather together the largest number of instructional resources? Why?
4. Would it be prudent to start instruction directed toward some of these objectives at the beginning of a new unit of instruction? Why?

---

nature of values. Collectively, the work of these specialists suggests that value formation is initiated when people open themselves to receiving and interpreting new ideas. Individual values become truly established only when people develop enough commitment to support them publicly. Several schemes have been developed to describe the different levels of the affective domain. Figure 4.2 is an example of one such framework.

As in the cognitive domain, pupils require more time to achieve high-level affective-domain objectives than to master low-level objectives. Not every objective can be at the level of "sharing." There simply is not enough time. Teachers must establish affective-domain priorities for their instructional objectives. (See Box 4–4.)

The whole area of affective learning poses dilemmas for social studies educators. Teachers do not want to intrude on personal and family values, and in some cases have been legally restricted from discussing such topics. Yet, teachers are reluctant to abandon all consideration of values and attitudes. Carried to its logical conclusion, abandoning values education could lead to pupils' accepting the ac-

Receiving

Behavior at the level of receiving is characterized by a pupil's willingness to be exposed to new content with an open mind. The intent is to remove any "blockages" that might be there because of misconceptions or general hostility to the content.

Objective: Each pupil will demonstrate a willingness to consider the study of new topics by not raising serious objections to more than five percent of the topics introduced during any one grading period.

Approaching

The level of receiving is concerned with a pupil's general willingness to take in new content. Approaching goes a step further. It refers to his or her predisposition to look at the individual aspects of content, one at a time. There should be no rejection of information before it has been seriously considered on its merits. Approaching involves a willingness to suspend judgment until evidence has been carefully weighed.

Objective: Each pupil will consider the individual issues on their merits and will not make statements to the teacher indicating that hasty prejudgments have been made on more than five percent of issues associated with any assigned topic of study.

Deciding

Deciding-level thinking is characterized by pupils' arriving at personal decisions that have been made without prejudgment and after consideration of the individual merits of issues.

Objective: Each pupil will orally inform the teacher of choices he or she has made after prejudice-free consideration of issues on at least ninety percent of those occasions when such judgments are possible.

Sharing

At the sharing level, pupils demonstrate a willingness to share their personal decisions with others. Sharing is characterized by commitments that run so deeply that pupils do not hesitate to state them publicly.

Objective: Each pupil will freely and without coercion make a public statement of his or her position regarding at least three social studies-related issues introduced during one grading period.

FIGURE 4–2
Affective categories and examples of objectives written at each level.

tions of a mass murderer on the grounds that the individual was simply following the dictates of his or her own conscience. A society must impose limits on the actions of people, and the broad social norms that limit these actions need to be taught to elementary school children.

In addition to building learners' commitment to widely accepted social norms, it is legitimate for social studies teachers to help pupils develop rational processes of thinking. Efforts to encourage interest in the social studies and in other parts of the school program are also appropriate.

Psychomotor Domain. Psychomotor development refers to learning that depends on fine-muscle coordination, including such activities as jumping a rope or hitting a baseball. But psychomotor development has implications for academic

---

BOX 4–4   **Table of Specifications for an Affective Domain Instructional Objective.**

		Affective Domain Level			
		Receiving	Approaching	Deciding	Sharing
	1	X	X	X	
Instructional	2	X	X	X	X
Objective	3	X	X		
Number	4	X	X	X	
	5	X	X	X	X

The terminal X indicates the affective level of each instructional objective. Note that the first objective is at the level of deciding, the second objective is at the level of sharing, and so forth. The Xs to the left of the terminal X imply that pupils are expected to be able to function at all of these levels when they finish the unit of instruction. For the first objective, pupils need to be able to function at the receiving, approaching, and deciding levels; for the second objective, pupils need to be able to function at all the levels; and so forth.

Think About This

1. For a grade level you would like to teach, identify some affective instructional objectives. For each objective, identify the intended outcome level. Arrange the objectives in an affective table of specifications. What does this table tell us about your priorities?
2. What kinds of social studies content do you believe best lend themselves to affective instructional objectives? Why?
3. Can you envision some topics for which you would include no affective instructional objectives? How could you justify not including affective learning outcomes in your planning?

---

learning as well as for physical education and purely recreational activities. For example, social studies lessons that require young pupils to measure distances with rulers require more than just an intellectual understanding of the task. Learners must also have sufficient control of their fine muscles to hold the pencil properly and to make marks where they need to be made.

Several schemes have been developed to illustrate the levels of the psychomotor domain. One of these schemes (Armstrong and Savage 1990) is illustrated in Figure 4.3.

As with cognitive and affective instructional objectives, higher levels of psychomotor objectives require longer teaching time. "Free practice" assumes a level of proficiency that allows pupils to perform tasks with no teacher supervision. This expertise requires much more learning time than the simple familiarization associated with the "awareness" level. Teachers must carefully establish priorities

Awareness

At this level, a pupil must be able to correctly describe what he or she must do to perform a given psychomotor task properly. This psychomotor level is closely related to the cognitive-domain levels of knowledge and comprehension.

Objective: Each pupil will tell the teacher, with no errors, how the tape measure will be held and the individual units of scale marked off when determining point-to-point distances of a map.

Individual Components

Psychomotor learning at this level requires pupils to demonstrate the individual parts of a complex activity one at a time. The pupil should be able to do each step called for with no errors.

Objective: Each pupil will demonstrate, with no errors, an ability to do each of the following on request: (1) align the tape on the map properly, (2) point to the lines indicating centimeters and millimeters, (3) mark the number of centimeters and millimeters representing 100 kilometers on the work map, and (4) count the number of 100-kilometer intervals between two locations on the work map.

Integration

At this level, pupils should be able to perform an entire sequence of psychomotor activities under the guidance of the teacher. The teacher should be available to provide help, if needed.

Objective: Each pupil will be able to measure the appropriate point-to-point distance (within five kilometers) of the actual distance between two given locations. This will be done on a work map, using a tape measure with a centimeter and millimeter scale.

Free Practice

At this level, pupils are expected to demonstrate a mastered sequence of psychomotor behavior in diverse settings, with no direct teacher assistance or supervision.

Objective: Each pupil, on request, will be able to measure point-to-point distances on a work map, using a tape measure with a centimeter and millimeter scale. In no case will the estimated distance be less than or greater than 100 kilometers of the actual point-to-point distance.

FIGURE 4-3
Levels of the psychomotor domain and examples of objectives written at each level.

among psychomotor domain objectives when developing their instructional objectives. (See Box 4–5.)

Interrelationships Among the Cognitive, Affective, and Psychomotor Domains of Learning

Though we sometimes isolate thinking about cognitive, affective, and psychomotor learning when planning for instruction, in reality the three domains are interconnected. *Every* instructional objective contains some element of learning from *each* domain. Think about this as you read the following account of a playground episode:

At 9:45, Joey, a second grader, was building his own snow fort on the playground. Robert, unseen by Joey, crept up quietly behind him. He scooped up a handful of

BOX 4-5   Table of Specifications for a Psychomotor Domain Instructional Objective.

		Psychomotor Domain Level			
		Awareness	Individual Components	Integration	Free Practice
Instructional	1	X			
	2	X	X	X	
Objective	3	X			
Number	4	X	X	X	X
	5	X	X	X	X

The terminal X indicates the psychomotor level of each instructional objective. Note that the first objective is at the level of awareness, the second objective is at the level of integration, and so forth. The Xs to the left of the terminal X imply that pupils are expected to be able to function at all of these levels when they finish the unit of instruction. For the first objective, pupils need to be able to function at only the awareness level; for the second objective, pupils need to be able to function at the awareness, individual components, and integration levels; and so forth.

Think About This

1. Which of the instructional objectives listed in the table of specifications above would take the longest to teach? Why?
2. Why might a teacher ever have an interest in teaching pupils only to the level of awareness?
3. For a grade level and topic that interest you, develop three or four instructional objectives in the psychomotor domain. Arrange them in a table of specifications. Why have you established the priorities reflected in your table?

---

fresh snow and, in a flash, pushed it down Joey's back. Joey jumped up, whirled around, and howled. He desperately tried to unzip his jacket, pull his shirttail loose, and shake out the cold snow.

What did Joey learn? First, he already knew that snow is cold. He knew that cold things do not feel good against warm skin. He had two cognitive understandings that helped him react.

Second, the experience triggered an emotional, or affective, response. Joey was unhappy about what happened. We know this from his "howl". Even if Joey did not long remain angry, he would probably want to play a similar prank on Robert.

Third, Joey had a psychomotor reaction. The nerve endings flashed the message to his brain that something was amiss. Reacting from past experience, he used

Manipulative activities help teachers involve the psychomotor domain.

his hands to unzip his jacket, began to pull his shirttail out of his pants, and tried to shake the snow out, all maneuvers requiring psychomotor abilities.

As with this playground incident, classroom learning involves interplay among the cognitive, affective, and psychomotor domains. What instructional planners mean when they refer to "cognitive," "affective," and "psychomotor objectives" is that one or another of these domains tends to be more heavily weighted in any given planned lesson. The others are always present to some degree.

For example, suppose a group of pupils were asked to read some information about Thomas Jefferson. On the surface, this exercise appears to be almost exclusively cognitive. However, depending on how the teacher structures the assignment, individual reading proficiency, the quality of the prose, the lure of competing activities, and other variables, the assignment will also have an affective dimension. Psychomotor skills (eye coordination, for example) will also play a role.

INFORMATION NEEDED IN MAKING INSTRUCTIONAL PLANNING DECISIONS

As they plan for instruction, teachers determine how to sequence instruction, how to pace lessons, which teaching techniques to use, and how to tie new content to previous learning. These decisions require knowledge about (1) learners to be taught, (2) content to be taught, (3) alternative instructional options, and (4) available resource materials.

Knowledge about Learners

Successful planning requires teachers to be knowledgeable about their learners. This point is widely recognized. Researchers have found that teachers spend more of their planning time thinking about characteristics of their pupils than about any other dimension of the planning process.

As teachers plan instructional objectives and lessons, one area of their concern is the personal expectations and perspectives individual children bring to the classroom. Pupils who come to school with positive expectations and who have strong parental support for their work at school react differently than pupils who lack these characteristics.

Learning Styles

Teachers must also consider the learning styles of their pupils when planning instructional experiences. Some children learn best through listening, others through exposure to reading and other visual media, and still others through manipulation of objects. There are pupils who do better when they work alone. Others blossom when they are assigned to work in groups. Certain pupils respond spontaneously and intuitively. Some tend to be more reflective and cautious. To the extent possible, teachers consider these differences when planning instructional objectives and learning experiences.

Special Needs of Handicapped and of Gifted and Talented Pupils

Educators must carefully consider the needs of exceptional pupils when preparing objectives and lessons. Public Law 94-142, the "Education for All Handicapped Children Act," requires that learners with handicapping conditions be *mainstreamed*, or placed in regular classrooms to the greatest extent possible.

Mainstreamed children add an important dimension to the elementary school social studies program. Their presence in the classroom provides an opportunity for teachers to help all children in the class develop sensitivity to the needs of people different from themselves.

Not all special pupils have handicapping conditions. Gifted and talented learners also constitute a special population within the school, and instructional programs must also attend to their needs.

Handicapped Pupils. Numerous physical handicaps may interfere with pupils' abilities to succeed in elementary social studies classes. These impediments include hearing impairment, sight impairment, physical handicaps, and certain emotional disorders. These handicaps must be considered when planning instruction.

For example, a film probably is a poor choice as a means of transmitting information to hearing-impaired children. If the film is well suited to the needs of others in the class, the least the teacher should do is provide hearing-impaired pupils with either an outline of the film's content or a general summary of the covered information.

Sight-impaired learners need to be seated near the front of the classroom so they can clearly see the chalkboard. Those with severe visual handicaps may need material in Braille, or they may require audio recordings containing information that is presented to other pupils visually. Pupils with certain other handicaps must be provided with open spaces for crutches or wheelchairs. Arrangements must be made to allow these pupils more time to move from place to place.

Other special requirements face teachers as they work with these learners. Good responses to special needs require teachers to stretch their creative talents as they seek to devise instructional opportunities that are suited to particular needs of mainstreamed learners.

Gifted and Talented Pupils. Gifted and talented learners also present special challenges to the classroom teacher. These children often complete their work quickly. A common mistake beginning teachers make is to assign more work to gifted and talented pupils who finish early. Bright pupils are quick to spot this pattern, and some of them will try to hide their talents by working more slowly than necessary to avoid the extra work. This is an undesirable pattern because it encourages these children to underuse their abilities. It is better to allow them to choose to engage in selected enrichment activities, or to assist other pupils with their studies. These choices enable them to feel rewarded for their talents.

Knowledge about Content

Teachers consider knowledge about the content to be taught as they plan learning experiences. The course textbook may provide some of this information, but it is inadequate as an exclusive source for content knowledge. Textbooks tend to provide very sketchy treatments of topics that are covered. Teachers find it necessary to identify key ideas they wish to emphasize and to gather information from a variety of sources to illuminate these ideas for children.

As the teacher becomes more knowledgeable about the specific content to be treated, he or she typically begins to develop personal ideas of sequencing. Because of special learner characteristics in a particular classroom, the sequence followed in the course text may not be appropriate for a given topic. The teacher may need to devise a different sequencing scheme. This may well mean that learners will be asked to skip around in the textbook as they read information in an order the teacher considers more appropriate than the one used by the textbook author.

Knowledge about Teaching Methods

As they plan instructional experiences for their pupils, teachers identify teaching methods they will use. They try to incorporate a variety of techniques. Changing teaching approaches helps maintain pupils' interest.

Appropriate available resources, such as records and tapes, need to be selected when planning lessons.

Careful selection of teaching methods requires teachers to have a good understanding of different approaches. In particular, they need to know strengths and limitations of each. For example, it is possible to give pupils a general idea of how a bill becomes a law by having them read about the process. However, this approach fails to communicate much about the human give and take that characterizes legislative debate. A simulation activity is better suited to giving pupils an "emotional feel" for the reality of legislative activity than is a passive reading exercise.

Knowledge about Available Resource Materials

Learning is facilitated when a variety of resource materials are available to support instruction. As teachers plan lessons, they try to find out what learning resources are available to supplement basic information in the textbook, such as supplementary reading material, visual material (films, filmstrips, videocassettes, and so forth), computer software, artifacts and objects, maps, globes, simulations, and reproducible materials. Materials selected should relate to the topic, be appropriate for the pupils to be taught, and support instructional objectives.

USING PLANNING INFORMATION

Information gathered about learners, content, alternative instructional options, and available resource materials is reflected in completed instructional plans.

Whether these plans are carefully laid out in complete written form or whether they are reflected as sketchy outlines is largely a function of a teacher's experience. Individuals who have been in the classroom a long time often are able to condense planning decisions into a highly abbreviated form, relying on notes containing only a few key phrases and terms to guide their instruction. Their years of experience allow them to fill in the gaps and deliver excellent sequential instruction.

Teachers with less experience, who have not had the benefit of years of class-room practice, need to refer to detailed products of instructional planning to be able to lead pupils smoothly through lessons. Carefully written lesson plans and unit plans document their planning decisions. They enhance their confidence, particularly when they teach content areas that they have not taught before. The following sections introduce procedures for preparing unit and lesson plans.

UNIT PLANS

Teachers engage in both long-term and short-term planning. Long-term planning involves laying out an instructional program for a period as long as an entire school year. Content to be taught over such a period must be subdivided. The most popular way of doing this involves preparation of units. An *instructional unit* is a coherent body of content that requires between two and four weeks to teach.

The unit-planning process for the year begins with a consideration of content that has been mandated by state and local authorities. This content must be assigned high priority. It has the force of lawful authority behind it.

After considering this high-priority content, additional content is identified that relates closely to major school and social studies program goals. Teachers at this point might ask themselves questions such as: What citizenship elements need to be covered? Which social science understandings relate to this topic? How can the topic be used to develop personal goals? What knowledge, skills, and values need to be included in each of these three major areas? Responses to these questions help identify units to be covered during the year.

Once units are identified, they become the basic building blocks of the instructional program. Individual lessons are developed for each unit. Once social studies unit titles are determined, teachers can refer to them as they make decisions about instruction in other curricular areas. This can result in a valuable integration of content from many subjects. For example, a fifth-grade teacher might decide to include a unit titled "Pioneers," and might then undertake efforts to find reading materials related to pioneers to be used in the reading program, music related to pioneers, science projects related to pioneer life (perhaps making soap), and so on. A unit approach to planning the social studies program can lead to an important unity across the entire elementary curriculum.

It is important that units be planned in advance. There may be materials to be ordered. Films may need to be reserved. Arrangements for speakers and field trips must be made. These tasks take time. Ideally, it is a good idea to allow at least a month between the time a unit is planned and the time when it must be taught. (There are times when this will be impossible.)

Units are formatted in many ways. The exact format chosen rests with the individual teacher. Good formats display information so that relationships among instructional objectives, teaching approaches, and needed learning materials are easy to see.

It is common to begin the unit-planning process by preparing a general *unit-planning document* that identifies (1) pupils' grade level, (2) the unit title or theme, (3) intended learning outcomes, (4) necessary prerequisite knowledge, (5) the organization of the unit, (6) evaluation information, and (7) how to review the new unit.

Identifying the Grade Level

The grade level for which the unit is intended needs to be identified. This information is for other teachers who might have an interest in using or modifying the unit.

Identifying the Title or Theme

The title or theme of the unit is a self-explanatory component. This element of the unit describes the general category of information it treats. The title will also be useful to other teachers who may, on the basis of the title or theme, decide the unit is something they might like to examine for possible use in their own classrooms.

Describing Intended Learning Outcomes

This section of the unit is important. Intended outcomes relate back to broad goals of the elementary social studies program. In the unit-planning document, teachers often respond to questions such as these:

    a. What will be the citizenship outcomes? What knowledge, skills, values, and decision-making opportunities associated with citizenship will be included?

    b. What will be the history and/or social sciences outcomes? What generalizations, skills, values, attitudes, and decision-making opportunities associated with history and/or the social sciences will be emphasized?

    c. What problem-solving opportunities will be included?

Identifying the Necessary Prerequisite Knowledge

Any prerequisite information pupils absolutely must have must be identified. If the teacher fails to note this information, it is possible a potential unit user (another teacher, for example) might begin teaching the material only to discover that pupils were unable to succeed because they lacked needed background information.

Organizing the Unit

The next step is to organize the body of the unit in a way that makes clear the interrelationships among its parts. Initially, this information does not have to be excessively specific. Details can be added later when daily lessons are prepared. The form shown in Figure 4–4 is one many teachers have found useful. It organizes information for quick visual reference.

Identifying Evaluation Information

In this section the unit planner provides specific information about how pupils' levels of performance are to be measured. Sample checklists, observation instruments, suggested test items, or descriptions of projects learners will submit are included. These evaluation suggestions are just that—*suggestions*. They may be modified later when actual instruction of the unit has begun, but they provide a good beginning point for thinking about the issue of evaluation.

Reviewing the New Unit

This section includes questions that will be answered after the first draft of the actual unit has been completed. Answers will provide a final quality check before the unit is taught for the first time. (Almost always, there will be revisions made after an initial teaching of the unit.)

    a. Is the whole range of social studies outcomes included?
    b. Is the unit sequenced logically? Does learning in the early part of the unit

Social Science Generalization(s): _____		
Specific Objectives	Teaching Approach	Materials

FIGURE 4–4
Planning format for organizing the body of a unit

Grade Level: Fifth
Unit Theme: Why Do People Move?

Intended Learning Outcomes

Social Science Understandings
1. The promise of increased economic opportunity, religious freedom, political freedom, adventure, or values associated with a given lifestyle motivates people to move.
2. Conflict often occurs when one group of people moves into an area where people of a different culture already live.
3. The advances and changes in technology change the opportunities that people see in certain places.

Citizenship Understandings
1. A variety of groups of people have contributed to the development of our nation.
2. The rights of minorities need to be respected by those who have power.
3. Whenever people live together in a group they must establish rules to govern their behavior.

Personal Understandings
1. The need for adventure and novelty is something that all individuals experience.
2. What might be the correct choice for one person may not be the correct choice for another.
3. The values that people hold shape their decisions.
4. The dignity of all human beings needs to be respected and preserved.
5. Change is a constant feature of life that everyone needs to understand.

Prerequisite Knowledge

1. Pupils need to be able to read maps and identify the significant features of the United States.
2. Pupils need to know how to work together in groups.
3. The basic concepts of time and chronology—such as year, decade, and century—need to be understood.
4. Pupils need to have an understanding of scale and distance.
5. Pupils need to understand direction and location.
6. Pupils need a basic understanding of the events preceding the westward movement.

Unit Outline

Focus Generalization(s)
A variety of motives cause people to move to new places. When two groups or cultures come into contact, conflict often results.

Specific Objective	Teaching Approach	Materials
Unit Initiation and Development The class will demonstrate an interest in the topic by seeking books or materials or by asking questions about the topic.	Pose a problem situation: How would you feel if your parents said you were going to move? Relate to the feelings of the pioneers.	Bulletin board with pictures of wagon trains, etc. Play tape of an interview with a pioneer woman.
Individuals can identify significant events and people who helped open the West to settlement.	Read from text; view filmstrips.	Text, supplementary books. Filmstrips: "Lewis and Clark," "Mormon Trek," "California!"
Individuals can identify at least three reasons why people moved west.	Large group discussion to share and relate material. Use music as a source of data by listening to songs of the West.	Records, record player. Large sheet of paper to record data.

FIGURE 4–5
Sample unit plan.

Specific Objective	Teaching Approach	Materials
Individuals can identify the different groups of people who already lived in the West, and their locations.	Read in text. Map exercise for homework.	Text. Outline maps of U.S.
Pupils can identify the values and lifestyle characteristics of those already living in the West.	Small groups view filmstrips; read resource material.	Filmstrips: "Indians of the Plains," "The Spanish in the West," "Old Fort Vancouver."
Pupils can identify how the values and lifestyle elements of those already in the West may have conflicted with the values and lifestyle elements of those moving West.	View film. Use chart to make inferences and generalizations.	Film: "Westward Ho!"
Individuals can provide at least two examples of conflicts that arose between those already in the West and those moving to the West.	Read text. Review in large group.	Text. Large sheet of paper to record data.
Pupils can cite at least two reasons that encouraged people moving to the West to cross the Great Plains before settling down.	Use inquiry to pose problem: Why did the pioneers seek to move farther west? Follow by reading in text to test hypotheses.	Text. Outline maps.
Pupils can identify the impact of an innovation on the settling of the Great Plains.	View film. Do homework on an invention.	Film: "The Iron Horse." Assignment sheet for homework.
Individuals can identify present problems resulting from the contact between cultures during settlement of the West and can suggest how new innovations affected settlement patterns.	Engaging in generalizing and inferring after charting data in small groups.	Newspaper and news magazines.
Pupils will state feelings and choices they might have made if confronted with the prospect of a move West.	Large group discussion.	
Pupils will identify criteria they used in deciding to move or not to move West.	Simulation activity.	Handouts, maps of imaginary land.
Culminating Activity Pupils will work in groups of 2-3 or individually to create a project that illustrates some aspect of moving West.	Group work on projects.	Art supplies, models.

Evaluation Procedures

1. Multiple-choice quiz on significant events, people, and innovations.
2. Checklist on work habits to evaluate each individual working with a group.
3. Checklist for evaluating the final product. The checklist should include knowledge of geography, knowledge of settlers, knowledge of values, knowledge of problems, etc.
4. Grade homework assignments for accuracy and completeness.

build a basis for learning in subsequent sections? Is material organized to facilitate mastery of generalizations as well as concepts and facts?

c. Are specific instructional objectives identified?

d. Is there a variety of suggested teaching approaches? Are teaching ideas consistent with the intents of the objectives to which they relate? Are there ample opportunities for children to apply what they have learned?

An example of a completed unit plan is given in Figure 4–5.

LESSON PLANS

Short-term planning results in the preparation of lesson plans. A lesson plan outlines what the teacher and pupils will be doing during one lesson. Many lessons will require only one instructional period. Some may last longer.

Because student teachers and beginning teachers have not had much experience managing the flow of instructional activity, their lesson plans tend to be more detailed than those of teachers who have been in the profession for many years. A rule of thumb is that lesson plans should include sufficient information for a substitute teacher to implement the lesson without difficulty.

Lesson plans usually reference the title of the unit of which the lesson is a part, specific lesson instructional objectives, a sequence of teacher activities (including information about classroom management and materials management), a tentative time allocation for each lesson part, and a listing of all needed materials. As teachers gain experience, the quantity of specific information they put in their lesson plans tends to decrease.

Lesson plans feature information about (1) the objective to be pursued, (2) instructional approaches to be used, (3) needed instructional materials, (4) time allocations, and (5) organization and management of learners.

Lesson Objective

An individual lesson focuses on one unit objective. Separate lesson plans are prepared for all objectives in a unit. Some objectives may be broad enough that several lessons will be needed to familiarize pupils with the associated content.

Instructional Approaches

Decisions about instructional approaches are made after consideration of components of the instructional act. Decisions about instructional approaches involve choices about (1) the entry point for instruction, (2) motivation, (3) procedures to be used to inform pupils about the objective, (4) approaches to introducing the new content, (5) ways of checking to determine levels of pupils' understanding,

(6) eliciting pupil behaviors that suggest learning has occurred, and (7) concluding the lesson.

Determining an Entry Point for Instruction

In thinking about the "flow" of a lesson, one important decision relates to determining an *entry point*. This decision requires the teacher to think carefully about individual characteristics of pupils and about what has been taught previously. Ideally, the entry point takes advantage of past learning and begins new instruction at the place where content begins to deviate from what has been previously taught.

Motivating Learners

A successful lesson often depends on a teacher's success in motivating learners. Motivation involves more than simply generating pupils' interest at the beginning of a lesson. Ideally, there should be teacher moves at various points throughout the lesson that are designed to maintain and rekindle learner interest.

Clever social studies teachers often are able to take advantage of children's natural curiosity about other people. One aspect of this curiosity is what psychologists call the "identification motive." People seek to be like people who interest them and whom they respect. If lessons emphasize appealing aspects of people who are studied, the identification motive sometimes can be triggered.

Motivation tends to increase when children see content as related to their own lives. Instructional approaches that help young people see these connections tend to enhance their interest. For example, a study of explorers may become more meaningful if explorers are introduced as individuals who, like the children in the class, have experienced personal doubts and fears.

Novelty has long been recognized as a powerful motivator. To the extent possible, it is a good idea to introduce elements of surprise and unpredictability into lessons. Teachers who dress up in period costumes, start a lesson with an explanation of a startling fact, or use a cartoon featuring an attention-getting element are hoping that students will be motivated by these actions.

One of the most powerful motivators of all is success. The better children do in school, the better they feel about themselves and about the school program. This basic principle applies also to individual parts of the school program. Teachers who plan their social studies lessons with a view to ensuring that the largest possible number of children succeed have few motivational problems.

Informing Pupils About the Lesson Objective

The unit instructional objective selected to guide an individual lesson needs to be communicated to members of the class in language appropriate to the age and developmental levels of the children. Often, the teacher will provide pupils with a simple oral version of the objective.

The objective provides learners with a sense of direction. It gives them a feeling for what the teacher's expectations are. This tends to reduce anxiety and to make pupils' learning more efficient.

Introducing New Content

Presentation of new information is the heart of the lesson. Procedures selected for this purpose bear directly on what pupils will learn, retain, and transfer to new situations. Teachers may select from any of numerous instructional techniques. These are selected in light of the content to be delivered, the age levels of the pupils, the range of individual abilities represented in the class, the specific interests of the learners, the availability of appropriate support materials, and other variables. Regardless of the technique or techniques selected, teachers tend to keep in mind some basic instructional principles as they implement their instruction.

For example, new content is more accessible to pupils when they recognize its relationship to what they already know. Good teachers place content into a meaningful context for their children. They help them see how it connects to and builds logically from previously mastered content.

Learners' attention spans are short. This is particularly true of pupils in the primary grades. Successful lessons respond to this reality by including a variety of activities. Children need opportunities to work actively with new information they have learned. Teachers' verbal activities can be varied to include such options as questioning, demonstrating new techniques, and modeling what learners are to do when they are asked to apply what they have learned.

Teachers' verbal presentations need to be organized to avoid vague and ambiguous terms. Phrases such as "a bunch of these" or "some time ago" are imprecise. They fail to communicate clearly to learners and indicate poor planning. Detailed preparation can greatly enhance teacher clarity by ensuring that references to quantity and time will be sharply defined.

Good lessons feature *planned redundancy,* or systematic repetition of critical information. Planned redundancy is often accommodated by providing pupils with multiple examples of new ideas. These examples afford additional opportunities for the teacher to review new information and reinforce learning.

Checking on Pupils' Understanding

Smooth, productive lessons include periodic teacher checks to determine how well learners are grasping new material. There are many ways to do this. For example, teachers sometimes intersperse questions throughout a presentation. These questions require learners to restate or clarify what has been introduced. If they are unable to do so, the teacher reviews information that pupils have failed to grasp. At the beginning of an application activity, it is useful to ask a member of the class to restate directions in his or her own words. This allows the teacher to determine how well instructions have been comprehended.

When learners are working on application activities, teachers regularly monitor their work. It is important for children not only to receive corrective information when they are making mistakes but to also receive encouragement when they are doing good work. This encouragement makes them more self-confident and improves their attitudes toward the lesson.

Eliciting Behaviors that Suggest Learning Has Occurred

Pupils need opportunities to "do something" with new information introduced as part of a lesson. Times for these application activities are referenced in lesson plans. Sometimes these application activities occur toward the end of a lesson. On other occasions, several application opportunities are interspersed at points throughout the lesson. When appropriate, this design has merit. Frequent application activities add variety to the lesson and generally are well received by learners.

Concluding the Lesson

At the end of the lesson, the teacher reviews and highlights key points. Lesson planners need to reserve adequate time for this important step. Recapitulation helps learners solidify their grasp of important new content. Once the review has been completed, the teacher commonly makes a brief reference to the next lesson, building a bridge between what pupils have learned that day and what they will encounter the next day.

Needed Instructional Materials

Lesson planning requires more than careful attention to the flow of basic instructional activity. Attention must also be devoted to identifying learning resources that will support instruction. Needed materials might include items such as books, paper, pencil, maps, globes, and teacher-prepared materials of all kinds. The lesson planner works to assure that all of these materials will be available when the lesson is taught. If needed materials are not available, even a carefully planned lesson may fail.

Allocating Time

Instruction delivered in a typical lesson has many parts. It is a common practice to indicate tentative time allocations for each part of a lesson plan, for example, gaining learners' attention, introducing new content, allowing for guided practice, and reviewing the lesson.

In general, lessons should be designed to unfold at a fairly brisk pace, but slowly enough so that most learners will profit from the instruction. It is critical to allow plenty of time for application activities. Good guided practice activities associate with high levels of pupil achievement.

Organization and Management of Learners

Depending on the specific content of a lesson, there may be a need to seat pupils in a certain way. Some physical arrangements make it easier for pupils to accomplish certain assigned tasks and also simplify the teacher's job of monitoring the classroom.

Some lessons may have activities that require pupils to be organized in different ways at different times. For example, it may desirable for pupils to work in small

Alternative methods of instruction, such as group work, should be included in teacher plans.

groups during an application activity. In such a case, the teacher needs to think through a procedure for explaining to pupils when and how they are to move. If this is not done, confusion and time loss are certain to result.

Formatting the Lesson Plan

Many acceptable lesson forms are used. The exact format adopted is largely a matter of teacher preference. The design selected should be easy to use and should be of a size convenient for quick reference as the lesson is taught. A sample lesson plan format is shown in Figure 4–6.

KEY IDEAS IN SUMMARY

1. Competent instructional planning is a hallmark of a professional teacher. During the planning process, among other things, the teacher establishes priorities

```
Unit Theme:_____ Lesson Plan Number:_____

Learner Objective:_____

_____

Needed Prerequisites:_____

_____

New Vocabulary or Concepts:_____

        Time              Lesson Sequence                  Materials
                   Gaining Attention/Informing Learners of Objective
                   Presentation of New Content
                   Checking for Understanding/Feedback
                   Eliciting Desired Behavior/Practice/Application
                   Lesson Conclusion/Evaluation of Learning

Teacher Evaluation of Lesson Effectiveness:_____

_____

_____
```

FIGURE 4–6
Sample lesson plan format

for instruction, considers alternative teaching approaches, identifies needed learning materials, considers organizational issues, and makes decisions related to pupil and program evaluation.

2. Instructional planning begins with a consideration of aims and goals. Aims are broad statements of purpose that describe what citizens and the society expect of the schools. For example, one aim of schooling with special relevance for the social studies is that schools should produce "good citizens." Goals are related to aims, but are much more specific statements. They point out specific directions for subjects and grade levels. For example, a grade-three goal related to the aim of promoting "good citizenship" might be for "pupils to become aware of rules that govern their behavior."

3. Instructional objectives amplify goals in terms that describe specifically what pupils should be able to do as a consequence of their exposure to instruction. They provide specific guidance to teachers. The *ABCD* format for developing instructional objectives is widely used. According to this format, an instructional objective must include an *A* component that describes the intended audience for the instruction, a *B* component that describes the behavior the pupil should be able to demonstrate at the lesson's conclusion, a *C* component

that describes the conditions under which the behavior will be demonstrated, and a *D* component that outlines the expected degree of proficiency.

4. Instructional objectives may be planned for each of the three major domains of learning: cognitive, affective, and psychomotor. Cognitive instructional objectives focus on learning of an intellectual or academic nature. Affective instructional objectives are concerned with feelings, values, and attitudes. Psychomotor instructional objectives describe desired behaviors that involve physical movement and fine-muscle control.

5. As they prepare to make planning decisions, teachers need information that relates to several important topics. Specifically, they seek information about (a) pupils to be taught, (b) content to be taught, (c) alternative instructional options, and (d) available resource materials.

6. Long-term instructional planning often culminates in the development of instructional units. Instructional units are major subdivisions of the academic year. A typical unit requires two to four weeks of instructional time. In preparing units, teachers must (a) identify the grade level of the pupils for whom the unit is intended, (b) select a title, (c) describe intended learning outcomes, (d) identify prerequisite knowledge, (e) organize the body of content to be covered, and (f) select evaluation procedures.

7. Lesson plans are the written results of short-term planning activities. Lesson plans provide a guidance system for teachers to follow as they provide instruction in the classroom. Typical lesson plans include information related to (a) the objective to be pursued, (b) instructional approaches to be followed, (c) needed instructional materials, (d) allocation of instructional time, and (e) organization and management of learners.

POSTTEST

Answer each of the following true/false questions.

1. Aims, goals, and objectives are different names for the same thing.

2. Nearly every learning activity has its cognitive aspects, affective aspects, and psychomotor aspects.

3. It is recommended that an instructional unit be written on the same day instruction on the unit is to begin.

4. Teachers should assign additional regular school work to gifted and talented pupils who finish their regular assignments quickly.

5. Learners' levels of motivation tend to increase when they believe lesson content relates clearly to their own lives.

QUESTIONS

1. Why is planning an important element of teaching?

2. What are some distinctions among aims, goals, and instructional objectives?

3. What kinds of information do teachers need as they make instructional planning decisions?

4. What are some basic components of instructional units?

5. What kinds of information are found in lesson plans?

6. Suppose you were hired to teach in a school district with no social studies curriculum guides. How would you begin the task of planning your social studies program?

7. The importance of careful planning is widely supported, but there are people who hold a contrary view. They argue that overemphasizing planning produces inflexible teachers who insist on mechanically moving through the steps of their lesson plans. They suggest that planning removes spontaneity from the classroom. How do you react to this perspective?

8. Pupils in elementary classrooms have many special needs. To which kinds of pupil needs do you feel least capable of responding? What might you do to prepare yourself to help these children?

9. Motivation is an issue that is widely discussed in educational circles. Some people argue that today's learners are less motivated to do school work than were learners in previous years. Do you agree or disagree?

10. Are instructional units as useful to teachers other than those who have developed them, or do they really function well as guidance systems only for teachers who have been directly involved in their preparation? Why?

EXTENDING UNDERSTANDING AND SKILL

1. Think about a grade level you would like to teach. For this grade level, identify a theme, and plan a unit centering on that topic. Include objectives written in the *ABCD* format.

2. For the unit you have developed, write at least two lesson plans that could be used to teach two different objectives.

3. Motivation should not occur only at the beginning of a lesson but should be included at various points. In your lesson plans, highlight how you will integrate motivation at the beginning, during, and at the conclusion of the lesson.

4. Teach a group of peers a social studies lesson of a few minutes' duration. Have them critique you on logical organization, clarity of presentation, checking for

understanding, and elicitation of behaviors that allow pupils to practice new learning.

5. For each of the handicapping conditions noted below, prepare a list of ways that the lessons might be adapted in order to accommodate these special needs.

learning disability
hearing impairment
sight impairment
physical handicap
emotional disorder

REFERENCES

Armstrong, D., and T. Savage. *Secondary Education: An Introduction*, 2d ed. New York: Macmillan, 1990.

Bloom, B. (ed.), M. Englehart, E. Furst, W. Hill, and D. Krathwohl. *Taxonomy of Educational Objectives: Handbook I: The Cognitive Domain*. New York: David McKay, 1956.

Borich, G. *Effective Teaching Methods*, 2d. ed. Columbus, OH.: Merrill, 1992.

Clark, C., and P. Peterson. "Teachers' Thought Processes." In M. Wittrock, ed. *Handbook of Research on Teaching*, 3d ed. New York: Macmillan, 1986, pp. 255–96.

Doyle, W. "Classroom Organization and Management." In M. Wittrock, *Handbook of Research on Teaching*, 3d ed. New York: Macmillan, 1986, pp. 392–431.

Krathwohl, D., B. Bloom, and B. Masia. *Taxonomy of Educational Objectives: Handbook II: Affective Domain*. New York: David McKay, 1956.

Raths, L., H. Harmin, and S. Simon. *Values and Teaching*. Columbus, OH: Charles E. Merrill, 1966.

SUPPLEMENTAL READING

Gunter, M., T. Estes, and J. Schwab. *Instruction: A Models Approach*. Boston: Allyn and Bacon, 1990.

Merkle, D. "Thematic Units for the Classroom." *New England Reading Association Journal* (Winter 1984), pp. 12–17.

Ochoa, A., and S. Shuster. *Social Studies in Mainstreamed Classrooms*. Boulder, CO: ERIC Clearinghouse for Social Studies/Social Science Education, 1980.

Orlich, D., R. Harder, R. Callahan, D. Kauchak, R. Pendergast, and A. Keogh. *Teaching Strategies: A Guide to Better Instruction*, 3d ed. Lexington, MA: D. C. Heath, 1990.

FUNDAMENTAL APPROACHES TO INSTRUCTION

5

CONCEPTS, GENERALIZATIONS, AND INDIVIDUALIZED LEARNING

This chapter provides information to help the reader:

1. distinguish between concepts and generalizations,
2. describe procedures followed in concept-attainment lessons and concept-formation/diagnosis lessons,
3. identify steps that are followed in an inducing-a-generalization lesson,
4. point out variables that can be altered when content is organized with a view to individualizing instruction, and
5. explain features of learning centers, learning activity packages, activity cards, and learning contracts.

PRETEST

Answer each of the following true/false questions.

1. In general, disjunctive concepts and relational concepts are more difficult for pupils to grasp than are conjunctive concepts.
2. In a concept-attainment lesson, the teacher begins by naming the focus concept.
3. Generalizations are statements about relationships among concepts.
4. Altering the pacing of instruction is one way teachers respond to the need to individualize instruction.
5. A learning contract is an agreement between a teacher and a school district according to which the teacher guarantees to cover certain content during the period of one academic year.

INTRODUCTION

Chapter 2, "The Content Sources: History, Geography, and Economics," introduced the structure of knowledge. Two of the content types included in the structure of knowledge, concepts and generalizations, are particularly important organizers of information. Because of their broad explanatory power, some instructional procedures have been designed specifically for the purpose of teaching concepts and generalizations to learners. This chapter introduces several examples of these techniques.

Because learners are diverse, teachers need to differentiate their instruction. Instruction that is individualized seeks to capitalize on pupils' individual characteristics. In the social studies, individualization does not necessarily mean that learners will be working in isolation. Much social studies learning requires interaction with others. Individualization often results in lessons that involve groups but that may allow individual learners to pursue some content in different ways. This chapter suggests alternatives for responding to learners' individual needs.

TEACHING CONCEPTS AND GENERALIZATIONS

As a preface to thinking about teaching concepts, we review here the meaning of the term. *Concepts* are labels applied to phenomena that share certain common characteristics or attributes. For example, something with the attributes of (a) a personal vehicle with four wheels, (b) a gasoline or diesel engine (also, but rarely, with an electric motor), and (c) a steering wheel is given the common label "automobile." This label helps people to group the many different kinds of personal vehicles into the common category, automobile. A concept, then, is a kind of shorthand that people use to recall many kinds of related information through the use of a common label.

Three basic types of concepts are important. These are *conjunctive, disjunctive,* and *relational concepts* (Bruner et al. 1962). *All* of the defining attributes of a conjunctive concept must be present in order for something to be considered a proper example of the concept. For example, the conjunctive concept "triangle" has these three attributes: (a) three sides, (b) a closed two-dimensional figure, and (c) three interior angles. If any attribute is missing, the "thing" is not a triangle.

In the case of disjunctive concepts, it is not always necessary for all possible defining attributes to be present for the "thing" to be considered a proper example of the concept. The "extra point" in football is an example of a disjunctive concept (Fraenkel 1980). There are several ways an extra point can be scored: (a) the ball can be run into the end zone; (b) the ball can be passed into the end zone; or, (c) the ball can be kicked through the goal posts. If any one of these attributes is present, it is legitimate to say that an extra point has been scored. The multiple attributes typically associated with disjunctive concepts makes them somewhat more challenging to teach than conjunctive concepts.

Relational concepts are defined by attributes that bear a specific relationship to one another. Consider the concept "miles per hour." There is a relationship between an attribute having to do with distance covered (miles) and the time required to so (hours). Mastery of concepts of this type requires pupils to understand not only each attribute by itself but also the relationship among attributes. Consequently, relational concepts also are somewhat more difficult for pupils to master than conjunctive concepts.

In addition to problems associated with disjunctive and relational concepts, pupils also frequently have difficulty with concepts of all types that feature large numbers of defining attributes. For example, concepts such as "democracy," "citizenship," "power," "socialization," and "industrialization" come up often in social studies lessons. Such concepts are difficult for elementary learners. Because these complex concepts often are included in powerful, explanatory generalizations, instruction that is designed specifically to teach basic, but complex, concepts is often a feature of elementary social studies classes.

Concepts can be taught in various ways. Sometimes teachers use direct-instruction approaches. One example of an approach to teach concepts directly is concept attainment.

Concept Attainment

Concept attainment focuses on teaching concepts that the teacher has selected for study. The approach is easily applied to a wide range of concept-centered lessons. The basic steps are as follows:

1. The teacher introduces the concept by name.
2. The teacher presents examples of the concept.

3. The teacher introduces nonexamples of the concept.
4. A mixture of examples and nonexamples is presented. Pupils are asked to point out the correct examples of the concept.
5. Next, pupils are asked to try to define the concept.
6. Finally, pupils try to apply their understanding by finding additional examples of the concept.

This process can be used to teach a variety of concepts. If a fairly simple concept such as "desert" were the focus, the teacher might begin by showing learners photographs of desert regions. Next, photographs of nondesert regions might be introduced. Then a display including photographs of both desert and nondesert regions would be made available. Learners would be asked to point out the ones depicting deserts. Next, the teacher would ask members of the class to try to define "desert." Finally, pupils might be asked to find photographs of deserts in sources such as old *National Geographic* magazines.

This basic approach can also be used to teach such complex concepts as "justice" and "democracy." When sophisticated concepts are taught, the process may take several class periods. Though the time required for teaching these complex concepts is longer than that needed for simpler concepts, the process remains basically unchanged.

At times, the teacher may be interested in having pupils develop concepts of their own. Often, when this is what the teacher has in mind, he or she is more

"I know you're all for individualizing, but Larry can't play his boom box here. Let's take a chance on the possibility that his psyche can take this kind of repression."

interested in teaching the *process* of concept formation rather than the meaning of a specific concept. One procedure, based on the work of the late Hilda Taba (1967), helps learners develop their thinking powers.* This is "concept formation/ diagnosis." This approach also helps teachers to identify some misunderstandings that some members of the class might have.

Concept Formation/Diagnosis

These are the basic steps in a concept-formation/diagnosis lesson:

1. In response to a stimulus provided by the teacher, often a question, pupils provide a number of responses. The teacher writes these where learners can see them.
2. Pupils organize responses into categories.
3. Pupils develop concept labels that define the common characteristics of the responses organized in each category established during step two.

To get the lesson started, a teacher might ask questions such as these: What are the types of jobs that people have today? What kinds of buildings are there in our town? What would you tell a friend who was going to move here about what our state is like? What do you think you would find if you visited Brazil? Additional sample questions are listed in Figure 5–1.

Pupil responses are listed on the chalkboard, butcher paper, a chart, an overhead transparency, or some other appropriate writing surface. The teacher should

---

*For information about several techniques designed to improve learners' thinking skills, see Chapter 7, "Thinking-Skills Instruction."

This strategy requires the teacher to plan some questions to prompt responses from the members of the class. Questions will vary with the particular topic the youngsters will be studying. The questions that follow are examples of those that function well when this strategy is being used.

1. What things can be bought at the store?
2. What jobs do people have?
3. Draw a picture of something we do in school.
4. Draw a picture of things for which families spend money.
5. What buildings do we find in our community or town?
6. If you were to tell friends about our state, what would you say?
7. What would you expect to see on a visit to _____ ?
8. What are some of the ways people earn money?
9. If you were a pioneer moving west, what would you take along?
10. What comes to mind when you hear the word "democracy"?
11. What do you think of when you think of summer?
12. What did you see on our field trip?

FIGURE 5–1
Suggested questions for concept formation/diagnosis.

restate contributions of each learner as his or her contributions are added to the list. No effort should be made to correct misinformation. Mistakes provide the teacher with important diagnostic information about what pupils believe to be true. These misconceptions suggest kinds of content that need to be addressed in future lessons.

Once the list is complete, the teacher initiates the next step in the activity by asking this question: Which things on our list go together in groups? As learners suggest groups, the teacher asks them their reasons for making their suggestions. The teacher takes care to remind pupils that it is acceptable for some items to belong to more than one group.

The final phase of the exercise is also begun by a teacher question. At this point the teacher might say, What could we call each group? As learners respond, the teacher urges them to think of labels that are neither too broad nor too narrow. Useful concept labels tend to strike a middle ground between excessive specificity and excessive breadth.

Inducing Generalizations

Social studies lessons often are directed at helping pupils acquire generalizations that summarize important information. Recall that generalizations are statements of relationship among concepts. They are succinct statements reflecting what the best available evidence has found to be "true."

Generalizations often concisely sum up volumes of scholarship on a given topic. Consider this generalization: The global location of a nation or region contributes to its importance in international affairs. This statement represents a distillation of a tremendous amount of scholarship, primarily from the field of political science.

Several approaches are available to teachers who are interested in having their pupils acquire important social studies generalizations. One of these is the inducing-a-generalization technique. This procedure seeks to help learners develop an understanding of a well-established generalization by considering evidence and following the logic of their own thought processes. The technique begins by the teacher selecting a powerful focus generalization. The idea is for the teacher to provide learners with evidence that supports the "truth" of the generalization in a way that will allow learners to infer the generalization on their own.

Prior to starting an inducing-a-generalization exercise, the teacher must assure that pupils understand basic concepts associated with the generalization. Consider again the generalization that the global location of a nation or region contributes to its importance in international affairs. Learners who are ignorant of the concepts "global location," "nation," "region," and "international affairs" would find it impossible to infer the generalization.

It is also necessary that the teacher gather together ample evidence that supports the truth of the focus generalization. If this information is unavailable, pupils will become frustrated, and they will fail in their attempts to infer the generalization.

Gathering data from a variety of sources is an important step in formulating concepts and generalizations.

These are the steps followed in an inducing-a-generalization activity. (For an example, see Figure 5–2).

1. Pupils look at evidence that the teacher has made available. They organize this evidence into appropriate categories.
2. Pupils compare and contrast information and note relationships.
3. They develop statements (generalizations) that can explain relationships and that seem capable of being applied to other situations.

In step one, the teacher introduces information that supports the "truth" of the focus information. (Remember, the pupils are not given the focus generalization. They get only evidence that tends to support it. The purpose of the exercise is for them to arrive at the focus generalization on their own.) At this point, the teacher may wish to help learners organize information into appropriate categories.

During step two, pupils look at all information that has been gathered. To accomplish this task, the information must be displayed so that all members of the class can see it. Writing the information, now frequently organized into categories, on the chalkboard works well. The teacher asks questions designed to prompt pupils to think about the information. These are examples of questions that might be asked: What do you notice about kinds of jobs people have in our community and kinds of jobs people have in other communities? What do you notice about the differences in climate between place A and place B? How were the conditions in this colony different from the conditions in that colony?

The following chart is a visual illustration of how the data for such a lesson might be displayed. This generalization might be selected by the teacher as a focus for this lesson: The types and varieties of services change as the size of a community changes. One axis of the chart displays communities of different types. The other axis indicates different types of businesses and services. Below the chart are the questions that the teacher might use in guiding the class session.

| | Types of Services Available | | |
Size of Community	Government Services	Types of Industries	Types of Stores
Small rural community			
Moderate-sized suburban community			
Large city			

Step 1: What do you notice about the types of government services, businesses and stores in the different communities?

Step 2: What are the similarities and differences you notice among these communities?

Step 3: Why do you think there are differences among these communities? What statements can we make that might help us explain what we might find in other communities?

FIGURE 5–2
Organizing an inducing-a-generalization lesson.

Step three requires pupils to develop a general statement that sums up the relationships noted in step two. This part of the exercise initially may frustrate some learners. At this time, they are asked to make inferences that go beyond the literal limits of the given information. Some pupils may feel they are "at risk" in venturing a response under these conditions. The teacher must do all possible to help learners lose their fear of making an inappropriate response. They must not feel that their ideas will be ridiculed.

This final step begins with questions from the teacher such as these: Why do you think different types of jobs are available in different types of communities? Why do places change at different rates? How can you explain all of these things? These questions prompt pupils to speak up about all relationships they see. The teacher probes gently to encourage pupils to justify their generalizations in terms of the available evidence. As this phase of the lesson unfolds, the teacher writes down all pupil-developed generalizations. These generalizations can be tested as learners encounter more information. As time goes on, learners will discover that many of their generalizations are "true." Some will need revision. Others may have to be abandoned in the light of contrary evidence. The following episode illustrates how an inducing-a-generalization activity might proceed (also see Figure 5.2).

LESSON
▪ IDEA ▪

The Changing Community

Grade Level: 2–5. *Objective:* Learners can state at least one generalization based on the comparison of data on a chart. *Suggested Procedures:* Following are the teacher's comments while guiding pupils through the process.

1. Each of your groups has studied communities of different sizes. We now have all of this information on this large sheet of paper. Let's look at it together. What do you notice about the population of each community? What services are available in each community? (Pupils respond to each question in this and subsequent steps.)

2. What do you notice about the different types of jobs in each community? What do you notice about the kinds of services available in each community? In what ways are these communities alike? In what ways are they different?

3. You have identified the important differences in jobs and services available in these communities. What explains these differences? Why do you think some services exist in all of the communities we studied? Why do some communities have so many different kinds of jobs available? What statements can you make that might help us understand other communities we might study?

Involving pupils in plays can reinforce their understanding of generalizations.

INDIVIDUALIZED LEARNING: BASIC FEATURES

Planning that serves the interests of all pupils in the classroom features lessons that respond to learners' special interests and needs. Several approaches to individualization that are appropriate for the elementary school social studies classroom are introduced in this section.

The term *individualized instruction* means different things to different people. Some people think of individualization as implying an independent study situation where each learner works alone. In our view, individualized instruction by no means suggests that a pupil must always work alone. Indeed, working alone may be totally inappropriate for many instructional tasks and may poorly serve the needs of some pupils. Many individual needs are best accomplished in group settings. In planning for individualized learning, several variables can be manipulated. These include (1) the rate of learning, (2) the content of learning, (3) the method of learning, and (4) the goals of learning.

Altering the Rate of Learning

The rate of learning refers to the pacing of instruction. In a classroom where only one instructional experience is available, it is assumed that all pupils will be able to learn the material at the same rate. The truth of the matter is that some pupils will grasp the material quickly, and others will be unable to learn it in the time allotted.

Individualized planning seeks to provide different experiences for different pupils. When the learning-rate variable is manipulated, the content and basic requirements are unchanged. What *is* altered is the time allowed for the completion of tasks.

When planning a lesson in which pupils are assumed to have different rates of learning, the teacher must break the learning sequence into small steps. Next, a test for each learning step needs to be developed. The basic arrangement is for an individual learner to go on to the next step only after he or she has passed the test over the previous one. Pupils who fail a test over a given step are allowed the opportunity to work on the material some more. This is called *recycling*. After additional work, the pupil is given a chance to take the test again. This approach allows pupils to progress as rapidly as they evidence learning of the material associated with each step.

Altering the Content of Learning

In individualized programs that have altered the content of learning, different people in the classroom study different content. There may be a common set of objectives guiding instruction; however, the specific information pupils study en route to mastering these objectives may vary.

When this approach is used, pupils are often given the freedom to select content from among several options. For example, when a major program objective focuses on the mastery of research and writing skills, individual learners may be given wide latitude in selecting their research topics.

One scheme that has been used to provide structure for this approach to individualized learning is the learning activity package. (A complete description of a learning activity package is given later in this chapter.) A learning activity package is a document that describes the important goals and objectives to be met and that suggests alternative learning experiences that pupils might pursue to achieve them. It is assumed that pupils will choose the learning experiences that are of most personal interest to them.

When the learning-content variable is manipulated to individualize instruction, some pupils may work alone. Others may work in groups. Small group work is likely to occur when several learners select the same learning activity. Successful lessons of this kind necessitate that a variety of learning options and resources be available. Much teacher planning and organization is required.

Altering the Method of Learning

Individualized instructional programs that focus on varying the method of learning seek to respond to pupils' differing learning styles. The objectives and the content are the same for all. Individualization occurs as pupils select how they will learn. The teacher provides options from which they are encouraged to choose. For example, pupils may be offered choices such as using a textbook, viewing filmstrips, building a project, interviewing an expert, or interpreting the content of a photograph or painting.

Alternative learning methods sometimes are included as parts of more general instructional approaches. Two examples that often provide options for learners are learning activity packages and learning centers. (Learning centers are discussed later in this chapter.)

Altering the Goals of Learning

Individualized instructional programs that alter the goals of learning are uncommon. These programs allow pupils to make major decisions about what they want to learn. The teacher acts as a facilitator who listens to pupils and helps them clarify their interests. This approach presumes each learner to be the best judge of his or her long-term needs. In recent years, pressures have mounted to hold pupils accountable for learning prescribed content. As a result, interest in approaches that alter the goals of learning has diminished.

Table 5.1 summarizes the ways in which the four given variables may be altered for individualized instruction.

TABLE 5–1
Altering the variables for individualized instruction.

Variable	Pupil Role	Teacher Role
Learning rate	Works at own pace; seeks assistance when needed.	Makes assignments; monitors work; provides assistance; checks for mastery.
Content	Chooses topics to be studied in working toward goals; works at own pace; finds materials.	Sets learning goals; provides alternative topics for study; monitors work; evaluates products.
Methods	Decides how to study a topic; arranges environment for study; works at own pace.	Establishes goals; identifies content to be studied; evaluates learning; provides learning alternatives; monitors pupils.
Goals	Chooses goals to be accomplished; helps establish criteria for evaluation; submits final product when satisfied.	Challenges pupils to consider what is important for them to learn; negotiates goals evaluation and timeline with pupils; provides assistance; evaluates product according to criteria jointly established with pupil.

INDIVIDUALIZED LEARNING: SOME INSTRUCTIONAL APPROACHES

Decisions about which variable or variables should be the focus of individualized lessons reflect teachers' values and priorities, the expectations of the school and community leaders, and the nature of the subject matter. Some methods of "packaging" individualized instruction are described in the pages that follow.

Learning Centers

Learning centers are frequently used to individualize instruction in elementary social studies programs. They are designated areas of the classroom that feature materials for learning and directions telling pupils what they are to do. Often there is an attractive visual display in the center that is designed to motivate pupil interest in the focus topic. Centers may include a wide variety of learning resources, among which are such information sources as books, pictures, filmstrips, tape recorders, worksheets, assignment sheets, computer software (and computers), and study guides.

Fold-down learning centers with cardboard sides, which include general instructions and information, are popular. These can be set up on tables when they are needed. They store easily once pupils have completed working on the focus topic. Figure 5.3 illustrates a learning center that features instruction on map and globe skills.

In the learning center displayed in Figure 5.3, a projector with a filmstrip and an accompanying audio tape recorder with a cassette containing basic information

Learning centers help teachers individualize social studies instruction.

are set up. Earphones allow individual learners to listen to the information without disturbing others. Pupils are asked to use this center one at a time. Each is free to go to the center when no other pupil is using it. There may several such centers available for pupil use. This allows several learners to be working in centers at the same time.

Study guides are typically included at a learning center. Figure 5–4 is a study guide designed for use in the center shown in Figure 5–3.

The learning center approach can accommodate different rates of learning. Some pupils typically will take a long time to accomplish all the tasks at the center. Others will complete the work quickly. Some learning centers provide pupils with alternative learning options. For example, the directions may allow pupils a choice of getting basic information from a cassette recording, a reading selection, or a videotape. Though there typically are differences in learning rate and though there may be a provision for alternative learning options, the same set of learning

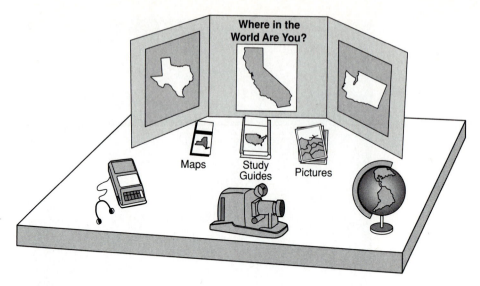

FIGURE 5–3
A learning center: map and globe skills.

objectives almost always guides the work of all pupils who work at a given learning station.

When several learning centers are set up in the classroom at the same time, it may be necessary for the teacher to set some general time limits. For example, pupils might be told, "All centers must be completed by Friday." The teacher needs to monitor pupils carefully to assure that all are using their time at the learning centers in a productive way. Some pupils will finish much before their classmates. They need to be provided with enrichment activities that they can pursue while others in the class are finishing work at individual centers. Sometimes teachers find it useful to have brighter learners who have finished their work function as tutors to help other learners who are still working on learning center tasks.

Learning Activity Packages

The learning activity package (LAP) is often used to organize individualized instructional programs. Sometimes LAPs are included as parts of learning centers. Sometimes various LAPs are given to different pupils to complete on their own. Occasionally, all learners in a class are assigned to work on the same LAP.

All LAPs share certain features. These include (a) a pretest, (b) a list of the activities to be completed, (c) an explanation of resources to be used, and (d) a posttest or other evaluation procedure. Sometimes the pretest is set up so that pupils with high scores are allowed to skip some of the listed learning activities.

If pupils are to succeed when they work with LAPs, they must have the prerequisite skills and knowledge needed to accomplish the assigned tasks. If LAPs

---

Where in the World are You?

Objective
When you complete this learning center, you should be able to identify the type of map that is needed to solve a given problem.

Sequence of Activities
1. Take a minute to look at all the material in the learning center. What do you think this center's purpose is? What do you already know about this topic? Think about this.
2. Pick up the worksheet that goes with the filmstrip. Look at the filmstrip and listen to the tape. When you have completed the worksheet, give it to your teacher. If you do not understand some part of the filmstrip, look at it again until you do. If you still have trouble, raise your hand and the teacher will come to help you.
3. Use the maps in the center as you answer these questions.
   (a) Which maps would be the best for identifying the populations of cities?
   (b) Which maps would be helpful if you wanted to know the elevation of a place?
   (c) Which maps would be helpful if you wanted to say something about the kinds of things grown in different places?
4. *Application activity.* Construct a map of our own community. In your map, show something that is not usually included on a street map. (Examples: the types of trees, the locations of apartment houses, the kinds of stores, and so forth.)

FIGURE 5–4
A learning center study guide, "Where in the World Are You?" *Grade Level:* 5–6.
Objective: Learners can identify the type of map needed to solve a given problem.

assume pupils know more than they really do, they quickly become frustrated. They may have great difficulty succeeding, and they are certain to require lots of teacher help.

All of the information a pupil might need to complete tasks outlined in the LAP is not always contained within the LAP itself. For example, the LAP may provide instructions directing the learner to another information source. The pupils might be asked to read part of a textbook or part of a book in the school library, to view an evening newscast, or to read an account of an event in a newspaper.

The LAP is basically an instruction management tool. It allows the teacher to organize instructions for pupils in a convenient package. The format allows teachers to individualize their instruction. Individual LAPs can be developed for learners who have different instructional needs. LAPs encourage responsibility. They place an obligation on learners to accomplish all assigned tasks. An example of a LAP is provided in Figure 5–5.

LAPs are especially useful for guiding pupils' work on research projects. They provide specific directions about what learners are to do. Pupils need to be carefully monitored by the teacher when they are working on LAPs. This monitoring is needed to keep learners working on their assigned tasks. Without this teacher attention, there is a tendency for some pupils to procrastinate. Close supervision of pupils' work also allows the teacher to help individual learners who may be experiencing difficulty with any of the assigned work.

Primary Sources

I. Pretest

This learning activity package is about primary sources. If you think you know what a primary source is, answer the following questions and take them to the teacher. If you do not know, proceed directly to the introduction.

1. What is a primary source?
2. Is our social studies textbook a primary source?
3. Why are primary sources important?

II. Introduction

When you read our social studies textbook, do you ever wonder how the writers found out about the events they describe? For some recent events, they may have observed or participated in the event. However, for events they did not participate in or see, they had to rely on the descriptions provided by others.

When you read an account of an event, it is important to know whether the writer personally observed the event or learned about it by reading a report written by someone else. Information tends to get confused as it is passed from person to person. You may recall that this has happened to you when you have heard something a friend heard from someone else. When this happened, the information your friend shared may have been quite different from what actually took place.

III. Objectives

When you complete this LAP, you should be able to:

1. Define a primary source.
2. Define a secondary source.
3. Identify examples of primary sources.
4. Identify primary sources, and use them in reporting about a historic event.

IV. Activities

Definition. A primary source is a person or a record written by a person who was either a participant or an observer of an event. For example, an eyewitness to an automobile accident would be considered a primary source. Other records, such as the repair bill and pictures of the damaged car would be considered primary sources. However, the reports of others about the accident, such as a newspaper account, would be secondary sources. If a friend saw the accident and told you about it, he or she would be a primary source. If you tell someone else about it, you are a secondary source.

1. Which of the following are most likely to be primary resources in learning about the Civil War?
    (a) A diary of a soldier who was in the war.
    (b) Our textbook.
    (c) The PBS series, "The Civil War."
    (d) The letters of one General to another General.
2. Read the story of the "Shot Heard Around the World" in our social studies textbook. Next, read the diary account of a British soldier. State the ways the two accounts differ, and explain why you think they differ.
3. What do these differences tell you about the uses of primary sources when trying to determine what happened?
4. If you were to write an account of how our school has changed in the past ten years, what would be some of the primary sources that you could use?

V. Evaluation Activity

Choose an event from the recent history of our nation or community. Identify a person or some records that could be considered a primary source. Prepare an account of the event. If you use a person, you may ask them to describe the event to you on a cassette tape. Before you do this you will need to develop some questions to ask the person. The teacher can help you with this. When you finish, give your teacher the account or the tape.

FIGURE 5–5

A learning activity package, "Primary Sources." *Grade Level:* 5. *Objective:* Learners can complete a learning activity package with minimal assistance. *Suggested Procedure:* Provide the LAP for learners to complete at their own pace.

Activity Cards

Activity cards provide pupils with choices of how they will go about learning assigned content. Each card points out several tasks that are to be accomplished. Typically, a set of activity cards pertains to a single objective. Each card in the set deals with a portion of the total learning associated with the objective.

Ordinarily, pupils are allowed to select one activity card from a set. If several learners select the same card, they often work as a group to accomplish the tasks outlined on the card. When work has been completed, the teacher checks it and credits each individual who has done it properly with completing the tasks described on the card.

Activity cards are easy to organize and store. Many of them can be kept conveniently in a small file or in a shoe box. Tasks listed on activity cards often seek to extend learners' understanding of content that, initially, has been introduced in other ways. Sometimes, too, tasks on activity cards are used for extra-credit assignments. Figure 5–6 illustrates examples of information included on three activity cards that were developed for use in an elementary social studies class. Sets of activity cards are often prepared by teachers at the same time they develop individual units of study. When this is done, activity cards are developed that can be used throughout the year to support instruction on all topics covered in the social studies curriculum.

Learning Contracts

A learning contract is an agreement between a teacher and a pupil. In very specific terms it describes what the pupil agrees to do to satisfy certain learning requirements. There are two basic types of learning contracts: open and closed.

Open learning contracts are those that give the learner a great deal of discretion concerning such issues as the learning objectives to be included, the specific assignments to be completed, the kinds of learning activities to be engaged in, and the types of evaluation procedures to be used to assess progress. Open learning contracts are suitable for use with motivated, independent, mature learners.

Closed learning contracts are much more common. The teacher plays a directive role in determining the contents of a closed learning contract. Based on his or her best professional judgment, the teacher will identify the objectives, determine the assignments and learning activities, and prescribe the sorts of assessment to take place to evaluate pupil progress. The teacher prepares the contract in light of information about special needs of the pupil who will be held to its terms.

Learning contracts are written in very specific language. They nearly always include clear descriptions of:

1. What the pupil is to do,
2. What resources are to be used,
3. What kind of a learning "product" the pupil is to prepare,
4. What evaluation procedures will be followed, and
5. What will be the latest acceptable date for all work to be completed.

An example of a learning contract is shown in Figure 5–7.

Activity Card 1

Topic: The Division of Labor
Grade Level: Primary
Purpose: The pupil will state examples of the division of labor.

Activities
1. Look through the magazines in the learning center.
2. Cut out five pictures of jobs that people are doing.
3. For each job, write one sentence describing how this job helps other people.
4. Draw a picture of a job that you have at home.
5. Write a sentence telling how your job helps your family.

Activity Card 2

Topic: Goods and Services
Grade Level: Upper Elementary
Purpose: The pupil will identify businesses that provide goods and those that provide services.

Activities
1. Look through the Yellow Pages. Make a chart like the one below. In the "Goods" column, place at least ten businesses that provide goods. In the "Services" column, place at least ten businesses that provide services. Identify at least three businesses that provide both goods and services.

Goods	Services	Both

2. Interview a relative or friend. Find out whether his or her job provides a good or service. Identify what she or he must know to provide this good or service.

Activity Card 3

Topic: Local History
Grade Level: Middle Elementary
Purpose: The pupil will research an event in local history.

Activities
1. Are there any historical markers or important historical sites in our community? If there is a marker, visit this site. Write down what the marker says. Talk with other people in the community to find out what they might know about the event described on the historical marker.
2. Once you have gathered information about the event, do one of the following:
   (a) Prepare an oral report about the event.
   (b) Draw a picture of the event.
   (c) Write a play about the event, and act it out for the class.

LESSON
▪ *IDEA* ▪

FIGURE 5–6
Three examples of activity cards.

Contract

Topic:

I _____ , agree to do the following:

1.

2.

3.

4.

The following criteria will be used in evaluating the activities and products of the contract.

1.

2.

3.

I agree that the activities will be completed by _____ .

_____   _____   _____
Student's Signature   Teacher's Signature   Date

FIGURE 5–7
An example of a learning contract.

KEY IDEAS IN SUMMARY

1. Concepts are labels that describe phenomena with certain common characteristics. Generalizations are statements of relationships among concepts that are based on the best available evidence. Because of the broad explanatory power of concepts and generalizations, some specific instructional techniques have been developed for teaching them in elementary social studies classes.

2. All of the defining attributes of the concept must be present for something to be considered a proper example of a conjunctive concept. A disjunctive concept has several attributes, but it is not necessary for all of them to be present for something to be considered a proper example of the concept. Relational concepts are characterized by attributes that bear a specific relationship to one another. In general, disjunctive concepts and relational concepts are more difficult for pupils to grasp than are conjunctive concepts. Concepts with many defining attributes also often cause problems for learners.

3. The concept-attainment technique focuses on teaching concepts that the teacher has selected for pupils to study. These steps are typically followed: (a) the teacher introduces the concept by name; (b) the teacher presents exam-

ples of the concept; (c) the teacher introduces nonexamples of the concept; (d) a mixture of examples and nonexamples is presented, and pupils are asked to point out the examples; (e) pupils are encouraged to name the concept; and (f) pupils apply their understanding by finding additional examples of the concept.

4. A concept-formation/diagnosis technique can be used when the teacher wishes pupils to develop concepts of their own. This procedure is used when there is an interest in having learners grasp the *process* of concept formation. These steps are typically followed in a concept-formation/diagnosis lesson: (a) pupils respond to a stimulus, often a question, provided by the teacher; (b) pupils organize responses into categories; and (c) pupils develop concept labels that define the common characteristics of the items gathered together during the previous step.

5. The inducing-a-generalization technique helps pupils understand a well-supported generalization by considering evidence and following the logic of their own thought processes. The teacher selects a generalization and provides learners with evidence that supports it. Learners look only at the evidence as they attempt to infer the explanatory generalization. These steps are typically followed: (a) pupils look at evidence that the teacher has made available, and they organize it into categories; (b) pupils compare and contrast information and note relationships; and (c) pupils develop explanatory statements (generalizations) that explain relationships and that are capable of being applied to other situations.

6. Individualized instruction seeks to meet needs of every learner. It does not mean, however, that pupils necessarily will be working in isolation from others. Particularly in social studies classes, an end result of assessing learners' individual needs is a decision to organize pupils into small groups, each of which includes students with similar interests and needs.

7. In general, approaches to individualized instruction manipulate one of four variables. Respectively, these are (a) the rate of learning, (b) the content of learning, (c) the method of learning, and (d) the goals of learning. Programs directed at altering the goals of learning are the least widely used.

8. Learning centers are frequently used to individualize instruction in elementary social studies classes. Learning centers are designated parts of the classroom that include materials for learning and directions for pupils. Learning centers can be designed that allow for different rates of learning and that provide for different learning options. Sometimes several learning stations are set up in the classroom.

9. Learning Activity Packages (LAPs) represent another approach to packaging individualized instruction. LAPs typically include (a) a pretest, (b) a list of activities to be completed, (c) an explanation of resources to be used, and (d) a posttest or other provision for evaluation. LAPs of different types can be developed for learners with varying interests and instructional needs.

10. Activity cards give pupils choices regarding what they can do to master a given body of content. Typically a set of cards is prepared. Each set ties to a single learning objective. Individual cards suggest different things that pupils can do to master content associated with the objective. Pupils are encouraged to choose a card from the set that includes a method of learning that appeals to them. When several pupils choose the same card, often they are organized into a small group. Group members may work together on the assigned learning task.

11. Learning contracts are agreements made between the teacher and individual pupils. The include descriptions of (a) what the pupil is to do, (b) what resources are to be used, (c) what kind of learning "product" the pupil is to prepare; and (d) what dates have been established for completing work.

POSTTEST

Answer each of the following true/false questions.

1. A concept-attainment/diagnosis approach would be appropriate when a teacher intends to teach learners the *process* of concept development.

2. In the inducing-a-generalization technique, the teacher uses a direct-instruction approach in which he or she simply tells students what the focus generalization is and then provides them with evidence to support it.

3. It is possible for several learning centers to be available for pupil use at the same time.

4. One advantage of having pupils work with Learning Activity Packages (LAPs) is that the teacher has few responsibilities to monitor them as they work on instructional tasks associated with the LAPs.

5. Typically, a set of activity cards pertains to a single instructional objective.

QUESTIONS

1. What basic kinds of concepts are there?

2. What is an *attribute* of a concept?

3. What are the purposes of concept attainment?

4. What instructional purposes can be met by a concept-formation/diagnosis approach?

5. What steps are followed in an inducing-a-generalization lesson?

6. What variables can be manipulated as teachers attempt to individualize instruction?

7. What are the features of a learning center?

8. What common components are found in most learning activity packages?

9. What are characteristics of activity cards?

10. What are elements often found in a learning contract?

11. Concepts with many defining attributes are considered difficult for learners to grasp. Think about some complex concepts that might be introduced in a social studies lesson at a grade level you wish to teach. Try to list all relevant attributes. What are some approaches you might use in helping your learners acquire these concepts?

12. Inducing-a-generalization lessons and concept-formation/diagnosis lessons often consume quite some class time. Would it be better for teachers to simply tell pupils about the generalizations and concepts? This could be done much more quickly. Why do you respond as you do?

13. If you were planning some individualized lessons, would you feel it more important to (a) alter the rate of learning, (b) alter the content of learning, (c) alter the method of learning, or (d) alter the goals of learning? Why did you arrive at this conclusion?

14. Social studies instruction tends to focus on relationships among groups. Given this orientation, is it really appropriate to think about individualizing instruction when social studies content is the academic focus of a lesson? Why do you take this position?

15. Learning contracts vary in content. Some pupils may be required to do more than others. Is this fair? Should teachers treat some pupils differently than others? Support your answer.

EXTENDING UNDERSTANDING AND SKILL

1. Much has been written about concept learning and concept teaching. Review some articles in journals such as *Social Education* and *The Social Studies* (your instructor may suggest alternatives) that deal with these issues. Take notes on one or two specific techniques. Bring them to class, and share them with others. Be prepared to explain how these techniques differ from those introduced in this chapter.

2. Individualized instruction requires a great deal of planning. Planning takes time. Interview several teachers who teach at a grade level that interests you. Ask them about their feelings about individualizing, particularly as it relates to the issue of time for planning. Share your information with your class in the form of an oral report.

3. Select an objective to guide pupil learning at a grade level and in a topic of your choice. Prepare a complete set of activity cards that present learners with choices they may pursue as they seek to master content associated with the objective. Ask your course instructor to critique your activity cards.

4. Prepare a design for a learning center. Ask your instructor to review a preliminary draft. Share the revised version with others in your class. Be sure to include all needed components. Develop a sketch that illustrates how the center will look after it has been set up.

5. Work with two or three others who are interested in teaching a given social studies topic at a given grade level. Develop a complete learning activity package (LAP). Ask your instructor to critique your work. If appropriate, consider sharing copies of this material with others in your class.

REFERENCES

BRUNER, J. S., J. J. GOODNOW, AND G. AUSTIN. *A Study of Thinking*. New York: Science Editions, 1962.

FRAENKEL, J. R. *Helping Students Think and Value*, 2d ed. Englewood Cliffs, NJ: Prentice-Hall, 1980.

TABA, H. *Handbook for Elementary Social Studies*. Reading, MA: Addison-Wesley, 1967.

SUPPLEMENTAL READING

ACKERMAN, P. L., R. J. STERNBERG, AND R. GLASER. *Learning and Individual Differences: Advances in Theory and Research*. New York: W. H. Freeman, 1989.

BEYER, B. K., AND A. N. PENNA, eds. *Concepts in the Social Studies*. Washington, DC: National Council for the Social Studies, 1971.

KEIL, F. C. *Concepts, Kinds, and Cognitive Development*. Cambridge, MA: MIT Press, 1989.

KNOWLES, M. S. *Using Learning Contracts*. San Francisco: Jossey-Bass, 1986.

LARKIN, J. M., AND J. J. WHITE. "The Learning Center in the Social Studies Classroom." In W. W. Joyce and F. L. Ryan, eds., *Social Studies and the Elementary Teacher: Promises and Practices*. Bulletin 53. Washington, DC: National Council for the Social Studies, 1977.

TANCK, M. L. "Teaching Concepts, Generalizations, and Constructs" In D. M. Fraser, ed., *Social Studies Curriculum Development: Problems and Prospects*. 39th Yearbook of the National Council for the Social Studies, 1969. Washington, DC: National Council for the Social Studies, 1968.

GROUP LEARNING

This chapter provides information to help the reader:

1. recognize the importance of group learning experiences in the elementary social studies program,
2. differentiate among basic group types,
3. describe procedures that can be used to prepare learners for group learning experiences,
4. point out what has to be done to plan and implement classroom debates, role-playing lessons, and simulations, and
5. recognize characteristics of several cooperative learning techniques.

PRETEST

Answer each of the following true/false questions.

1. Learners take "naturally" to small-group learning; hence, teachers do not have to do anything specific to get pupils ready for learning experiences of this kind.
2. Buzz sessions are sometimes used when a new topic is introduced to generate questions that pupils might like to have answered.
3. Classroom debates adapt the basic debating format in a way that allows more people to be actively involved.
4. Jigsaw is an example of a cooperative learning technique.
5. In a tutoring group the teacher works with a small group much in the way he or she might work with the class as a whole.

INTRODUCTION

Nearly all school instruction is group instruction. The term *group learning* will be used in a more restricted sense in this chapter, referring to instructional groups ranging in size from about half of a regular class to as small as two learners.

The numbers of pupils assigned to a given group vary in terms of the purposes of the group activity. Some group activities can accommodate fairly large groups of learners. Others demand very small numbers. Many classroom groups function well with four to six pupil members. This number seems to work well when the expectation is that group members will discuss content (Cohen 1986).

Group learning has several advantages for the elementary social studies classroom. The very name *social studies* implies a focus on human interaction. Instruction that organizes learners to facilitate idea exchange and high participation levels helps to refine learners' abilities to work well with others.

Learners in individual classrooms vary greatly in ability and aptitude. Lessons directed at an entire class often fail to meet needs of some class members. Organizing pupils into smaller groups allows teachers to respond more directly to particular needs of individual learners.

There is evidence that group learning helps to develop warmer relationships between teachers and learners (Olmstead 1974). This occurs for several reasons. First of all, small groups allow learners to sit quite close to the teacher. This allows pupils to hear better and to feel they are more important as individuals. Additionally, the teacher is better able to appreciate how pupils are reacting to lesson content. This allows for quicker responses when learners signal confusion or disinterest. The ability of the teacher to adjust instruction, as needed, often results in enhanced levels of learner motivation.

Group learning helps develop positive relationships between teachers and learners.

Learners tend to participate more frequently in small groups than in large groups. In part, this occurs because it is difficult to avoid participating when so few people are involved. Second, participation is less intimidating. Many learners who hesitate to speak before the entire class willingly participate as members of a small group.

An important side effect of enhanced levels of learner participation is an increase in individual learners' commitment to decisions made by their group. This occurs because the group experience fosters a sense of "ownership" in decisions. In large-group instructional settings pupils are less likely to develop such allegiances to conclusions emerging from discussions of issues.

Certainly there are some difficulties associated with group learning approaches. For example, careful planning is essential for these approaches to be successful. Pupils need to understand exactly what they are to do and what the expected learning outcome is. Care, too, needs to be exercised in assigning specific individuals to groups. For example, little is to be gained by organizing a group to "discuss" a controversial issue if, at the outset, each group member holds the same opinion.

Despite potential pitfalls, a strong case can be made for incorporating some group learning experiences into the elementary social studies program. This chapter introduces some basic group types, suggests procedures for introducing learners to group work, discusses ways to implement classroom debates, role-playing exercises, and simulations, and points out several cooperative learning approaches.

BASIC GROUP TYPES

Successful group learning lessons are preceded by careful planning. An important consideration during this planning phase is the purpose to be served by the group activity. A clear view of purpose helps to clarify kinds of responsibilities to be required of learners, learning objectives they are to pursue, and the role or roles to be played by the teacher.

Many group organizational schemes represent modifications of three basic group types: (a) the tutoring group, (b) the equal roles group, and (c) the assigned roles group.

Tutoring Group

This basic type may be used for two distinctive purposes. First, it may be organized to help learners who may be having trouble mastering content introduced in a large-group setting. Second, it may be organized to provide enrichment experiences for pupils who are capable of doing more sophisticated work than that introduced to the class as a whole.

In the tutoring group, the teacher's role does not vary greatly from the role he or she plays when working with the class as a whole. In general, it is a role of directive leadership. The teacher provides general instructions, explains content, and leads discussions.

Pupils are encouraged to participate actively during tutoring-group sessions. Often, because of the relatively small number of pupils involved, learners are more inclined to speak up in small-group situations when a discussion is being conducted with members of an entire class. In the tutoring group, pupils are usually seated close to the teacher. This physical proximity also tends to increase their willingness to participate actively in lessons.

Preparing learners for a tutoring-group experience is not difficult. In a large measure, they will be doing work similar to what they have always done in larger, whole-class settings. A few learners may experience some initial discomfort as they realize there is "no place to hide" and that they will be expected to participate. Supportive comments from the teacher can overcome these anxieties.

Instructing a tutoring group demands the teacher's undivided attention. This means that he or she must make arrangements for members of the class who are not in the group. These arrangements must not be made casually. Other pupils must have meaningful tasks to work on while the tutoring group is in session, and they must be supervised. (See Box 6–1.) Sometimes it is possible for some learners to work with aides or other paraprofessional personnel. Parent volunteers occasionally are available to work with some learners. Others might be involved in work with the school librarian or at a media center.

Equal Roles Group

The equal roles group is used most frequently in elementary social studies classes to involve learners in solving a problem. Learners are organized and provided with

---

BOX 6-1   **Planning Meaningful Work for Other Learners**
            while Working with a Tutoring Group

Working with a tutoring group is an intensive activity for both teacher and learners. The teacher must devote undivided attention to the group members. This means that plans must be made to occupy other learners in a meaningful way.

Suppose you had twenty-five pupils in your class, and you are thinking about working with a tutoring group that includes five of them. If the tutoring-group activity is to succeed, you must have special plans for the other twenty students. Perhaps you will have all twenty do a common activity, or perhaps you will involve them in several small-group activities.

Think   1. Develop two separate plans for dealing with these twenty learners. What features will
About   each plan have?
This   2. How will they be supervised?

---

experiences designed to make them more familiar with systematic approaches to resolving issues. One widely used problem-solving scheme involves these steps:*

1. identify the problem
2. consider possible approaches
3. select and apply approaches
4. reach a defensible conclusion

In the equal roles group, all pupils are required to participate in each step of the process. Often, a group leader is assigned to take general charge of the investigation. The teacher might also wish to assign a group recorder to take notes on decisions that are reached.

The teacher begins by explaining the problem to be solved. The following problem might be given to a group of sixth graders who were beginning a unit of study on Eastern Europe: "Why is Romania the only country in Eastern Europe with a language based on ancient Latin?"

Once the issue is identified, the teacher explains steps to be followed. He or she must also ensure that sufficient learning materials are available for pupils to use. As the activity develops, the teacher circulates among members of the group to assure that all are participating and to respond to questions.

The teacher plays a particularly important role at the conclusion of the exercise. At this time, he or she challenges conclusions, calls on pupils to defend ideas by referring to evidence they have gathered, and asks why other solutions to the "problem" might not be equally good. This phase of the lesson needs to be handled sensitively. For many pupils, the experience of developing conclusions of their own will be unfamiliar. Their ideas need to be supported at the same time they are asked to think about alternatives.

---

*For more information on problem solving, see Chapter 7, "Thinking-Skills Instruction."

As was true with the tutoring group, arrangements need to be made for other learners when an equal roles-group instruction is contemplated. Sometimes, it is possible for the entire class to be organized into four or five separate equal roles groups. When this happens, the teacher moves quickly from group to group to monitor pupils' activities. This can tax the teacher's energies, but, with careful planning, this arrangement can be made to work. Alternatively, some learners might have their work monitored by aides, other paraprofessionals, or parents.

Assigned Roles Group

In the assigned roles group, each member has a particular task assignment (Cohen 1986). This means that each pupil must do his or her work if the group as a whole is to have complete information at the conclusion of the activity. There are many kinds of lessons for which assigned roles groups might be appropriate. The scheme is often used when the teacher wants learners to be exposed to complex content that can be conveniently divided into parts. For example, fifth graders usually study American history. Often, information about the English colonies is introduced under the headings "New England Colonies," "Middle Colonies," and "Southern Colonies."

A fifth-grade teacher might organize members of the class into assigned roles groups of six or so pupils each. Individual members would be assigned to answer certain questions about (1) family life and religion and (2) locations of major towns and settlements in each of the three colonial regions (a total of six topics).

Sometimes assigned roles groups are organized to familiarize learners with perspectives of groups who see a common problem in different ways. Often controversial current events lend themselves well to lessons of this kind. For example, in early 1990, a teacher might have organized learners into groups of four to focus on varying views of the United States's invasion of Panama. Each learner could have been assigned to become familiar with perspectives about public opinion in the United States, in Panama, elsewhere in Latin America, or in Spain.

Successful assigned roles-group lessons require careful preparation. It is especially essential that learning materials be available for learners to use as they work to become "experts" on topics associated with their assigned areas of responsibility.

The teacher plays an important role during the debriefing phase of the lesson. She or he must assure that all pupils have an opportunity to share their information and that all members of the group understand it. The teacher, too, responds to questions and clarifies points of confusion. Sometimes, teachers encourage students to write some major points they have gathered on the chalkboard or on a large piece of butcher paper. (For the above example, the labels "United States," "Panama," "Elsewhere in Latin America," and "Spain" would be written. Pupils would write major points at the appropriate places under these labels.) This procedure allows the teacher to help learners make comparisons and contrasts using information written under the various categories.

Identify an elementary school grade you would like to teach. Talk to your course instructor about social studies content that is typically taught at this grade level. (You may also wish to review Chapter 1, "An Introduction to the Social Studies.") Next, identify a topic that might be suitable for presentation via an assigned roles-group activity. Suggest roles that might be assigned to each of five learners in your group.

FIGURE 6–1
A plan for an assigned roles-group activity

As is true for all small-group learning lessons, the teacher must make plans for pupils who will not be participating in the small-group activity. Procedures followed when using assigned role-group techniques parallel those used with tutoring-group and equal roles-group lessons (Figure 6–1).

PREPARING PUPILS TO WORK IN GROUPS

Experiences of learners in different classrooms vary. Some may not have had much experience in working in groups except during reading lessons. Consequently, it is often desirable to put learners through some experiences designed to more thoroughly orient them to group work.

This teacher is monitoring group work. This is one of the most important roles of teachers during group work time.

Working in Groups: Two-by-Two's

Grade Level: 3–6, earlier grades with clear instructions and careful monitoring.

Objectives: Learners can (1) gain information about their classmates, (2) learn how to work together, and (3) develop a sense of cohesion and friendship in the classroom.

This exercise is particularly useful as an "ice breaker" at the beginning of the school year when learners in a class may not know each other well. The example is designed for a class of thirty-two; group size must be adjusted for smaller or larger classes.

Suggested Procedures: The teacher gives the following instructions for each of the seven steps of the exercise.

1. Listen carefully. Do not do anything until I say "ready . . . go." I want each of you to stand up. Then, walk over and find somebody you don't know well. You will have half a minute to do this. Any questions? (Teacher responds to questions, if any.) Ready . . . go! (Each pupil finds a partner.)

2. I want you to find out three things about your partner. First, find out your partner's name. Second, find out your partner's birthday. Third, ask what your partner would do if someone gave him or her $300.00 that had to be spent this Saturday. You will have two minutes to do this. (Pupils follow instructions in this and each subsequent step. The teacher monitors activities and calls "time" after it expires.)

3. You have done very well. Now let's make things more interesting. I want you and your partner to get together with another pair of partners. This will make a group of four. When you have formed your groups of four, I want each of you to tell the three other members of the group the things you learned about your partner. Remember these are (1) your partner's name, (2) your partner's birthday, and (3) what your partner would do with $300 that must be spent this Saturday. I want everybody in the group to try to remember the answers for each group member. You will have four minutes to do this. Are there questions? Ready . . . go!

4. Now you are *really* going to be challenged. I want each group of four to get together with another group of four. This will create a group of eight. Do the same thing in the group of eight as you did in your groups of four. That is, take turns providing information about your partner. I want all of you to try and remember information about everybody in your group. Are there questions? You will have six minutes to do this. Ready . . . go!

5. Now let's find out who our memory champions are. I want each group of eight to get together with another group of eight to make a group of sixteen. Follow the same procedure as before. You'll have eight minutes this time. Ready . . . go!

6. Now it's time to really stretch our memories. Let's all get together in a giant circle. Then, I want you to use the same process as before. Let's do this for about eight minutes. Are there any questions? Ready . . . go!

7. Now, who wants to start. Is there anybody who can provide all three items of information about everybody in the group? (If there are learners willing to try, the teacher calls on them. The teacher provides supporting comments. If no one wants to try this, the teacher asks if anyone can provide one or two items about each person in the class.) Are there others who would like to try? (Process continues until as many pupils as wish to volunteer have had a chance to participate.)

Teachers who have never used two-by-two's before are often astonished at the large number of learners who will be able to provide information about everybody in the class at the end of the activity. The exercise makes learners more comfortable with one another, and it builds a sense of cohesiveness. Learners who know something about one another tend to settle into academically oriented group work better than those who are assigned to work with comparative strangers.

LESSON
▪ *IDEA* ▪

Working Together: Inside-Outside

Grade Level: 4–6. *Objectives:* Learners can participate in a class discussion and identify behaviors that contribute to a productive discussion. *Suggested Procedures:* To begin, the teacher divides the class into two large groups. If there are twenty-four pupils in the class, there will be twelve learners in each group. Enough chairs are arranged in a circle to seat all twelve members of one of the groups. Members of one of the groups are asked to sit in the chairs. The seated group is called the "inside group."

Members of the other group arrange themselves behind the circle of chairs. This is the "outside group." Each member of the outside group is assigned to observe what one member of the inside group does during a discussion and to take notes on this person's behavior. After these instructions have been given, the teacher gives the inside group a controversial topic. This should be a matter of genuine interest to learners. For example, a group of fourth graders might be asked to discuss this idea:

"It should be the law that every fourth grader is in bed no later than 9.00 P.M. on school nights."

Before the discussion begins, the teacher provides additional information to members of the outside group regarding kinds of information to note. Pupils might be asked to observe the extent to which their assigned person does each of the following:

▪ takes an active part in the discussion;
▪ makes comments that logically follow what the previous speaker says;
▪ summarizes something said earlier in the discussion;
▪ makes comments that keep the group from arriving at a premature conclusion;

- supports comments made by someone else in the group;
- refers to evidence to support a point he or she makes.

At this point, the discussion begins. The teacher allows it to go on for eight to ten minutes. At this point, members of the inside group and the outside group change places. The teacher reminds members of the new outside group what they are to do. The new inside group begins discussing the topic. This second discussion also continues for eight to ten minutes.

To conclude the activity, the teacher leads a debriefing discussion with the whole class. Information gathered by the notetakers is introduced. The teacher points out the kinds of verbal behavior that help keep discussions going in a productive way (supportive comments, willingness to listen, careful attention to points made by previous speakers, and so forth).

Learners who go through an exercise of this type tend to work more productively when they are assigned to participate in group learning activities than are those who have not. Sometimes teachers use inside-outside several times during the school year to reinforce good group participation skills. Pupils tend to like the activity.

Buzz Session

Two-by-two's and inside-outside focus on the development of attitudes and thought processes conducive to effective group participation. The buzz session can tie directly to academic content. It is a very simple procedure that can be used to introduce pupils to doing group work in social studies. Often the buzz session is used when a new unit of study is about to begin.

The buzz session results in high levels of verbal interchange. It lasts only about ten minutes. This helps maintain pupil participation throughout the activity. The teacher begins by organizing class members into groups. Four or five pupils should be assigned to each group. If possible, members of each group should arrange chairs in a circle so members can face one another. Each group is asked to select a recorder. This person will write down group responses. At the end of the activity, the teacher will collect these.

LESSON
• IDEA •

Buzz Session: Moving to America
Grade Level: 5. *Objective:* Learners can list questions they have about the settlement of America. *Suggested Procedures:* The teacher begins by explaining what the groups are to do:

We are going to be learning about the lives of some of the first permanent settlers to come to North America. These people came from England. (Teacher points out location of England on a large globe or world map.) They landed and established settlements here. (Teacher points out location of New England.)

I want you to suppose that you were living in England in the early 1600s. You are thinking about coming to America, but you know very little about what America might be like. I want members of each of your groups to write down

---

BOX 6–2   **Do Buzz Sessions "Rob" Valuable Instructional Time?**

A critic of buzz sessions recently made these comments:

> Buzz sessions should be banned from elementary social studies programs. They promise more than they deliver. It is claimed they motivate pupils. I'm not totally convinced on that point. But, even if they do, they simply allow teachers to waste too much time.
>
> Some people claim that a buzz session can be completed in ten minutes. I'm somewhat dubious about teachers' abilities to restrict them to so short a time. But, even if they do so, ten minutes can add up to a lot of time over a year's time. Suppose a teacher uses buzz sessions twice a week. That is eighty minutes a month when learners aren't working hard to master new academic content. The result can be a reduction of overall pupil learning. We simply cannot afford to let this happen.

Think   1. Do you think this person has a reasonable concern? Why, or why not?
About   2. Other might argue that buzz sessions, by helping learners establish a focus for later
This   learning, in the end will increase pupils' levels of achievement. Do you agree?
               3. Specifically, how would you respond to this critic?

---

as many questions as you can that a person thinking about moving to America might have had at this time. The recorder should write down your answers.

Don't start until I give you the signal. This is going to go fast. I will give you ten minutes. I would like every member of each group to think of at least one question. Now, before we start, do you have any questions? (Teacher responds to questions, as necessary). All right, let's begin. (Learners begin to talk or "buzz" in their respective groups. Teacher calls "time" after ten minutes.)

After the buzz period has concluded, the teacher picks up the question lists from each group. These are shared with learners. The teacher may wish to write some of these on the board or on an overhead transparency. The class in the example above might develop questions such as these:

- How will I get to America?
- How long will the trip take?
- What kinds of animals will I find?
- What will I eat?
- Where will I get my clothes if there are no stores?
- What will happen if I get sick?
- What will the weather be like?

These and other questions can provide a focus for the study of the new unit. Since pupils have developed the questions themselves, they frequently are eager to find some answers. The buzz session often motivates students to learn new material. The interest it generates helps them master content and, at the same time, may increase their interest in doing additional work in groups.

THREE POPULAR GROUP TECHNIQUES: CLASSROOM DEBATE, ROLE PLAYING, AND SIMULATION

Many different forms of group learning are employed in elementary social studies classrooms. Three widely used examples are classroom debate, role playing, and simulation.

Classroom Debate

People whose only exposure to debates has been formal debate tournaments in high schools and universities might wonder how debate might be regarded as a useful group activity. The classroom debate is organized differently from the format used in tournament debates. It features teams of pupils who prepare positions on each side of an issue and who each participate actively during the debate itself.

There are many ways classroom debates can be organized. One version features teams of seven pupils each. Assignments are made as follows:

- Three learners are assigned to take the "pro" position
- Three learners are assigned to take the "con" position
- One learner is assigned to play the role of "critic."

"I agree that, in general, learning in groups is a sound approach for upper graders, but we've had complaints about this particular lesson."

The teacher explains that members of the pro team will gather as much information as they can that supports a controversial proposal. Each member will be expected to play an active role in arguing the pro team's case. Similarly, members of the con team will gather information that can be used to attack a controversial proposal. Each member will play an active role in arguing the con team's case. The critic will learn as much as she or he can about positions of both the pro team and the con team. This critic's function will be to ask probing questions toward the end of the debate that will highlight weaknesses of the positions of both the pro and the con teams.

The teacher selects a controversial issue that will serve as a focus. Then, the teacher ensures that adequate background materials are available for team members. Time must be provided for team members to prepare their case. The teacher needs to monitor pupils during this time to render assistance and to assure that learners are staying on task.

The controversial issue is usually described in terms of a proposal that implies a change. The following are examples:

"Resolved that all people in this school should be required to wear uniforms to school."

"Resolved that the environment of Antarctica should be protected by forbidding tourists to visit that continent."

"Resolved that schools should be in session at least eleven months of the year."

"Resolved that families should be required to pay children for taking out the garbage."

"Resolved that classroom rules should be made by teachers, not members of the class."

The classroom debate follows a general sequence. The following example reflects what might be done in an upper-grades class during a fifty-minute period:

1. Each member of the pro team and each member of the con team speaks for two minutes. (Two minutes *each*.) Individual pro and con speakers alternate. Approximate time: twelve minutes.

2. Members of the pro team cross examine members of the con team for a team total of six minutes. Then, members of the con team cross examine members of the pro team for a team total of six minutes. Approximate time: twelve minutes.

3. Members of each team make final statements. All team members are encouraged to speak. Total time allotted to each team is three minutes. Approximate time: six minutes.

4. The critic is invited to ask probing questions of both pro team and con team members. The critic, at his or her discretion, may choose to direct a question at either some or all members of each team. The function of the critic is to point out weak spots in arguments made by members of both teams. Approximate time: eight minutes.

5. At this time, the class as a whole votes to determine a winner. Approximate time: two minutes.
6. The teacher debriefs the class. It is important that comments be as supportive as possible. Learners need to understand that speaking up is not going to elicit negative teacher reactions. During the debriefing phase, the teacher might use focus questions such as these:

What were the best arguments you heard?
What impressed you about those arguments?
What other points would you have brought up if you had been on the pro team? the con team?
Should the critic have asked some other questions? If so, what should the critic have asked?

Classroom debate is a technique that can generate high levels of interest. It provides an opportunity for large numbers of pupils to get actively involved in the learning process.

Role Playing

Role playing serves several purposes that are consistent with objectives of the elementary social studies program. The technique can help learners (1) develop their interpersonal relations skills, (2) appreciate perspectives of others, (3) recognize the impact of one person's decision on others, and (4) master academic content by replicating roles of people who participated in "real" events. Role playing is adaptable for use with learners at all elementary grade levels.

Role playing begins with a problem. It is often useful to introduce pupils to the technique by presenting them with a problem they or members of their family might have faced. Competition for a parent's time is a situation that many young people face.

LESSON
▪ IDEA ▪

Role Playing: How Can Needs Be Met?
Grade Level: 4–6. *Objectives:* Learners can identify perspecitves of different characters and state the impact of one person's actions on others. *Suggested Procedures:* This simple role-playing lesson might present participants with the following situation.

Mr. Jones is a single parent. He has four children. These are Jill, a fourteen-year-old high school freshman. The twins, Tom and Sid, eight-year-old third graders, and seven-year-old Jessica, a second grader.

It is five o'clock on a Thursday evening. Mr. Jones has had a difficult day at work. He had many interruptions, and he wants to get back to the office no later than six thirty to catch up on some paperwork.

Jill is panicked about an algebra test she must take on Friday morning. She wants Mr. Jones to go over the material with her. She needs help right after dinner. At seven o'clock she will have to stop studying algebra and watch a special public television service production of *The Merchant of Venice* for her English class.

The twins, Tom and Sid, have a cub scout meeting that begins at six thirty, where they are both receiving awards. They are hopeful that their father be there to see them receive the awards.

Jessica's church group will be having a short meeting from six thirty to seven thirty. The meeting is at the church, about four miles from the house. She will need to be taken to the meeting and picked up after it is over.

The problem is, How can needs of each person be met? Pupils are needed to play the roles of Mr. Jones, Jill, Tom, Sid, and Jessica.

Once a situation has been developed and presented to learners, participants need to be selected. Sometimes the teacher asks for volunteers, sometimes he or she appoints pupils to play each part. It is desirable to allow learners the option to refuse an invitation to play a role. The role-playing exercise does not work well when learners feel they are being required to do something they would prefer not to do. More often, the teacher will find that more pupils want to participate than there are roles available.

Once players are selected, the teacher provides them with background information about their parts. They need a little time to think about how the individuals they are playing would react to the basic problem.

A good role-playing lesson involves the entire class, not just the pupils playing parts. Pupils who are not playing roles should be assigned to look for specific things as the enactment procedes. ("How realistic were Mr. Jones's responses to Jill?" "What other arguments could the twins have made to make a stronger case?") Pupils should be told to be ready to comment during the discussion following the role-playing enactment.

Sometimes, teachers find it useful to have two or three enactments of the same basic situation. When this is done, numerous learners can be actively involved as role players. Knowing they may be called upon to play roles in a subsequent reenactment, pupils pay closer attention during the initial enactment.

These steps have been found useful in implementing role playing (adapted from Joyce and Weil 1986):

1. *Enactment.*   Role players act out responses. They are encouraged to be as realistic as possible. The teacher may intervene occasionally to remind learners of their roles, of the basic "problem," and of issues relevant to the situation.

2. *Discussion and Evaluation:*   The teacher leads a discussion. Pupils who were asked to look for specific things are asked to speak. The teacher highlights motives and priorities of individual characters. Courses of action different from those that came out during the enactment are sometimes discussed.

3. *Reenactment.*   When feasible, reenact the situation to give additional pupils opportunities to play roles. Such reenactments also allow for more responses to the problem to be considered.

Identify an issue you might teach as part of your elementary social studies program that could be taught via a role-playing exercise. Describe the problem as clearly as possible. Then, indicate specific roles to be played by the participants. Be sure to indicate participants' unique perspectives on the problem. If circumstances permit, you might ask students in your social studies methods class to assume roles and go through the exercise as part of a class activity. You might play the teacher and take the remainder of the class through the entire role-playing sequence (enactment, discussion and evaluation, reenactment, final discussion and debriefing).

FIGURE 6-2
Preparing a role-playing exercise

4. *Final Discussion and Debriefing.*   If there have been reenactments, this phase begins with a discussion and evaluation similar to the one that follows the initial enactment. This phase concludes with the teacher summarizing some major points players made during the enactments. Learners' ideas are actively solicited at this time. Some teachers use this final phase to ask learners about other issues they would like to study using the role-playing technique (Figure 6–2).

Simulations

Simulations are designed to place participants in situations that closely parallel those found in the real world. Simulations simplify reality to highlight certain key ideas. For example, a simulation designed to focus on the legislative process may emphasize negotiation and deemphasize other features of legislative decision making.

Learners are intensely involved during simulations. Often they have opportunities to talk and to move to different parts of the room. Many pupils find simulations to be highly motivating. They have the potential to add an important real world dimension to elementary social studies instruction.

Simulations vary enormously in their complexity. Some are simple board activities that have been derived from popular commercial games such as Monopoly™. Others are very elaborate schemes that require computers to manage and many days to play.

Often simulations divide participants into several groups. For example, there might be a simulation of an international conference on the control of terrorism. Individual groups may be assigned to play the roles of diplomats from individual countries or groups of countries.

Most simulations that are suitable for use in elementary social studies classrooms are not excessively complex. They typically can be played in one or two class sessions, though a few require more time. Many simulations are available from commercial sources. Simulations suitable for use in elementary schools are included in the annual "Grades K–6 Social Studies Catalog," available on request and free of charge from: Social Studies School Service, 10200 Jefferson Boulevard, P.O. Box 802, Culver City, CA 90232-0802.

Simulations require learners to assume roles, make decisions, and face the consequences of their actions. They tend to be more complex in their organization than role playing. Hence, more time typically is required to prepare pupils to participate in them and more support material may be required.

There are four basic parts to a complete simulation activity. These are the (1) overview, (2) training, (3) activity, and (4) debriefing phases.

Overview.   During this phase, the teacher introduces pupils to the simulation to be used. Parts to be played by individual learners are described, and assignments to these parts are made. General rules of the simulation are introduced at this time.

Training.   This amounts to a "walk through" of processes to be followed once the simulation begins. The teacher selects several learners, assigns them parts, and uses them to illustrate how class members will be involved once the simulation begins. Learners are invited to ask questions as the teacher explains how the simulation will operate.

Following this introductory information, pupils should be allowed to review their roles. If the simulation features several groups, group members should be allowed to meet to discuss their roles and to plot preliminary strategy.

Activity.   This is the phase when the actual simulation activity takes place. During this time, the teacher plays the roles of discussant, coach, and referee. At times, pupils may not grasp the point of the simulation. The teacher may find it necessary to stop the action for a moment to help pupils think about their decisions and to explain the purpose of the activity.

Some pupils may not know how to respond to certain developments. The teacher can coach them as they consider their options. Teacher ideas can help inexperienced simulation participants gain in confidence. As pupils' expertise grows, the teacher gradually disengages from the coaching role.

It is common for disputes to arise during simulation activities. Often there are situations for which the rules fail to provide a specific action guideline. When this happens, the teacher needs to intervene and make a ruling that will allow the simulation to continue.

Debriefing.   This is a critically important part of any simulation activity. During debriefing, the teacher leads a discussion highlighting various events that occurred during the activity. The discussion helps pupils recall things that might have escaped their notice during the fast pace of the activity itself.

Debriefing discussions sometimes focus on specific decisions that were made and their desirability relative to alternatives. Sometimes debriefing concerns the design of the simulation. What issues were forced to the front because of the rules of the simulation? What did the designers of the simulation omit? Often, individuals will want to critique their own performances and suggest ways they might act differently were they to do the exercise another time.

COOPERATIVE LEARNING TECHNIQUES

Cooperative learning is an approach that emphasizes working together. This approach to teaching is particularly appropriate for use in social studies lessons, as it replicates the kind of cooperative activity that characterizes much of adult social, economic, and political life.

Many cooperative learning techniques involve groups of learners who work toward a common objective. Evaluation of individual members of each group depends, at least in part, on the overall quality of the group's work. For example, if a test is used to assess the quality of learner performance, the average grade of pupils in a given group may be used to evaluate the overall effectiveness of the group's effort. When group members understand that individual grades will be determined, in part, by the quality of the work of the group as a whole, there is an incentive for group members to help one another learn.

Researchers have found that cooperative learning approaches often result in higher levels of mastery and better retention of concepts than situations in which pupils compete against one another as individuals. Learners tend to be better motivated, and their attitudes toward school tend to be more positive. As a result, their self-esteem tends to be higher.

A number of cooperative learning approaches have been developed. Three popular approaches are introduced here.

Jigsaw

The jigsaw method is a group learning technique that requires each person in a group to accomplish part of a larger assignment. The entire assignment cannot be finished until all parts of the "jigsaw" are fitted together. There are many possible applications of the jigsaw method in elementary social studies classrooms.

LESSON
▪ IDEA ▪

Jigsaw: South America

Grade Level: 6. *Objectives:* Each learner can become an "expert" on one aspect of a particular subject and, in turn, can teach others in the group about the material learned.

Suppose a sixth-grade teacher was about to begin a unit on South America. One purpose of such a unit might be to familiarize pupils with several countries. For example, the teacher might decide to focus on Brazil, Argentina, Columbia, Paraguay, and Peru. For each of these countries, the teacher might like learners to learn something about religions, languages, major income sources, major terrain features, and educational systems.

Suggested Procedure: Teaching this content using the jigsaw method begins by organizing pupils into groups with responsibilities for learning content related to one country. In a class with twenty-five learners, five would be assigned to each country. Within each group, one pupil would be assigned to become an expert on religions. Another would be assigned to become an expert on the country's languages. Other members would be assigned, respectively, to become experts on their assigned country's major income sources, major terrain features, and education system.

Once these assignments have been made, the groups organized around the individual countries break up. Pupils are organized into new groups by subject, rather than country, e.g., one new group is comprised of all five learners assigned to become experts on religions. These new "expert groups," with teacher guidance, discuss how they will gather their information. They begin working, either together or alone, to gather the needed information. The teacher ensures that necessary information is available.

When the expert groups have completed their work, pupils rejoin the original groups organized by country. Each expert shares information with others. At this time, each learner assembles the information.

Teachers sometimes provide a blank data chart that learners can use to record information. Such a chart for this example would have the names of the five countries listed across the top. The terms "religions," "languages," "major income sources," "major terrain features," and "educational system" would be written down the left side. Pupils would be invited to write notes in the appropriate cells of this matrix.

When pupils in a given group have completed their work, they let the teacher know they are ready for their evaluation. The teacher assesses their work and provides reactions to members of the group.

In summary, the jigsaw method promotes the development of productive group behavior. Pupils learn to listen attentively to others. This is encouraged because contributions of all group members will be needed to complete the assigned task. The procedure also helps develop cooperative, mutually supportive attitudes among class members.

Learning Together

The learning together method features a less formal organizational structure than the jigsaw method (Johnson and Johnson 1975; Johnson et al. 1984). In learning together, the teacher organizes pupils into groups whose members reflect a variety of interests and abilities.

Once the groups are formed, each group receives an assignment that requires the attention and involvement of each person. The technique works best when many talents and enthusiasms are represented in each group. This allows individual pupils to work on parts of the overall project that are compatible with their own interests. The assignment usually requires pupils to develop a "product" of some kind. This might be a set of written responses to questions, a research report, a play to be presented to the class, or a group oral report. Members of a group receive grades based on the quality of this final product.

Roles of individual pupils within each group can be quite varied. For example, if a teacher wants a group of fifth graders to write a short play about life in colonial New England, pupils could be assigned roles as head writer, general manuscript editor, set designer, and sound effects chairperson. All could assist in preparing the actual content of the play.

In learning together lessons, each pupil receives the same grade. This feature of the technique encourages individuals to pool their talents. There is incentive for each learner to do his or her best to assure that all members of the group receive a good final evaluation. Johnson and Johnson (1985) report that learners who have had some experience in working together tend to support the idea that it is fair to award the same grade to each group member.

During a learning together lesson, the teacher monitors each group carefully. Pupils may have problems that have to be resolved. The teacher tries to be available to clear up misunderstandings and to help group members complete the required learning product.

Teams Achievement Divisions

Teams achievement divisions begins with the teacher dividing the class into four- or five-member teams (Slavin 1978). Each team includes some high achievers, some low achievers, some boys, some girls, ideally from different ethnic backgrounds. After the teacher introduces new content through traditional large-group instruction, each team is given a set of study worksheets. These worksheets describe tasks to be accomplished and problems to be solved. These tasks and problems relate to the content that has been introduced to the class as a whole.

At this point, each team begins to work. Team members may quiz each other, tutor each other, or take other action they feel is necessary to accomplish the assigned work. Once a group has finished its work, team members take a test over the material. They may not help one another on the test. Scores of group members are scored separately.

There are several approaches to computing team scores. Teachers who have worked with their pupils for some time have a good idea of each pupil's expected test score. The teacher makes a list of these expected or "base" scores. When tests are scored, one point is awarded toward the team's score for every point a member of the team exceeds his or her base score. Usually there is a maximum number of points that any one pupil can contribute to the team total (often this is set at ten points.) This would mean, for example, that a learner with a base score of thirty-two who scored eighty still would contribute only the ten-point maximum to the total team score.

An example of a group score for an achievement team is given in Table 6–1.

Note in the table that Calvin, although he had the lowest actual test score, still contributed ten points to the team total. This happened because his test score of thirty-five was much higher than his base score of twenty.

Student teams achievement divisions encourages slower pupils. They have an incentive to do as well as they can. Even though their individual scores may not be high, they have opportunities to make important contributions to the total scores of the teams to which they are assigned. This technique also encourages brighter pupils to assist less talented members of their group to master the con-

TABLE 6-1
Group Score for an Achievement Team

Student	Base Score	Quiz Score	Team Points
Alan	49	56	7
Bertha	50	48	0
Calvin	20	35	10
Dinah	85	90	5
Carlos	75	100	10

tent. This is true because all members of the group will profit when these slower youngsters perform at levels that exceed the expectations reflected in their base scores. Indeed, each member of a teams achievement divisions group has a stake in the learning of each member of the group. Hence, there is an incentive for all group members to help each other.

In summary, cooperative learning techniques require these teacher decisions:

1. selecting a topic that lends itself to group work,
2. making decisions about group size and composition,
3. providing appropriate materials,
4. identifying the parts of the lesson and sequencing the lesson,
5. monitoring the work of pupils in groups,

This chart shows the scoring of teams participating in a cooperative learning exercise.

6. intervening when necessary to solve problems, and

7. evaluating outcomes.

Because of the social nature of many aspects of the subject, cooperative learning approaches are particularly suitable for use in elementary social studies programs. Many teachers find these techniques enhance pupils' interest and improve general levels of achievement.

KEY IDEAS IN SUMMARY

1. Group instruction refers to instruction that is directed at classroom groups ranging in size from about half of the total class to as few as two pupils. Many group instruction techniques feature high levels of interaction. They have the potential to improve learners' abilities to work with others at the same time they promote learning of new content.

2. Successful group learning requires that teachers plan carefully. For example, pupils must understand exactly what they are to do, and they must know what expected learning is to result from the activity. Teachers must exercise care in assigning individuals to groups. Many group procedures work well when each group includes pupils with diverse academic abilities, interests, and points of view. Materials to be used in group activities must be prepared in advance, and they must be easily accessible to group members. Finally, teachers need to monitor groups carefully when they are working on assigned tasks.

3. Tutoring groups tend to be used (a) to help pupils who have difficulty mastering material when it is introduced in a large-group setting, and (b) to provide enrichment experiences for bright learners. This is an arrangement that features a teacher who plays a strong leadership role as a provider of instruction, disseminator of information, and leader of discussions.

4. In equal roles groups, learners are grouped together for the purpose of working on a common problem. All members of a given group participate in these general problem-solving steps: (a) identifying the problem; (b) considering possible approaches; (c) selecting and applying approaches; and (d) reaching a defensible conclusion.

5. In assigned roles groups, individual members work on a unique task that represents part of a larger problem assigned to their group. This scheme works well when teachers want pupils to work on complex issues having many parts.

6. Teachers who want to use group learning techniques with their learners sometimes find they have had little prior experience in working together in small groups. To facilitate learner functioning in groups smaller than the class as a whole, teachers sometimes use several introductory techniques. Among these are two-by-two's, inside-outside, and buzz sessions. The first two procedures focus almost exclusively on developing learners' techniques for working pro-

ductively in groups. The third technique, the buzz session, also has potential to help learners establish a focus on academic content.

7. There are many group learning techniques that are suitable for use in elementary social studies classrooms. Three popular techniques are (a) classroom debate, (b) role playing, and (c) simulation. Classroom debate features teams of pupils who are assigned to prepare positions to either support or oppose a controversial proposition. Role playing allows learners to appreciate perspectives by others by responding to situations in a manner consistent with the views of a character they are assigned to play. Simulations help pupils learn by involving them in structured simplifications of reality that help them to grasp the complexities of important processes and issues.

8. Cooperative learning techniques seek to replicate in the classroom many of the kinds of cooperative activities that characterize adult social, economic, and political life. Numerous cooperative learning approaches have been developed. Three that are widely used in elementary social studies classes are (a) the jigsaw method, (b) learning together, and (c) teams achievement divisions. Many of these methods seek to give each learner a personal stake in the learning of all members of his or her group.

POSTTEST

Answer each of the following true/false questions.

1. In an equal roles group lesson, each group member participates in each step of a sequence designed to develop a solution to a common problem.

2. When members of a class are organized into several assigned roles groups, each group studies a different aspect of a problem, but members of any one group study the same thing.

3. One important purpose of role playing is to help pupils identify with the perspectives of someone else.

4. Generally it is accurate to say that lessons featuring simulations require more class time than lessons featuring role playing.

5. In teams achievement divisions, members of each group have an incentive to see that each group member learns as much as possible.

QUESTIONS

1. To what does the term *group learning* refer?

2. What are some purposes of tutoring groups?

3. How does two-by-twos work, and what purposes are served by the technique?

4. What are the characteristics of a buzz session?

5. How might a class be organized for a classroom debate?

6. What steps are followed in a role playing lesson?

7. How does the jigsaw method work?

8. What are characteristics of the learning together approach?

9. What steps are followed when a teacher implements teams achievement divisions?

10. What differences might there be in problems you would face as a teacher when (a) you assigned pupils to work in equal roles groups and (b) you assigned pupils to work in assigned roles groups?

11. Two-by-two's and inside-outside are used primarily to improve learners' skills at working in groups. Is it defensible to take time away from content-oriented teaching to focus on the development of such skills?

12. Suppose you were planning to involve members of your class in some role-playing exercises. What are some problems you might anticipate? How would you respond to them?

13. Think about some social studies topics you might teach at any selected grade level. Are these topics ones that could be taught using the jigsaw method? If so, describe how you might apply this technique.

14. Many cooperative learning approaches emphasize cooperation and mutual support. At the same time, they downplay competition. Some people argue that much of life features competitive activity. If this is true, does it make sense for teachers to involve pupils in procedures that are not designed to encourage competitive behavior?

EXTENDING UNDERSTANDING AND SKILL

1. Prepare a list of group learning techniques that are introduced in this chapter. Interview an elementary teacher. Ask whether he or she uses any of these procedures to teach social studies lessons. Also, ask whether the teacher uses other group approaches. Summarize what you learn in your interview in an oral report to your social studies methods class.

2. In recent years, there has been an explosion of interest in cooperative learning. Review educational journals for articles focusing on specific cooperative learning techniques. (You might want to begin by looking up "cooperative learning" in the *Education Index*, available in your library. Your instructor also may be

able to direct you to some specific sources of information.) Identify one or two cooperative learning techniques that were *not* introduced in this chapter. Be prepared to explain to your instructor how these techniques work. If time permits, you might involve other class members in a lesson featuring one or more of these approaches.

3. Identify content from this chapter that might be taught to social studies methods students using the jigsaw method. Show your suggested ideas to the course instructor. He or she might be interested in having you involve class members in your suggested approach.

4. To familiarize yourself with two-by-two's, use the technique as means to break the ice when a large group of people get together. You might try it at a party, at a church function, at an orientation session for new university students, or in some other setting. Share your experiences in using the procedure with members of your social studies methods class.

5. Following procedures for a classroom debate, organize some members of your methods class into teams to debate this issue: "Resolved, that exposing learners to cooperative learning techniques in school will diminish their abilities to succeed in a competitive society." Ask other members of the class to observe the debate and to critique the technique.

REFERENCES

Cohen, E. G. *Designing Groupwork: Strategies for the Heterogeneous Classroom.* New York: Teachers College Press, 1986.

Johnson, D. W., and R. T. Johnson. *Learning Together and Alone.* Englewood Cliffs, NJ: Prentice-Hall, 1975.

Johnson, D. W., R. T. Johnson, E. Holubec, and P. Roy. *Circles of Learning: Cooperation in the Classroom.* Alexandria, VA: Association for Supervision and Curriculum Development, 1984.

Johnson, R. T., and D. W. Johnson. "Structuring Conflict in Science Classrooms." Paper presented at the annual meeting of the National Association of Research in Science Teaching." French Lick, IN: April, 1985.

Joyce, B., and M. Weil. *Models of Teaching,* 3d ed. Englewood Cliffs, NJ: Prentice-Hall, 1986.

Olmstead, J. A. *Small Group Instruction: Theory and Practice.* Alexandria, VA: Human Resources Research Organization (HumRRO), 1974.

Slavin, R. E. "Student Teams and Achievement Divisions." *Journal of Research and Development in Education* (Fall, 1978), pp. 39–49.

———. *Using Student Team Learning.* Baltimore, MD: Johns Hopkins Team Learning Project, Center for Social Organization of the Schools, Johns Hopkins University, 1980.

SUPPLEMENTAL READING

GREENBLATT, C. S. *Designing Games and Simulations*. Newbury Park, CA: Sage Publications, 1988.

JONES, K. *Simulations: A Handbook for Teachers and Trainers*. New York: Nichols, 1987.

LADOUSE, G. P. *Role Play*. New York: Oxford University Press, 1989.

PARISE, J., AND W. CULP. "Enhancing Leadership Qualities through Small-Group Activities." *The Gifted Child Today* (November–December, 1988), pp. 46–48.

ROY, P. A., ED. *Structuring Cooperative Learning Experiences in the Classroom, the 1982 Handbook*. Minneapolis, MN: A Cooperative Network Publication, 1982.

SHARAN, S., AND Y. SHARAN. *Small Group Teaching*. Englewood Cliffs, NJ: Educational Technology Publications, 1976.

SLAVIN, R. E. "Synthesis of Research on Groups in Elementary and Secondary Schools." *Educational Leadership* (September, 1988), pp. 67–77.

VERMETTE, P. J. "Cooperative Learning in the Classroom: Turning Students into Active Learners." *The Social Studies* (November–December, 1988), pp. 271–73.

THINKING-SKILLS INSTRUCTION

This chapter provides information to help the reader:

1. describe the positions of those who favor and oppose direct teaching of thinking skills,

2. point out approaches to developing pupils' metacognitive abilities,

3. cite general features of inquiry teaching,

4. identify steps followed in an a lesson developing learners' critical-thinking skills,

5. suggest an instructional sequence appropriate for a problem-solving activity,

6. state characteristics of creative-thinking lessons, and

7. describe what a teacher might do to improve learners' decision-making skills.

PRETEST

Answer each of the following true/false questions.

1. Some critics have argued that school lessons designed to teach thinking skills rob time from instructional focusing on academic content.
2. The thinking aloud technique is based on the principle of modeling.
3. Inquiry approaches are based on deductive rather than inductive logic.
4. Data charts can be used to help learners compare, contrast, and generalize.
5. Problem solving and critical thinking are different names for the same basic approach.

INTRODUCTION

Should schools improve children's thinking skills? Of course. Is there agreement about how this should be accomplished? No. Today many educators argue that time should be devoted to teaching thinking skills directly. This view seems to be gaining ground, but it is not universally endorsed.

Lynn V. Cheney, in *American Memory: A Report on the Humanities in American Schools* (1987) argues that teachers spend too much time teaching children learning processes and too little time teaching them substantive content. The argument of Cheney and other critics (Ravitch 1985; Hirsch 1987) is that time devoted to teaching children skills, including thinking skills, robs time from instruction that could better be devoted to teaching important academic content. As a result, these critics contend, learners are not mastering important bodies of information.

The view that there is too much process instruction in American classrooms has been challenged. Social studies specialist Walter C. Parker (1988) reports that numerous studies of teachers' practices in American classrooms reveal that very little time is spent on teaching thinking skills. The vast majority of instructional time is devoted to teaching "facts" associated with academic content areas.

The lack of attention to teaching learners cognitive skills has prompted some authorities to suggest that more school time should be directed to skills-oriented lessons. Nickerson, Perkins, and Smith (1985) argue that "thinking skills are more critical today than ever before. The world is more complex and so are the challenges it presents. Meeting those challenges will require not only considerable knowledge but the skill to apply that knowledge effectively" (p. 4).

The view that teachers should devote some attention to teaching children how to think probably represents a majority position today. However, this does not imply an attempt to deemphasize the importance of academic content. The purpose of thinking-skills instruction is to develop learners' abilities to use thinking processes that will enable them to more fully appreciate important aspects of academic content. As researchers Garner and Alexander (1989) note, "'knowing,' and 'knowing how to know' both matter for all sorts of academic tasks, and both can be enhanced with instruction" (p. 152).

Many approaches to teaching learners to improve their thinking skills can be applied in the elementary social studies classroom. Among them are ideas for improving children's abilities to (a) monitor their own thinking patterns, (b) use inquiry approaches, (c) engage in creative thinking, (d) think critically, and (e) solve problems.

TEACHING CHILDREN TO MONITOR THEIR THINKING

Learning psychologists use the term *metacognition* to refer to conscious thought about how we think about a problem or dilemma. It is important for learners to learn how to monitor their own thinking. Chances are then better that they will use thinking approaches that are appropriately suited to the task they are trying to accomplish. Several instructional approaches have been developed to help learners better monitor their thinking patterns. Examples of these include thinking aloud and visual thinking.

Thinking Aloud

The thinking aloud approach is based on the principle of modeling. Research has shown modeling to be a powerful instructional tool. As applied to thinking aloud, modeling requires the teacher to verbalize thought processes followed as he or she approaches a task.

For example, suppose a teacher plans to have a group of fourth graders use maps to find distances (in miles) between selected pairs of United States cities. In preparation for this activity, the teacher might prepare the class with a think aloud approach.

LESSON
▪ IDEA ▪

Finding Distances

Grade Level: 4–6. *Objectives:* Learners can (1) locate selected cities on a map and (2) use scale to calculate the distance between two points. *Suggested Procedure:* The teacher gives the students the following example.

TEACHER: Let's pretend that someone has given me the same assignment I've given you. This is how I would go about it.

I have to find the distances between several pairs of cities. The first pair is Chicago and San Francisco. The first thing I need to think about is where these two cities are. If I don't know, I'll need to look in the back part of the atlas, in the index. I need to find Chicago and San Francisco. For Chicago, I find a reference to B9. This tells me to go back to the map of the United States and

---

BOX 7–1   Preparing a "Thinking Aloud" Lesson

**Think
About
This**

There are many places where a thinking-aloud approach may be appropriately used in teaching elementary social studies content. The procedure is particularly important when a learning task will require pupils to follow a predictable series of steps. For example, such a thinking-aloud approach would be useful to a teacher as a way to introduce class members to a task requiring them to identify elevations of various places by using a map showing physical relief. The teacher could begin by pointing out one place on the map and talk through the thinking processes involved in arriving at an answer. ("Let's suppose I wanted to know the elevation of the central part of the Tibetan Plateau. The first thing I would do would be to. . .")

When planning a thinking-aloud lesson of your own, first select a topic. Then, indicate what you would say to your class to explain each step they would need to follow to achieve your learning goal.

---

find the letter B. (Teacher does this.) There it is on the left side. Then I need to find the number 9 at the top. (Teacher does this.) Now, I'll simply move my finger even with the B until it is under the 9 at the top. Chicago should be near this spot. (Teacher does this.) And there it is! Now I know where Chicago is.

I'll follow the same procedure to find San Francisco. The index tells me it is at C1. (Teacher proceeds to find San Francisco.)

Now what I have to do is figure out the distance between them. The first thing I am going to do is look at the scale at the bottom of the map. Remember we learned that the scale tells how many miles are represented by a given distance on the map. When I look at the scale, I learn that one inch on the map is equal to about 300 miles.

The next thing I need to do is to measure the distance on the map between San Francisco and Chicago. This is about six inches. Now, I know that one inch equals 300 miles. Six inches, then, has to be six times as far. So, I multiply six times 300 to find out about how far it is from San Francisco to Chicago. This turns out to be 1,800 miles. (Teacher briefly explains this is a point-to-point air distance. Because of curves in highways, mountains, and other variables, the highway distance between Chicago and San Francisco is longer.)

Now that I know how to compute the distance between one pair of cities, I can use the same procedure to compute distances between other city pairs.

Thinking aloud provides children with a model they can follow as they attempt a new task. Further, it points out to them the importance of thinking about how they are going to approach a learning activity before they actually begin working on it.

Visualizing Thinking

Visualizing thinking is another technique that is used to help learners monitor their own thinking processes. It helps them focus on the specific nature of an assigned task. This approach encourages learners to develop diagrams that reflect their understanding of the task and kinds of information they will need. These diagrams often are used by pupils to take brief notes about what they have read and learned.

**LESSON
▪ IDEA ▪**

The Unhappy Tale of the Mongoose

Grade Level: 6. *Objectives:* Learners can (1) recall specific information from a reading selection and (2) identify cause and effect relationships using a visual diagram. *Suggested Procedure:* Have all class members read the following selection.

> Pests have always bothered farmers. Crop damage from pests can be costly. At various times and places, landowners have tried to get rid of pests by introducing other animals that will eat them.
>
> For example, in the 1800s farmers in Argentina imported cases of sparrows from England. These small birds were brought in to eat moths. This did not work out as expected. The moths were eaten all right, but the sparrows grew so numerous that they themselves became a serious problem.
>
> Several attempts were made in the 1700s and 1800s by farmers in the West Indies to get rid of rats that lived in their sugar cane fields. Some farmers imported weasels. Unfortunately, the weasels were attacked by a certain kind of fly, and they did not survive. Farmers even tried bringing in a species of ant that was famous as a "biter." It was hoped that the ants would make life miserable for the rats. The rats didn't suffer as much as the farmers had hoped, and the rats stayed in the fields. One group of farmers went so far as to import a number of giant toads, said to be aggressive rat eaters. The toads, too, failed to get the job done.
>
> In the early 1870s, West Indian farmers finally found a solution that seemed to work. A small meat-eating animal called a mongoose was brought to these islands and released. The mongooses multiplied. Soon farmers noticed that the number of rats in their sugar cane fields had gone down. But this good news was not to last.
>
> After about 10 years, rats were becoming a problem again. The mongooses had discovered chickens. They preferred to eat chickens, and many flocks were lost. By 1900, the mongoose, itself, had come to be viewed as a dangerous pest. Governments in the West Indies even paid hunters to kill them. The solution to the pest problem had become an even bigger problem for authorities.

Children in any class vary greatly in their abilities. As a result, teachers may ask some learners to focus on different information as they read a common selection. To help pupils focus on their tasks as they read the selection, visual-thinking diagrams might be developed as shown in Figure 7–1. The teacher who assigned the reading about the mongoose might ask some students to accomplish this task:

Learning Task: Name some examples of animals that were released to control pests. What pests were they supposed to control?

Class members can write their notes in the appropriate places as they read the selection. When a class has not previously worked with visual-thinking diagrams, the teacher usually prepares them. Once pupils get used to working with them, they can be encouraged to prepare their own. Developing them requires close attention to the specific nature of the required learning task. It can help pupils

Animals and Pests They Were to Control

Animals   Pests to be controlled

_____   _____

_____   _____

_____   _____

_____   _____

Others in the class might be asked to read the selection for the purpose of accomplishing this task:

Learning Task: What happened when the mongoose was first introduced? What happened that was expected? What happened that was not expected? How do you explain peoples' feelings about the mongoose by 1900?

Changing Attitudes toward the Mongoose

What happened when the mongoose was first introduced?

_____

_____

_____

What happened that was

Expected?   **Unexpected?**

_____   _____

_____   _____

_____   _____

How did people feel about the mongoose by 1900?

_____

_____

Why did they feel this way?

_____

_____

FIGURE 7–1
Visual thinking diagram.

174

monitor and adjust their own thinking processes as they do their assignments. Improved understanding and enhanced feelings of self-confidence often result.

INQUIRY APPROACHES

Inquiry teaching introduces concepts to learners inductively. *Inductive learning,* which involves reasoning from the particular to the general, first introduces a number of specific examples. Pupils study the examples and try to pick out general patterns. They conclude by identifying a broad principle that will sum up characteristics of the examples.

Suppose a teacher working with a group of kindergartners wanted to teach the concept "bird." The teacher might begin by showing these youngsters pictures of different birds. A series of questions would prompt members of the class to identify common features in the pictures. To conclude the lesson, the teacher would help learners develop their own definition of the concept "bird." Additional pictures of birds might be shown to pupils to help them determine the adequacy of their definition.

Inquiry learning might be thought of as an exercise in knowledge production. Learners are asked to develop conclusions in the light of their own consideration of evidence. The kinds of reasoning involved in inquiry learning parallels the kind of rational thinking learners will be called upon to exercise throughout their lives. The processes pupils learn in inquiry lessons is every bit as important as the lessons' academic content.

Inquiry Teaching: The Basic Steps

Inquiry teaching is the application of the scientific method to a variety of learning problems. It is a method widely used in elementary social studies programs. The eminent American educational philosopher John Dewey suggested basic steps for sequencing inquiry instruction in his classic *How We Think*, originally published in 1910. The following steps parallel closely those suggested by Dewey.

1. Describe essential features of a problem or situation.
2. Suggest possible solutions or explanations.
3. Gather evidence that can be used to test the accuracy of these solutions or explanations.
4. Evaluate the solutions or explanations in light of this evidence.
5. Develop a conclusion that is supported by the best evidence.

Inquiry lessons can be used at all elementary grade levels. A very simple lesson might be directed at learners in the early primary grades who are beginning to work with maps and globes.

BOX 7–2   **"Inquiry Lessons Slow my Class Down."**

Two elementary teachers were discussing their social studies lessons in the school's faculty lounge. One of them made these comments.

> I like the *idea* of inquiry teaching. I mean, I think it really can improve how my people think. But I just can't cover much content when I use an inquiry technique. It takes a long, long time for them to see patterns and make generalizations. I'm afraid I'm falling way behind. We may never finish the book at this rate.

Think   1. Do you think this teacher has a legitimate concern? Why, or why not?
About   2. Are the benefits associated with learning higher-level thinking skills worth the "cost"
This   of giving up some content coverage? Why, or why not?
              3. How would you have responded to this teacher's comments?

LESSON   *Inquiry Lesson: Maps and Globes*
▪ IDEA ▪   *Grade Level:* K–2. *Objectives:* Learners can (1) identify what selected map symbols represent and (2) state reasons for using different symbols on a map. *Suggested Procedure:* The teacher guides pupils through the following steps.

   1. TEACHER: How many of you have ever been to a lake? To a river? Have any of you seen an ocean? How are all of these alike? (Pupils respond to each question. Teacher keeps probing until learners mention that all have water.) Did you know that there is more water in our world than land?

      People who make maps and globes have a problem. They have to have a way to make people recognize what areas are land and what areas are water.

Inquiry activities provide for a great deal of student involvement. These pupils are using a map as a data source for their inquiry activity.

2. TEACHER: How do you think people who make globes have solved this problem? How do you think they might indicate where areas of water are located?
   Sample pupil responses:

   ▪ Maybe they neatly print the word "water" at places where there is water.
   ▪ They may draw pictures of waves in areas where there is water.
   ▪ They may use a special color to show where the water is.

3. TEACHER: Now we're going to act like scientists as we see which of our ideas
   are best. Let's look at this globe? (Teacher holds up globe.) Can anyone give
   me the name of an ocean? (If not, the teacher helps.) All right, let's look at
   the Atlantic Ocean. Here it is on the map. How is it shown? (Pupils respond,
   "It's blue.") Let's look at the Pacific Ocean. How is it shown? (Pupils respond, "It's the same color—blue.")
   (The teacher puts down the globe and points to a large U.S. wall map at
   the front of the room.) Here is the Atlantic Ocean and here is the Pacific.
   What do they look like? (Pupils respond, "They're blue.") These are what we
   call the Great Lakes. What do they look like? (Pupils respond, "They're
   blue.") This long thin part of the map represents our longest river. How is
   it shown? (Pupils respond, "It's blue, too.")

4. The teacher asks learners to reflect on evidence they have seen. They are
   encouraged to consider the possible explanations they have put forward in
   light of this evidence.
   TEACHER: Based on what we have seen, what do you think most map and
   globe makers do when they want to show water? (Pupils respond: "They
   color it blue.")
   Do you have any ideas about why they have chosen this solution to the
   problem? I mean, why wouldn't they write "water" at various places or draw
   in waves? (Pupils respond. Possible answers include: "If they had to write
   water, they would have to write the word over and over again." "Because
   some areas of water are small, it might be difficult to squeeze the word
   'water' in the space." "It would be hard to have enough room to write the
   word 'water' on rivers." "Drawing little waves might be all right for an ocean,
   but it would be hard to see on rivers." "Drawings of little waves might make
   it hard to print other information."

5. This step concludes the lesson. It is designed to produce a general explanation or principle that can be applied in many different situations.
   TEACHER: From what we have learned, what can you say about how areas of
   water are indicated on maps and globes? (Pupils respond: "They are shown
   in blue.")
   Let's work with this idea a little more. We'll spend a few minutes looking
   at some other maps and globes to see if this idea works. (Teacher and pupils
   look at some other maps and globes. The teacher concludes by praising
   learners' work and telling them that they have discovered a principle they
   can remember: "On most maps and globes, the color blue is used to show
   water."

Using Data Charts to Compare, Contrast, and Generalize

A major purpose of many inquiry lessons is the development of pupils' abilities to compare, contrast, and generalize. *Data charts* are useful organizers of information that learners can use as they engage in these thinking processes.

LESSON
• IDEA •

Nations of Latin America
Grade Level: 6. *Objective:* Learners can state a generalization explaining the relationship between literacy, income level, and life expectancy by comparing data presented on a chart.

Suggested Procedure: Suppose an elementary teacher were about to introduce a unit focusing on nations of Latin America to a group of sixth graders. A data chart constructed for this lesson would include information pupils would use to develop some generalizations. Part of subsequent unit study would be devoted to testing the accuracy of these generalizations. The data chart might look something like that shown in Table 7–1.

The teacher distributes copies of this chart to each pupil. As an alternative, a large version can be drawn on the chalkboard or projected from an overhead transparency. The teacher begins by asking pupils to look carefully at the information and to respond to this sequence of questions:

1. What are some similarities you note among these countries?
   Possible pupil responses:

   - The label at the top refers to all of them as Latin American countries and the United States. So they're all in the same part of the world.
   - Spanish seems to be spoken by some people in each of these countries.

2. What differences do you notice?

TABLE 7–1
Selected Characteristics of Four Countries in Latin America and the United States

Country	Languages	Percentage of People Who Can Read and Write	Average Annual Income (Dollars)	Life Expectancy (Years)
Bolivia	Spanish and various Indian languages	63	470	53
Costa Rica	Spanish	93	1,290	74
Ecuador	Spanish and various Indian languages	85	1,160	65
Honduras	Spanish	56	730	63
United States of America	English and other languages, including Spanish	99	16,400	75

Possible pupil responses:

- More people are able to read in and write in some of these countries than others. Honduras has the highest percentage of people who can't read and write.
- The life expectancies are very different. In Bolivia, the age is only 53.
- The average incomes are very different. In Bolivia it's only $470. In the United States it's over $16,000 a year.

3. You have identified several important differences. Can you identify some possible causes?
Possible pupil responses:

- It seems that where income levels tend to be higher, people live longer.
- People also seem to live longer in places where higher percentages of the people can read and write.
- It seems to me that incomes go up when more people in a country can read and write.

(These are examples only. Members of a real class may develop different generalizations from the chart.)

TEACHER: These are all good ideas. Let me write them on the board. We are going to be studying Latin America for the next couple of weeks. As we do, let's try and find evidence that we can use to test the accuracy of these statements. I want each of you to take notes about these ideas. When you find new information, think about whether it supports or does not support these generalizations. When we finish studying the unit, we'll look again at these ideas to see whether we need to revise any of them.

The data chart helps learners develop insights of their own. They engage directly in the creation of new information. This information, in turn, provides a point of departure for further study. The opportunity to test their own generalizations often motivates learners to pursue additional study of a topic more enthusiastically.

Delimiting and Focusing Pupils' Thinking

Pupils sometimes are overwhelmed with the volume of information they confront when they study social studies topics. This is particularly likely to be true when they are introduced to inquiry lessons. These lessons typically begin by presenting learners with a great deal of specific information that, at least in the minds of the pupils, may appear fragmented and disjointed.

J. Richard Suchman (1962) developed an approach designed to help learners to focus on relevant information and to dismiss irrelevant details as they begin to solve a problem. Suchman's approach builds on learners' natural curiosity. It begins by presenting learners with a puzzling or perplexing situation (Suchman calls this a *discrepant event*), something that does not quite fit learners' under-

"Today, I'm going to teach you a unique new behavior."

standing of reality. Once confronted with the puzzling situation, pupils ask the teachers questions about it. The major rule of the exercise is that the question must be one that can be answered either "yes" or "no." The technique has a certain parlor-game flavor that many young people like. These are the basic steps:

1. Pupils are presented with a discrepant event.
2. They are encouraged to explain it by asking the teacher questions that can be answered either "yes" or "no."
3. The exercise ends with a general discussion of explanations that students have suggested and of the processes followed in arriving at them.

To illustrate how Suchman's approach might be used, suppose a teacher were interested in developing the idea that many of the foods we consume change form before we eat or drink them. A good lesson could be built around the case of cocoa. The drink will be familiar to most pupils; few, however, will know that it comes from seeds or beans that grow in a pod on a tropical tree. Fewer, still will know that a roasting process must intervene before cocoa can be consumed.

An interesting thing about cocoa beans is that they are white. This makes an ideal discrepant event for the exercise. Few children will associate the color white with cocoa. To prepare for the lesson, the teacher must find a color photograph of a cacao pod that has been cut open to reveal the seeds. The lesson begins with the teacher reminding children of the "rules" and asking a simple focus question such as: "What are these things and what do we use them for?"

BOX 7–3   **Preparing Suchman Inquiry Lessons**

Many elementary pupils enjoy participating in Suchman inquiry lessons. There is a gamelike quality to the approach that is very appealing. Additionally, everybody is encouraged to be an active participant.

   Good Suchman inquiry lessons begin with a discrepant event, something that learners find does not quite fit with their previous knowledge. Think about some social studies lessons you would like to teach. Choose at least five topics you could introduce using the Suchman procedure. Identify the discrepant event you will use to capture learners' attention and interest.

After they have experienced several Suchman lessons, pupils become adept at asking questions that eliminate enormous quantities of irrelevant information. Soon, members of the class become quite good at focusing on issues that are central to the solution of the problem with which they have been confronted.

CREATIVE THINKING

Creative thinking features novel approaches to perplexing problems. Many inventors are creative thinkers. For example, the inventor of the forklift truck was inspired to build it after watching mechanical fingers remove donuts from a hot oven (Ruggiero 1988).

   Creative-thinking abilities are not widespread among the population of learners in the schools (Perkins 1981). In part, this situation may represent an instructional failure. Perhaps schools provide too few experiences designed specifically to encourage the development of learners' creative-thinking powers. One widely used technique that has been used is *brainstorming*.

   Brainstorming developed first in the world of business. The technique seeks to prompt participants to develop original solutions to problems, placing an initial premium on volume. Teachers use brainstorming in social studies classes to unleash learners' mental powers in ways that prompt the development of unusual ideas. Pupils are encouraged to develop large numbers of responses to a focus problem. The rules for brainstorming are as follows:

1. Learners are provided with a focus problem.
   Focus Problem (sample): Suppose, because trees release great quantities of oxygen into the air, all nations in the world decided to ban all further cutting of trees for lumber. What might result from this decision?
2. Learners are asked to call out ideas as rapidly as possible. A person is free to speak out whenever any silence occurs. The idea is to generate a rapid outpouring of ideas. Learners are encouraged to say whatever comes to their minds as long as it is relevant.

3. Participants are cautioned not to comment positively or negatively on any ideas suggested by others. All ideas are accepted. This rule helps break down learners' fear of "saying something stupid."
4. The teacher or a designated recordkeeper writes down every idea, often using the chalkboard. The person so selected should be able to write quickly. Ideas come at a rapid rate.
5. The exercise should be stopped when the rate of presentation of new ideas noticeably declines.
6. A general discussion of the ideas concludes the exercise. This discussion may prompt ideas for additional study by the class. (For the given focus problem, there might be followup research activities on such topics as alternative fuels, substitute materials for furniture, new construction materials for houses, and so forth.)

CRITICAL THINKING

The purpose of critical thinking is to *evaluate* ideas. It always involves judgment. These judgments must be based on informed opinion. Properly, they should rest on defensible criteria (Lipman 1988).

Creative thinking focuses on the generation of new ideas. This activity is sometimes tied to critical thinking. When this is done, the creative thinking part of the lesson occurs first, during which pupils generate new ideas. During the second part of the lesson, they use critical-thinking skills to make judgments about these ideas.

Dunn and Dunn (1972) have developed an adaptation of the basic brainstorming technique. Their procedure encourages learners to think critically about ideas generated in an early part of the activity. An analytic brainstorming activity that requires pupils to use critical thinking skills might include the following steps. Pupils brainstorm responses to each step. The teacher writes them so all class members can see them.

1. As a focus, the teacher encourages pupils to consider what the "best" solution to a problem might be. An elementary teacher might use this as a focus statement for a class of fifth graders: "The best thing we could do to assure that the first graders don't get hurt on our school playground would be to . . ."
2. With the ideas produced during the step one brainstorming activity in plain view, the teacher asks the class why the responses mentioned have not already been done: "What things are preventing us from doing those things to solve this problem?"
3. Step three focuses pupils' attention on thinking about what might be done to overcome obstacles noted in the step two responses: "How could we overcome some of these difficulties?"

4. During step four, the teacher asks pupils to note problems that might be encountered in doing things mentioned during step three: "What might keep us from overcoming any difficulties we may face in trying to keep first graders from getting hurt on the playground?"

5. The final step requires learners to decide what should be the first step toward a realistic solution of the problem: "Let's think about everything we have considered. What action should we take first to solve this problem? Be prepared to explain your choices." (Class members respond and defend their choices by referring to appropriate criteria.)

PROBLEM SOLVING

Some problems have a "best," "correct," "right," or "appropriate" solution given the evidence that is available. In working with these situations, teachers often encourage students to follow a problem-solving approach. A typical problem-solving lesson includes steps such as these:

1. Identify the problem
2. Consider possible approaches to its solution
3. Select and apply approaches
4. Reach a defensible conclusion

LESSON
▪ IDEA ▪

Weather Patterns

Grade Level: 5. *Objective:* Learners can identify variables that explain differences in climate and weather between two places. *Suggested Procedure:* A fifth-grade teacher interested in having learners understand weather patterns in different parts of the United States, for example, might engage pupils in the following dialogue.

TEACHER: I am going to write some information about temperatures in Boston and Seattle on the board. (Teacher writes the following information on the board):

City	Average January low
Boston	23°
Seattle	34°

Does everybody remember where Boston and Seattle are? (Teacher points out locations of the two cities on a large wall map of the United States.) Now let's be detectives. I want you to explain these differences. Why is Seattle warmer than Boston in the winter?

Let's start by reviewing what we already know about things that influence a place's climate. Who'll tell me one thing that is important?

JOSE: Well, places farther north sometimes are colder than places farther south.

TEACHER: Yes, that is true. What term did we learn to describe how far a place is north or south of the equator?

LaSHANDRA: Latitude.

TEACHER: Latitude. Good. So one thing we might want to look at is latitude. That is, how far north of the equator Boston and Seattle are. All right, what else might we want to know?

SAMUEL: It makes a difference how high these places are. I mean, a place way up on a mountain is going to be colder than a place lower down.

TEACHER: That's a good idea. Remember we use the term "altitude" to talk about how high a place is. Remember, too, we always compare its elevation to sea level. So, we may want to find out how high both Seattle and Boston are above sea level. Good. Now, what other things might we want to know?

RHEA: We might want to know if there is a lot of water close by and the direction the winds blow. That could make a difference.

TEACHER: That's a good idea, Rhea. For your information, class, winds that blow over a place mostly from the same direction are called "prevailing winds." Now let's think about our ideas. There are three of them. First of all, we will want to know how far each city is north of the equator. Second, we will need to find out how far each city is above sea level. Finally, we'll need to look for information about nearby bodies of water and prevailing winds.

I want people at each table to find out information that will let you answer these three questions:

1. How far north of the equator are Seattle and Boston? You can use the back part of the atlas to find out.
2. How far above sea level is each city? Look at page 326 in the almanac on your table to find out.
3. Are there large bodies of water near each city, and what are the prevailing wind patterns? Use your atlas and see pages 78–81 in your text to find this information. (The teacher monitors pupils as they work.)

All right, let's see what we learned. Who will tell me how far north each city is?

ANDRE: Boston is 42°21' north and Seattle is 47°36' north of the equator.

TEACHER: Thank you, Andre. Now, does this information explain differences in minimum January temperatures or not?

SUZANNE: No, it doesn't make sense. I mean, Seattle's farther north. It should be colder. But it's not.

TEACHER: Yes, it's a bit puzzling, isn't it? Let's go on to another possible explanation. Let's take a look at the question of altitude. What did you find?

GRACIELLA: Seattle's about ten feet above sea level and Boston's about twenty-one feet.

TEACHER: Does this difference explain differences in winter temperature?

ROLAND: It doesn't seem so to me. There isn't much difference. I mean, eleven feet doesn't seem like much to me.

Newspapers are a good source for problems that are of interest to pupils.

TEACHER: I think you're right, Roland. The ceiling of this room is about twelve feet higher than the floor. If we keep the air circulating in the room, there probably is not much of a temperature difference between the part of the room near the floor and the part near the ceiling. So, let's go on to our third question. Who has an answer?

DEJUAN: Well, both cities are on water. The winds generally blow over both cities from the same direction—out of the west. I'm not sure that this means anything. I mean, why should this make winter temperatures different?

TEACHER: That's a good question, DeJuan. Let's think about it for a minute. Let me give you a hint. In the winter time, areas of water are warmer than areas of land. Now, where is the wind coming from in the winter that blows over Seattle and Boston?

RENEE: Out of the west.

TEACHER: Keep working with that idea, Renee. What is west of Seattle? What is west of Boston?

RENEE: Well, it's mostly Pacific Ocean west of Seattle. It's just land, other states and stuff, west of Boston.

Are Problem-Solving Lessons Appropriate for Younger Elementary School Learners?

Recently, after his son's first-grade teacher had explained some simple problem-solving lessons that had been introduced to the class, a parent made these comments:

> I appreciate what you are trying to do. I certainly want my son to learn how to think. But, I wonder whether introducing these formal skills is appropriate for first graders. It seems to me that the process takes time. I realize that they generally will come to see what the "right" answer is, but some kinds of learning are so important that any delay may be dangerous. For example, I don't want my son to go through an elaborate lesson to figure out that a red light means stop. I want him to be told this immediately. If there is a delay in getting young learners to immediately understand that they should just listen and accept some things as true, we may be asking for trouble.

**Think
About
This**

1. Specifically, what are this parent's concerns?
2. How would you respond to them?
3. How do you personally feel about the issue involving younger elementary pupils in problem-solving lessons? Why do you feel this way?

TEACHER: And why might that be important? What effect might their locations have on the two cities?

STEWART: Well, you said that water stays warmer than land in the winter. In Seattle, the wind blows east over water. Maybe the wind warms up a little before it gets to Seattle.

TEACHER: Stewart, you're on the right track. Now what about Boston's situation?

STEWART: Well, in the winter time, the winds out of the west blow over cold land before they get to Boston. Maybe that's why its colder in the winter than Seattle.

TEACHER: Class, I think we've solved our problem.

DECISION MAKING

Many questions people face have no "right" answers. A number of responses might be appropriate. Issues of this kind force people to choose from among alternatives. They do this by thinking about available options, weighing evidence, and considering personal values. Thinking of this kind is known as *decision making* (Beyer 1988).

The following seven steps are found in many decision-making lessons:

1. Identify the basic issue or problem
2. Point out alternative responses
3. Describe evidence supporting each alternative
4. Identify values implied in each alternative

5. Describe possible consequences that might follow selection of each alternative
6. Make a choice from among available alternatives
7. Describe evidence and values considered in making this choice

There are many possibilities for using decision-making lessons in elementary social studies classes. For example, many elementary schools, as part of their commitment to developing learners' citizenship skills, have a student council. Suppose a group of fifth and sixth graders decided that upper-grade members (from grades five and six) ought to be pupils who had been attending the school for at least three years. Their idea is that newcomers are unfamiliar with school traditions and won't be able to represent the true interests of the school. Present school policy allows any student in grade five or six to run for election to the school council. This situation could be used as the basis for a problem-solving lesson.

LESSON
▪ *IDEA* ▪

Decision Making: Electing School Officers
Grade Level: 5–6. *Objective:* Learners can apply the steps of the decision-making process to a problem. *Suggested Procedures:* The teacher guides students through the following steps.

Step 1: The issue could be framed as a proposition, worded in this way: "No fifth or sixth grade student should be allowed to run for the student council unless he or she has been in this school at least three years."

Step 2: In this case, there are only two alternatives. Alternative one is to support this policy. Alternative two is to maintain the present policy, which allows any fifth or sixth grader to seek election to the student council.

Step 3: Some of the following evidence might be used to *support* the idea that only fifth and sixth graders who have been in the school three years should be allowed to run for the student council.

- This is a special school different from all others. Learners who have been here for at least three years tend to appreciate its special qualities.
- Learners who have been in the school for at least three years tend to know more people than those who are relative newcomers. They will be better able to represent the interests of all people in the school.
- Some issues such as deciding how to keep first graders from getting hurt on the playground have been considered before. Fifth and sixth graders who have been in the school for at least three years will know what has been tried before and what has and has not worked.

Some of the following evidence might be used to *oppose* the idea that fifth and sixth graders on the student council should have been in the school at least three years.

- Bright people who are new to the school quickly learn about its special qualities.

- It makes more sense to have a fifth or sixth grade student council member who really wants to work on the council than another student who may have been in the school longer but who really isn't especially interested in being a member.
- New people may bring new ideas that can be used to solve problems that others have been unable to resolve.

The following values might be among those expressed by people who *support* the new proposal.

Step 4:
- Traditions are important; they are likely to better be appreciated by people who have years of familiarity with them.
- People with more experience make more responsible decisions than people with less experience.

The following might be among values cited by people *opposing* the new proposal.

- Maintaining broad interest in student government is more important than assuring individual members meet strict qualifications for office.
- Years in the school does not necessarily translate to a commitment to the school and its traditions.

Step 5:   The following consequences might be noted by a *supporter* of the three-year requirement.

- If fifth and sixth grade council members have been in the school at least three years
  a. council decisions are likely to please a higher percentage of the school population.
  b. the council will move more efficiently because these members will be more familiar with school procedures and with ideas tried before.

The following consequences might be cited by an *opponent* of the three-year rule.

- If there is a change in the rules to require fifth and sixth graders on the student council to have been in the school at least three years, then
  a. Many in the school will become apathetic about the student council. They will not have any sense of "ownership" in the organization and will be little inclined to support its decisions.
  b. The decision will create two categories of pupils. One category, the politically powerful "upper class" will be those fifth and sixth graders who have been in the school here three or more years. The second, or "lower class," will include all other fifth and sixth graders.

Step 6:   At this point, a decision is made. In this example the decision would be to either support or oppose the idea of requiring fifth and sixth grade members of the student council to have been members of this school for at least three years.

BOX 7–5   Decision-Making Issues for Different Grade Levels

Think
About
This

Decision-making lessons are widely used in elementary social studies programs. Because of developmental differences and interest differences, kinds of problems used as a focus for these lessons tend to vary across grade levels. Based on what you know about developmental levels of children and about kinds of issues addressed in social studies classes, identify some issues that might be appropriate for decision-making lessons. Identify three issues that might be appropriate for some learners in grades K through three and three issues that might be appropriate for some learners in grades four through six.

Step 7: A person *supporting* the idea might identify the evidence and values he or she found relevant in this way:

"I like the idea that people who have been in school here for at least three years know what the school is really like. I like the school pretty much as it is. I think they feel more like I do than someone new would. These people are also likely to know a lot of people in other grades. I think that's important, too."

A person *opposing* the idea might identify the evidence and values he or she found relevant in this way:

"I think we need to have the smartest people in the fifth and sixth grade on the student council. Some of them haven't been in the school all that long. I want to be sure that we don't have a rule that would keep them from running. Also, if I ever had to go to another school, I wouldn't like being shut out of things simply because I hadn't gone there as long as some of the other people."

In summary, the decision-making sequence allows learners to think through alternative solutions to problems. Teachers, as they encourage class members to think about these alternatives, relevant evidence, and related values, involve children in a pattern of thinking demanded of adults daily. As a link to the adult world, decision-making lessons have a legitimate place in the elementary social studies program.

KEY IDEAS IN SUMMARY

1. Few dispute that one outcome of schooling should be an improvement in learners' thinking abilities. Some authorities, however, have argued against teaching thinking skills directly. Among other things, partisans of this position feel that time devoted to teaching pupils thinking skills will detract from the study of academic subject matter. Others argue that time devoted to teaching thinking skills will make it possible for students to engage academic subjects in more sophisticated ways. Though debates continue, today there is widening

support for the idea that it makes sense for instructional time to be devoted both to teaching thinking skills and to teaching academic content.

2. Metacognition is a term learning psychologists use to refer to conscious thought people have as they confront problems or dilemmas. Several instructional approaches have been developed to help learners more carefully monitor their own thinking processes. The thinking aloud technique, based on the principle of modeling, requires the teacher to verbalize the steps followed in approaching a task similar to the one the learners will be asked to do. The visualizing thinking technique helps learners to develop diagrams prepared in ways that will enable them to take notes clearly relevant to the assigned learning task.

3. Inquiry approaches are inductive learning processes. They begin by introducing pupils to isolated pieces of information. Learners are led through a series of steps that culminates in their development of a broad explanatory principle or generalization. General steps for an inquiry lesson are (a) describing essential features of a problem or situation, (b) suggesting possible solutions or explanations, (c) gathering evidence to test these solutions or explanations, (d) evaluating solutions or explanations in light of this evidence, and (e) developing a conclusion based on the best evidence.

4. Data charts are often used to develop learners' abilities to compare, contrast, and generalize. They typically feature information displayed in a matrix. Individual cells in the matrix are used as learners look for patterns, identify similarity and differences, and draw general conclusions.

5. J. Richard Suchman developed an inquiry approach that is useful for helping pupils reduce the volume of information they must consider. It features a problem introduced by the teacher and pupil interrogation of the teacher with questions that can be answered either "yes" or "no." Through this procedure, pupils learn to reject broad categories of irrelevant information and to focus on information that will help them solve the problem.

6. Creative thinking requires learners to think about perplexing problems in novel ways. Brainstorming is one technique teachers use to develop pupils' creative thinking skills. This procedure encourages learners to generate responses to a problem in a lively, uninhibited way.

7. Critical thinking is thinking that is used to evaluate. Learners are introduced to techniques that allow them to make judgments in the light of defensible criteria. Dunn and Dunn (1972) have developed an analytic adaptation of the brainstorming technique that is useful for developing pupils' critical-thinking skills.

8. Problem-solving techniques are used when issues have "correct," "right," or "most appropriate" answers or solutions. A typical problem-solving lesson includes these steps: (a) identify the problem, (b) consider possible approaches to its solution, (c) select and apply approaches, (d) reach a defensible solution.

9. Some problems have several possible acceptable responses. The specific decision an individual reaches will result from considering evidence and weighing

personal values. Decision-making lessons can be used in a variety of circumstances in elementary social studies programs.

POSTTEST

Answer each of the following true/false questions.

1. Visual-thinking exercises encourage learners to develop diagrams they will use to take notes that are clearly related to the assigned learning task.
2. The Suchman approach requires the teacher to ask pupils questions that they must answer either "yes" or "no."
3. The analytic brainstorming technique introduced by Dunn and Dunn (1972) can be used to develop learners' critical-thinking skills.
4. Critical thinking involves a consideration of personally-held values.
5. A problem-solving approach is inappropriate when the situation learners confront has no "best," "correct," "right," or "appropriate" answer.

QUESTIONS

1. What are some concerns of people who have opposed direct teaching of thinking skills?
2. What are some classroom procedures that are useful for helping learners to monitor their own thinking processes?
3. Describe the basic features of inquiry approaches.
4. Name some thinking processes that can be encouraged through the use of data charts.
5. What are general guidelines for using the Suchman inquiry approach?
6. What are basic characteristics of creative thinking?
7. What is the purpose of critical thinking?
8. What steps do teachers commonly follow when teaching a problem-solving lesson?
9. Point out basic features of decision making.
10. How would you respond to critics who suggest that direct teaching of thinking skills irresponsibly takes time away from lessons devoted to important academic content?
11. How might you explain the purposes of inquiry instruction to a parent who is unfamiliar with the approach?

12. Do creative-thinking lessons have a legitimate place in the elementary social studies classroom? Why or why not?

13. Compare and contrast critical thinking and problem solving.

EXTENDING UNDERSTANDING AND SKILL

1. Think about a topic you might like to teach in an elementary social studies class at a grade level of your choice. Find a passage in an elementary text that deals with this issue. Then, think about at least two learning tasks that you might develop for pupils of different ability levels. For each, prepare a visual-thinking diagram. Ask your instructor to critique your work.

2. There have been dozens of articles on inquiry lessons published over the years. Look for such articles in journals such as *The Social Studies* and *Social Education*. Copy two or three articles that describe the use of inquiry at the elementary level. Share these with others in your class. Use material from one of the articles as a model for developing a lesson plan of your own that features inquiry learning.

3. Review chapter material on the analytic brainstorming technique. Identify a social studies topic suitable for presentation via this technique. Develop a plan outlining what you would do at each phase of the lesson.

4. Review material in this chapter on data charts. Prepare a data chart that will facilitate making comparisons and contrasts among creative thinking, critical thinking, and problem solving. Share the chart with others in the class. Class members may keep copies as review material for a quiz.

5. Suppose you were called upon to make a presentation to a meeting of your school's parent-teacher organization on approaches to improving thinking skills. Prepare a draft of your remarks. Share it with your instructor.

REFERENCES

BEYER, B. K. *Developing a Thinking Skills Program.* Boston: Allyn and Bacon, 1988.

CHENEY, L. V. *American Memory: A Report on the Humanities in the Nation's Public Schools.* Washington, DC: National Endowment for the Humanities, 1987.

DEWEY, J. *How We Think.* Boston: D. C. Heath, 1910.

DUNN, R., AND K. DUNN. *Practical Approaches to Individualizing Instruction.* New York: Parker, 1972.

GARNER, R., AND P. A. ALEXANDER. "Metacognition: Answered and Unanswered Questions." *Educational Psychologist* (Spring 1989), pp. 143–58.

HIRSCH, E. D., JR. *Cultural Literacy: What Every American Needs to Know.* Boston: Houghton Mifflin, 1987.

LIPMAN, M. "Critical Thinking—What Can it Be?" *Educational Leadership* (September 1988), pp. 38–39.

NICKERSON, R. S., D. N. PERKINS, AND E. E. SMITH. *The Teaching of Thinking*. Hillsdale, NJ: Lawrence Erlbaum Associates, 1985.

PARKER, W. C. "Restoring History to Social Studies—Had It Ever Left?" *Educational Leadership* (April 1988), p. 86.

PERKINS, D. *The Mind's Best Work*. Cambridge, MA: Harvard University Press, 1981.

RAVITCH, D. *The Schools We Deserve*. New York: Basic Books, 1985.

RUGGIERO, V. R. *Thinking Across the Curriculum*. New York: Harper & Row, 1988.

SUCHMAN, J. R. *The Elementary School Training Program in Scientific Inquiry*. Report to the U.S. Office of Education, Title VII, Project 216. Urbana, IL: University of Illinois Press, 1962.

SUPPLEMENTAL READING

BEYER, B. K. "Developing a Scope and Sequence for Thinking Skills Instruction." *Educational Leadership* (April 1988), pp. 26–30.

COSTA, A. L., ed. *Developing Minds: A Resource Book for Teaching Thinking*. Alexandria, VA: Association for Supervision and Curriculum Development, 1985.

DERRICO, P. J. "Learning to Think Philosophy for Children." *Educational Leadership* (April 1988), p. 34.

HEIMAN, M., AND J. SLOMIANKO, eds. *Thinking Skills Instruction: Concepts and Techniques*. Washington, DC: National Education Association, 1987.

POGROW, S. "Teaching Thinking to At-Risk Elementary Students." *Educational Leadership* (April 1988), pp. 79–85.

DEVELOPING PROSOCIAL BEHAVIOR

This chapter provides information to help the reader:

1. point out the importance of prosocial behavior as a desired outcome of the social studies program,

2. identify the relationship between values and attitudes and prosocial behavior,

3. describe sensitive issues related to teaching values and morality,

4. recognize the components of a four-level framework that can be used to organize learning associated with values and morality,

5. explain the use of a moral dilemma approach in developing moral reasoning, and

6. prepare role-playing experiences for use in the elementary classroom.

PRETEST

Answer each of the following true/false questions.

1. Teachers should be cautious about dealing with values in the classroom because, in general, the public does not believe schools should deal with these topics.

2. Aesthetic values tend to reflect personal preferences, not general issues of "right" and "wrong;" hence, they need not be addressed in social studies classrooms.

3. When using techniques such as rank ordering and open-ended sentences, it is important that the teacher neither forces pupils to respond as he or she might prefer nor requires them to reveal their personal responses.

4. Role-playing approaches are especially useful in lessons designed to develop pupils' moral sensitivity.

5. A stronger value commitment is associated with moral decision making than with moral action.

INTRODUCTION

As the decade of the 1980s drew to a close, the world witnessed extraordinary political changes throughout Eastern Europe. People in nation after nation forced changes in their governments as they sought liberation and freedom. These changes came about because committed individuals were willing to become directly involved in the attempt to redirect the political directions of their countries.

At the same time these remarkable events were unfolding in Europe, some critics lamented what they believed to be an increase in apathy and disillusion among citizens of the United States. There were calls for higher levels of political interest and involvement in the affairs of our country (Broder 1990).

An important purpose of the social studies is to help pupils acquire a deep sense of social concern. Learners should understand what they can do to take actions directed at the improvement of our country. Collectively, behaviors that contribute to the betterment of society are termed *prosocial behavior.*

Developing prosocial behavior requires more than providing information to pupils. It involves consideration of values and personal ethics. People rarely take actions based exclusively on factual information. Action occurs when there is a strong sense of personal commitment and belief. This means that the social studies program, as it attempts to promote the development of prosocial behavior, must permit pupils to consider individual values and morality and allow opportunities for them to act on their beliefs.

Beginning in the middle and late 1980s, interest in the importance of values and morality in the school program revived. One national survey revealed that 68 percent of the public school parents felt that a major objective of the schools should be to help children develop a sense of right and wrong. The poll revealed this concern to rank second in importance only to the school's obligation to teach children how to read and write properly (Gallup 1984, p. 37).

In the first half of the 1990s, there continues to be broad support for the general idea of teaching moral behavior patterns in school. However, some schools are criticized for programs they have adopted to promote the development of prosocial behavior. This criticism often comes from individuals who may approve of the general idea of teaching moral behavior but do not like the specific types of prosocial behavior that school programs are encouraging. For example, some parents may be concerned that values and patterns of morality being espoused in some school programs will conflict with those being stressed at home.

Lessons that deal with issues associated with values and morality must be prepared and presented carefully. School experiences should encourage learners to act in informed and intelligent ways as they seek to bring about productive change. This chapter offers suggestions about how the social studies program can contribute to the development of these behaviors.

VALUES, MORALITY, AND PROSOCIAL BEHAVIOR

Prosocial behaviors include those individual actions that contribute to the general well-being of humankind. They are directed toward the good of others as opposed to a primary concern for self.

Prosocial behavior rests on the values and sense of morality of the individual. *Values* are those bedrock beliefs that give direction to a person's life. They are convictions that are so deeply rooted that they guide individuals as they make decisions about how they spend their time, talents, and money. There are different types of values. These range from aesthetic values that are concerned with issues relating to beauty and style to moral values concerned with broad questions of right and wrong.

Aesthetic Values

Aesthetic values tend to reflect personal choice. They do not carry connotations of right and wrong or of good and bad. For example, one person may prefer classical music, and another may prefer country western music. Neither preference is "right" or "wrong." Each is a simple aesthetic preference of an individual. Aesthetic values add a stimulating variety to life.

Aesthetic values deserve attention in the social studies curriculum. First of all, pupils must recognize that others may have aesthetic preferences that are different from their own. Tolerance for a diversity of aesthetic perspectives is an important outcome of social studies instruction.

Second, pupils need opportunities to clarify their own aesthetic values. Individuals who are clear about those things they prize and value need to be encouraged to develop commitments and take actions in support of those values. For example, a person who strongly values the beauty of nature might choose to spend time on community beautification projects.

Third, though individuals have different sets of aesthetic values, there tend to be groups of people who share them. Comparative study of aesthetic values of different cultures and societies is an important dimension of lessons in many elementary social studies programs.

Moral Values

Moral values *do* carry connotations of right and wrong. Moral values influence patterns of interpersonal relationship, and they help people define appropriate and inappropriate behavior. Among moral values that are of particular interest to the social studies teacher are those focusing on justice, equality, fairness, basic rights such as life and liberty, freedoms such as religion and speech, respect for human worth and dignity, and the rule of law. Some moral values are deeply held throughout the world. For example, all world cultures hold human life to be sacred. The murder of a member of the culture is everywhere considered to be an immoral act. These basic moral values ought to be an essential ingredient in any social studies program. The actions and lives of others and the study of other cultures has little meaning unless it is related to these concepts of morality.

James Rest's Framework

James Rest (1983) developed a four-level framework that identifies the elements that might be included in lessons focusing on values and morality. This framework includes (a) moral sensitivity, (b) moral judgment, (c) moral decision making, and (d) moral action.

Moral Sensitivity

At the moral sensitivity level, people must understand that they are faced by a situation calling for the application of values and moral thinking. In the elementary social studies program, this stage would require pupils to appreciate that making a decision demands more than a simple consideration of evidence. They need to understand that a value or a moral judgment precedes the final act of deciding.

Moral Judgment

At the moral judgment level, there is analysis of previous decisions that have implications of right and wrong embedded within them. In the social studies classroom, lessons focusing on this level engage pupils in considering decisions they or others have made and in analyzing the principles or values that led to these

Moral action involves doing something about a moral issue. These young pupils are involved in picketing for the homeless.

decisions. Pupils are taught that people who have different basic values will have different conceptions of moral behavior. Hence, it is possible for very different decisions to be defended on moral grounds.

Moral Decision Making

The moral decision-making level requires people to move beyond the analysis of decisions based on the values of the decision maker. Individuals are confronted with problems that are not yet solved. They are introduced to evidence related to the problem. Next, they are challenged to consider a number of different value positions that relate to issues associated with the problem. They are asked to describe decisions that would be consistent with the different value positions. Typically, they are also required to comment on the possible consequences of these decisions. Finally, they are asked to make personal decisions about the problem and to defend their positions.

Moral Action

At the moral action level, an individual is asked to move beyond a statement about what he or she would do about a given problem. He or she must go beyond "talking" to "doing." Some action that supports the decision is required. For example, in an elementary classroom, if a pupil (or several pupils) decided that the best way to "improve the school" was to eliminate the trash on the playground, the

BOX 8–1   **Should Young Children Learn About Values?**

A State Board of Education recently held public hearings on a proposed new elementary social studies program. The members of the public were invited to testify. The following comments were made by one person who spoke at the hearing.

> The proposed new social studies program asks children to inquire into the personal values of some of the historical people they're reading about. These children will even be asked to comment about whether they personally approve of the values of these people.
>
> It seems to me that this sort of thing is going to lead to boys and girls asking parents about their attitudes and values. I don't think this is appropriate for children this young. It may be all right when they are older. But their job now is to accept their parents as they are. I think the social studies program should just stick to teaching youngsters the facts.

Think   1. Why do you think the designers of the program included lessons focusing on values?
About   2. The person giving this testimony felt that such instruction might cause problems for
This   parents. Do you agree?
                   3. What is your personal reaction to this testimony?
                   4. How does your reaction reveal some of your own deeply held values?

moral action level would require them to remove it. Merely indicating that trash removal would be their preferred action will not suffice. The level of moral action reflects a stronger value commitment than the moral decision-making level.

APPROACHES FOR DEALING WITH VALUES, MORALITY, AND PROSOCIAL BEHAVIOR IN THE CLASSROOM

Many approaches are available for addressing values issues and morality issues in the classroom. The best of them call for active pupil participation and demand high levels of personal involvement. Some approaches to values and morality are appropriate for developing moral sensitivity and moral judgment. Others are more appropriate for decision making and moral action. The subsections that follow introduce approaches elementary teachers have found useful.

Clarifying Personal and Aesthetic Values

Clarifying those things that are important in one's life is an essential step in developing commitments and taking action. People are often confused about the values that influence the choices they make. Instructional techniques that are designed to heighten pupils' sensitivity to their own values do not focus on issues that have right or wrong answers. Neither do they force them to select any one position. Their purpose is to help learners think about what values are important to them and whether their behaviors are consistent with these values. Raths, Harmin, and Simon (1978) outlined several procedures that are useful for this purpose.

Rank Ordering

This approach begins by the teacher giving pupils several alternative courses of action. The learners are asked to rank these alternatives in terms of their individual preferences. With younger learners, teachers often present two or three alternatives verbally. Learners are given a minute to think and are then invited to share their rankings (and their individual reasons for making their choices). Older pupils are usually given a larger number of alternative actions to rank. They may be invited to share their rankings with others, but they should not be forced to do so. The following example illustrates how a rank-ordering lesson might develop in an elementary classroom.

LESSON
▪ IDEA ▪

What Would You Do With Your Time?

Grade Level: 3–6. *Objective:* Learners can identify the influence of values on the choices people make. *Suggested Procedure:*

1. Focus Component
    TEACHER: All of us have made decisions about what we do with our free time. Today, I would like you to pretend that it is Saturday morning. You have three things you can do. I would like you to think about these three things. Then, decide which one would be your first choice, which one would be your second choice, and which one would be your third choice. When we finish, if you want to share your choices with others in the class, you may. But, you may also keep your ideas to yourself if you want to. Here are the three choices:
    1. You can watch your favorite program on television.
    2. You can play with your best friend at his or her house.
    3. You can spend the day with your family at the park.
    Think for a minute about your choices. Would anyone like to share his or her ideas with us?
2. Discussion Component

    JOSE: I would want to go and play with my friend.
    TEACHER: Why did you choose that first?
    JOSE: Well, I don't get to see my friend very much anymore, and I think playing with friends is more fun.
    SHARON: I would want to go with my family because we always have fun when we do things together. I think a person's family is more important than friends or TV.

    (Discussion continues until all who want to respond have had an opportunity to do so.)

3. Debriefing

Teacher: Today we have discussed how people might make different choices about what to do with their time. Some think that spending time with their families is important. Others think that spending time with friends is a good idea. Others feel that it is a good idea sometimes to do something just by yourself. All three of these are reasonable ideas. When we make choices we have to think about what is most important to us. We also need to consider the consequences of our choices. For example, will spending time with a friend cause us to develop a poor relationship with some member of our own family? If so, we might need to rethink our choice.

**LESSON
• IDEA •**

Open-Ended Sentences

Grade Level: 5–6. *Objective:* Learners can state the things they value by completing sentences.

Suggested Procedure: Open-ended sentences help learners think about what they value. The teacher begins by preparing some partial sentences, or *sentence stems*, relating to ideas that interest pupils. Learners are told to complete the

Taking a stand and being willing to publicly affirm a position is an essential ingredient in clarifying values.

sentences. Younger learners usually are asked to respond orally. Older pupils may be directed to write complete sentences that incorporate the given stems.

1. Focus

   TEACHER: Today I am going to read you the first part of a sentence. I would like you to complete the sentence using your own words. Write your new sentences on your own paper. We will do several sentences. When we finish, I will ask any of you who wish to share some of your sentences to read what you have written. Here are the partial sentences I would like you to complete. (The teacher reads these one at a time, giving learners ample time to add their own words to build complete sentences.)

   a. "If I could describe myself to someone else, I would say that I am . . ."
   b. "The person we have read about that I would most like to be like is . . ."
   c. "The thing I am best at is . . ."
   d. "I am happiest when . . ."

2. Discussion

   TEACHER: Who would like to share some sentences with us? Chou.
   CHOU: I am happiest when I draw pictures.
   TEACHER: Why does that make you happy?
   CHOU: Well, people tell me that I draw good pictures, and I like to hear them say so.
   TEACHER: Are there other reasons why some people might like to draw?
   BILLY: Some people can tell about what they feel better by drawing pictures than by talking. It makes them feel good to draw about their feelings.
   TEACHER: Does anyone else wish to share a sentence? (Discussion continues as long as some pupils are willing to share their sentences.)

3. Debriefing

   TEACHER: Today we have all had an opportunity to respond to some sentence stems that allowed us to think about ourselves. If we think about the kinds of people we want to be and the things we enjoy, then we need to think about what we can do to become those kinds of people. Some of you might want to spend more time thinking and writing about these sentences. You may do so during the rest of the day when you have finished other work. If some of you want to talk to me individually about your sentences, I will be happy to talk with you.

Teaching for Moral Sensitivity: Values-Situation Role Playing

As pupils begin to develop a personal sense of morality, they become more sensitive to situations where moral principles need to be applied. Role-playing activities help them recognize these situations. These exercises call on learners to make value judgments as they make decisions consistent with their understanding of the worldview of the person whose part they are playing.

Learners' moral sensitivity levels can also be enhanced by lessons calling on them to look for values and moral issues as they occur in history and in present political and economic conflicts. Values-situation role playing is a technique that helps learners become more sensitive to moral and values issues. The exercise places pupils in situations that call upon them to test alternatives and to explore possible consequences when they are faced with values and moral dilemmas.

Values-situation role playing can take several forms. Commonly, the exercise begins when pupils are confronted with a situation in which several alternative actions are possible. Each action represents a different value choice. Learners are invited to act out their responses. In a short debriefing session, the teacher and members of the class discuss each response. These are the typical steps:

1. Introduce pupils to a situation.
2. Select individuals to role play their responses.
3. Discuss each response with the class as a whole.
4. Debrief at the end of the exercise. Draw attention to the pros and cons of each response, and call attention to other possible responses that learners might not have thought about.

There are several ways to introduce pupils to a situation to be used as a focus for a values-situation role-playing activity. The teacher might propose a simple situation, or pupils might respond to a question such as, "Can you think of a time when you had a hard time deciding what was the right thing to do?" Another approach that many teachers have found useful is to provide class members with an unfinished short story. Typically, a character in the story is faced with making a difficult choice. Pupils role play this character and make a choice that seems sensible to them. The short-story approach works well because, when they are well written, the stories themselves capture pupils' interest and generate enthusiasm for the role-playing activity.

Values-situation role playing can focus on several issues. In the lower grades, many of these activities focus on self-understanding and the understanding of others. In the middle and upper grades, pupils are exposed to more content from history and the social sciences. At these grade levels, values-situation role-playing lessons often are used to help them grasp value dilemmas faced by people in other times and places.

LESSON
▪ IDEA ▪

Values-Situation Role Playing: Self-Understanding

Grade Level: K–2. *Objective:* Learners can identify the complexity of solving personal problems and state alternative choices. The purpose of values-situation role playing that focuses on self-understanding is to help learners think through some of their personal problems. These lessons might relate to such issues as self-doubt, worries about the future, concerns about grades, fears of the dark, and others. *Suggested Procedure:*

1. Focus story

Joel *hates* the dark. When his mother tucks him in at night and turns off the light, he waits quietly until she leaves the room. Then he leaps out of bed and silently runs to the light switch. When he hops back into bed, he feels good and goes right to sleep.

Joel's parents have told him that there is nothing scary about the dark. His father has offered to take Joel fishing this weekend if he can go a whole week without turning on the light in his room after his mother has tucked him in and left. Joel really wants to go fishing. His father has never taken him along before. But he *knows* something terrible will happen to him and that he'll never sleep if he's alone all night in a dark room.

On Monday night, Joel's mother puts him to bed, reminds him about the possible fishing trip, turns off the light, and leaves the room. Joel is nervous. What should he *do?*

2. Role playing and discussion

TEACHER: John, you go first. Pretend that you're Joel. You're in the bedroom trying to decide what to do. Tell us your idea.

JOHN: I really want to go fishing, but there's no way I can go to sleep in the dark. I'm going to stuff a pillowcase along the bottom of the door and turn the light on. That way, my mom and dad won't know I've turned it back on.

TEACHER: All right, class, we've heard John's idea. How do we feel about it?

ROSA: I don't think Joel will be able to sleep. He'll worry about whether his father or mother will look in the room to see if the light's out.

JAMES: Maybe Joel won't feel good inside. I mean, he may fool his mom and dad, but he'll know he's done something wrong.

(Other comments follow.)

TEACHER: Sarah, why don't you play Joel this time?

SARAH: I really want to go fishing, but I am so scared of the dark that I just can't stand it. I'd tell my mom and dad that I just can't go to sleep with the light off.

TEACHER: How about some ideas about Sarah's approach to the problem?

RODNEY: That idea is going to make Joel unhappy (he's not going to go fishing) and his parents unhappy (Joel still won't go to sleep in the dark). I don't think it's much of an answer.

JILL: Maybe Joel's mom and dad should make a new plan. If Joel is this afraid of the dark, a whole week is going to be tough. Maybe they should expect only one or two nights of sleeping in the dark at first. (Other comments follow.)

3. Debriefing

TEACHER: Let me list some of the ideas we've identified:

  (a) Joel should give up on the fishing trip because he's too afraid of the dark.
  (b) Joel should pretend he's sleeping in the dark by putting a pillowcase at the bottom of the door so that his parents won't know the light is back on.
  (c) Joel's parents should be asked to set a more reasonable number of nights with no light. This will give Joel a better chance of succeeding.

(Other pupil responses are listed in the same way.) Are there some other ideas we need to think about?

PAULA: Maybe Joel's parents should talk to him more about why he's so afraid of the dark.

JOYCE: It might help if his mom and dad said they used to be afraid of the dark, too. Maybe they could tell him what helped them.

LUIS: I think Joel's parents should buy him one of those small night lights. You know, the kind that uses a Christmas tree light bulb. Maybe they'd let him keep this small light on when they turned off the main light.

TEACHER: These are interesting ideas. Any others?

(Discussion continues.)

TEACHER: Have any of you faced a situation similar to Joel's? What did you do? Why did you act in this way?

(Discussion continues.)

This lesson helps pupils realize that many personal problems are complex. There are no absolutely right or wrong answers. Solutions depend on many factors, including personal values.

LESSON
• IDEA •

Values-Situation Role Playing: Using Content from History

Grade Level: 5. *Objectives:* Learners can (1) identify conflicting values when confronted with choices and (2) state the possible consequences of making a choice. Values-situation role-playing lessons with a historical focus seek to help pupils

---

BOX 8–2   **Should Pupils Be Taught that Some Things Are Absolutely Right or Wrong?**

The following editorial appeared in a local newspaper.

We applaud the efforts of local school authorities to put some important new substance in the elementary social studies program. The new curriculum provides these youngsters with specific training in making complex decisions.

The program works like this. Pupils are given unfinished stories. At the end of each story episode, a major character faces a very difficult situation. There is no clear-cut "right" answer. The elementary youngsters are asked what they would do in this situation. They role play responses. Then the teacher follows up with a discussion focusing on the values implicit in the decision they have made.

This kind of activity is outstanding, as far as it goes. Clearly, it can help young people understand that many of life's issues are complex. For many of them, there are no simple solutions.

On the other hand, there *are* some issues that our society refuses to acknowledge are debatable. For example, we do not countenance a discussion that murder might be right. As a society, we have decided this is an issue beyond dispute.

We at *The Journal* would be pleased if the present elementary social studies program would supplement what it is doing now with a few lessons pointing out to youngsters that there are positions we do not debate. All truths are not relative. Youngsters should learn this as part of their elementary school experience.

Think
About
This

1. What dangers does the editorial writer see associated with the existing elementary social studies program?

2. What kinds of things might be taught as being "beyond debate"?

3. What would you say in a letter to the editor commenting on this editorial?

appreciate value dilemmas people have faced in the past. These lessons help learners understand that value conflicts have always been a part of human existence.

Suggested Procedure:

1. Focus Story

Joseph Fender was 17 years old. In 1862, he lived with his mother and father in central Kentucky. For months, talk had been of little else other than the Civil War. Joseph looked forward to June when he would become a soldier. But which side should he choose?

Joseph's mother's family, the Gibsons, came from central Ohio. All of his Gibson cousins were fighting in the Union army. His father's family came from Tennessee. His uncles and cousins on his father's side were fighting in the gray uniforms of the South.

"Joseph," his mother called, "here's a letter for you from Grandfather Fender." Grandfather Fender lived in Memphis in western Tennessee. Joseph's grandfather wrote, "Your father writes that you will be going off to join the war in June. In my heart, I know you will remember your southern roots. All of the Fenders are fighting for the South. Your father's Kentucky tobacco lands are really part of the South. Your speech is like that of the rest of the family here in Tennessee. You belong in a gray uniform. May God give you the insight to make the right decision."

Grandfather Fender's letter certainly didn't make matters easier. Just yesterday, Joseph had received a letter from Cousin Norman, mother's nephew, who lived in Cincinnati. Joseph recalled again the words of Cousin Norman's letter: "I am home on leave from the Union forces. Believe me, I'm proud to be in a blue uniform. With all of our factories here in the North, we have excellent equipment and supplies. There is little doubt we will win. But even more important, we have 'right' on our side.

"All of the Gibson people have joined up. We expect to see you in a blue uniform soon. The Ohio River joins Ohio and Kentucky. Kentucky really has many more common interests with Ohio and the North than with Tennessee and the South. Remember that even our brave President, Abe Lincoln, was born in Kentucky. When you join up, let me know what outfit you are with."

2. Role Playing and Discussion

TEACHER: I am going to ask several of you to pretend that you are Joseph. I want you to tell us what you would have done and why. Who wants to be first? (Several pupils play the role of Joseph. After each portrayal, there is a followup discussion.)

3. *Debriefing*

During this phase of the exercise, the teacher and the members of the class discuss all of the positions mentioned by the several role players. The teacher steers the discussion so that there is a thorough understanding of the value conflicts inherent in the focus situation.

These role-playing exercises actively involve pupils in making choices that involve conflicts of values, and help them recognize that choices have consequences. Often, even the "best" choice has accompanying results that are not

"No, I don't think sending President Bush a get-well card will help the federal deficit."

completely desirable. These exercises help learners think seriously about alternative consequences associated with each of several courses of action. They help them, too, to realize that difficult problems rarely have easy solutions. Role playing develops an appreciation for the difficulties people face in making decisions about complex issues.

One key to success in values-situation role playing is using good focus stories. Many teachers write these themselves. Several other sources are available. One that is particularly good is *Role Playing in the Curriculum*, by Fannie R. Shaftel and George Shaftel (1982).

Developing Moral Judgment: The Work of Lawrence Kohlberg

When they make moral judgments, people make subjective decisions about right and wrong. In doing so, they apply certain criteria. Lawrence Kohlberg (1975) has identified six stages of moral development. People at each stage tend to apply certain kinds of criteria and to use certain kinds of logic when they make moral judgments.

1. The Punishment and Obedience Orientation Stage
People at this stage make decisions based on their respect for raw power. They may feel that if they make a decision that runs counter to the views of perceived authority something terrible may happen. An elementary child at this stage might

---

BOX 8–3   **Do Lessons Focusing on Values Help or Hinder Elementary Pupils?**

Two teachers recently exchanged these views:

TEACHER A: Our elementary learners are going to have to make difficult decisions all of their lives. We need to provide them with lots of opportunities to think about complex issues. They need to practice making decisions now. It is not too early for them to learn that not all questions have easy answers.

TEACHER B: We push our elementary learners too fast. Are these youngsters really capable of thinking about sophisticated values conflicts? I think many of them become confused by lessons that consider values. Perhaps we should leave the job of dealing with values to the parents.

Think
About
This

1. Are elementary pupils too young for lessons focusing on values?
2. What personal experiences can you draw upon to support your position?
3. Suppose you were to join these teachers in this discussion. What would you say?

---

say something like this: "I made my bed this morning because my father would have spanked me if I hadn't made it."

2. The Instrumental Relativism Stage

People who are this stage make their decisions based on feelings that they might receive a certain advantage if they make a particular choice. It is logic of the reciprocal back-scratching variety: "If you help me with my arithmetic, I'll help you write your theme."

3. The Interpersonal Concordance Stage

At this stage, individuals make decisions that are consistent with the feelings of a group with which they identify: "If I give to the charity drive, then our class will have 100 percent participation, and we can display the special door banner."

4. Law and Order Orientation Stage

People at this stage decide issues based on their respect for established rules, regulations, and traditional social practices. They prize duty and formal authority: "I may not like the speed limit, but if that's the law, I'll drive no faster."

5. Social-Contract Legalistic Orientation Stage

Decisions at this stage are not based exclusively on laws. Rather, they involve consideration of the formal rules and guidelines of the entire society, and of personal values and opinions. When no guidelines for a specific situation are available, people at this stage rely on personal insights. Their reasoning is characterized by a willingness to take action to change formal rules: "I'm going to challenge the way the school district has drawn these attendance boundaries. They are unfair to some people."

6. The Universal Ethical Principle Orientation Stage

At this stage, people make decisions based on individual conscience, taking into account such universal principles as respect for human life, love, and dignity. There is no necessary reliance on formal rules, traditions, or other guidelines. The universal principles guiding decisions are chosen by people making the decisions; they are not suggested by others: "I know what I say will not be popular, but my words are not my real message. I want to take a stand in support of the idea of freedom of speech. In the long run, respect for this principle will make people happy, even though, in the short run, my words may anger them."

According to Kohlberg's theory, people progress through these stages sequentially. No one can be a third-stage decision maker who has not previously passed through the first and second stages. Moral development stops at different stages for different people. A few people never go beyond the first stage. Relatively few people attain the highest stages of moral development.

Much of Kohlberg's research has been devoted to testing the existence of these theoretical stages. Kohlberg has had difficulty finding stage-six moral reasoners (Kohlberg 1980). This does not mean there are none, but does suggest their numbers are few. Kohlberg has also found few people at the fifth stage.

There is a suggestion in Kohlberg's work that schools, as a realistic goal, should strive to develop pupils' moral development through stage four (Kohlberg 1980, p. 463). If large numbers of learners leave school at stage four, chances improve that, in time, some of them will move to higher levels of moral reasoning.

According to Kohlberg's theory, a person at a given stage is capable of making decisions based on the logic of this and all lower stages. A high percentage of decisions will display reasoning patterns associated with the uppermost stage attained. People are not thought capable of making decisions based on the logic of stages they have not attained.

Movement upward from one moral stage to another is believed to be facilitated by exposure to higher-stage moral reasoning. People are thought to be capable of understanding the logic of one stage above their own highest-attained stage. If moral reasoning involves higher-level logic, it is not likely to be understood.

Because there is generally more concern for others associated with each higher moral stage, followers of Kohlberg are interested in techniques that will help people move to these higher stages. One approach that has been used in social studies classes is the moral dilemma discussion.

Moral Dilemma Discussions

A moral dilemma discussion involves these four steps:

1. Introducing the moral dilemma.
2. Asking pupils to suggest tentative responses.
3. Dividing pupils into groups to discuss their reasoning.
4. Discussing the reasoning and formulating a conclusion.

BOX 8–4   **Moral Reasoning and Individual Pupil Counseling.**

Moral reasoning can be used to counsel individual pupils as well as to consider moral dilemmas as a class. In listening to pupil's explanations of misbehaviors, the teacher notes the logic and tries to identify the moral reasoning stage it represents. The teacher attempts to respond with logic that is a single stage higher than that of the pupil. Consider the following examples.

Episode 1   TERESA: Yes, I did look at Anne's paper. I mean I did it just a little.
TEACHER: Tell me exactly what happened.
TERESA: Anne's terrible in math, and I'm pretty good. I said I'd let her peek at a few of my math answers if I could see a few of her social studies quiz answers.
TEACHER: Teresa, I'm concerned about your reputation. Do you want all of your friends thinking you're a cheater?

Episode 2   TERESA: Yes, I did look at Anne's paper. I mean I did it just a little.
TEACHER: Tell me exactly what happened.
TERESA: Anne's terrible in math, and I'm pretty good. I said I'd let her peek at a few of my math answers if I could see a few of her social studies quiz answers.
TEACHER: Teresa, I want to read you a section from our school handbook. It says that "any pupil who cheats may be subject to appropriate punishment as designated by the principal and the district policy." We simply must follow the rules.

Think   1. What moral stage is suggested by Teresa's response?
About   2. What moral stages are reflected in the teacher's response in each episode?
This   3. Which teacher response is the more appropriate? Why do you think so?

Introducing the Moral Dilemma

The dilemma selected should be an issue that has meaning for pupils. It should also have some of the complexity of the issues they will face as adults. The material introducing the dilemma should be short and tightly focused on the situation. A dilemma can be introduced in prose form, on film, on cassette tapes, or in some other suitable manner. The following is an example of a moral dilemma that might serve as a focus for a moral reasoning discussion.

Kim Kamatsu is in the sixth grade. She has an older brother in junior high school. Her twin sisters are in the third grade.

Kim's father Henry used to make a good living as a steelworker. The plant where he worked closed six months ago. He has taken odd jobs here and there, but has not found anything permanent. The family has had a difficult time financially. Savings are gone. Kim's mother Katherine works at a low-paying job. She worries about how she will feed and clothe her family.

Today, Kim is shopping with her mother in a large grocery store. As she walks down an aisle, Kim notices seventy-five dollars worth of food stamps that have fallen from a shopper's purse. She stoops to pick them up. She looks at them and thinks about what they will buy. Should she keep them, or should she return them to the person who lost them?

Asking Pupils to Suggest Tentative Responses

After the class has been introduced to the dilemma, each pupil is asked to write down what he or she would do, along with brief explanation of the decision. Next, the teacher asks (for the above example) for a show of hands of those pupils who think Kim should keep the food stamps and of those who think she should return them.

Dividing Pupils into Groups to Discuss Their Reasoning

The teacher then divides the class into five or six groups, taking care to assure that each group includes pupils favoring keeping the food stamps and pupils favoring returning them. The teacher instructs pupils to take turns in their groups explaining their choice, emphasizing that the discussion is to focus on *why* pupils made their decisions, not on what they chose. The teacher circulates from group to group to keep learners on task.

In a group setting, there is a good chance that there will be pupils who are at different moral reasoning levels. Pupils have opportunities to be exposed to logic that is at least one stage above their own. This can help them move up to a higher moral reasoning stage.

These discussions should be kept brief. With fifth and sixth graders, for example, five or ten minutes is plenty. The idea is to maintain intense interaction. When the teacher senses the discussions have gone on long enough, he or she asks each group to select a spokesperson.

Discussing the Reasoning and Formulating a Conclusion

During the concluding phase of the exercise, the teacher provides either a large chalkboard area or strips of butcher paper and marking pens. The spokespersons write their group's reasons supporting each viewpoint. The reasons are displayed for the whole class to examine.

The teacher leads a discussion covering all noted reasons, being careful to remain nonjudgmental and accepting of each pupil's idea. The teacher tries to elicit comments reflecting a mixture of moral reasoning stages.

After this discussion, the teacher asks each learner to take a piece of paper and write down the three or four best reasons that support the position he or she does *not* support personally. This requires pupils to think carefully about logic other than their own. Each leaner is then directed to write down the three or four most compelling reasons supporting the position he or she has taken. The teacher does not collect these papers, but may choose to elicit this information from learners during individual conferences.

In summary, moral reasoning discussions help learners think about their own logic as well as that of others. During the exercise, there are opportunities for them to be exposed to levels of reasoning different from their own. This exposure may help some learners advance to higher moral reasoning levels.

Teachers should not set their expectations of moral reasoning discussions too high. There are many variables over which the teacher has little control. For example, there may be little disagreement among class members about the course of action to be taken in the focus situation presented. It is also possible that there will be only a limited range of moral reasoning levels represented among learners in the classroom. Finally, some pupils may not be able to articulate their reasons for selecting a given response to a moral dilemma.

Despite these limitations, moral reasoning discussions can be valuable. They have the potential to sensitize pupils to the perspectives of others. And, for some, there may be growth toward higher stages of moral reasoning.

Teaching for Moral Decision Making: Issues, Values, and Consequences Analysis

Teaching for moral decision making is designed to help learners to make decisions that are consistent with their own values and understandings of morality. Lessons with this purpose typically require learners to analyze several value positions with respect to an issue. They are asked to suggest decisions consistent with these value

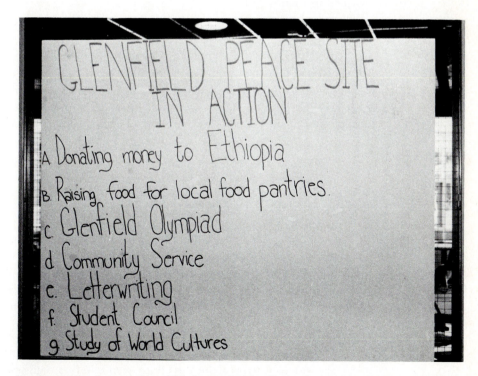

Social studies lessons should help pupils identify issues and possible actions.

positions and to suggest probable long-term consequences of these decisions. These exercises often conclude with requiring learners to make and defend a personal decision about the issue.

Issues, values, and consequences analysis seeks to help pupils recognize that the decisions individuals make reflect their values by giving them personal experience in making decisions of their own. The technique is applicable in a variety of situations. It can be used in lessons designed to promote learners' self-understanding, and in those promoting appreciation of decisions made by others. For this latter purpose, teachers often draw subject matter content from history or the social sciences.

When the objective is to work with content focusing on self-understanding, these steps are followed:

1. identifying the issue
2. gathering evidence from appropriate sources
3. considering the values that are relevant to the issue
4. identifying the possible solutions
5. pointing out the consequences of the possible solutions
6. making a decision and providing a rationale

A diagram illustrating these steps and indicating the general flow of this activity is provided in Figure 8–1.

Let us look at an example of how this procedure might be applied to a lesson focusing on self-understanding.

LESSON • IDEA •

Self-Understanding: Worry about the Future.

Grade Level: 5–6. *Objectives:* Learners can (1) state values relevant to a given issue, (2) state possible actions and probable consequences for each action, and (3) apply their values to choosing a course of action. *Suggested Procedure:*

1. *Identifying the Issue.*

Evidence suggests that many young people in the upper elementary grades worry a great deal about the future. They wonder whether they will be able to "make it" in junior high school and high school. Older brothers, sisters, and friends tell them how difficult the work there is. Some pupils in the fifth and sixth grades even worry about their future social lives. Will they have good personalities? Will they be popular? Will they find a job? Many other concerns bother young people in this age group.

Some authorities suggest that these anxieties will resolve themselves as these young people grow older. They contend that these worries will naturally disappear as these fifth and sixth graders mature and increase in their confidence to cope.

Other authorities feel that these worries will not just go away. At least, they suggest, some of these young people will continue to be plagued by very serious worries about the future even into their late senior high school years. These authorities believe strongly that fifth- and sixth-grade pupils

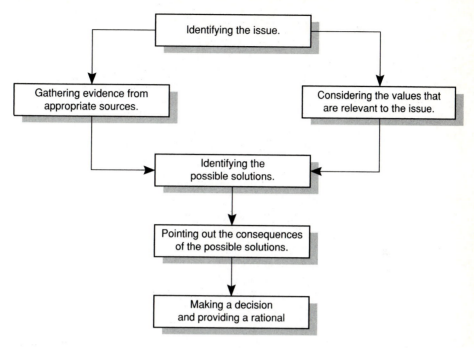

FIGURE 8–1
Lessons focusing on self-understanding or social understanding: a framework for issues, values, and consequences analysis.

should receive systematic help to relieve them of anxiety brought on by excessive worry.

The issue, then, is simply this: Should there be specific programs for fifth- and sixth-grade pupils to help them deal with their worries?

2. *Gathering evidence from appropriate sources.*
Information introduced at this point is directed toward shedding light on both sides of the issue. In looking for information to present to pupils, some teachers find it useful to develop some guiding questions. These questions suggest the kinds of information that might be needed. The following are some examples.
What is worry? Is all worry bad?
Do adults worry, too?
What conditions bring on worry?
What ways are there to reduce worry?

3. *Considering the values that are relevant to the issue.*
Teacher questions at this point can help pupils identify the values relevant to the discussion. The following are some examples.
If a person says people should not have worries, what does this tell us about what this person considers to be important in life?

Some people say worries will go away in time. Others say they won't and that we need to help people with worries right now. What differences are there in what each of these two groups thinks is really important in life?

4. *Identifying the possible solutions.*

A number of possibilities might be suggested in a discussion. The following possibilities might occur after the teacher asks, What should be done about the worries of fifth and sixth graders?

The school should have special "worry" counselors.

Parents should take these problems seriously and make time to listen to their children as they talk about their worries.

The school should introduce a course on dealing with worries about the future.

Nothing should be done. Worrying will go away in time.

5. *Pointing out the consequences of the possible solutions.*

At this point, the teacher asks pupils to think about the consequences of the possible solutions to the problem they have suggested. The following are teacher questions and a few illustrations of potential pupil responses.

What might happen if we established special "worry counselors" in each school?

Possible responses:

(a) More people might have worries because now there is somebody to talk to about them.

(b) Worries would not bother people so much because the "worry counselor" could help.

(c) Counselors maybe couldn't do some of the things they do now because they would be so busy dealing with worry problems.

(d) People might worry just as much but not be so concerned about these worries. This would be true because they would know that the counselors could help.

What would happen if we did nothing at all about this problem? Possible responses:

(a) Some would continue to worry so much that it would interfere with their ability to do well in school. That's what happens now.

(b) When they get to high school, most people will have outgrown the worries they had in the fifth and sixth grade.

(c) Some people will always worry no matter what is done. So if we do nothing, it really won't make much difference.

6. *Making a decision and providing a rationale.*

At this point, the teacher asks some questions designed to force pupils to make a personal decision about the problem. Further, pupils are asked to suggest their rationale for making this decision. The teacher might ask the following questions.

What should we do about the "worrying" issue?

Why do you make this choice?

What convinced you this choice was better than any other?

What would your choice tell others about the things in life you consider to be really important?

Lessons that focus on helping pupils appreciate the decisions made by others often draw on material from history and the social sciences. They help pupils understand that many historical events required agonizing choices among competing values. An issue that is suitable for a lesson of this type must be one for which at least two opposing viewpoints can be found. The steps to be followed are slightly more complex than for lessons that focus on personal or social understanding. These steps are listed here:

1. identifying the general issue
2. describing Faction A
3. identifying the information perceived as relevant by Faction A
4. describing the relevant alternatives open to Faction A
5. pointing out the possible consequences of each Faction A alternative
6. describing Faction B
7. identifying the information perceived as relevant by Faction B
8. describing the relevant alternatives open to Faction B
9. pointing out the possible consequences of each Faction B alternative
10. relating and comparing the alternatives open to each Faction; relating and comparing the probable consequences of each alternative; making decisions
11. applying to another setting

A diagram graphically depicting the flow of a lesson of this type is provided in Figure 8–2.

A lesson that focuses on helping pupils appreciate the decisions made by others might develop along the following lines.

LESSON
▪ IDEA ▪

Appreciating Decisions Made by Others
Grade Level: 5. *Objectives:* (1) Learners can state views, possible actions, and conflicts between two competing viewpoints. (2) Learners can apply the steps of this analysis to a new problem.
Suggested Procedure:

1. *Identifying the general issue.*
   Pupils are provided with the following information:
   In 1710, when today's United States was still a colony of Great Britain, John Peter Zenger came to New York from Germany. He started a newspaper called *The New York Weekly Journal.* All went well until 1732. In that year, a new governor, William Cosby, came to the New York colony from England. When he arrived, he found that the man who had been acting as temporary leader in New York had been drawing his salary. Cosby wanted the man to pay him the money, even though, in truth, the man had been doing Cosby's job. By using some shady tricks, Cosby succeeded in having a court decide in his favor, and there was a decision that Cosby should get the money.

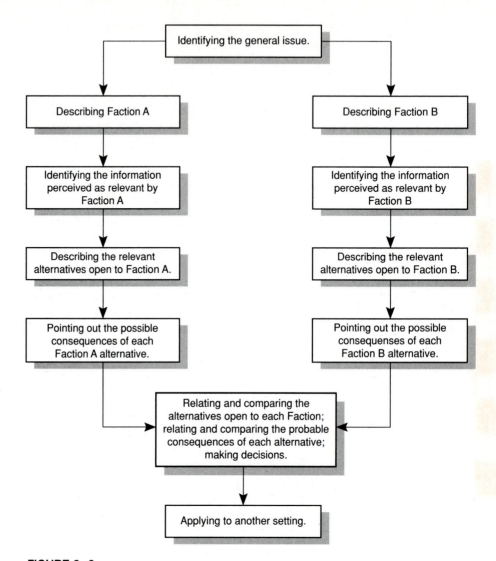

FIGURE 8–2
Appreciating the decisions made by others: a framework for issues, values, and consequences analysis.

After this had happened, John Peter Zenger reported in his newspaper about all of the questionable things Cosby had done. Cosby was furious. He accused Zenger of libel. *Libel* means damaging a person's reputation by publishing defamatory information about him or her in something like a newspaper. Zenger denied that he was guilty of libel because the things he printed were true.

Should John Peter Zenger have been found guilty of libel?

2. *Describing Faction A: Cosby and his judges.*
   Pupils are provided with the following information.
   Cosby was the Governor of New York, the king's own representative. He had responsibility for the overall administration of the colony. He was concerned about letting the colonists develop the idea that they had any real powers of their own. He felt that any attack against him was also an attack against the king.

3. *Identifying the information perceived as relevant by Faction A.*
   The teacher asks questions and provides information to assure pupils are familiar with the following facts.
   The judges selected by Cosby felt that Zenger had committed libel. English law at this time did not allow a jury to make this decision. The judges decided whether a given act was libelous. For example, it was up to the judges to decide whether something written in a newspaper was libelous. The only job of the jury was to decide whether the person accused of writing the article had actually written it.

4. *Describing the relevant alternatives open to Faction A.*
   The teacher asks pupils some questions about these alternatives. They might generate answers similar to the following.

   They could do nothing. This might just be an episode that would "blow over" in time.
   They could bring Zenger to trial.
   They could banish Zenger from the colony.

5. *Pointing out the possible consequences of each Faction A alternative.*
   The teacher asks questions. Pupils might identify the following consequences.

   If they did nothing, these attacks on the governor might escalate. They could lead to real problems.
   If they took Zenger to trial, it was always possible some unexpected outcome might result. But Cosby had had a good record of managing judges and juries.
   If they sent Zenger out of the colony, he could make trouble elsewhere in America. If he went to England, he might make trouble for Cosby by planting vicious rumors among his enemies there.

6. *Describing Faction B.*
   The teacher provides pupils with the following information.
   John Peter Zenger was a journalist. He was anxious to increase his paper's circulation over that of the rival *New York Gazette*. He was interested in appealing to those interested in extending the rights of the colonists.

7. *Identifying the information perceived as relevant by Faction B.*
   The teacher helps pupils grasp the following information.
   Zenger and his attorneys felt that the old English idea that judges should decide whether something was libelous should be changed. Judges were

too easy for the English to control. Juries, on the other hand, were something else. They tended to be made up of colonists. Zenger and his lawyers felt that juries, not judges, should decide whether the crime of libel had been committed.

Zenger's people also felt that someone should not be able to claim he had been libeled if the information printed in a newspaper could be shown to be true. Thus, they were very interested in demonstrating the truth of what Zenger had written.

8. *Describing the relevant alternatives open to Faction B.*
The teacher asks questions about alternatives. Pupils provide responses such as the following.

Zenger could have retracted what he had originally printed and published an apology to the Governor in the hope the libel suit would be dropped.
Zenger could have agreed to stand trial in the hope that he might win his case.
Zenger could have fled the colony.

9. *Pointing out the possible consequences of each Faction B alternative.*
The teacher asks questions about the consequences of each alternative. Pupils might respond in the following way.

If Zenger had retracted what he had said, he would have weakened the case the colonists were trying to make to extend their authority.
If Zenger had agreed to stand trial, he stood a chance to be found guilty. On the other hand, a trial would provide an opportunity for him to share his views with a larger audience. Also, he might win the case.
If Zenger fled, he would lose any immediate influence he might have in New York in support of increasing the authority of the colonists. On the other hand, he might be able to make life uncomfortable for Cosby if he could get to England and talk to some of Cosby's enemies.

10. *Relating and comparing the alternatives open to each faction: Relating and comparing the probable consequences of each alternative making decisions.*
The teacher asks questions to help pupils contrast the positions of the two factions. The following are questions and possible responses.
What similarities and differences do you see between the alternatives open to each side?
Possible responses:
(a) both sides consider having Zenger leave.
(b) Both sides seriously consider the merits of a trial. Both ultimately decide to choose this alternative.
What differences in viewpoint are represented on each side?
Possible responses:
(a) Cosby and his people feel that a libel had already been committed. The trial would be simply to see whether Zenger had written the libelous

article. Zenger and his people deny that a libel has been committed. They claim there was no libel since the material printed in the newspaper was true.

(b) Cosby and his people are afraid of extending the power of the colonists.

(c) Zenger favors extending the colonists' power.

What is most important to each side?

Possible responses:

(a) Cosby sees preserving his authority as most important. He sees Zenger as a threat to his authority and that of the king.

(b) Zenger wants to extend the rights of the colonists. He wants to do this by establishing the idea that anything can be printed about a person so long as its truth can be proved.

Did Zenger have a right to print articles critical of the Governor?

Possible responses:

(a) I don't think so. The governor was the king's representative. Zenger was a threat against law and order.

(b) Yes. If he couldn't be critical, then very bad governors could have done all kinds of terrible things and few people would know about them.

(c) He might have had this right, but not in New York. If he wanted to print critical articles, he should have gone to England.

What do you think really happened in this case?

The teacher conducts a discussion on this issue. To conclude the discussion, information about what happened is shared with the class.

The outcome of the Zenger case was shocking to Governor Cosby. First, the jury was convinced by the arguments of Zenger's attorney that judges should not decide when something is libelous or not. This should be left to juries. Second, the jury decided that there was no libel in a case where the person writing the article could prove the truth of what he or she had written. John Peter Zenger, as a result, was found innocent.

The Zenger case established the principle that juries, not judges, decide when a libel has occurred. Furthermore, the case established the important freedom-of-the-press principle that there is no libel when material printed can be shown to be true.

11. *Applying to another setting.*

This last phase is an attempt to tie an episode from another time or place to something more familiar to pupils' own experiences. Teachers might ask questions such as the following.

The Zenger case changed some rules that courts had followed for a long time. Can you think of any new rules that have changed how we have done things? (If pupils have trouble, provide some examples—the 55-mph speed limit, integration in the schools, changes in local school rules, and so forth.)

How do people react to changes? Do some people like them and some people oppose them? Why might there be differences?

Are newspapers today free to criticize public officials? Is this right a result
of the famous Zenger case?

How do you feel personally about what can be printed in the press? What
does your answer tell us about what things in life you believe to be really
important?

Issues, values, and consequences analyses have diverse applications. They actively involve pupils in thinking about values as well as the evidence associated with alternative positions. They deserve a place in the elementary social studies classroom.

KEY IDEAS IN SUMMARY

1. Prosocial behavior contributes to the betterment of society. Prosocial behavior rests on the values of sense of morality of individuals. One purpose of the social studies is to encourage pupils to develop a sense of concern that will lead them to act to improve their community, state, and nation.

2. In general, there is agreement that schools have some obligation to promote the development of moral patterns of behavior among learners. Some school programs that have attempted to do so have been criticized for allegedly encouraging patterns of behavior inconsistent with those espoused in some learners' homes.

3. Aesthetic values reflect personal choices and do not carry connotations of right or wrong. Moral values, on the other hand, do carry connotations of right and wrong. They help people define what kinds of behavior are appropriate and what kinds of behavior are inappropriate.

4. James Rest has developed a four-level framework that identifies components that may be included in lessons emphasizing values and morality. The levels are (a) moral sensitivity, (b) moral judgment, (c) moral decision making, and (d) moral action.

5. Many instructional techniques are available for helping learners clarify their personal and aesthetic values. Raths, Harmin, and Simon (1978), for example, recommend a rank ordering activity. Another widely used technique involves the use of open-ended sentences.

6. A widely used approach to increasing pupils' levels of moral sensitivity is values-situation role playing. This technique allows learners to become more sensitive to moral and values issues. It is applicable to issues ranging from those focusing on present personal problems of learners to those drawn from historical contexts and centering on moral dilemmas faced by others.

7. Lawrence Kohlberg has developed a six-stage framework for analyzing individuals' stages of moral development. Individuals at each stage are thought to

apply certain kinds of criteria to problems and to use certain patterns of logic as they seek solutions. The stages are (a) the punishment and obedience orientation stage, (b) the instrumental relativism stage, (c) the interpersonal concordance stage, (d) the law and order orientation stage, (e) the social-contract legalistic orientation stage, and (f) the universal ethical principle orientation stage.

8. According to Kohlberg, individuals progress through the stages sequentially. Because people at the higher levels are thought to have more concern for others than those at lower levels, followers of Kohlberg are interested in helping people move to the higher stages. One instructional approach that has been developed with this end in view involves the use of moral dilemma discussions. These attempt to expose learners to moral reasoning at stages higher than their own, a process thought to facilitate movement to higher moral reasoning levels.

9. Moral decision-making activities seek to help pupils make decisions consistent with their own values and personal understandings of morality. Lessons with this focus tend to involve learners in analyses of issues featuring a problem and a number of potential solutions. Each potential solution tends to be associated with a different set of value priorities. Learners are taught to recognize the values underlying the alternative solutions, to predict long-term consequences of each possible solution, to make a choice among the alternative solutions, and to defend this choice. Issues, values, and consequences analysis is an example of this technique that is applicable to a broad range of issues.

POSTTEST

Answer each of the following true/false questions.

1. Some common moral values are deeply held throughout the world.

2. To operate properly at the level of moral sensitivity, pupils must understand that making a decision about a complex issue requires only careful consideration of the evidence.

3. Values-situation role playing is never used when the teacher wishes to focus attention on values conflicts faced by people in the past.

4. Lawrence Kohlberg has found that a majority of elementary school pupils, by the time they complete grade six, are operating at the universal ethical principle orientation stage of moral reasoning.

5. Moral reasoning discussions can help pupils think seriously about the logic used by people other than themselves.

QUESTIONS

1. What does recent evidence tell us about parents' attitudes about teaching the concepts of "right" and "wrong" in school?

2. What are the four levels in Rest's (1983) framework for studying values and morality?

3. What are the steps in a values-situation role-playing exercise?

4. Who is Kohlberg and what are his six stages of moral reasoning?

5. What steps are followed in a moral reasoning discussion?

6. What are the general characteristics of issues, values and consequences analysis?

7. Why might some people object to dealing with values in the elementary classroom? How might you respond to these concerns?

8. Suppose a friend scheduled to do student teaching in the second grade told you that he or she was interested in doing a series of lessons focusing on the clarification of personal and aesthetic values. What would you advise?

9. Would it be wise to choose an issue that was being hotly debated in the local community as a focus for an issues, values, and consequences lesson? Why or why not?

10. How do you think the issue of including discussions about morality in the classroom can be resolved so that parental concerns can be eliminated?

11. Should the teacher always keep his or her personal values out of a values discussion or should these values be made public? Why do you think so?

EXTENDING UNDERSTANDING AND SKILL

1. Interview a district-level social studies curriculum director (if that cannot be arranged, find an elementary teacher involved in social studies curriculum development) about the emphasis in programs on lessons focusing on attitudes and values. Ask about the nature of instruction provided, any problems with patrons and other school patrons, and teachers' reactions to working with this kind of content. Prepare a report to share with your class.

2. Survey several elementary social studies textbooks. Find out how many of the suggested activities concern attitudes or values. Prepare a chart that displays your finding for your course instructor.

3. Read ten articles in professional journals that provide practical ideas for dealing with attitudes and values in the elementary social studies classroom. (You may wish to use the *Education Index* to locate your articles.) Write a brief description of each suggested approach. Share what you have found with others in your class.

4. Prepare three role-playing situations, two moral reasoning dilemmas, and one situation for an issues, values, and consequences analysis lesson. Develop these for a grade level you would like to teach. Write a description of each approach. Ask your instructor to review your descriptions.

5. Start a newspaper-clipping file featuring conflicts between people having different value priorities. Try to include at least twelve items. Discuss some of the items with others in your class. Point out how they might provide beginnings of elementary social studies lessons.

REFERENCES

BRODER, D. S. "Goal for the 90's: Reviewing Democracy at Home." *Los Angeles Times*, 3 January 1990, p. B-11.

GALLUP, G. H. "The 16th Gallup Poll of the Public's Attitudes Toward the Schools." *Phi Delta Kappan* (September 1984), pp. 23–38.

KOHLBERG, L. "The Cognitive-Developmental Approach to Moral Education." *Phi Delta Kappan* (June 1975), pp. 670–75.

KOHLBERG, L. "Education for a Just Society: An Updated and Revised Statement." In B. Munsey, ed., *Moral Development, Moral Education, and Kohlberg*. Birmingham, AL: Religious Education Press, 1980, pp. 455–70.

RATHS, L., M. HARMIN, AND S. B. SIMON. *Values and Teaching*, 2d ed. Columbus, OH: Charles E. Merrill Publishing Company, 1978.

REST, J. "Morality." In P. Hussen, ed., *Handbook of Child Psychology*, vol. 4. New York: Wiley, 1983.

SUPPLEMENTAL READING

DAMON, W. *The Moral Child: Nurturing Children's Natural Moral Growth*. New York: Free Press, 1988.

EISENBERG, N., AND P. H. MUSSEN. *The Roots of Prosocial Behavior in Children*. New York: Cambridge University Press, 1989.

KRACHT, J. B. "Values Clarification: Some Observations." *Lutheran Education* (May/June 1984), pp. 274–81.

POWER, F. C., A. HIGGINS, AND L. KOHLBERG. *Lawrence Kohlberg's Approach to Moral Education*. New York: Columbia University Press, 1989.

RYAN, K., AND G. F. McLEAN. *Character Development in Schools and Beyond*. New York: Praeger, 1987.

SHAFTEL, F. R., AND G. SHAFTEL. *Role Playing in the Curriculum*, 2d ed. Englewood Cliffs, NJ: Prentice-Hall, 1982.

SIMON, S., L. W. HOWE, AND H. KIRSCHENBAUM. *Values Clarification: A Handbook of Practical Strategies for Teachers and Students*, 3d ed. New York: Dodd, Mead & Co., 1985.

A SELECTION OF THEMES

LAW-RELATED EDUCATION

This chapter provides information to help the reader:

1. state reasons for including law-related education in the social studies curriculum,
2. define law-related education,
3. list the goals of law-related education.
4. define curriculum topics related to law-focused education,
5. find information and material related to the teaching of law-related topics,
6. explain how the case study method can be applied in the elementary classroom,
7. define the steps for using mock trials in the classroom, and
8. state how the local community can be used for teaching law-related topics.

PRETEST

Answer each of the following true/false questions.

1. A basic purpose of law-related education is to help pupils think rationally and critically about social problems and conflicts.

2. The curriculum of law-related studies should be restricted to the study of the Constitution and Bill of Rights.

3. A prerequisite for use of the case study method is considerable pupil knowledge of the law.

4. Mock trials require little advanced planning and preparation and are, therefore, easily implemented in the classroom.

5. Commercially available resources for law-related studies are scarce; therefore, teachers themselves must develop many of the needed materials.

INTRODUCTION

Have you ever had a defective product that the maker refused to fix? Have you ever been frustrated while trying to read the small print on a contract or warranty? Did you ever receive a class grade that you believed was an unfair measure of your performance? Have you ever felt that you were wronged by someone to the extent that you wanted to file a lawsuit?

Nearly all of us have had some of these experiences. When these situations occur, we often do not know what to do and end up feeling powerless, frustrated, and angry. At such times, an understanding of the law is helpful. The law has an enormous influence on our lives. Laws govern television advertising, products we purchase, the way we drive our cars, and the social relationships we have. The law provides processes to resolve disputes and to respond to perceived injustices. It helps individuals to live secure and peaceful lives.

Some people feel frustrated when they attempt to respond to unjust circumstances. Some have resorted to illegal and violent means to solve problems and bring about change. When individuals understand the laws and legal system that underpin a democratic society, there is less likelihood that they will engage in destructive, antisocial behavior. Dissemination of such information is a basic obligation of American education. The issue, then, is not *whether* elementary school children should learn about the law, but rather *what* they need to know and *how* they should learn it.

WHAT IS LAW-RELATED EDUCATION?

Some forms of law-related education have been found in social studies classrooms for many years. Instruction in "civics," for example, has been a common feature of many school programs. Traditional civics instruction has placed a heavy emphasis on the study of the United States Constitution and its first ten amendments, the Bill of Rights. Even when this traditional content has been well taught, the relatively narrow focus of the instruction has made it difficult for some learners to appreciate its relevance for their daily lives.

Modern law-related education programs have a broader focus than traditional civics. They attempt to teach pupils about the importance of the law in their everyday lives. The intent is to help them to think rationally and critically about important social problems and conflicts. This by no means suggests that emphases on the Constitution and the Bill of Rights have been abandoned. It does suggest that these documents are studied in different ways. Today, the focus is on them as living documents that embody many of our basic values and that very much influence how we live.

Law-related education, by helping learners to appreciate more fully how our legal system works, seeks to produce future citizens who will participate actively in the democratic political process. It is hoped that pupils who are exposed to such instruction will develop a personal commitment to working within the structure of the American system of governance. It is hoped, too, that they will more fully appreciate the roles of those who make, administer, and enforce the law.

Law-related education programs emphasize both common values of our society that draw us together and values conflicts that divide us. Pupils are invited to examine social problems and controversial issues. Lessons are designed to help children understand that difficult problems seldom have absolute right or wrong answers and that decisions result as much from a consideration of values priorities as from a consideration of evidence. Teaching children processes associated with legal conflict resolution is an important feature of law-related education programs.

GOALS OF LAW-RELATED EDUCATION

The following goals guide law-related education programs in the elementary school classroom.

Law-related programs should help pupils:

1. identify the basic functions of law in society
2. develop an appreciation of the need for a society governed by law
3. develop an ability to think critically about issues related to laws and the legal system

---

BOX 9–1   What Is the Purpose of Law-Related Education?

A parent was informed that the teacher was integrating law-focused content into the social studies program of a fifth-grade classroom. The parent wrote these comments to the school board.

> I am very concerned about this so-called emphasis on law-related education. I have been told that one of its purposes is to teach children critical thinking. There is already too much criticism of the laws of this nation. It is time we stopped being critical and simply told the children that it is their patriotic duty to abide by the laws that have been established. I do not want my youngster to grow into some irrational fanatic who protests every law and rule. The schools have enough to do without encouraging this sort of disruptive behavior.

Think   1. Do you see any validity in the arguments of this parent?
About   2. What points would you make in response to this person?
This   3. How would you approach issues that might prove to be controversial?

---

4. apply problem-solving skills in proposing solutions to legal issues and problems
5. identify societal values that guide the development of laws and legal processes
6. accept the rights and responsibilities of a citizen
7. develop realistic and honest views of our legal system, its strengths, and its weaknesses

Law-related education is not intended to turn pupils into miniature lawyers. Its purposes are consistent with the overall goals of the social studies. They include emphases on learning substantive content, identifying and clarifying values, and applying critical-thinking and problem-solving skills.

Some basic questions related to the goals of law-related education are the following:

1. What are rules and laws?
2. Why do we need rules and laws?
3. Who makes them?
4. What do I do if I think a rule or a law is unfair?
5. What happens if a person breaks the law?
6. What are my obligations as a citizen to follow the laws?
7. How does the law protect me and my rights?
8. What do I do if I feel I have been wronged?
9. Why does the legal system seem so complicated?

LAW-RELATED EDUCATION TOPICS

Historically, the curriculum topics that could be considered law-related education were quite limited. In recent years, however, the list of topics has expanded dramatically, and now ranges from basic legal concepts, the Constitution and the Bill of Rights, and the legal system to criminal, consumer, and family law.

Basic Legal Concepts

The intent of this topic is to help pupils understand the function of law in society. Lessons often focus on where laws come from, limitations of laws, relationships between values and laws, and a free society's need for laws. The basic concepts of fairness, justice, liberty, equality, property, due process, and power are highlighted.

The Constitution and Bill of Rights

The Constitution and the Bill of Rights are the basic documents around which our legal system is built. Pupils need to understand how these two important documents embody key legal concepts that influence our lives every day. Lessons often emphasize the relationship of these documents to situations familiar to learners. For example, they may focus on issues related to education, discrimination, and privacy.

The Legal System

This topic focuses on how our legal system operates. Lessons with this emphasis may consider law enforcement agencies, courts, lawyers, judges, and juries. Learning experiences that emphasize the duties of police officers and the nature of and limitations of their power help pupils develop an honest and realistic understanding of the roles these individuals play in our society.

Lessons focusing on what attorneys do are often featured when the nature of the legal system is being considered. Children who do not understand how the system works, often view lawyers as extremely powerful individuals who "have all the answers." This perception, no doubt, is influenced by television programs that glamorize the roles attorneys play. Young people need to understand that attorneys are not magicians who can "get you off," but that rather they are professionals who must operate within limits prescribed by law.

Young people often also have mistaken understandings of the roles of judges and juries. (See Figure 9–1 for a suggested method for identifying these misconceptions.) It is common for them to believe that judges and juries make laws. They need to understand that judges act to interpret laws made by others and that they do not personally have the power to convict or acquit those who have been charged. Similarly, it is important for children to recognize that there are important limitations on what juries can do.

Criminal Law

The high crime rate in the United States has become a much-discussed national problem. Serious students of this situation point out that law enforcement alone

A good beginning point for teaching law-related material is to identify pupils' misconceptions. Interview several learners at different grade levels to identify their understandings of the roles of police officers, attorneys, and judges. You may wish to use the following questions. When the interviews are complete, compare them with those conducted by other class members. Try to identify common misconceptions and any pattern that might be related to the developmental levels of the children.

1. What types of things do _____ do when they are working?
2. How does a person get to be a _____?
3. Where did you get your information about _____?
4. When might you need a _____?

FIGURE 9–1
Identifying misconceptions

can never reduce the crime rate. A low crime rate depends on a population committed to lawful behavior. Lessons focusing on criminal law help pupils understand what constitutes a crime, why society has defined certain acts as crimes, and what can happen to individuals who choose to violate the law. Of special importance here are topics related to the typical problems youth have and how the juvenile justice system works. Other topics of interest include trial and courtroom procedures, punishment, probation rehabilitation, and rights of the accused.

Consumer Law

Young people in our society have disposable income and have considerable influence in the national marketplace. As consumers, they need to know their rights and responsibilities. There are laws that protect them from fraud as well as laws that protect producers from irresponsible consumers. Some areas that often are covered under the heading of consumer law are advertising, contracts, guarantees, labeling, and consumer fraud. Lessons also often inform learners about options that are open to them when they find they have purchased a defective product or when they feel they have been pressured into buying something that they really do not need or want.

Family Law

The family is a basic unit in society, and there is a body of law that governs family relationships. Pupils tend to be very interested in issues associated with family law. Lessons related to this topic often emphasize laws governing marriage, parental responsibility, adoption, child abuse, spouse abuse, divorce, wills, and death. The personal nature of many of these issues require teachers to be sensitive in their instructional approaches. They must know their pupils well and deal with the content in an honest, nonjudgmental way.

BOX 9–2   **Understanding Legal Documents**

Collect a number of different documents such as warranties, contracts, copies of advertisements, product labels, and so forth. Examine these for clarity and for explanations of legal responsibility and liability.

Think   1. What do you see as common problems in these documents?
About   2. What do you think needs to be done to protect the rights of consumers?
This   3. Write a sample warranty that would be clear and understandable.
             4. How could you use these documents in teaching about consumer law?

Abundant resources are available to help teachers work with these topics. Organizations, including bar associations, have developed programs that sometimes include speakers as well as resource materials.

SOURCES OF INFORMATION

One key to the success of any social studies program is the availability of quality learning materials. Several organizations have been actively developing materials for teachers to use in law-related education programs. These materials cover many subjects and are written for a variety of grade levels. Individual organizations will be happy to provide information about the specific materials they have available. Several excellent information sources are identified here.

BOX 9–3   **Demonstrating Sensitivity when Dealing with Family Law**

Many family law issues, such as divorce, death, child abuse, and spousal abuse, are highly personal. Teachers need to treat them sensitively.

Think   1. Suppose you have several children in your classroom whose parents have divorced.
About   How might you handle the legal aspects of divorce without upsetting the children or
This   the parents?
             2. When dealing with wills and death, how could you demonstrate sensitivity to the
                feelings of a child who had recently experienced a death in the family?
             3. Suppose you were dealing with the issue of child abuse or spousal abuse and a
                youngster volunteered that it was common in his or her home. What would you do?
             4. Legal issues surrounding abortion are hotly debated. Would you teach the legal
                issues related to abortion in your classroom? Why or why not?

Special Committee on Youth Education for Citizenship

For several decades, the American Bar Association has actively promoted law-related education in the schools. It has sponsored several publications for teachers. One of these, *Update on Law-Related Education,* includes articles introducing new topics, and provides examples of classroom techniques for teachers at all grade levels. The American Bar Association also publishes other classroom materials and a special catalog of law-related audiovisual material. For information, write to: Special Committee on Youth Education for Citizenship, American Bar Association Administration Center, 1155 East 60th Street, Chicago, IL 60637.

Constitutional Rights Foundation

This organization has developed material on the Bill of Rights and other law-related topics. Published material includes simulations, filmstrips, resources for learners, and lesson plans. In addition, the foundation publishes the *Bill of Rights Newsletter,* available to teachers and students. Although much of the material is written for learners in grade seven and above, some of it can be useful to teachers in the upper elementary grades. The foundation also sponsors conferences and workshops for teachers. For information, write to: Constitutional Rights Foundation, 6310 San Vincente Blvd., Los Angeles, CA 90048.

Law in a Free Society

This organization has been very active in developing high quality materials for use in K–12 classrooms. These include case studies and lesson plans that promote the sequential development of the concepts of authority, justice, freedom, participation, diversity, privacy, property, and responsibility. The group also provides materials and assistance for people charged with planning and administering in-service training workshops for teachers. For information, write to: Law in a Free Society, 606 Wilshire Blvd., Santa Monica, CA 90101.

Consumer Law Resource Kit

This resource kit contains units on topics of interest to consumers. Titles include "Avoiding Gyps and Frauds," "How to Use Advertising," "Spending," "Borrowing," "Saving," "Budgeting," and "Safeguards for Shoppers." Although much of the material was published several years ago, it is still useful as a resource for teachers planning lessons focusing on consumer issues and consumer law. For information, write to: Consumer Law Resource Kit, Changing Times Educational Service, 1729 H Street, N.W., Washington, DC 20006.

Opposing Viewpoints Series

Over the past twenty years this series has addressed a wide variety of topics that are useful in teaching law-focused studies. These materials are especially valuable because they give opposing viewpoints on each of the issues. They can be used to stimulate classroom debates and critical-thinking skills. For information, write to: Opposing Viewpoints Series, Greenhaven Press, Box 831, Anoka, MN 55303.

National Institute for Citizen Education in the Law

This organization was created to promote the teaching of law in the schools. Its programs focus on teacher training and on the development of curriculum materials and courses. The institute also assists individuals interested in starting law-related education programs. One noteworthy publication is a set of materials on family law. For information, write to: National Institute for Citizen Education in the Law, 605 G Street N.W., Suite 401, Washington, DC 20001.

Public Affairs Pamphlet Series

Although these pamphlets are not specifically designed for teaching law-related content to elementary school learners, they provide a wealth of background for the teacher on a wide range of issues such as job discrimination, delinquency and the law, abortion, justice for the poor, and consumer issues. For information, write to: Public Affairs Pamphlet Series, Public Affairs Pamphlets, 381 Park Ave. South, New York, NY 10016.

Law in Action Units

This series of units includes materials and lesson plans on these topics: "Lawmaking," "Juvenile Problems and the Law," "Courts and Trials," "Youth Attitudes," and "Police and Young Consumers." The units are planned for learners in grades five to nine. For information, write to: Law in Action Units, West Publishing Company, Inc., 50 West Kellogg Blvd., St. Paul, MN 55165.

Cases: A Resource Guide for Teaching about the Law

This book includes juvenile crime cases covering a wide variety of topics. The cases are designed for learners between the ages of eight and sixteen. In addition to the cases, questions are posed for learners. Presentation ideas and a discussion guide are also provided. Sample test items are also included. For information, write to: Cases: A Resource Guide for Teaching about the Law, Good Year Books, Scott, Foresman and Company, 1900 East Lake Avenue, Glenview, Illinois 60025.

CLASSROOM APPROACHES TO LAW-RELATED EDUCATION

Law-related education can be integrated into the social studies classroom in several ways. As with other approaches, it is important for teachers to consider the background, interests, and developmental levels of their pupils in deciding how to introduce the content. Case studies and simulations have been found to be particularly effective in law-focused education programs. Many commercially prepared materials encourage the use of these techniques.

Using Case Studies

Case studies have long been used to introduce people to the law. Most law schools use this approach in teaching prospective attorneys. This method was extended to

Role playing and visiting a court can provide pupils with insights into the legal system.

the elementary and secondary schools when law-focused programs began to appear in public school programs. Cases prepared for use in elementary schools tend to be short, often only two to three paragraphs in length. Reading difficulty is also reduced to make them accessible to elementary school readers.

Sometimes cases used in elementary schools are derived from famous and important cases that have been decided by the Supreme Court. Others focus on cases that have been heard by lower courts but that feature situations that are particularly interesting to younger learners. The case study approach helps children to identify key issues and to make decisions about where they stand.

Selecting Cases for Classroom Use
There are several guidelines that teachers should follow when selecting or creating cases to be presented to learners. First, the cases selected should be ones that

focus on significant issues of enduring value. For example, the issue of the right to privacy was included in the Bill of Rights over two hundred years ago. Although the original writers had specific events in mind that are no longer of major concern, the issue continues to be relevant, such as with cases concerning eavesdropping. Cases focusing on freedom of speech, religion, the press, and other Bill of Rights concerns continue to be litigated in our courts. These issues remain very important.

In addition to having the potential to focus on significant and enduring legal issues, cases selected for study should also be of interest to the learners, and should allow for a variety of viewpoints. Legal cases centering on trivial matters that have little interest for people other than the litigants will not generate much pupil interest. For example, although the case of Zsa Zsa Gabor slapping a police officer received considerable media attention, it presented few issues of enduring significance. It would not make much sense as a case to be developed for use in the elementary school.

Preparing a Case

Cases that have been prepared for classroom use are available from several commercial sources. Individual teachers often find it necessary to make some modifications of these materials to make them suitable for their own learners. When modifying a case that has already been prepared for classroom use or when developing a case from original sources, there are useful guidelines teachers can follow.

First, basic facts need to be introduced. Language used in doing this needs to be uncluttered, jargon free, and appropriate for the learners who will be studying the case. New terms need to be identified and explained. Often it is worthwhile to apply a readability formula to any prose material to be sure that reading levels are consistent with pupils' abilities.

Next, important legal issues raised in the case need to be identified. Often this is accomplished by developing a sequence of questions to which learners must respond. For example, a case focusing on the issues of privacy rights and powers of the police might feature questions such as these:

- Do the police have the right to stop anyone walking down the street?
- Do individuals stopped by the police have the right to refuse to be searched?
- Can the police protect citizens if they lack the freedom to go about their work as they see fit?

LESSON
▪ IDEA ▪

A Case Study: Police Search

Grade Level: 5–6. *Objective:* Learners can apply the principles of the Bill of Rights to a hypothetical situation. *Suggested Procedure:*

The Event. At 1.30 A.M. on the morning of November 7, two men were seen walking down the street. Both wore dark clothing. As they walked, they made frequent stops. They seemed to be looking into houses each time they stopped. A police officer sitting in an unmarked car watched them for about five minutes. He was in the neighborhood because there had been reports of house burglaries. The officer approached the two men, stopped them, and asked them why they were in the neighborhood. Then, he proceeded to search them.

Legal Issues.

1. Did the officer have a right to search the two men?
2. Under what conditions do you think the police should have the right to search someone?
3. What right or rights do you think would be involved in a case such as this?
4. If you were to write a law that would protect the rights of people and still allow the police to do their job, what would it say?

The previous case study began with a narrative of events. An alternative beginning is to present a situation's events from the viewpoints of individuals who are involved. The following example illustrates how this might be done.

LESSON
• IDEA •

A Case Study: Hurt on the Job
Grade Level: 4–5. *Objective:* Learners can interpret conflicting viewpoints and apply legal considerations to a hypothetical case. *Suggested Procedure:*

The Facts as seen by Mr. Chiu. "I arrived in the United States just a couple of years ago. I came looking for a better life. I didn't have much money when I arrived. Finally, I found a job working in a warehouse. It was hard work. But, I was willing to do what I had to do to make money.

"One day my boss told me to get some boxes from the back of the warehouse and take them to the loading dock. I don't know how to drive the mechanical loader most of the people use to move boxes. I usually use a hand cart. This day the boss was in a big hurry. He insisted that I use the mechanical loader. I told him I didn't want to, but he insisted. He told me he'd fire me if I didn't do it. So, I got on the loader and tried to use it. Because I didn't know what I was doing, a large crate fell. It hit me and broke my arm. Now the boss says it was my fault. He fired me. I can't pay my medical bills, and I can't get a job right away because my arm is broken."

The Facts as seen by The Boss. "Mr. Chiu worked hard for me from the minute he was hired. But, he was afraid of machinery. He always wanted to do everything by hand. I suppose this is how it is done in his native country. We tried to teach him to use our machinery, including the mechanical loader. But he wasn't eager to learn, and he always went back to doing everything by hand. On the day of his accident, we had to get out an important order in a hurry. The truck was at the loading dock and was about ready to leave. I told Mr. Chiu to use the mechanical loader to save time. When he started to operate it, he got very nervous. A box fell. It hit him and narrowly missed another employee.

"I have a business to run. I have to operate efficiently. Also, I can't put up with an employee who does things that might endanger the safety of others. For this reason, I had no choice but to fire Mr. Chiu."

Legal Issues

1. Who do you think was responsible for the accident?
2. Should the boss pay for Mr. Chiu's medical treatment since he was hurt on the job?
3. Did Mr. Chiu have a right to refuse to operate the mechanical loader?
4. Did the boss have a right to fire Mr. Chiu because he could not operate the machinery properly?
5. Did Mr. Chiu have obligation to learn how to operate the mechanical loader?
6. In general, can an employer require an employee to do something that might be dangerous?
7. To what extent must employers justify their reasons for firing someone?

In using a case formatted in this way, teachers often find it useful to summarize information on both sides of the issue. This helps class members recognize that each side has reasonable arguments favoring its position.

When preparing a case for classroom use it is helpful for the teacher to identify the factors that the courts take into account when deciding similar issues. Most legal issues involve a clash between two or more rights. Teachers need to understand how the courts go about balancing these two rights and reaching a decision. Many commercially prepared classroom cases provide information for teachers about lines of legal reasoning that the courts have used in past cases. Although this material need not be presented formally to the class, it is helpful for answering pupils' questions.

If the classroom case is based on an actual court case, information about the final decision is useful. However, the decision should not be shared with class members until they have had ample time to discuss the case and to reach their own decision. At this time, the decision can be shared and used to begin a discussion of the strengths and weaknesses of the reasoning learners used in arriving at their conclusion.

Presenting Case Studies

The case study approach seeks to get learners actively involved in discussing a case, identifying important issues, and making decisions. These purposes are best met when the teacher exercises indirect rather than direct leadership in the classroom. The teacher needs to motivate the pupils by pointing out the importance of the case, presenting the facts of the case, making sure they understand the facts, prompting discussion and exploration of legal issues, and getting learners to think about their own reasoning and to make a decision.

Debriefing is an important part of lessons featuring case studies. During debriefing, learners evaluate their own reasoning. They may compare their thinking to the thinking of others, including the judge who may have decided the case in a real court of law. The teacher makes sure that the basic legal principles and issues are summarized and understood by the class members. During this time, it is important for teachers to keep their personal views to themselves until pupils have had ample opportunities to share their own points of view.

Teachers who use case studies frequently report that pupils find them to be motivating. Case studies do not require learners to come up with answers that are right or wrong in any absolute sense. Further, activities require them to deal with challenging and puzzling situations. Many children find these learning activities to be a welcome change from the more traditional read-and-recite fare they have come to associate with social studies lessons.

A good followup to the use of case studies in the classroom is a classroom visit by an attorney. Often attorneys are asked to discuss basic legal principles that would be used in deciding cases similar to the ones used in the class.

In summary, the case study approach is an especially good vehicle for introducing law-related issues to children in elementary school classrooms. It motivates pupils. More importantly, the approach has excellent potential for introducing them to principles related to the function of law in society and to their rights and responsibilities as citizens.

Mock Trials

The mock trial is widely used in school law-related education programs. Mock trials are simulation activities that feature enactments of trials, and can be very engaging learning experiences. Because they include an element of competition between the contending parties, mock trials frequently stimulate high levels of pupil enthusiasm. Although mock trials have been used more widely at the secondary level, they have been applied successfully at the elementary level (Hickey 1990).

Mock trials can either be developed from actual trials that have taken place or around controversial issues that, at some point, might result in litigation. Teachers interested in engaging learners in experiences based on actual trials can draw upon an enormous volume of materials developed by firms that produce learning materials for schools. These include complete sets of directions for mock trials based on real court cases, videocassettes, and classroom simulations. Increasing numbers of these materials are directed toward elementary school learners. An excellent general source for such materials is Social Studies School Services. For their elementary school social studies catalog, write to: Social Studies School Service, 10200 Jefferson Boulevard, Room 1, P.O. Box 802, Culver City, CA 90232-0802.

Many options are available for teachers who wish to develop mock trial lessons based on controversial issues that may not have resulted in court cases. Recently, for example, large sections of southern California were sprayed with malathion, a chemical insecticide, to eliminate an infestation of the Mediterranean fruit fly.

Many citizens became alarmed about potential danger to the human population from this spraying program. Government agencies in California insisted that the chemical spraying program posed no serious health threat to human beings. However, people were urged to keep their pets inside. People observed that school playground equipment in sprayed areas was covered with a sticky substance, and they became very concerned about possible harm to children. In addition, they noticed that thousands of beneficial insects were dying along with the Mediterranean fruit fly. A tremendous controversy over the spraying program developed, and letters to the editor in newspapers and callers to radio talk shows kept the issue alive for many weeks.

Such lively public controversy can serve well as a focus for a teacher-developed mock trial. Because the media give heavy exposure to an issue of this type, pupils (and certainly their parents) may well be familiar with the basic situation. This gives credibility to the mock trial experience in that it focuses on something that is of clear concern to the world beyond the school classroom.

In addition, by assisting learners to focus carefully on arguments on both sides of a divisive issue, mock trial experiences help pupils learn basic information about how our legal system operates. For example, they learn something about the operation of courts and trials and the roles of participants. They also afford excellent opportunities for guest speakers from the community to come in to broaden learners' understandings. For example, there may be good opportunities for attorneys and judges to share information with learners about how trials operate and about more general aspects of our justice system.

Developing Mock Trials

Using mock trials in a classroom involves the three stages of (1) preparation, (2) enactment and (3) debriefing. The success of a mock trial depends on careful teacher attention to each of these stages.

Preparation. One of the first steps is to introduce the learners to the purpose of a mock trial. They need to know something about the focus of the trial and what they will do to prepare for it. The basic purpose of this step is to motivate students and to teach them any rules or procedures that they will need to know.

The teacher then provides basic information concerning the facts of the case, preparing and distributing facts related to both sides of the disputed issue. This often takes the form of a simple fact sheet. Once it is distributed, the teacher takes time to check for pupil understanding and to respond to questions.

Next, the teacher identifies roles that are needed and assigns them to individual members of the class. Typically, these roles include a judge (or panel of judges), attorneys for both the prosecution and defense, jurors, and court assistants such as court reporters and bailiffs. Some trials require witnesses and people to play the accused person or persons.

Once roles have been assigned, the teacher gives each pupil specific information about his or her role and responsibilities. Often this is done by providing each person with a sheet that summarizes the role to be played and provides some

"I think his fifth graders put a bit too much realism into their mock trial on teacher liability."

specific suggestions. Often learners are asked to do some additional research in preparation for the trial. This preparation may require one or two class days.

If pupils have never been involved in a mock trial before, often it is helpful to stage a short rehearsal trial. When this is done, the teacher selects a focus issue that will not require pupils to do much by way of background preparation. Learners are assigned roles. The teacher guides them through the process, answers questions, and generally helps them understand the flow of the trial process.

Enactment.   The enactment stage involves the actual running of the trial in the classroom. This general sequence is followed:

1. the opening of the court
2. opening statements by attorneys with the prosecuting attorney going first and the defense attorney second
3. witnesses for the prosecution with cross examination by the defense attorneys
4. witnesses for the defense with cross examination by the prosecuting attorneys
5. closing arguments with the defense going first and the prosecution second

6. jury deliberations
7. the verdict and adjournment of the court

Certain specific statements are made by the clerk and the judge at each step of the process. The teacher usually provides these to pupils playing these roles so the enactment more closely resembles a real court session. During the enactment the teacher serves as an adviser and a monitor. The teacher's basic task is to keep the enactment on track.

Debriefing.   Teachers need to monitor time carefully so ample opportunity remains for this important component of the learning process. During debriefing, the teacher focuses pupils' attention on issues that have been raised, logic that has been used, and processes that have been implemented.

Typically, the teacher leads a discussion in which observations and feelings of the different participants are solicited. Learners are asked about what they have learned. Often, pupils are tempted to dwell only on the verdict. Although this is an important component of the experience, discussion of the verdict should not be allowed to overshadow significant learning about the general trial process.

Mock trials require a considerable amount of class time. Often a full week will be required. The need to commit such a substantial block of time is an important drawback to their use. Realistically, most teachers find that they can conduct a mock trial only once or twice during a school year. Those who use them find the commitment of time is more than repaid in terms of pupil learning and excitement.

In addition to formal mock trials, there are numerous simulations that can be used to teach law-focused content. Simulation is a very useful approach for teaching processes and decision-making skills. A number of simulations have been

---

BOX 9–4   Are Mock Trials Worth the Time?

Two teachers were discussing approaches to social studies lessons. One mentioned a plan to use a mock trial. The other made these comments:

> I tried mock trials once. I just don't think they are worth the effort. It took me two weeks to get the material together and another two weeks of class time to implement. I just don't think my people learned much from it. Let's face it, the classroom is nothing like a courtroom, so they don't really learn what a trial is like. In addition, the class was difficult to control. There is so much content to cover that I just can't put up with the time and hassle of another mock trial.

Think   1. What strengths do you find in this argument?
About   2. What weaknesses?
This   3. How would you try to avoid some of the problems mentioned by this teacher?
                   4. How would you respond to this teacher?

Getting to know and developing respect for individuals involved in enforcing the law helps pupils overcome the fear that is often associated with law enforcement.

developed that focus on topics such as juvenile hearings, constitutional conventions, mediating conflicts, and even serving as a police officer on patrol. Chapter 6, "Group Learning," provides guidelines for using simulations in the classroom.

COMMUNITY RESOURCES

In nearly every community there are people who can be invited to school to share their insights with learners involved in law-related activities. Resource people who are available in nearly every community include those working for such governmental agencies involved in law enforcement and corrections as police departments; highway patrols; corrections institutions; city, county, and district attorneys' offices, and all levels of courts.

Representatives from these agencies are often willing to come to a classroom to talk to pupils. Their visits often add an important dimension of reality to the content of law-focused lessons. For example, the problems of law enforcement and the decisions that must be made by a police officer take on added significance when they are explained by a police officer who comes to the classroom to talk about his or her role.

Bar associations and law schools are possible sources of attorneys who may be willing to come to the school. (There also may be an attorney who is a parent of a child in the class and who would like to talk to a group of elementary school learners.) Attorneys are in a position to share information related to a wide range of legal topics, and often are willing to assist teachers interested in creating mock trials or simulations. Some may even be willing to help debrief learners after they have experienced a simulation on a law-related topic.

Judges are also frequently willing to serve as guest speakers. Their comments can help learners understand difficulties judges face as they grapple with complex issues. They can also help pupils understand that judges face certain constraints as they do their work.

A field trip to view a court in session is often an enlightening experience for learners. In planning for a court visit, it is important that the teacher understand that not all courtrooms are open at all times to the public and that there are some cases that are not appropriate for young learners. Usually, court visits should be arranged through the court clerk. This person is able to help the teacher work out details for a visit.

There may be branches of the Better Business Bureau and the American Civil Liberties Union in the local community. The Better Business Bureau has information that may be of interest to teachers developing lessons focusing on consumer law and consumer fraud. The American Civil Liberties Union is particularly interested in civil rights cases.

The local newspaper is a very important community resource. The newspaper provides information about local controversial issues that might be used by teachers as bases for preparing mock trial and simulation experiences. Many newspapers are willing to provide classroom sets of newspapers to schools at a reduced rate. A temporary class subscription sometimes is very useful when pupils are preparing for mock trials or simulations focusing on hotly debated local issues.

Many newspapers, particularly in larger communities, have their own Newspaper Education programs. Though programs vary, often they feature classroom materials and a list of speakers from the newspaper. These are made available to teachers who are interested in using the newspaper as an instructional resource. Newspaper Education programs typically include ideas for using newspapers in many different content areas. However, many of them contain useful ideas for law-focused lessons.

In summary, there are many community resources teachers draw upon as they plan and implement law-focused studies. This also happens to be an area of the social studies curriculum that is well served by commercial sources. There are vast quantities of instructional materials available from publishers. Teachers who develop an interest in law-focused education have little difficulty in finding good classroom resource materials.

KEY IDEAS IN SUMMARY

1. Law-related education programs, particularly those labeled "civics," have been in public schools for many years. These traditional programs have placed a

great deal of emphasis on the study of the Constitution and the Bill of Rights. Contemporary law-focused programs, available both in secondary and elementary schools, are broader in their focus. They emphasize topics that try to explain to learners how various aspects of the legal system influence their daily lives.

2. Law-related programs seek to help pupils (a) identify the basic functions of law, (b) think critically about issues related to laws and our legal system, (c) develop problem-solving skills related to solving legal issues, (d) identify values that guide the development of laws and legal processes, (e) accept the rights and responsibility of citizenship, and (f) develop realistic and honest views of our legal system, including both its strengths and weaknesses.

3. Law-related lessons often focus on basic legal concepts; the Constitution and the Bill of Rights; our legal system; and criminal, consumer, and family law.

4. Teachers with interest in law-related education are able to choose from many materials that have been developed by organizations and commercial publishers. Organizations with materials and information of interest to public school teachers include (a) the Special Committee on Youth Education for Citizenship, (b) the Constitutional Rights Foundation, (c) Law in a Free Society, (d) Changing Times Educational Service, (e) the Opposing Viewpoints Series, (f) the National Institute for Citizen Education and the Law, (g) the Public Affairs Pamphlet Series, (h) Law in Action Units, and (i) Cases: A Resource Guide for Teaching about the Law.

5. Case studies are excellent instructional vehicles for teaching law-related content. Many cases are available from commercial sources. Teachers also write cases of their own. Cases sometimes are devised from important cases that have already been heard and decided by the courts. At other times, cases are built around controversial issues about which formal court decisions have yet to be rendered. Cases selected for classroom study should focus on issues of enduring value. For elementary school learners, cases should not be excessively long. Sometimes a few paragraphs of information will suffice. Cases typically introduce learners to important facts related to the case and to relevant legal issues. Following the enactment of the case, the teacher leads a debriefing discussion to clear up misunderstandings and to reinforce learning.

6. The mock trial is another instructional approach that teachers often find useful. Mock trials are simulations that feature enactments of trials. Mock trials involve preparation, enactment, and debriefing phases. A sequence is followed that to some degree parallels the flow of activity in an actual trial. Mock trials are time-intensive activities. Often a full week of instructional time is required. For this reason, many teachers find it practical to use mock trials only once or twice during a given school year.

7. There are resources in local communities that can supplement law-related programs in the schools. Human resources appropriate for this purpose include law enforcement officials, attorneys, and judges. Organizations such as the Better Business Bureau and the American Civil Liberties Union produce some

materials that may prove useful to teachers planning law-related lessons. The local newspaper is an excellent source of information about current controversies that might serve as bases for preparing case studies or mock trials.

POSTTEST

Answer each of the following true/false questions.

1. Law-related studies should seek to avoid controversial issues and conflict.
2. Mock trials are always based on cases that have previously been decided by the courts.
3. When selecting case studies for use in classrooms, cases focusing on significant and persistent issues should be used.
4. Case studies feature little active learner involvement. Basically, the teacher lectures to pupils about what the courts decided.
5. The debriefing step should be omitted when using mock trials because the verdict is the same as the debriefing.

QUESTIONS

1. What is meant by law-related education?
2. What are some of the purposes of law-related programs?
3. What are some examples of basic topics that might be included in law-related lessons?
4. What criteria should be used when selecting case studies for classroom use?
5. What are the three stages involved in using mock trials in the classroom?
6. How would you respond to the argument that law-related education is an interesting frill in the social studies program that might promote pupil interest but that is not central to the purposes of social studies instruction?
7. Do you think law-related studies might help prevent alienation, apathy, and hostility? Why or why not?
8. How would you respond to the argument that using case studies in the classroom when students have little legal knowledge amounts to little more than a sharing of ignorance?
9. What do you see as the advantages and disadvantages of using mock trials and simulations in the classroom?
10. Some people feel that case studies focusing on unresolved community controversies can stir up trouble for the schools. They argue that only issues that

have already been decided should be used as the focus for case studies. What is your reaction?

EXTENDING UNDERSTANDING AND SKILL

1. Interview two or three elementary teachers who teach at a grade level that interests you. Ask them to comment on the extent of their use of law-related lessons. Also, ask them about their views regarding the relative importance of such studies in the classroom.

2. Write to one or more of the information sources identified in the chapter. Ask for a list of the materials and services available for assisting teachers in implementing law-related content in the classroom. Share information you receive with others in your class, and begin developing a materials file for teaching law-focused content.

3. Develop a case study related to criminal, consumer, or family law that could be used for teaching law-related content to a group of pupils. Prepare a lesson plan that outlines how the case study will be taught.

4. Develop a plan for using a mock trial in the classroom. Identify the case to be discussed, the role profiles that will be needed, and the format that will be used in presenting and debriefing the mock trial. Share your mock trial ideas with others in the class. Keep ideas provided by others in a "mock trial teaching ideas" notebook.

5. Collect newspaper articles on law-related study topics. Suggest how these articles might be used to motivate discussion of law-focused topics, or how they might be developed into case studies.

REFERENCES

GERLACH, R., AND L. LAMPRECH. *Teaching About the Law.* Cincinnati, OH: W. H. Anderson, 1975.

HESS, R., AND J. TORNEY. *The Development of Political Attitudes in Children.* Chicago: Aldine, 1967.

HICKEY, M. "Mock Trials for Children." *Social Education* (January 1990), pp. 43–44.

THOMAS, R., AND P. MURRAY. *Cases: A Resource Guide for Teaching about the Law.* Glenview, IL: Scott, Foresman, 1982.

SUPPLEMENTAL READING

BONAR, D., A. FRANCIS, AND R. HENDRICKS. "Encouraging Law-Related Education at the Elementary Level." *The Social Studies* (July/August 1989), pp. 151–52.

Furlong, M., and E. McMahon. *Family Law: Competencies in Law and Citizenship*. St. Paul, MN: West, 1984.

Hodge, W. "The Eleven Commandments of Writing Effective Law-Related Education Proposals." *The Social Studies* (January/February 1988), pp. 4–9.

Katsh, M., ed. *Taking Sides: Clashing Views on Controversial Legal Issues*, 3d ed. Guilford, CT.: Dushkin, 1989.

Moshman, D. *Children, Education, and the First Amendment*. Lincoln, NE: University of Nebraska Press, 1989.

Schuncke, G., and S. Krogh. "Law-Related Education and the Young Child." *The Social Studies* (May/June 1985), pp. 139–42.

Strazzella, J. "Legal Eaglets." *Learning '88* (n.d., 1988), pp. 60–61.

GLOBAL EDUCATION

This chapter provides information to help the reader:

1. recognize the interdependence of people living in different world places and cultures,

2. understand arguments that have been made in favor of increasing global education experiences in the elementary social studies program,

3. describe the relationship between citizenship training and international understanding,

4. develop alternative schemes for infusing global education experiences into the elementary social studies program,

5. identify sources of information that can be used to support global education instruction, and

6. describe classroom activities for helping learners increase their sensitivity to perspectives of people in other places and cultures.

The United Nations building is a symbol of the need for international cooperation in approaching global problems.

PRETEST

Answer each of the following true/false questions.

1. Because most people in the United States do not travel outside the country, it makes little sense to place strong emphases on international understanding in elementary social studies classrooms.

2. Technological developments, particularly those related to communications, are increasing the likelihood that people throughout the world will become more aware of cultures other than their own.

3. Global education has been found to be incompatible with the objective of training future citizens to have strong commitments to core American values.

4. Though a strong emphasis on global education makes sense for more sophisticated learners at the junior high school and senior high school levels, experts generally agree that global education should not be introduced to less sophisticated elementary school learners.

5. Today, a number of groups are encouraging elementary school teachers to increase their emphases on lessons designed to promote learners' sensitivity to different world peoples and cultures.

INTRODUCTION

In early June 1989, television viewers throughout the world witnessed hundreds of thousands of young Chinese crowding into Tiananmen Square in Beijing. In the name of democracy, these young people demanded a greater voice in making decisions affecting their lives. These courageous students jeopardized their reputations and their economic futures. Sadly, some of them lost their lives when troops unexpectedly opened fire on the protesters.

In the days before troops were called in to clear the square, Chinese governmental authorities tried a time-honored method of dealing with dissent. They attempted to control the news. Transmissions to satellites carrying broadcasts of foreign journalists throughout the world were banned. Official government media began painting a picture of "bands of young hooligans" who, it was alleged, were irresponsibly undermining the nation's hallowed traditions. The army, so said the state-controlled media, had been brutally attacked by the students.

The approach was a familiar one, one with a long history of success. But, this time the old device failed. Despite every effort of the Chinese government to control the news, information from "unauthorized" sources continued to get through. FAX machines scattered throughout China's cities printed entire articles from Western news magazines. These articles were transmitted by sympathetic supporters of the students in other countries, including the United States. Once these materials arrived in China, their volume increased a hundredfold as Chinese students raced to make copies. Miniaturized transmitters, orbiting communication satellites, and a dozen other workhorses of the electronic communication age allowed information to move easily in and out of China. The old totalitarian ploy of crushing the media and spreading an official lie through a limited number of controlled communications' channels failed. Within hours of the event, people in even the remotest sections of the planet knew that the government of China had ordered its troops to fire on its own young people.

The unhappy events at Tiananmen Square underscore how technological advances, particularly in communications, are drawing the world together. One hundred years ago, people living in the central United States had only the haziest notion of what was happening in far-off countries. Today, television allows us to see and hear events happening tens of thousands of miles away. This communication capability is complemented by a growing international economic association.

The degree of the United States's involvement with other countries has increased tremendously in recent years. Today, fully one-third of American corporate profits are generated by international trade. Even more impressively, four out of every five new jobs in this country are created as a direct result of foreign trade (*Educating for Global Competence* 1988). Ten percent of the nation's manufacturing base and twenty percent of the banks are owned by foreign firms (Colman 1989). It is clear the United States has become a part of a planet-wide economy. What goes on in other countries has a profound impact on our lives.

We must become sensitive to other people and cultures. In this regard, writers of *The United States Prepares for Its Future: Global Perspectives in Education* (1987), a report of the Study Commission on Global Education, pointed out that "effective citizens must have knowledge and understanding of the world beyond our borders . . . its peoples, nations, cultures, systems, and problems; knowledge of how the world affects us, and knowledge of how we affect the world" (p. 12). In schools, this concern has been reflected in instruction that often is organized under the general heading *global education*.

WHAT IS GLOBAL EDUCATION?

Global education seeks to sensitize learners to perspectives of people in other lands and cultures. A leader of the American Forum has suggested that this be accomplished through school programs that emphasize (a) values that are unique to individual cultures as values that are common to all, (b) differing world political, economic, technological, and ecological systems, (c) broad international problems such as peace, international security, and human rights, and (d) aspects of world history emphasizing that contacts between peoples of different cultures have occurred for centuries (Colman 1989, p. 59).

Writers of *The United States Prepares for Its Future: Global Perspectives in Education* (1987) included recommendations for emphases in global education programs in elementary schools similar to the following:

1. Examination of present and past world cultures, including those at home and abroad.
2. Instruction focusing on values expressed in American political and economic institutions and how they fit in a global context.
3. Familiarity with and sensitivity to the history, art, literature, and languages of our own and other cultures.
4. Understanding of basic physical and cultural geography.

Subsequent sections of this chapter will illustrate more specific applications of these general characteristics of global education programs.

GLOBAL EDUCATION: ISSUES

There has not been universal agreement that an increased emphasis on global education is a good idea. Particularly, some people have wondered whether such an emphasis is appropriate for elementary school learners. They have argued that a longstanding priority of the elementary school program has been developing pupil commitment to American ideals. They wonder whether this commitment can be developed in a program that provides a great deal of exposure to non-American values and perspectives. John O'Neil (1989) frames the issue in this way: "Is it possible to teach students to appreciate the diversity and pluralism of other cultures while still maintaining their commitment and loyalty to democratic ideals?" (pp. 39, 90).

One response to this question is that there is nothing incompatible between global education and citizenship education. Indeed, American values may be more adequately appreciated when seen in contrast with values of people in other lands and cultures. Because of the widespread commitment here to such values as toleration for diverse opinion, learners sometimes find it difficult to suppose such values are not universally accepted. Exposure to situations where this is not the case may highlight unique features of our own worldview.

Today, global education programs are increasing in number. One recent survey found that thirty-eight states were either requiring or strongly recommending global education experiences in the schools (Colman 1989). Professional journals in education reflect great interest in this approach. Some foundations and private organizations underwrite global education programs. Many major universities have undertaken to develop instructional materials with this focus. Among these are (a) the Center for Public Education in International Affairs at the University of Southern California, (b) the Global Education Center at the University of Minnesota, (c) the Center for Teaching International Relations at the University of Denver, (d) the Social Studies Development Center at Indiana University, (e) the Stanford Program on International and Cross-Cultural Education at Stanford University, and (f) the Global Awareness Program at Florida International University.

Two excellent sources of information about global education activities for schools are: The American Forum for Global Education, 45 John Street, New York, NY 10038 (phone: 212-732-8606); and the Stanford Program on International and Cross-Cultural Education (SPICE), Littlefield Center, Room 14, 300 Lasuen Street, Stanford University, Stanford, CA 94305-5013 (phone: 415-723-1114).

This broad base of support suggests that global education instruction will remain an important component of elementary school social studies programs.

Studying other cultures helps pupils develop a global perspective.

ORGANIZING GLOBAL EDUCATION LEARNING EXPERIENCES

Global education learning can be integrated into the elementary social studies program in several ways. One flexible approach, developed by a group of Australian educators (Gael et al. 1983), identifies a number of organizational alternatives, abbreviated and modified here:

1. monocultural emphasis
2. experience emphasis
3. contributions emphasis
4. intercultural emphasis
5. personal emphasis

The developers point out that these emphases allow teachers at every grade level to develop global experiences that respond to learners' needs and to teachers' personal and professional backgrounds. Further, they allow for the development of global education lessons that are consistent with a variety of grade-level social studies programs. For example, in a traditional expanding horizon program featuring a grade-two emphasis on "the family," lessons can be prepared that study families in different world settings.

Monocultural Emphasis

The monocultural emphasis features an in-depth study of a single culture. The purpose is not so much to teach another culture's unique characteristics as to suggest how people from different cultures share characteristics. The idea is to help students develop a sensitivity to the existence of a broad global human community. Though there are interesting local differences, people in all cultures have, for example, developed mechanisms for nurturing the young to maturity, for providing shelter for their members, and for administering justice.

Depending on the grade level of learners and the nature of the local community, global education lessons with a monocultural emphasis might focus on issues such as these:

- a brief history of a particular group of people in their native land and a brief history of the group since members began arriving in the United States
- values and traditions that are particularly important to members of the culture
- how members of the group living in the United States retain their cultural identity
- influences members of the group may have had on American life
- influences the United States and its people may have had on the place from which members of the group originally came

Lessons built around a monocultural emphasis can be easily fitted into the traditional elementary school social studies curriculum. The following are examples of questions that might be considered by learners at selected elementary grade levels:

Grade 1: Do both mothers and fathers sometimes have jobs outside the home in this country? How is this similar to or different from what we have here?

Grade 4: What is the geography like of these people's native country? In what ways is it similar or different from our geography? What ideas do you get from this country's geography about what people there might do?

BOX 10–1   **Surveying Community Cultures**

To plan good lessons with a monocultural emphasis, it is necessary to know something of the cultural and ethnic makeup of the local community. The following questions may serve as useful guides as this information is gathered.

Think
About
This

1. What are the major cultural and ethnic groups in this community?
2. Approximately how large is each?
3. Are there any individuals who are widely regarded as leaders or spokespersons for these groups?
4. Are there clubs or other organizations that draw their membership from members of individual cultural and ethnic groups?
5. Are there ethnic neighborhoods in the community?
6. Who are some people from one or more groups whom you have contacted and who have expressed a willingness to talk to pupils in your class?

Grade 6: How is this country similar or different from other countries you have studied? How might you explain similarities and differences?

Some monocultural lessons build on the experience immigrants have had in coming to terms with their new country. Teachers often find it helpful to invite members of the focus group to their classes to talk to learners about problems of adjustment they faced.

Many recent immigrants to this country have come from Southeast Asia. If the teacher selects the Vietnamese as the focus for a monocultural study, members of the local Vietnamese community might come to school to share their experiences with the children. These visitors could point out similarities and differences between their lives in Vietnam and their lives as residents of the United States.

Experience Emphasis

The monocultural approach, ideally, tries to provide learners with a comprehensive picture of one cultural or ethnic group. The experience approach tends not to look at members of a single group but rather at how events experienced by people throughout the world influence their attitudes and priorities. The power of events to mold individual perspectives is presented as a characteristic shared by human beings everywhere.

Global education lessons with an experience emphasis often focus on a number of different cultural or ethnic groups. Many teachers have found it useful to organize these lessons around (a) oral history and (b) case studies.

Oral History

Oral histories are particularly popular with fifth- and sixth-grade learners. They can prepare these oral histories as a class project, possibly basing them on pupil interviews with people from different groups who have immigrated to this country. Questions such as these might be used in the interviews:

- What was it like to leave your old country? What were your feelings when you left?
- What things in this country were pretty much as you had imagined them? What things were different? What surprised you the most when you came here?
- How did your experience as an immigrant change you as a person? Do you think your reaction to this experience was typical? Why, or why not?

Case Studies

Case studies involve learners in the study of a limited number of aspects of one or more cultures. For example, a second-grade class might focus on neighborhood life in several countries. The lesson might introduce learners to housing patterns in neighborhoods, how letters are mailed (does a mailperson come to the door, must mail be taken to a central deposit, or is there some other arrangement?), and typical patterns of interaction among residents.

A grade-five class might examine how governments operate in one or more foreign lands. Such a lesson could be included as part of their regular study of the government of the United States. The contrasts between the practices of selected foreign governments and more familiar U.S. practices may help learners appreciate some special features of their own government.

Regardless of the focus of the case study, these general questions function well to guide learners' thinking:

- What similarities to what we have in this country do you see?
- What differences do you see?
- What are some of your ideas about why these differences might exist?

Contributions Emphasis

As the title suggests, this approach focuses on contributions to our world by people in different lands and cultures. Sometimes, teachers choose to emphasize contributions of people who have come to this country from original homelands elsewhere. Such lessons may be built around topics such as "Distinguished African Americans," "Famous Italian-Americans," "Contributions of German Immigrants," "French Influences in America," "Hispanic Americans: A Proud Legacy for America," and so forth. The following focus questions may be useful.

- In what ways have people from other lands and cultures helped our country?
- In what ways have people from our country influenced other lands?
- Are people from other lands and cultures continuing to influence us today? Are we continuing to influence them? Can you think of some specific examples?

It is important that learners not be left with the impression that the only important contributions were made by people who chose to move to the United States. Global education seeks to help young people appreciate contributions that have been made in the past and that continue to be made by people living in many parts of the world. Some possible topics for lessons with this broad focus include:

- African origins of iron smelting
- The work of Louis Pasteur
- Tea: An agricultural gift from Asia
- South America's wonderful potato
- Brave navigators of Portugal and Spain
- Japan's haunting "Noh" plays
- Speaking different languages and working together: Switzerland's special story

Intercultural Emphasis

The intercultural emphasis involves learners in lessons that help them compare and contrast how different cultures respond to common issues. Lessons are de-

"Multicultural education is great as an idea, but . . ."

signed to help learners appreciate that people in many parts of the world face common challenges and have developed different ways of responding to them.

Some teachers find it convenient to use *retrieval charts* in organizing lessons featuring an intercultural emphasis. A retrieval chart is simply a grid. One axis might list several countries whose people and cultures are being studied. The other axis lists common challenges faced by people in each country. For example, all people have a need for food, shelter, clothing, and recreational outlets. Hence, this axis might include such labels.

Certainly other focus issues could be selected. Some teachers, for instance, might be interested in comparing several countries in terms of their attitudes toward women, their views on capital punishment, and the nature of their school systems. In such a case, this axis might include these headings. Figure 10–1 illustrates a simple retrieval chart.

The retrieval chart has several advantages. Large versions printed and distributed to learners can be used to take notes, pupils writing information in each of the cells as they learned it. Some teachers use retrieval charts to differentiate assignments, having learners find information related to specific cells. A poster-sized

	Food	Shelter	Clothing	Recreation
Country A				
Country B				
Country C				

FIGURE 10–1
Sample retrieval chart.

version of the chart can be displayed on one wall. Learners can take turns writing information they have gathered in the appropriate places. The completed chart can be used as a basis for debriefing. Using the chart in Figure 10.1 as an example, the teacher might ask questions such as these:

- What are some similarities among countries *A*, *B*, and *C*?
- What are some differences?
- Do these differences necessarily mean people are "better" in some of these countries than in others? (The teacher must be prepared to deal with an occasional "yes" response to this issue. Learners need to be helped to understand that responses to life's challenges in one country may be different than in another, but that this difference does not imply inferiority. It speaks rather to the rich diversity that is one of our world's real treasures.)
- How might you explain any differences?

This general sequence helps students to move beyond given information to make inferences. Such a lesson has the advantage of both deepening learners' sensitivity to differences among peoples and cultures and of developing their higher-level thinking skills.

Another intercultural approach that some teachers use teaches children games that are played by young people in other cultures. Cynthia Sunal (1988) has written that "learning about a facet of childhood in another culture is likely to be the most concrete means by which children can come to form an initial understanding of that culture" (p. 232).

LESSON
▪ IDEA ▪

Intercultural Emphasis: Hide and Seek
Grade Level: 3–6. *Objective:* Learners can identify selected features of a culture by playing a game popular in the culture.

Suggested Procedure: In one of many examples from Nigeria, Sunal describes a game similar to our familiar hide and seek. This version is often played by children who are members of a small Nigerian group, the Unemeosu. In this game, the blindfolded person who is "it" counts silently while other children hide. After a reasonable period of time, the person who is "it" starts looking for the children who have hidden. While trying to keep from being spotted by the child who is "it," the children who are hiding try to run quietly and touch a small mound of stones that they have built in the middle of the area of play. If they succeed in touching the stones (and if they are undetected by the person who is "it"), then they must say a phrase meaning "I have touched the earth." When the person who is "it" finds someone, that person becomes "it" for the next round.

This version of hide and seek is "supposed to remind children of Unemeosu history. The hiders are like heroes of the past who were believed to be smart enough to seem to disappear from an attacking enemy, hide, and reappear quickly in a position to defeat the enemy" (p. 234). Since this game is so similar to the hide and seek many children will have played, learners take to it quickly. The teacher may organize a game, perhaps during recess, and have a followup discussion to pinpoint differences between the Nigerian and American versions. As Sunal suggests, children might be reminded that many Nigerians are farmers and for this reason the phrase "I have touched the earth" might be especially important to them. A discussion of this phrase might lead children to consider whether there are special phrases American children sometimes say at certain times during their games.

Individuals who are interested in specific directions for playing other games from foreign lands should read Sunal's article. (See the complete citation in the "References" section at the end of this chapter.) In addition to directions for playing the games, the author provides excellent ideas for followup discussions.

Personal Emphasis

Some elementary school learners have regular contact with people from other countries. They may have relatives with whom family members correspond, or may be fortunate enough to travel regularly outside the United States. They may live in a community where large numbers of people have come relatively recently from other lands.

On the other hand, children in many other families and communities have had very little direct personal contact with people from other lands and cultures. Though their lives are very much influenced by people outside the United States, they may not be aware of the extent to which they are members of an interactive international community. Some direct instruction can help underscore this point. Teachers have developed approaches designed to help pupils appreciate how much they personally are affected by other cultures. Three of these approaches are illustrated by the following activities.

LESSON
• IDEA •

The Parking Lot Survey
Grade Level: 5–6. *Objectives:* Learners can (1) locate nations on a map and (2) state the interdependence and influences of various nations on each other.

BOX 10–2   **Is There Time for Global Education Lessons?**

Recently, a critic of elementary school global education lessons made these comments.

> The elementary program is choked with too much content. Some say we can still give our children a good basic grounding in Americanism and, at the same time, teach them about other cultures. I disagree. There simply is not time to do both. What we are going to end up with is a group of young people who are ignorant both of their own traditions and of those of other cultures. It makes good sense to defer the study of other cultures until junior or senior high school. By this time, most young people will be well informed about the proud heritage of our own country.

Think   1. What strengths do you find in this argument?
About   2. What weaknesses?
This   3. How would you respond to this critic?

Suggested Procedure: This activity works particularly well with older elementary school youngsters. Ask each student to look at twenty-five to fifty cars parked in a row at a shopping center. (For safety's sake, suggest that a parent accompany them.) Have the students write down the name of the make, not the model, of each car (not Thunderbird, but Ford, for example). Ask students to bring the results of their survey to class.

Prepare a master list of all the car makes the children saw. Write these on the board. Next to each make, indicate the number of cars of this kind that pupils saw. Continue by asking learners to name the countries where each make is manufactured. Be prepared to help if learners are unsure.

Next, use a large world map to indicate locations of other countries in which cars are made. It is probable that the learners' lists will include cars from Japan and Germany. Often, there will also be some that came from Sweden, England, France, Italy, and Korea. Perhaps there will be a few from Yugoslavia and other countries. Conclude with a discussion that helps make these points:

- Many countries now manufacture automobiles.
- Usually countries that manufacture automobiles have many highly skilled workers and access to needed raw materials.
- Because large ships can easily transport cars throughout the world, consumers enjoy a wider choice than they would if they had access only to cars made in their country.

LESSON   *Where Clothing is Manufactured*
▪ IDEA ▪   *Grade Level:* 4–6. *Objectives:* Learners can (1) locate places on a map, (2) give reasons why different countries manufacture different items, and (3) state the impact of importation on a nation's economy.

This activity can be combined with a family trip to a local discount department store such as K-Mart. In preparation, provide learners with a short list of clothing items, such as shirts, socks, and jackets, to look for during their trip to the store. At the store, pupils (assisted by their parents) should attempt to determine the countries that manufactured these items. They will find that many of these familiar pieces of clothing are manufactured in other countries.

Suggested Procedure: Have pupils take notes on their observations. Notes should include the category of each item observed and the name(s) of the countries where it was manufactured. When these notes are shared with the class, the teacher may write the names of items and countries of manufacture on the chalkboard or on an overhead transparency. Countries should be pointed out to pupils on a globe and on a large wall map of the world. Additional activities may be directed at highlighting certain aspects of these countries and their people.

A followup discussion can help learners develop insights such as these (specific information emphasized will vary with grade level, academic ability, and interests of learners):

- Common items of clothing are manufactured in many countries outside of the United States.
- Much clothing comes to this country from countries in Asia.
- Foreign makers of clothing know a great deal about likes and dislikes of American buyers. Hence, it often is not possible to distinguish between clothing made in this country and clothing made in other countries on the basis of styles, fabrics, and colors.
- It costs something to ship clothing from another country to the United States. Often this means that clothing comes from areas where wages paid to workers in clothing factories are less than they are in the United States. (If they weren't, transportation charges would require sellers to sell these clothes at prices higher than American buyers are willing to pay. Lacking buyers, foreign manufacturers soon would stop shipping clothing here.)

LESSON
▪ IDEA ▪

Where Do Different Dog Breeds Come From?

Grade Level: 3–6. *Objectives:* Learners can (1) gather data from available resources, (2) identify patterns in data, and (3) state possible explanations for observed patterns.

Nearly all elementary-aged children like dogs. Some teachers have used this interest to stimulate interest in learning about other world places and peoples. Several approaches can be taken to this activity; the one suggested here is representative.

Suggested Procedure: Planning requires access to a source of information about dog breeds that includes specific details about where each breed originated. One excellent source is Gino Pugnetti's *Simon & Schuster's Guide to Dogs* (New York: Simon & Schuster, 1980). Select five to ten breeds. These need not necessarily be breeds that each child has seen, but it is not a good idea to select rare breeds that children may never see. The idea is to emphasize that the local and the familiar, represented here by the humble dog, has important international ties. Dogs should be selected whose roots trace to a number of different countries.

After acquiring a basic reference book on dogs, select several breeds as a focus for the lesson. The following list shows a sample selection.

Breed	**Presumed Country of Origin**
Boxer	Germany (originated in Munich)
Poodle	France
Chihuahua	Mexico
Shih-Tzu	China
Basenji	Egypt
Cocker Spaniel	England

Place photographs of these dogs around the borders of a large wall map of the world. Then help the class to locate the countries from which these dogs came. Finally, invite individual pupils to place brightly colored yarn between the photographs of the dogs and their countries of origin.

A number of followup activities and lessons can be pursued. For example, help the class to notice that large number of breeds originated in European countries. This does not mean that there have not always been large numbers of dogs elsewhere. What it suggests is that Europeans were among the first to keep breeding records and become concerned about the purity of breeds. Attitudes of people in other lands toward dogs might be a productive avenue of inquiry. Do people everywhere like dogs? This is an interesting question to pursue.

Learners can be encouraged to do some research of their own to determine where other breeds originated, and may bring in photographs of these dogs. When they find this information, the new photographs can be added to those around the map. Additional colored yarn can be strung between these dogs and their probable countries of origin.*

KEY IDEAS IN SUMMARY

1. Technological developments are drawing peoples of the world closer together. The increasing internationalization of life makes a strong case for school programs that increase learners' sensitivity to other countries and cultures.

2. Global education seeks to familiarize learners with perspectives of others. Programs emphasize, among other things, values of individual cultures; differing world political, social, and economic systems; challenging international problems such as the search for peace, international security, and human rights; and aspects of world history that stress the long history of contact among peoples of different places and cultures.

---

*Authorities do not agree about where some breeds of dogs originated. Thus, it is possible that two children may have researched origins of the same dog and found different information. The teacher needs to be prepared for this situation and to explain that there are some matters about which even qualified authorities disagree.

3. Some critics have charged that global education programs may undermine the effort of elementary programs to develop learners' appreciation for the unique qualities of their own country. Supporters of global education argue that American values can be better understood when seen in contrast with values of other peoples and cultures. Today, supporters of global education seem to be prevailing. Global education experiences are increasingly included within elementary social studies programs.

4. Some global education lessons reflect a monocultural emphasis, designed to provide pupils with an appreciation of characteristics of a single culture. Such lessons may focus on the history of the focus group, its values and traditions, and its past and present interactions with the United States.

5. Lessons featuring an experience emphasis are designed to help learners appreciate that attitudes and perspectives of people everywhere are influenced by what they have experienced in life. Often teachers who plan lessons with this emphasis use oral history and case studies as vehicles for delivering instruction.

6. The contributions emphasis in global education focuses on contributions that have been made to our world by people from different cultures. Lessons are designed to help learners understand that the quality of our lives today has been greatly enhanced by contributions made by people living in other countries and cultures.

7. The intercultural emphasis helps learners grasp how people in different cultures may respond to common issues in different ways. These lessons help young people understand that problems may have several effective solutions.

8. The personal emphasis attempts to take advantage of experiences learners may have had personally with influences from other countries and cultures. People living even in isolated inland areas of the United States have more contact with other lands and peoples than they may realize. Personal emphasis lessons help students to appreciate that exchanges of ideas and goods among the world's peoples have become commonplace.

POSTTEST

Answer each of the following true/false questions.

1. There is less interest in global education today than there was when communication technologies were less sophisticated.

2. The most important objective of a monocultural emphasis is to teach pupils the unique characteristics of one other culture.

3. Events experienced by people in different cultures influence their sense of what is important in life.

4. Some global education lessons seek to familiarize learners with contributions made to our world by people in different places and cultures.

5. An important purpose of global education lessons with a personal emphasis is to help pupils understand that, increasingly, our world has become an interactive, multicultural international community.

QUESTIONS

1. What is global education?

2. What are some arguments that have been made in support of including global education experiences in the elementary social studies program?

3. What are some criticisms that have been made of global education experiences in elementary schools?

4. What are the purposes of global education lessons with (a) a monocultural emphasis, (b) an experience emphasis, (c) a contributions emphasis, (d) an intercultural emphasis, and (e) a personal emphasis?

5. Describe some approaches to global education learning experiences that are organized to provide an experience emphasis.

6. Describe some approaches to global education learning experiences that are organized to provide a personal emphasis.

7. How would you respond to critics who suggest that global education lessons interfere with the effort to develop elementary school pupils' sense of patriotism?

8. In addition to some of the ideas presented in the chapter, what might you do to provide learners with global education learning experiences having a personal emphasis?

9. How would you go about the task of identifying people in your local community who came to this country from other lands and cultures?

10. How would you rate the relative importance of lessons having monocultural, experience, contributions, intercultural, and personal emphases? How did you arrive at this conclusion?

EXTENDING UNDERSTANDING AND SKILL

1. Invite a social studies director or coordinator from a local school district to your class. Ask this person to comment on the extent to which the local elementary program emphasizes global education. Inquire about any special difficulties teachers may have had in implementing such lessons.

2. Survey the professional journals in education for articles focusing on global education. (You may wish to begin by referring to the *Education Index* in your library. Your course instructor may have other ideas about article sources.) Make copies of three articles that you feel contain good ideas. Share these ideas with others in your class.

3. Review a social studies curriculum guide for an elementary grade level you would like to teach. (Such guides may be available in the library, or at local school district offices. Your instructor may also know where to find them.) Prepare a brief oral report for your class on the extent to which this document reflects a global education emphasis.

4. Prepare a lesson with one of the following global education emphases: (a) monocultural; (b) experience; (c) contributions; (d) intercultural; and (d) personal. Present your lesson to your course instructor for review.

5. Organize a debate on this question: "Resolved that an increased emphasis on global education will irresponsibly take away from other important social studies content." Select teams of individuals to prepare a case in support of both the pro and the con positions. Conduct the debate as a class, and conclude with a general discussion of the merits of including global education experiences in the elementary social studies program.

REFERENCES

COLMAN, P. "Global Education: Teaching for an Interdependent World." *Media and Methods* (January/February 1989), pp. 21–23, 59–61.

Educating for Global Competence. Report of the Advisory Council for International Educational Exchange. New York: Council on International Educational Exchange: August, 1988.

GAEL, J., G. GROVE, and P. HENRIKSEN,; with B. CIGLER. *Changes: Developing Multicultural Perspectives in the Primary School.* Richmond, Victoria, Australia: Hodja Educational Resources Co-Operative, 1983.

O'NEIL, J. "Confronting Controversy in Global Education." *Media and Methods* (March/April 1989), pp. 39, 90.

PUGNETTI, G. *Simon & Schuster's Guide to Dogs*, E. M. Schuler, ed. New York: Simon & Schuster, 1980.

SUNAL, C. S. "Studying Another Culture Through Children's Games: Examples from Nigeria." *The Social Studies* (September/October 1988), pp. 232–38.

The United States Prepares for Its Future: Global Perspectives in Education. Report of the Study Commission on Global Education. New York: Global Perspectives in Education, 1987.

SUPPLEMENTAL READING

DRAKE, C. "Educating for Responsible Global Citizenship." *Journal of Geography* (November/December 1987), pp. 300–306.

EVANS, C. S. "Teaching a Global Perspective in Elementary Classrooms." *Elementary School Journal* (May 1987), pp. 544–55.

PICKLES, J. "A Report on the American Forum on Education and International Competence held May 13–16, 1988 in St. Louis, Missouri." *Journal of Geography* (November/December 1988), pp. 229–31.

SELLEN, R. W. "How to Internationalize a Parochial Curriculum." *The Social Studies* (March/April 1987), pp. 80–84.

VOCKE, D. E. "Those Varying Perspectives on Global Education." *The Social Studies* (January/February 1988), pp. 18–20.

WEAVER, V. P. "Education That is Multicultural and Global: The Imperative for Economic and Political Survival." *The Social Studies* (May/June 1988), pp. 107–9.

CHAPTER

11

MULTICULTURAL AND SEX-EQUITY EDUCATION

This chapter provides information to help the reader

1. recognize the diverse character of American society,
2. describe issues that need to be considered when designing and implementing multicultural education lessons and sex-equity lessons,
3. state basic goals of multicultural and sex-equity education,
4. point out differences between single-group studies and multiple-perspective studies,
5. describe classroom activities that can help learners become more sensitive to multicultural and sex-equity issues, and
6. identify information sources for resources that might be used in multicultural and sex-equity lessons.

PRETEST

Answer each of the following true/false questions.

1. Multicultural and sex-equity lessons are primarily directed at children who are members of ethnic minorities.
2. All classroom methods and processes are bias free and, hence, equally suitable for all pupils.
3. In preparation for single-group approach lessons, the teacher must spend time learning about the perspectives of the chosen group.
4. A single-group lesson provides learners with extensive information regarding the perspectives and general worldview of one group.
5. Multiple-perspective studies, while having a place in the elementary social studies program, are not recommended for use in multicultural or sex-equity lessons.

INTRODUCTION

Olivia Escobar is beginning her teaching career in a largely white, affluent community. She has become painfully aware that most of her pupils have little understanding of cultural groups other than their own. Many seem to think that minorities are less deserving and less intelligent. They have little appreciation of the diversity that characterizes American society.

Steve Stepanovich teaches in a very different community. The majority of learners in his class come from a cultural background very different from his own. Many seem not to understand the importance of arriving at school on time and are seldom prompt in turning in assignments. Others appear to have little respect for his own personal property. These attitudes contrast sharply with those shared by people in the small, all-white town where he grew up. The attitudes of his fifth graders make Steve uncomfortable, and he is not sure what he should do.

The challenges facing Olivia Escobar and Steve Stepanovich confront many teachers in today's schools. The diversity of American society virtually assures that many teachers will confront learners coming from cultures that are unfamiliar to them. Responding to this diversity requires more than simply learning something about perspectives of individual ethnic groups. Individuals in our society have their behavioral patterns shaped by many influences in addition to ethnicity. A given child in the classroom may at the same time be a member of a black culture, an urban culture, a youth culture, and a poverty culture. Many influences contribute to the diversity of today's elementary school population. Of first-year students in school year 1986–1987,

25 percent were from families living in poverty;

14 percent were children of teenaged mothers;

15 percent were children of non-English-speaking immigrants;

30 percent were nonwhite;

40 percent would be living in a one-parent home before their eighteenth birthday;

25 percent lived in homes where the resident adults were still at work when children came home after school; and

15 percent were in special education programs. (Grant and Sleeter 1989, pp. 1–2)

Schools must serve *all* children who attend. An important obligation of the social studies is to help learners understand the diversity of their society. Lessons focusing on multicultural and sex-equity issues can help them develop sensitivity to the reality of the society in which they live. Such lessons must be directed at the entire school population. The future stability of the nation demands citizens who appreciate perspectives of others and who recognize that their own cultural groups are parts of a larger, more diverse whole.

The issue of equity is a central theme in school social studies instruction. It is a concept that extends beyond the perspectives of individual ethnic groups, and embraces gender as well. Historically, women have been denied opportunities available to men. Though this situation has begun to change, much remains to be done. The encouragement of the maximum development of learners, regardless of gender, is an important commitment of social studies educators.

Multicultural and sex-equity education form a natural partnership, linked by the social goals of equality and fairness. The elementary social studies program seeks to produce young people who, as they begin assuming their responsibilities as citizens, will work to overcome injustice and inequality wherever they are found.

BOX 11–1   **Are New Roles for Women Undermining the Family?**

A speaker at a recent parent-teachers organization meeting made these comments:

> We hear much these days about how important it is to encourage girls to think about many kinds of employment options. I am not at all sure this is a good idea. There are too many women working hard to build careers as professionals today. Their work is taking them out of the home and away from their children. As a result, too many children are being left to "raise themselves." It would be better for larger numbers of brighter women to stay home where they can give their children the nurturing they need as they grow to adulthood.

Think   1. What are the strengths of this argument?

About   2. What are the weaknesses?

This   3. How would you respond to this person's comments?

ATTORNEY

Karen Kai, attorney, in her office in San Francisco, California. She is holding one of the prize-winning baskets she designs and crafts.

Photo: Thomas Wing Wo   Design: Anne Gibbons

"One's work should be both beautiful and useful. I try to apply that to both art and law."

FIGURE 11-1
Poster used in multicultural and sex-equity education.

Copyright 1987, Organization for Equal Education of the Sexes, Inc., 744 Carroll St., 2nd fl., Brooklyn, NY 11215. Used by permission.

THE SEVERAL FACES OF MULTICULTURAL EDUCATION

The increasing diversity of the nation's population of learners has been recognized for many years. School authorities, too, early noted that many children from minority cultures were not doing well in school. One early explanation for this situation attributed lack of academic success to a "genetic deficit." According to this view, learners from minority ethnic groups and cultures simply lacked the basic intellectual equipment to profit from instruction. Not surprisingly, people with this point of view were reluctant to commit resources to serve the needs of minority learners.

By the 1960s, the "genetic deficit" perspective had given way to a "cultural deficit" view. Proponents suggested that many learners from minority groups did not achieve "because they did not experience a cognitively stimulating environment" (Erickson 1987, p. 335). Frederick Erickson, reporting on changing attitudes toward minority learners in schools, points out that the cultural deficit view allowed educators to place the blame for minority children's failure on the home rather than on the school program.

Among more contemporary explanations for school difficulties of minority children have been the "communication process" explanation and the "perceived labor market" explanation (Erickson 1987). According to the communication process explanation, language patterns of minority students are so different from those of their teachers that they do not understand much of what goes on in the classroom. The perceived labor market explanation suggests that minority learners do not feel that a job awaits them at the end of their schooling and that, hence, they fail to take schooling seriously and frequently drop out.

The communication process explanation has been criticized because it fails to suggest why some students from ethnic and cultural minorities do extremely well in school. Similarly, some minority students continue to be highly motivated by the prospects of getting a better job at the conclusion of their schooling.

Critics have argued that these "explanations" are, at best, excuses that have allowed school officials to shift the blame for the failure of many minority learners to succeed in school. They argue that the real culprit has been a failure of educators to plan seriously for the success of youngsters from all of the ethnic and cultural groups that make up today's student population. Erickson (1987) argues that educators must work hard to be seen as credible in the eyes of minority learners and their parents. This demands an effort to avoid instructional practices that may undermine learners' self-confidence and to work hard to appreciate the social benefits of a culture that encourages diversity.

School programs that have responded successfully to needs of learners from varied cultural and ethnic backgrounds sort into several types. Gezi (1981, p. 5) summarizes these basic approaches as: (a) lessons and programs directed specifically at culturally different children for the purpose of equalizing educational opportunities for them, (b) lessons and programs designed to promote an appreciation for cultural differences among all learners, (c) lessons and programs designed to preserve and maintain perspectives of individual cultures and ethnic groups, and (d) lessons and programs that seek to help children function in multiple cultural contexts.

These approaches place important obligations on teachers. They must plan experiences that support an acceptance of multiple perspectives. It is particularly important to emphasize the contributions that have been made by people who are members of the many cultural and ethnic groups that make up the fabric of American society. Educators must eliminate teaching practices that seem to devalue certain individuals or groups.

Teachers who respond to these challenges must know a good deal about the backgrounds of their learners. This information can help them select appropriate teaching approaches. Consider, for example, pupils recently arrived from Southeast Asia. Many cultures in this part of the world expect young people to acquire new information through rote learning, and schools there tend to rely heavily on this kind of teaching (Grant and Sleeter, p. 35). If these learners encounter a teacher who fails to rely on this method, they may well be confused. Teachers of such youngsters need to take time to instruct them in other learning approaches and to help them understand that rote memorization, while a worthy way of learning some content, is not the only reasonable approach.

Teachers need to consider teaching methods, grouping practices, and expectations for individual learners in light of the cultural perspectives of individual pupils. Teachers who seriously consider the cultural diversity among learners in their classroom are much more likely to succeed with youngsters from minority cultures than teachers who fail to take important cultural differences into account.

SEX-EQUITY EDUCATION: ITS PURPOSES

For many years, certain occupational roles were widely believed to be restricted to members of one sex. Many more roles were open to males than to females. Today, employers have begun to remove gender-based employment barriers, and are now attempting to focus solely on each applicant's qualifications.

Despite considerable progress toward sex equity in all areas of our national life, residual attitudes persist. Such myths as "females are not good in mathematics," and "males tend to be poor writers" still have their adherents. Some people, too, continue to feel that males simply should not do such work as teaching kindergarten, nursing, and so forth, and that females in turn should not attempt firefighting, carpentry, surgery, and so forth. An important purpose of the social studies is to confront these gender-based biases openly. Learners need to understand that many social and occupational roles will be open to them as adults.

Gender discrimination in general has restricted choices more for women than for men. Social studies programs, therefore, have an obligation to provide examples to learners of females who discharge a wide variety of responsible roles. Girls

Occupational roles once open to one gender
are now opening to both genders.

must recognize that increasing numbers of females are today holding down leadership roles in government, engineering, the physical sciences, and medicine.

The standard of living in the United States is being challenged by economic successes of other nations. Consequently, there is a pressing need to develop *all* of our nation's intellectual resources. To this end, young people must feel free to pursue personal and vocational objectives unconstrained by gender-related barriers.

BASIC GOALS OF MULTICULTURAL AND SEX-EQUITY EDUCATION

The following are among the most important social studies goals addressed by multicultural and sex-equity lessons.

1. The social studies program should help learners develop a respect for cultures other than their own. This implies a preliminary need to help pupils identify their beliefs and attitudes toward other groups and cultures. This diagnostic information can help the teacher recognize pupils' initial levels of sensitivity to others. From this baseline of understanding, lessons can be developed that challenge stereotypes and extend learners' appreciation for diversity.

2. Pupils should be provided opportunities to work directly with members of different ethnic and racial groups. Direct contact with members of other groups fosters appreciation not only for these individuals themselves but also for the groups of which they are members. The purpose of these experiences is to promote the idea that certain rights and roles should neither be accorded nor denied simply because a person is a member of a given cultural group or gender.

3. Pupils need to recognize the validity of different cultural perspectives. This goal seeks to expand learners' conception of what it means to be human. Lessons directed toward this end celebrate the richness and diversity of the human experience. Pupils should emerge with a view that different people have developed

---

BOX 11–2   **Diagnosing Stereotypes**

This procedure can be used with all but the very youngest elementary school children. Younger children should respond orally; middle and upper grades pupils can write their responses.

To prepare for the exercise, gather together eight to twelve photographs of members of different racial and ethnic groups. Ask learners to view each photograph in turn and assign one of the following characteristics that they believe might "fit" the person in the photograph:

a. helpful	k. energetic
b. troublesome	l. hard-working
c. doctor	m. poor
d. teacher	n. wealthy
e. janitor	o. dirty
f. delivery person	p. kind
g. friendly	q. ignorant
h. hot-tempered	r. wise
i. lazy	s. sad
j. generous	t. helpless

Terms a, c, d, g, j, k, l, n, p, and r are associated with people viewed positively or perceived as having higher status. Terms b, e, f, h, i, m, o, q, s, and t are associated with people viewed negatively or as having lower status.

Think About This

If large numbers of pupils assign negative/low-status terms to photographs of blacks and women, this suggests that a negative stereotyping problem exists. Lessons can be planned to break down these narrow, unrealistic views.

Perform this exercise before and after a series of lessons designed to eradicate stereotyping. Comparing the results can indicate whether learners have developed more appreciation for members of groups that they initially negatively stereotyped.

many acceptable responses to common human problems. This goal aims to attack the ethnocentric view that one's own cultural experiences represent the "right" or "natural" way to live.

4. The social studies program should help pupils develop pride in their cultural heritage. This goal seeks to help learners understand that there is no one "American way." Though as a nation we are committed to such core values as toleration of minority opinion, the right to choose one's occupation, and so forth, the fabric of our society has been enriched by many cultural threads. It is quite proper for pupils to take pride in their own cultural roots. Lessons directed at this goal help learners develop a positive self-image. This, in turn, usually contributes to the development of better feelings toward the school and results in higher levels of academic achievement.

5. The social studies needs to emphasize the resolution of values conflicts between and among groups. Many issues that are in dispute in our society are not based on factual disagreements, but result because people whose values differ interpret facts differently. Values orientations often cause conflicts between and among members of different cultural groups. Social studies teachers have an obligation to help learners recognize that not all groups share the same values and priorities and to recognize that such issues are often at the heart of conflicts. (For

This picture of a girl in Thailand carving a wooden box for sale to tourists can be used to stimulate multicultural as well as sex-equity discussions

a general instructional approach that can be used to highlight values' differences, refer to the discussion of decision making in Chapter 7, "Thinking-Skills Instruction.")

MONITORING CLASSROOM PROCEDURES

Multicultural and sex-equity purposes of the social studies program require teachers to think carefully about the procedures they use for lessons in all subject areas. These procedures can greatly affect how individual learners feel about themselves. Attention to the following guidelines result in a classroom atmosphere that supports successful multicultural and sex-equity-oriented learning experiences.

1. *Learners of different ethnic, cultural, and social backgrounds should be included when learners are organized into groups.* There is evidence that this kind of mixing is not as a common as one might expect. Often race, socioeconomic status, and sex have been found to contribute to teachers' decisions about which learners should be included in a given group (Rist 1985). Grouping based on these variables can inhibit academic development and can induce low self-images.

2. *Teachers need to be aware of their own perspectives and to recognize how these may vary from those of some of the pupils they teach.* If teachers fail to grasp that they have certain attitudes that may differ from those of some of their learners, they may unintentionally create problems for themselves. For example, a teacher may believe that touching a pupil lightly on the head is a sign of friendship and personal warmth. A pupil from a traditional Thai family might regard such a touch as an impolite invasion of privacy.

3. *Teaching methods need to be varied to accommodate a variety of learning styles.* Researchers have found that individuals differ in their learning styles, and that cultural background seems to contribute to a person's preference for a given style (Grant and Sleeter 1989). In a classroom that includes a cross-section of learners from different ethnic and cultural groups, many style preferences will be represented. Some learners will need to manipulate objects, others will learn better by reading about them, still others may need graphic representations. Lessons that accomodate learning style differences are more likely to help pupils learn than are those in which content presentation assumes all youngsters learn in the same way.

4. *Evaluation procedures need to be monitored to assure that they are as free as possible from cultural and social bias.* Improper testing and evaluation procedures can present serious obstacles even to highly motivated learners from minority cultures. Standardized tests pose particularly difficult problems. The vocabulary used and assumptions made about the life experiences of those who take standardized tests often are unsuitable for learners from certain cultural backgrounds. Some of these tests even reflect a regional bias. For example, a test item developed in Texas that asked pupils to identify an armadillo might totally bewilder a pupil in New England, where armadillos are not a common roadside sight.

A general prescription for avoiding test bias is for teachers, to the extent possible, to develop their own assessment procedures. This allows them to take into account particular characteristics of their learners. Multiple techniques, including informal evaluation, also help to increase the accuracy and fairness of teachers' assessments of pupils.

5. *Teachers need to monitor their classroom behavior to assure that they are not favoring any one group of learners.* Researchers have found that teachers' attitudes toward and expectations of individual learners can have a great influence on achievement (Good and Brophy 1987). These expectations are often communicated to learners through teachers' actions. For example, the teacher may tend to ask more challenging questions, provide more feedback, and spend more time with certain pupils. Other learners are quick to note this pattern, and pupils not in the select group may do more poorly. Often their attitudes toward both school and the teacher take a turn for the worse.

Teachers frequently are not aware that they are favoring certain learners. Soliciting observations from other teachers or videotaping lessons can often highlight this problem. Usually, teachers do not find it difficult to adjust their procedures once they learn that they have unconsciously been "playing favorites."

Professional teachers approach their work deeply committed to the view that all pupils have the potential to learn. A teacher who believes that "it is natural for girls to have trouble with mathematics," or that "pupils from poor homes can't be expected to read well" cannot be effective. Such limited expectations influence teachers to adopt classroom behaviors that reflect these *a priori* biases. In the end, the children will fail to learn not because of any innate problems, but rather because the teacher has failed to teach.

BOX 11–3   **The Problem of "PigeonHoling"**

Some people have a tendency to assign certain allegedly fixed characteristics to whole groups of individuals. Often these characteristics are negative stereotypes. Occasionally teachers are guilty of this practice. The term *pigeonholing* refers to evaluating people based on characteristics thought to be associated with their ethnic group or gender.

Think back on your own experiences in school. Were there occasions when you felt the teacher had prior conceptions about what you could do even before he or she had an opportunity to observe your real abilities? Did you ever see it happening to another learner?

Think
About
This

1. If you ever felt yourself to be pigeonholed, describe your feelings. If you saw it happening to others, what were their reactions?
2. In your opinion, what might cause a teacher to pigeonhole a pupil?
3. As a beginning teacher, what are some things you might do to minimize the possibility of assigning certain expectations to a given student based on nothing more than ethnic group membership or gender?

CLASSROOM APPROACHES TO
MULTICULTURAL AND SEX-EQUITY STUDIES

Approaches used in developing these lessons either focus on a single group or feature a multiple-perspectives focus. The single-group approach looks at a single group or culture in depth. For example, one instructional sequence might center on women's roles during a key historical period and another might focus on experiences of immigrants from Southeast Asia.

The multiple-perspectives approach typically takes a given problem or event and concentrates on how it is seen and interpreted by people from two or more groups. These lessons help learners to "step into the shoes" of others and to become more sensitive to their views. The settlement of the United States, for example, might be the subject of a multiple-perspectives study. English, French, Spanish, and native American points of view, of both men and women, could be included.

Single-Group Studies: General Characteristics

It is particularly important that single-group lessons be free from damaging stereotypes and distortions. In preparing for lessons of this kind, teachers must become well informed about the group to be studied. Single-group studies are designed to help learners become better acquainted with the special perspectives of the group they are studying. Optimally, pupils will be able to appreciate how group members interpret reality. To accomplish this objective, lessons must go beyond superficial introduction of the group's food, clothing, and religious preferences, and examine their values, ethics, and traditions.

Single-group studies should provide general information about the group's history. This content is designed to help learners identify with struggles and experiences that, over time, have helped to shape members' perspectives. Additionally, historical content highlights relationships between the group and the larger society of which it is a part. Changes in this relationship over time often provide insights into present perspectives of group members. For example, individuals who are suspicious of the motives of others may be members of groups that have been systematically and officially repressed in the past by representatives of a larger, majority culture.

Contributions of the focus group in such areas as art, music, literature, science, mathematics, and government are often included in these lessons. Studying cultural adaptation provides opportunities for pupils to understand that some groups have made innovative responses to trying conditions. For example, studies of certain Eskimo groups often highlight their successful adjustment to extremely cold climatic conditions. Many of their practices were adapted by early European explorers of the far north. Without the contributions of the Eskimos, successful European and American exploration of the world's polar regions would have been impossible.

Single-group studies also focus on issues of import that highlight the values of the group. Positions taken on key issues help define the group's perspectives and priorities, and helps pupils to recognize that individual groups tend to have their own agendas. This recognition contributes to pupils' understanding that healthy conflict is a hallmark of our democratic society.

Single-Group Studies: Examples of Classroom Approaches

A group's music reveals a great deal about the worldview of its members. In the following example, the national anthem of Mexico is used as a beginning point for learning about Mexican values and culture.

LESSON
▪ IDEA ▪

What Does a National Anthem Tell Us about People?

Grade level: 4–6. Objectives: Learners can (1) develop one or two hypotheses about the history of Mexico, (2) identify two or more values or basic beliefs of the Mexican people, and (3) identify two or more sources that they can consult to validate and clarify their hypotheses.

Suggested Procedures: Ask class members if they know what is meant by the term *national anthem.* Discuss the "Star-Spangled Banner" with the class. Ask learners why the song is important. Go over the words. Ask pupils to try to identify what the song tells us about the history and the values of the people of the United States.

Provide learners with copies of the English translation of the words of "Himno National," the national anthem of Mexico. (If available, play a recording of the anthem to familiarize pupils with the music as well as the words.) Review some of the unfamiliar words and symbols. Answer any questions learners might have. Ask learners to state several hypotheses about what the anthem reveals about the history of Mexico. Write these hypotheses on an overhead transparency and project them for all to see or, alternatively, write them on the chalkboard.

Himno National

Mexicans when the trumpet is calling,
Grasp your sword and your harness assemble.
Let the guns with their thunder appalling
Make the Earth's deep foundations to tremble.
Let the guns with their thunder appalling
Make the Earth's deep foundations to tremble.
May the angel divine, O Dear Homeland,
Crown thy brow with the olive branch of peace;
For thy destiny, traced by God's own hand
In the heavens, shall ever increase.
But shall ever the proud foe assail thee,
And with insolent foot profane thy ground,
Know, dear country, thy sons shall not fail thee,
Ev'ry one thy soldier shall be found, thy soldier
    ev'ry one shall be found.

Blessed Homeland, thy children have vowed them
If the bugle to battle should call,
They will fight with the last breath allowed them
Till on thy loved altars they fall.
Let the garland of life thine be;
Unto them be deathless fame;
Let the laurel of victory be assigned thee,
Enough for the the tomb's honored name.
> Lyrics by Francisco Gonzales Bocanegra
> Music by Jaime Nuño

Ask members of the class what they think the anthem suggests is important to the Mexican people. Write their ideas on another transparency or on the chalkboard.

Ask pupils where they think they might get information about Mexico that they could use to test the accuracy of their ideas. Encourage them to think about such resources as books, films, interviews with people who have traveled to Mexico, and guest speakers of Mexican descent.

Divide the class into cooperative learning groups. Ask each group to work with one or more of the hypotheses generated by the class. Have each group find information relating to their hypotheses and reporting back to the class.

Challenge group members to present their information in interesting and creative ways. Encourage them to use pictures, murals, charts, or role playing. After each group reports, have the class decide whether the focus hypotheses should be retained, modified, or rejected. This portion of the activity may generate new hypotheses, which can also be discussed.

As a followup, some pupils might enjoy learning the Spanish words of the anthem.

Another rich source of material for lessons focusing on single groups is children's literature, which typically has more appeal for learners than their school texts. The growing trend of using children's literature to teach reading ought to have a counterpart in the social studies. Good children's literature can be particularly useful as a vehicle for teaching the perspectives of particular cultural groups. The following lesson, focusing on native Americans, draws on two well-written, popular books for young people, *The Legend of the Bluebonnet* by Tomie DePaola and *The Girl Who Loved Wild Horses* by Paul Goble.

LESSON
▪ *IDEA* ▪

How Do Legends Help Us Understand People?
> *Grade Level:* 1–3.
> *Objectives:*

1. Learners can identify two or three specific aspects of native American culture as reflected in their legends.
2. Learners can cite one or more examples that illustrate how native Americans view their relationship with nature.

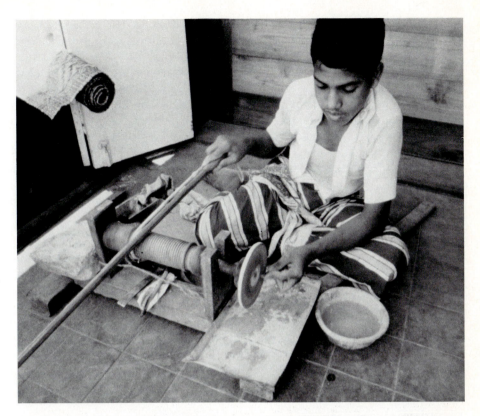

This boy from Sri Lanka is polishing gems. Relating the activities of children in other cultures to our own can stimulate some exciting multicultural learnings.

3. Learners can point out one or more aspects of native American culture that might conflict with aspects of the dominant Western culture.

Materials needed: *The Legend of the Bluebonnet*, by Tomie DePaola (New York: G. P. Putnam's Sons, 1983), and *The Girl Who Loved Wild Horses*, by Paul Goble (New York: Bradbury Press, 1978).
Suggested Procedures:

1. Begin by asking the class whether anyone has had experience riding a horse or taking care of horses. Encourage pupils to share their experiences. Ask them to tell how they feel about horses. Introduce them to *The Girl Who Loved Wild Horses* by Paul Goble. Tell the class that you are going to read them a native American legend about a girl who loved horses.
2. Read the story. Stop as necessary to clarify meanings of words, respond to pupils' questions, and share illustrations with the class.
3. Ask questions such as these: "What do you think this story means?" "What does it tell us about how native Americans felt about their world?" "What things were important to them?" Read aloud the two songs at the end of the

book. Then, ask questions such as: "What do these songs tell us?" "Do they reveal feelings that are different from those most of us have?" "What are the differences?"

4. Read aloud *The Legend of the Bluebonnet* by Tomie DePaola. Ask questions similar to those asked about *The Girl Who Loved Wild Horses*. Ask pupils what they think these people would have felt if others arrived and began hunting the wild horses and plowing under the bluebonnets to make room for houses and factories.

5. Conclude the study by helping pupils find other books dealing with lives of native Americans. Ask them to think about traditional native American customs as they read these materials. Particularly, urge pupils to consider how these customs might conflict with dominant Western cultural practices.

Using language appropriate for learners, explain that when two different cultures come together changes occur. Sometimes these changes can bring harm to members of cultural groups. Often this happens because people in the larger or dominant culture fail to understand aspects of the other culture. As a class, consider what might be done to minimize this kind of damage to members of minority cultural groups.

To help pupils understand that females, today, have many occupational roles open to them, a single-group lesson can focus on stereotyped views of what jobs are "proper" for women. Pupils should learn that the situation today is different from the past, when relatively few employment roles were thought "suitable" for females.

LESSON
▪ IDEA ▪

What Jobs Can a Woman Have?
Grade level: 4–6.
Objectives:

1. Learners can understand that all jobs are open to women for which they are qualified and that their gender is no longer a critical factor.
2. Learners can describe differences in kinds of jobs open to women today and those open to them thirty or more years ago.
3. Learners can suggest two or more reasons why women enjoy more employment choices today than they did thirty or more years ago.

Suggested Procedures:

1. Ask class members to think about kinds of jobs women can have today. Write ideas on the chalkboard under the heading "Jobs women can hold." Then, ask if there are any jobs women cannot hold. Write any pupil responses on the chalkboard under the heading, "Jobs women cannot hold." Save this information.
2. Divide class members into groups of about five learners each. Provide each group with one or two copies of magazines that are at least thirty years old. (These can frequently be had at rummage or garage sales. Often they are

available at modest cost from used book stores and from resale shops such as Goodwill Industries.) Ask learners in each group to look for pictures of women at work. For each woman pictured, ask pupils to write down the nature of the occupation shown (teacher, nurse, steelworker, and so forth).

3. Ask a spokesperson from each group to report the group's findings. Write this information on the chalkboard next to the information generated during step one. Lead a discussion that requires pupils to examine both the original lists and the list developed after their work with the magazines. Ask them to note any differences and similarities between the lists.

4. Have students re-form into groups. Give each group several copies of current magazines. Again, ask them to look for illustrations of women at work and to note the occupational roles.

5. Ask a representative from each group to share the group's findings. Write the information on the chalkboard. Repeat the discussion outlined in step three. Pupils should find more job roles represented in the current magazines than in either the step one or step three list.

6. Next, ask pupils to compare the kinds of jobs for women found in magazines thirty or more years old with those found in current magazines. Ask them if they can account for any differences. Ask each pupil to write a short paragraph beginning: "As I think about jobs available to women thirty years ago and today, I conclude that . . ."

7. As a followup activity, some pupils may enjoy preparing a bulletin board featuring women in a wide variety of roles. (The teacher may also wish to display some of the excellent posters available from the Organization for Equal Education of the Sexes, Inc. Their address is listed at the end of this chapter.)

Multiple-Perspectives Approach: General Characteristics

The multiple-perspectives approach focuses on a single issue that is presented from the perspective of several different groups. The approach lends itself to easy integration within the elementary social studies program. When a given event or issue is being studied, such as the early European settlement of the Atlantic coast of what is now the United States, lessons can be developed that examine this settlement from the perspectives of both the settlers and indigenous Americans.

In general, multiple-perspectives lessons help pupils grasp the idea that events tend to have varied interpretations. Often these interpretations are tied to the values of individual groups. Solutions that make good sense to people in one group because they uphold this group's values, may not be endorsed by members of another group because they are not consistent with this group's worldview.

Multiple-Perspectives Approach: A Classroom Example

Many films and books have romanticized the westward movement of settlers across the lands that today comprise the continental United States. Accounts of

---

BOX 11-4   Ideas for Multiple-Perspectives Lessons

**Think
About
This**

Events in history quite frequently were viewed in surprisingly different ways by various groups that experienced them. Such events work well as focal points for multiple-perspectives lessons. Think about two events from American history. Identify perspectives on these events of at least two different groups.

---

this settlement process are only beginning to give serious attention to the impact of this wave of settlement on people who were already living in these lands.

**LESSON
• IDEA •**

Moving Westward

Grade Level: 3–6. *Objectives:* Pupils can (1) identify two or more groups of people who were living in the West prior to the arrival of pioneers from the eastern United States, (2) identify several customs and ways of living of these people, and (3) state at least two influences on the ways of life of these people that were a direct result of the pioneers' arrival.

Suggested Procedures:

1. Have the class view a film or read a romanticized account of the Westward Movement or of the Old West. Ask the class to think about what they saw or read. Would pupils like to have lived at this time? Ask if their opinions are based on what they have just seen or read. Introduce them to the idea that there were people already living in the West before the arrival of the pioneers.

2. Divide the class into several groups. Ask each group to find locations of people inhabiting the west in the early 1800s. One group might be assigned to locate where different groups of native Americans lived. Another might focus on locations occupied by settlers who originally entered the area from Mexico. Others might focus on European groups such as the British, French, and Russians. Each group should be furnished with a small outline map of North America. A spokesperson from each group should be assigned to plot the location of the assigned population on the group's map. Be sure materials are available that will allow each group to complete its work successfully.

3. After the group work has been completed, reconvene the class as a single group. Have spokespersons from each group plot the location of its assigned population on a large map. If possible, make copies of this map and distribute it to all members of the class.

4. Next, reconstitute the small groups. Ask each group to find additional information about its assigned population. Particularly, members should find out (a) when members of the assigned population first began to occupy the area they settled, (b) what their motives for coming were, (c) how they made a living, and (d) interesting customs and lifestyles of these people.

5. Reconvene the class. Pose the possibility that pioneers from the eastern United States are about to move into the lands occupied by the people each group has studied. Challenge each group to think about probable reactions of people occupying these lands to the arrival of these newcomers. Give pupils an opportunity to meet again in their groups. Tell them their task is to respond to the movement of the pioneers. Give groups options regarding how they want to make these responses. For example, some groups may wish to write a simulated editorial about this situation. Others may choose to have one or two students present a short speech summarizing reactions.

"Rhonda, your story about the hard-driving woman who rises to become president of a major corporation is good *in general.* But, I wonder about the scene where you have her turning to her subordinates to say, "Just call me 'Little Lady'.""

6. To follow up on the presentation of the individual groups, add the perspective of yet another group involved in the Westward Movement: the women. Read the class the following account, taken from the diary of a young woman who moved west with her husband.

Only women who went west in 1859 understand what a woman had to endure. There was no road, no stores, and, many times, no wood for a fire. I had a new baby, and it was teething and suffering from fever. The child took nearly all my strength. I became very weak. My weight fell and fell. In the end, I was all the way down to ninety pounds.

After reaching Denver, we heard that gold had been discovered in the mountains. On the nineteenth of February, 1860, I was taken from my sick bed and placed in a wagon and we started for the new mines. No woman had yet been there. After several days travel we came late at night to Salt Creek. We tried the water and found that it was not good. We tied the oxen to the wagon so that they could not drink the water and went to bed with nothing to eat. That night it got very cold.

The next day we moved to Trout Creek and found the water good. Several men had left Denver a few days ahead of us. We wanted to join up with them but had seen no signs of them. The men decided to search for them, so they shouldered their rifles and started out in search of footprints. Each went in a different direction. The men had not returned by dark, and I felt very alone. I allowed the small donkey to come into the tent with me. I put my head on him and cried in the loneliness of the soul. (Adapted from W. M. Thayer, *Marvels of the New West*. Norwich, CT: Henry Bill Publishing Company, 1888, pp. 246–53.)

7. After pupils have finished making their group reports and have read and thought about the diary excerpt, ask them to make some general statements about the impact of the Westward Movement on different groups of people. As a culminating activity, involve learners in developing a play, drawing a wall mural, or writing a personal history of the Westward Movement.

Other multiple-perspectives lessons can be developed that introduce pupils to conflicting accounts of historical events, use letters to the editor or editorials from different newspapers that present conflicting views of contemporary issues, and expose learners to opposing view points by scheduling class speakers from groups with different views on controversial issues.

SOURCES OF INFORMATION

Multicultural Lessons

There are many idea sources for both single-group and multiple-perspectives approaches to multicultural learning. The *Education Index* includes many listings of articles in professional education journals that provide guidelines for such lessons. Specific examples frequently appear in journals such as *Social Education* and *The Social Studies*. Books are also available that include ideas for multicultural lessons. One that is particularly good is Carl A. Grant and Christine E. Sleeter's *Turning on Learning: Five Approaches for Multicultural Teaching—Plans for Race, Class, Gender, and Disability* (Columbus, OH: Merrill, 1989). This volume contains eminently detailed directions for implementing a variety of multicultural lessons.

A particularly useful classroom supplement for multicultural lessons is the Ethnic Cultures of America Calendar. This calendar is published annually and is available from: Educational Extension Systems, P.O. Box 259, Clarks Summit, PA 18411. The calendar features information for each day of the year about celebrations and events that are meaningful to different ethnic groups residing in the United States. In addition, there are several pages of information about the ethnic cultures of America, about various calendars in use throughout the world, and about holidays of many world religious groups.

Some additional places to write for information that might be included in multicultural lessons are:

The Balch Institute for Ethnic Studies
18 South 7th Street
Philadelphia, PA 19106

Center for Migration Studies
209 Flagg Place
Staten Island, NY 10304

Center for the Study of Ethnic Publications
Kent State University
Kent, OH 44242

Immigration History Research Center
University of Minnesota
Minneapolis, MN 55455

Institute of Texan Cultures
University of Texas
San Antonio, Texas 78294

Sex-Equity Lessons

There are many sources of information for sex-equity lessons, particularly those that focus on women's issues. The Upper Midwest Women's History Center for Teachers makes available a long list of information sources. This document can be obtained by requesting Handout 11, "Resources and Selected Bibliography," from: The Upper Midwest Women's History Center for Teachers, Central Community Center, 6300 Walker St., St. Louis Park, MN 55416.

An especially good source of visual materials is the Organization for Equal Education of the Sexes, Inc. This organization makes available more than one hundred 11-by-17-inch posters. Many feature women from history, and contemporary women in nontraditional occupations. The collection is multicultural and includes women with disabilities. Each poster includes a brief biography of the woman or women depicted. The materials are inexpensive. For a complete catalog, send $2.00 (as of this writing) to: Organization for Equal Education of the Sexes, Inc., 744 Carroll Street, 2nd Floor, Brooklyn, New York 11215.

The Population Reference Bureau publishes "The World's Women: A Profile." This large wall chart contains information about women throughout the world. For ordering information, write: Population Reference Bureau, Inc., 2213 M Street N.W., Washington, DC 20037.

Following are other organizations that provide materials of interest to teachers planning lessons with a sex-equity focus:

National Women's History Project
P.O. Box 3716
Santa Rosa, CA 95402

WEAL: Women's Equity Action League
1250 I Street N.W.
Washington, DC 20005

ISIS—Women's International Information and Communication Services
P.O. Box 25711
Philadelphia, PA 19144

KEY IDEAS IN SUMMARY

1. Schools must serve the needs of all learners who attend. In an increasingly diverse society, this means that many different cultural and ethnic perspectives must be supported. Negative stereotypes relating to ethnic minorities and females must be eliminated. A priority for social studies education is to develop the full potential of each learner.

2. At various times, minority group children have been viewed in different ways. The "genetic deficit" explanation, the "cultural deficit" explanation," the "communication process" explanation, and the "perceived labor market" explanation have all been offered as reasons many children from minority cultures have not done well at school. Today, these explanations have largely been dismissed as weak excuses for the system's failure to serve the needs of minorities. What is needed is a commitment to serve the needs of minority learners in a serious, accountable way.

3. To the extent possible, multicultural and sex-equity lessons should (a) help learners develop a respect for cultures different from their own, (b) provide pupils with opportunities to work with people from different groups, (c) help pupils to recognize the validity of different cultural perspectives, (d) help all learners develop a pride in their own cultural heritage, (e) assist pupils to appreciate that values differences are often the source of conflicts between and among groups.

4. Among general classroom procedures that can help pupils become sensitive to diversity are: (a) Learners of different backgrounds should be included in each group when the class is divided into smaller units for special projects. (b) Teachers need to be aware of their own perspectives and how these might vary from those of their pupils. (c) Teaching methods should be modified to accommodate a variety of learning styles. (d) Evaluation procedures must be as free as possible from cultural and social bias. (e) Teachers need to monitor their own behavior to assure they are not unconsciously favoring any one group of learners.

5. Classroom approaches to multicultural and sex-equity learning include the single-group approach and the multiple-perspectives approach. The single-group approach is designed to help learners become so familiar with one group that they can appreciate how its members interpret reality. The multiple-perspectives approach focuses on a single issue, which is introduced in a way that highlights views of several different groups.

6. Many sources of information are available for teachers wishing to implement multicultural and sex-equity lessons. These include examples of lessons, background materials for learners, instructional support items, and background information for classroom teachers.

POSTTEST

Answer each of the following true/false questions.

1. The most contemporary and most widely supported explanation for the poor academic performance of many minority learners is the "genetic deficit" view.

2. An important purpose of lessons with a multicultural emphasis is helping pupils develop a respect for cultures other than their own.

3. When they assign pupils to groups, teachers are strongly urged to include only members of a single ethnic or cultural group within any one group.

4. Standardized tests sometimes cause problems for learners from minority cultural groups.

5. Multiple-perspectives lessons can help learners appreciate that some problems have no answers that are universally acknowledged to be correct.

QUESTIONS

1. What social studies goals link multicultural and sex-equity education?

2. How well have minority group learners done in school as compared to majority group learners?

3. What are some basic goals of multicultural and sex-equity education?

4. What are some things teachers can do in their classrooms to provide a general atmosphere that is supportive of multicultural and sex-equity learning?

5. What distinguishes a single-group approach from a multiple-perspectives approach?

6. How would you respond to someone who proposed that the major goal of the social studies should be to eliminate differences among groups for the purpose of creating a single "American" culture?

7. Some people have explained low academic achievement of some minority students as being caused by (a) a genetic deficit, (b) a cultural deficit, (c) a communications problem, or (d) a perceived labor market problem. What criticisms have been made of these views by people who feel that schools should commit strongly to meeting the needs of learners from minority cultural groups?

8. In what ways might your personal cultural heritage inhibit your ability to develop good multicultural lessons in your classroom?

9. How might an emphasis on multicultural education be different in classes composed largely of pupils from the majority culture and classes composed largely of minority group pupils?

10. How would you defend sex-equity lessons in a community where many parents hold the view that certain social roles and jobs should be reserved for males and that others should be reserved for females?

EXTENDING UNDERSTANDING AND SKILL

1. Make arrangements to observe in an elementary social studies class. Note how the teacher interacts with male pupils, female pupils, and pupils from different cultural groups. Can you identify patterns that may cause difficulties for some learners?

2. Take time to reflect on your own cultural background and your personal life experiences. What values are most important to you? What are your images and expectations of members of different cultural groups? How might your perspectives affect your ability to teach individuals with different world views?

3. Prepare a report for your instructor on images of minority cultural groups and females included in photographs in an elementary school social studies text. Choose a text used at a grade level you might like to teach. Be certain to look for kinds of jobs being performed by minority group members and females. If time permits, you might wish to do this with two books, one published recently and one published twenty or more years ago.

4. Prepare a plan for a single-group lesson for a cultural group different from your own. Be certain to include a variety of proposed instructional approaches. Ask your course instructor to critique your plan.

5. Organize a group of five or six people from your class. Identify two or three key episodes from American history. (settlement of the West, initial legalization of slavery in some states, the Homestead Act and its provision of free lands, the annexation of Texas, the Gadsden Purchase, the Boston Tea Party, and so forth.) For each selected episode, brainstorm to identify as many approaches as you can to teach pupils how these events were viewed by members of different cultural groups. Prepare a copy of all ideas generated, and distribute the information to others in the class.

REFERENCES

ERICKSON, F. "Transformation and School Success: The Politics and Culture of Educational Achievement." *Anthropology and Education Quarterly* (December 1987), pp. 335–56.

GEZI, F. "Issues in Multicultural Education." *ERQ: Educational Research Quarterly* (Fall 1981), pp. 5–14.

GOOD, T. L., AND J. E. BROPHY. *Looking in Classrooms*, 4th ed. New York: Harper & Row, 1987.

GRANT, C. A., AND C. E. SLEETER. *Turning On Learning: Five Approaches for Multicultural Teaching—Plans for Race, Class, Gender, and Disability.* Columbus, OH: Merrill Publishing Company, 1989.

RIST, R. C. "On Understanding the Process of School: The Contributions of Labeling Theory." In J. A. Ballentine, ed., *Schools and Society: A Reader in Education and Sociology.* Palo Alto, CA: Mayfield, 1985, pp. 88–106.

THAYER, W. M. *Marvels of the New West.* Norwich, CT: Henry Bill Publishing Company, 1888.

SUPPLEMENTAL READING

ALLEN, J. P., AND E. J. TURNER, EDS. *We The People: An Atlas of America's Ethnic Diversity.* New York: Macmillan, 1988.

BAPTISTE, H. P. J. *Multicultural Education: A Synopsis.* New York: University Press of America, 1979.

HAMILTON, V. *The People Could Fly: American Black Folktales.* New York: Alfred Knopf, 1985.

HARVEY, K. D., L. D. HARJO, AND J. K. JACKSON. *Teaching About Native Americans.* Bulletin No. 94. Washington, DC: National Council for the Social Studies, 1990.

KENDALL, F. E. *Diversity in the Classroom: A Multicultural Approach to the Education of Young Children.* New York: Teachers College Press, 1983.

LEACOCK, E., AND H. SAFA. *Women's Work: Development and the Division of Labor by Gender*. South Hadley, MA: Bergin and Garvey, 1986.

SANDAY, P. R. *Female Power and Male Dominance—On the Origins of Sexual Inequality*. London: Cambridge University Press, 1981.

SEAGER, J., AND A. OLSON. *Women in the World Atlas*. New York: Touchstone Books, 1986.

STERLING, D., ED. *We Are Your Sisters*. New York: W. W. Norton, 1984.

THERNSTROM, S., ED. *Harvard Encyclopedia of American Ethnic Groups*. Cambridge, MA: Belknap Press, 1980.

12

ENVIRONMENTAL AND ENERGY EDUCATION

This chapter provides information to help the reader:

1. point out recent events that have focused increasing attention on the environment,

2. describe specific environmental problems including global warming, deforestation, toxic waste pollution, and ozone depletion,

3. suggest likely long-term results of failure to respond to threats to the environment,

4. develop instructional activities designed to sensitize learners to environmental concerns,

5. describe progress that has been made in utilizing alternative, renewable energy sources, and

6. point out some classroom procedures that might help learners more fully grasp issues associated with electrical energy conservation.

PRETEST

Answer each of the following true/false questions.

1. In the late 1980s and 1990s, public interest in environmental issues appeared to be declining.
2. Some scientists believe that use of carbon-based fuels contributes to a global warming trend.
3. Because global warming will enable crops to be grown in areas now too cold to support agriculture, this trend is expected to increase the world's food supply over the next few years.
4. There are suspicions that deforestation, reduction in the total world acreage of trees, will lead to a buildup of carbon dioxide in the atmosphere.
5. Toxic waste problems have affected people in many parts of the world.

INTRODUCTION

Environmental issues commanded much public attention in the late 1960s and early 1970s. During the 1980s, less was heard about these concerns. Committed environmentalists continued to press their case, but the federal government took a much less active environmental role during the Reagan presidency.

During the 1988 election campaign, environmental issues again moved to center stage, emphasized by both Democratic and Republican candidates. After the election, the Bush administration suggested that a commitment to protecting the environment was a national priority. This renewed federal interest has stimulated increasing environmental interest by others.

In part this broadened public awareness has resulted from extensive media coverage of threats to the environment beginning in the mid 1980s. Such coverage notably increased after the Soviet Union's nuclear disaster at Chernobyl in 1986. Radiation from this explosion crossed national frontiers. It underscored the multinational nature of environmental issues. What impacts the environment in one nation also affects the broader, global environment. Recognizing that irresponsible action in one location may undermine the planet's ability to sustain life, citizen concerns worldwide now range across a broad spectrum of issues.

These concerns will be even more important in the future. It is important for young people in the schools to be introduced to them. Resolving pressing environmental problems will require social, political, economic, and personal adjustments. Hence, environmental and energy questions have a legitimate place in the elementary school social studies program.

Dramatic incidents such as the sinking of an oil tanker can be used to develop environmental and energy issues.

PRESSING ENVIRONMENTAL AND ENERGY CHALLENGES

Global Warming

Large numbers of scientists believe that the world is experiencing a global warming trend (Jacobson 1989, p. 71), resulting from widespread use of carbon-based fuels such as coal and petroleum products. Burning these fuels releases carbon dioxide and other gases, causing a *greenhouse effect* as these gases retain heat in the lower atmosphere.

Warming poses a number of serious challenges. If the trend continues, large volumes of water that are now locked in the polar ice caps may be released. Brown, Flavin, and Postel (1989) note that "a temperature rise of three degrees Celsius by the year 2050 would raise sea level by 50–100 centimeters. By the end of the next century, sea level may be up as much as two meters" (p. 10). This will pose a tremendous threat to low-lying, densely populated lands where much of the world's rice and other crops are grown. It is estimated that as many as 17 million people in Bangladesh and as many as 8.5 million in Egypt could be forced from their homes (Brown et al. 1989).

Global warming may also influence kinds of crops that can be grown. Tree crops are particularly likely to be affected. Tress take years to develop, and cannot adapt to rapid climatic change. Some of the world's great orchard areas may be destroyed. Replacement of tree crops by planting new areas will take decades.

Deforestation

Deforestation, destruction of the world's supply of trees, has been occurring at an astonishing rate. In 1987 alone people cleared Amazon rainforest acreage equal in area to the entire country of Austria (Brown et al. 1989). This represents a severe reduction in the earth's total green plant cover. There are fears this reduction may be contributing to the buildup of atmospheric carbon dioxide widely thought to be responsible for the greenhouse effect and global warming. Green plants take in carbon dioxide and give off oxygen. Burning fossil fuels produces carbon dioxide. At the same time world forest acreage has gone down, fossil fuel consumption has gone up. In other words, fewer leafy surfaces are available to absorb the carbon dioxide and to produce oxygen, contributing to ever-greater concentrations of carbon dioxide and to rising average temperatures worldwide.

In addition to the reduction in the world's oxygen-generating capacity, global deforestation has had other negative consequences. For example, the ability of mountain areas to hold rainwater has diminished as the forest cover has been removed. Floods in Bangladesh have been made worse in recent years by the deforestation of the Himalayan mountains and a resultant decrease their capacity to hold back runoff water (Brown et al. 1989).

Industrial abuse and resource mismanagement are responsible for much of this loss. Deforestation has also resulted from high rates of population growth. For example, destruction of Amazon forest lands has been attributed to a population increase that has led people to move away from high-priced lands to create new affordable farms elsewhere in the Amazon Basin. In other world areas, population pressure has resulted in desperate searches for inexpensive fuels, often leading people to cut down available timber.

Toxic Waste

The problem of toxic waste is one of chemical contamination. As Jacobson (1989) points out, this can result suddenly from a specific event, for example a wreck involving a truck carrying dangerous chemicals, or it can develop slowly over time. This latter condition has been found in many places throughout the world where dangerous chemicals have been dumped over a period of years. In time, water supplies, food products, and even the surrounding air may become contaminated.

Toxic waste contamination has brought disaster to people in many parts of the world. In this country, 900 people were forced to move from their homes built along the Love Canal, a filled-in chemical dump site in New York State. Soviet authorities announced in 1987 that the city of Ufa had become so chemically contaminated that it was virtually unfit for human occupation. The government of Poland is offering to resettle villagers from one area of the country where chemical pollution has become a severe problem (Jacobson 1989).

BOX 12–1   Teaching the Concept "Deforestation"
            at Different Grade Levls

Think   Think about what you have learned in your teacher preparation program about learning
About   characteristics of pupils of different ages. Develop a list of ideas for introducing the
This   concept "deforestation" to learners in (a) grades K to two, (b) grades three and four,
            and (c) grades five and six. Share your ideas with your instructor and the class, and
            solicit their comments.

In recent years, the world's major industrial countries have tightened regulations governing dumping of dangerous chemicals. One unpleasant result has been a tendency for industries to ship these dangerous wastes to less developed countries for disposal. Increasingly, these countries are becoming more sophisticated about the dangers of these chemicals. More and more governments throughout the world are acting to place severe restrictions on the kinds of wastes they will accept for disposal.

Ozone Depletion

Ozone is a form of oxygen with an altered atomic structure. A large ozone layer exists in the upper atmosphere. This layer helps to keep dangerous ultraviolet radiation from reaching the earth's surface. In recent years, evidence has been accumulating that points to a gradual destruction of this atmospheric ozone. Scientists first noted that a hole in the ozone layer was occurring periodically over Antarctica. More recent evidence has suggested that the ozone layer around the entire globe is eroding (Shea 1989).

A primary cause of this erosion is release into the atmosphere of chlorofluorocarbons, or CFCs. CFCs are used predominantly as refrigerants in air conditioning units and as aerosol propellants. They also are used in some forms of insulation, and in certain important commercial solvents.

Destruction of the ozone layer can have serious consequences for animal and plant life. A diminished ozone layer poses the probability of increased levels of ultraviolet rays striking the body, which can lead to skin cancer and to eye cataracts. Cynthia Pollock Shea, an authority on the threat to the ozone layer, states that "reduced crop yields, depleted marine fisheries, materials damage, and increased smog are also attributable to higher levels of radiation. The phenomenon is global and will affect the well-being of every person in the world" (1989, p. 78).

Nations of the world have recognized the seriousness of this problem. More than thirty countries have signed the Montreal Protocol on Substances that Deplete the Ozone Layer. This agreement calls for nations of the world to work to cut CFC emissions in half by 1998. Some experts hope that replacement chemicals can be developed that will allow for a total ban on CFCs by the year 2000.

Among actions taken to deal with the CFC problem are efforts to prevent their release directly into the atmosphere. It has been a common practice for CFCs in car air conditioners to be released into the atmosphere when units are taken for repair. New equipment has now been developed that allows service personnel to recapture CFC coolant, store it, and recharge it back into units once they are repaired.

Serious efforts are under way to find replacement chemicals for CFCs that retain their useful properties without posing threats to the environment. Some chemicals for air conditioners have been discovered that will not harm the ozone layer, but these alternatives are less efficient coolants. They may require larger car engines to drive the air conditioning unit. This, in turn, could pour additional pollutants into the atmosphere from the larger volume of exhaust gases produced by the bigger engines.

Scientists agree that a solution to the ozone layer problem will not come quickly or easily. But the effort is drawing increasing attention from governments and scientists throughout the world. It appears likely that governments will allocate additional resources to finding a remedy to this continuing threat to life and health.

Issues Associated with Energy

Concerns about energy have come in for special attention in recent years. Many energy sources that are used today produce side effects that can damage plants, soils, and even human health. Common fuels such as coal, oil, natural gas, and wood produce huge quantities of carbon dioxide as a byproduct of combustion. As has been noted previously, this buildup is associated with a dangerous global warming trend.

Additionally, many widely used fuels are nonrenewable. The supply of coal and oil, for example, is finite. Quantities of these nonrenewable fuels are not likely to be sufficient to meet future energy needs (Flavin 1988). Nuclear energy is not an attractive alternative because of serious safety concerns. Today, the search is on for safe, renewable energy sources.

Hydropower, power generated through water, is an energy source that is safe, and its capacity does not diminish over time. One difficulty with hydropower is that sites suitable for development of hydroelectric plants are limited. Most of the best ones have already been utilized.

Many other renewable energy sources trace back to forces set in motion by the sun. Shea (1988) states that "uneven heating of the earth's surface produces wind, yesterday's winds are today's waves, and a season worth of solar energy is trapped in plants whose residues can be burned as fuel" (p. 62).

Efforts appear particularly promising for increasing the use of renewable plants and animal wastes as fuel. Shea points out that energy from these sources already contributes 15 percent of the energy used worldwide (p. 62). In some tropical areas, measures are being taken to increase acreage devoted to fast-growing varieties of sugar cane. Alcohol fuels derived from the sugar provide a reliable renewable energy source as well as a dependable market for farmers. Brazil has worked particularly hard at increasing use of alcohol-based fuels. In 1986, half of the nation's automobile fuel came from this source (Shea 1988).

Rice is one of the world's most abundant agricultural products. In preparing rice for market, husks are removed. Every five tons of finished rice yields about one ton of rice husks. These husks have an energy content about equal to wood, and have great promise as a fuel source. Other crop byproducts that are potential fuels include coconut shells, cotton stalks, fruit pits, and seed hulls of all kinds (Shea 1988).

In addition to energy from plants, work is being done to tap more directly into the sun's energy. Solar collection devices are being promoted as a means of transferring this energy to air and water. Research is underway that may result in large-scale production of electricity produced by the *photovoltaic effect,* a term scientists use to describe electricity generated when the sun's rays strike certain substances.

In some parts of the world, wind power is being harnessed to drive electricity-generating turbines, though this is possible only in areas where winds blow relatively consistently. Today, groups of windmills are providing substantial quantities of electricity to parts of California and to other world areas as well.

Scientists are seeking still other alternatives to traditional energy sources. Exploratory work is underway to determine if it is feasible to exploit temperature

"If we could harness all of this energy, our reserves of coal, oil, and natural gas would last forever."

differences between shallow and deep ocean water to produce energy. A priority for those interested in practical use of renewable energy is the development of systems to store energy from windmills and solar devices for later use. Pollution problems and dwindling supplies of coal, oil, natural gas, and wood demand that research into dependable renewable energy sources increase in the years ahead.

These environmental and energy concerns are but a few of those that are attracting attention of people throughout the world. Others include such issues as acid rain, general air pollution, general water pollution, desertification of productive agricultural lands, and maintaining environments to sustain the continued existence of endangered species.

Good information sources are available for teachers interested in general environmental education and energy education. Publications of the World Watch Institute are particularly recommended. This respected organization publishes the annual *State of The World* report, which contain well-researched articles that provide up-to-date reports on environmental issues of all kinds. World Watch Institute also publishes *World Watch*, a bimonthly journal. Each issue features a number of articles centering on important environmental topics. For information write to: The World Watch Institute, 1776 Massachusetts Avenue, N.W., Washington, DC 20036.

Many other organizations and government agencies publish materials related to the environmental and energy education. A particularly fine program has been produced by the Missouri Department of Conservation. The materials, entitled Conservation Seeds, include environmentally related activities for kindergarten

---

BOX 12–2   **Should Elementary School Pupils Deal with Difficult Environmental Issues?**

A parent who was informed about a school district's interest in requiring an instructional unit on "environmental challenges" in the elementary social studies program made these comments.

> I am very sensitive to the need to preserve our environment for future generations. But, I also recognize that many environmental issues are extremely complex. Often, proposed "solutions" seem to produce more problems than they are solving. In fact, even experts are discouraged by the magnitude of the problems we will be facing in the next ten to twenty years.
>
> Are young elementary children ready to confront these discouraging problems? I don't think so. I am afraid that this instructional unit might leave them with terribly negative feelings about the future. Let's reserve this kind of content for the high school years when they will have a more mature perspective on these issues.

Think   1. What are the major concerns of this parent?
About   2. Do you believe they are valid?
This   3. How would you respond to this person?

and early primary-grades pupils and are outstanding. For information about available materials, write to: Missouri Department of Conservation, Education Section, P.O. Box 180, Jefferson City, MO 65102.

CLASSROOM APPROACHES TO BUILDING
ENVIRONMENTAL AND ENERGY AWARENESS

Elementary social studies lessons focusing on the environment and on energy seek to develop youngsters' sensitivity to these issues. Maura O'Connor (1983, pp. 2–3) has developed a useful list of purposes for such lessons, which we have adapted here.

Environmental lessons seek to help learners

- develop an appreciation for the immediate environment,
- note the existence of interrelationships that tie together all living things,
- point out what individuals can do to maintain healthy local, regional, national, and global environments,
- appreciate the necessity of protecting certain natural areas, and
- point out threats to environmental quality and how they might be met.

Suggestions introduced in this section are not meant to be exhaustive in scope. They simply illustrate kinds of approaches some teachers have found to be successful. Specific lessons need to be tailored to age levels, interests, and levels of sophistication of children in individual classes.

Sensitizing Learners to the Problem of Unnecessary Waste

Most elementary school children (and many adults, too) have not thought much about how much garbage we generate. More specifically, few have considered whether too much is being thrown away and whether some items that end up in the trash might have additional uses.

Elementary teachers have developed several approaches to helping their pupils become more aware of problems associated with excessive litter and waste. Two widely used lessons are "Contents of the Wastebasket" and "The Dreaded Litter Creature."

LESSON
▪ IDEA ▪

Contents of the Wastebasket
Grade Level: 6. *Objective:* Learners will develop a plan for conserving resources. *Suggested Procedure:* This activity can be organized in many ways. One alternative involves a careful examination of all trash contained in the wastebasket at the end of the school day. In preparation for this activity, the teacher needs to bring a large plastic garbage bag to school. At the end of the day, contents of the class

wastebasket are emptied into the garbage bag and kept in a safe place until needed (usually the next day). The following steps are involved in the activity.

1. Organizing learners and displaying the contents of the wastebasket.
2. Sorting contents of the wastebasket into categories.
3. Describing sources of litter in each category.
4. Discussing what items might have been more effectively used or might be capable of reuse.
5. Establishing an action plan.

Organizing Learners and Displaying Wastebasket Contents. At the appropriate time, the teacher gathers members of the class around and carefully empties the garbage bag containing the wastebasket contents onto newspapers or sheets of butcher paper spread on the floor (or on the surface of a large table).

Sorting into Categories. Members of the class are invited to suggest categories into which items might be sorted. Sometimes teachers will ask one or more learners to move individual items into piles that are then organized. Categories may be of many kinds. Some learners may decide to put all paper items in one pile, wooden ones in another, and items made of plastics and other materials in still another pile. Some children may decide to sort objects by color. The teacher may decide to write category names on the board or on an overhead transparency and to list all items from the wastebasket belonging to each category. The teacher may ask children to speculate on why some categories have more items than others.

Describing Sources of Litter. The teacher asks children to suggest where litter in each category may have come from. Additional questions include "Do you think the amount of litter we found in this category today is more, less, or about the same that we would find on any day? Why do you think so? If we wanted to reduce the amount of litter in any one of these categories, what could we do?"

Discussing Reuse or Better Use of Items. This step flows logically from the previous one. The teacher asks questions designed to focus learners' attention on conservation-related issues, such as: "Are there some things we found that were thrown away too soon? Could people have used them more before throwing them away? For example, there is only writing on one side of this paper. How might this paper have been used longer before being thrown away? Could some of these things that have been thrown away been used for other things? What other things might they have been used for? If too many people throw away things that still might be used for something, what do you think might happen?"

Establishing an Action Plan. The teacher asks learners to make some decisions that will result in behavioral changes that reflect the need to conserve resources. The class might decide to try to reduce the amount of paper being thrown away. Pupils may then recheck the wastebasket contents periodically to see if less paper was going out each day. Another possibility might be to retrieve all paper not written on both sides. The blank sides could be placed in a "scratch paper" bin. Class members could be encouraged to use paper from this source for practice drawings, informal note taking, and so forth.

Other followup activities are sometimes used to conclude the wastebasket activity. Some teachers involve learners in schoolwide or neighborhood cleanup projects. Sometimes these feature similar analyses of the sources of litter and what might be done to decrease the volume of litter produced. Teachers also often have pupils prepare posters with a litter-reduction theme.

LESSON
▪ IDEA ▪

The Dreaded Litter Creature

Grade Level: 2–4. *Objectives:* Learners can (1) identify ways of preventing litter, and (2) demonstrate that they understand the importance of cleaning up litter. *Suggested Procedure:* This activity sometimes is designed to be used in conjunction with the wastebasket lesson or with a campaign to cleanup the school and its immediate neighborhood. Children are provided with large plastic garbage bags in which to collect litter. After they have followed the teacher's directions and have filled the bags with litter, pupils bring them back to the classroom. The teacher organizes class members into teams, each of which includes three or four pupils.

Each team is challenged to create a "dreaded litter creature" using items in their bags. The teacher provides paste, staples, poster board, pipe cleaners, and other art supplies that might be used by team members as they make their creature. Often teachers find it useful to show class members a "dreaded litter creature" that has been completed previously. The example may suggest to pupils ways in which the project might be approached.

As a final assignment, the teacher asks each group to make a sign to accompany their creature. The sign should focus attention on the issue of litter elimination. Signs might include such phrases as "Zap the Litter Creature!" "Make the Litter Creature an Endangered Species!" "No Litter Creatures Allowed Here!" "Let's Starve the Litter Creature!" To conclude the lesson, the class can display their "dreaded litter creatures" and accompanying signs in the classroom or in a hallway where others in the school can see them.

Developing Environmental Sensitivity through Children's Literature

Many books directed at elementary school pupils deal with environmental education issues. O'Brien and Stoner (1987) identify several of these books. One title they recommend is Brian Wildsmith's *Professor Noah's Spaceship* (New York: Oxford University Press, 1980). This book features content relevant to the topic of pollution.

O'Brien and Stoner point out that this book can provide an excellent starting point for classroom discussion focusing on effects of pollution on human beings and on specific animal species. They suggest followup activities centering around efforts to make records of evidence of pollution in and around pupils' homes, in the school, and in local neighborhoods, and suggest that class members might also make collages or engage in other art projects that will illustrate problems associated with pollution. Reading and discussing the book might also prompt interest in a class-sponsored environmental cleanup project.

O'Brien and Stoner list many other books and include suggestions for developing related environmental education activities. Their article is well worth reading. (See the complete citation in the "References" section at the end of this chapter.)

Learning What is Biodegradable

The adjective *biodegradable* means "capable of being broken down by natural processes such as the action of bacteria." The biodegradable characteristic of grass clippings, for example, make them suitable for use in compost piles. In time, they break down and become part of enriched new soil. Litter and waste products that are biodegradable produce fewer threats to the environment than those, such as many plastics, that are not biodegradable.

To help pupils determine whether some common items are biodegradable, Sisson (1982) suggests a classroom exercise based on burying different items in small containers of soil. This lesson is modified here.

LESSON
▪ IDEA ▪

Biodegradable Litter

Grade Level: 5–6.*Objectives:* Learners can (1) define the term *biodegradable,* (2) state the importance of using biodegradable products, and (3) develop a course of action to reduce nonbiodegradable litter. *Suggested Procedure:*

1. Select six containers, and fill each with garden soil.
2. Bury selected items.
3. Dig up and examine each item once a week for two months and make notes on conditions of the items.
4. Discuss differences in conditions of items as observed over time.
5. Consider further action.

Select Containers. Half-gallon ice cream containers work well. Fill each container with moist garden soil. Assign individual pupils to keep soil watered to maintain moisture levels. This must be done throughout the entire two months of the activity.

Bury Selected Items. Select items to be buried in each container. Take care to select some items that are biodegradable and some that are not. The following items work well:

a. a leaf
b. a piece of a paper bag
c. a foil wrapper from inside a pack of cigarettes or gum
d. a piece of orange peel
e. a pull-top from an aluminum can
f. a small plastic spoon

Bury one item in each half-gallon carton. Label the container with the name of the item it contains. Bury items approximately in the center of each container.

Object	Condition and Comments			
	Week One	**Week Two**	**Week Three**	**Week Four**
Leaf				
Paper bag				
Foil wrapper				
Orange peel				
Can pull-top				
Plastic spoon				

Duplicate chart with appropriate changes for weeks five through eight.

FIGURE 12–1
Sample note-taking chart for an exercise on biodegradable litter

Dig Up and Examine. Once a week, involve the class in digging up and examining the buried items. To do this, gather the class around a large table. Place a plastic sheet over the table top. Select a pupil to dig up each item. Do one container at a time. Caution the pupils to dig carefully to minimize the amount of dirt spilled and to prevent unnecessary damage to the item.

Provide each learner with a note-taking chart. A sample chart is provided in Figure 12.1. Prompt pupils to observe changes in the condition of each item and to take notes on their charts.

Discuss Observed Differences. At the conclusion of the eight-week period, lead a discussion. Encourage learners to refer to their note-taking charts. Ask questions such as these to guide the discussion:

- What things changed the most?
- What things changed the least?
- How might we explain why some things changed a lot and others didn't change much at all?
- What do our observations tell us about differences in how some kinds of litter might harm the soil?
- Why do you think we should be concerned about harming the soil?

Learners should be helped to appreciate that environmentalists generally believe biodegradable litter poses fewer threats to soil quality than nonbiodegradable litter. The teacher should point out that the breakdown of biodegradable material sometimes even provides additional nutrients to the soil.

Consider Further Action. To conclude the activity, ask members of the class to think about things to do to reduce the amount of nonbiodegradable litter. Have them consider actions they might take personally as well as what they might do to encourage others to do. For example, the group might decide to urge their parents to ask for paper bags at the grocery store rather than nonbiodegradable plastic ones. Or they may encourage their parents to take their own reusable fabric or plastic shopping bags to the store. They might suggest ways of reusing aluminum can pull-tops that would make people less likely to throw them away. They might wonder whether items such as chewing gum that are often wrapped in foil might be wrapped in a more biodegradable substance. They might make a personal inventory of the trash basket in their own bedrooms to determine which items are more biodegradable than others. As a result, they might decide to try to reduce the amount of nonbiodegradable trash they throw away each week.

The purpose of this final phase is to help learners understand that biodegradable alternatives are often available for many commonly used nonbiodegradable items. If more biodegradable materials were used, the threat to the world's soils could be reduced.

Much of the effort of environmentalists who are concerned with the negative impact of nonbiodegradable litter focuses on recycling material. Recycling reduces the volume of material that is thrown away and also reduces the demand for new raw materials. Sisson has developed a number of practical classroom lessons focusing on littering and recycling. These lessons appear in her book, *Nature with Children of All Ages.* (See the complete citation in the "References" section at the end of this chapter.)

LESSON
▪ IDEA ▪

Pollution

Grade Level: K–2. *Objective:* Learners can state the impact of automobiles on air pollution. *Suggested Procedure:* Sherri Griffin (1988) suggests a lesson designed to introduce pupils in kindergarten or the earliest primary grades to the concept of pollution. Begin by taking the class outside to the school parking lot. (It is a good idea to have some parent volunteers or another teacher along to monitor learners during this exercise.) Children gather around the car of a parent who has volunteered to help.

Take a piece of clean white cloth and attach it to the car's tailpipe with a strong rubber band. Ask learners to share ideas about what the cloth might look like if the car were driven with it attached to the tailpipe. Accept all ideas.

Next, tell pupils that they are going to be scientists and conduct an experiment. The parent volunteer is going to drive the car around the block. The class will then remove the white cloth and look at it. When the white cloth is removed, ask learners to report what they observe. Compare the condition of the cloth with what they said would happen before the experiment began.

Point to the dark smudges on the cloth and explain that it is pollution. Ask class members their thoughts on what happens to the air when there are lots of cars. Conclude the lesson by discussing some ideas, such as car pooling, that can reduce the amount of air pollution.

LESSON
• IDEA •

Electric Appliance Survey

Grade Level: 4–6. *Objective:* Learners can develop an action plan for conserving energy. At the elementary school level, an important objective of energy education lessons is to help pupils understand that, ultimately, many energy resources are used for the production of electricity. Demand is especially high in societies such as ours that are heavily dependent on electricity sources to run sophisticated equipment, light homes and businesses, and operate heating and cooling systems. Our reliance on electricity can be highlighted during an appliance survey activity.

Suggested Procedures: This activity can be organized in several ways. Sowards (1985) suggests that the teacher ask pupils to draw a rough floor plan of their house or apartment. When they have done so, ask them to draw in locations of household appliances, such as washing machines, dryers, electric stoves, refrigerators, lamps, radios, televisions, vacuum cleaners, ceiling lights, and hair dryers. Alternatively, pupils may simply develop a list indicating numbers of such items in their homes. This procedure should produce a list such as the following:

Appliance	Quantity
Stove	1
Refrigerator	1
Vacuum cleaner	1
Ceiling lights	7
Lamps	9
Radios	4
Televisions	2
Washing machine	1
Clothes dryer	1
Hair dryers	2
Room air conditioners	3

From individual student lists, compile a master list. Use this information as the basis for a discussion focusing on such questions as these:

- Which of these items do you regard as essential?
- Which items would you give up?
- If you didn't have to give up an item, but did have to use it less often, which item or items might you select?
- Which items seem to be turned on for the longest period each day?
- How do you account for differences in amounts of time individual items are used?
- Do you think that because an item is "on" longer during a given day than another item that it necessarily uses more electricity? (Point out here that some appliances use less electricity than others).
- If you wanted to save electricity in your home, what might you do?
- What could we do here at school to save electricity and to encourage others to do so as well?

LESSON
▪ IDEA ▪

Making Energy-Collage Posters
Grade Level: 2–4. *Objectives:* Learners can (1) identify different sources of energy, and (2) classify items according to the type of energy they use. *Suggested Procedure:* An energy-collage poster activity serves well to help younger learners

Understanding alternative energy sources such as this solar unit helps students investigate alternative energy sources.

appreciate that there are different kinds of energy resources. To begin, point out that energy is provided to us in many forms including electricity, natural gas, oil, coal, solar, and wind. Divide learners into teams of about four each. Provide each group with the following materials: (a) several old magazines or catalogs, (b) paste or glue, (c) scissors, (d) light poster board, and (e) marking pens or pencils.

Ask pupils to draw a line across the bottom of the poster board about five inches from the bottom. Tell them not to paste anything on this part of the poster. (They will write information here later.)

Next, instruct pupils to go through the magazines and catalogs and find pictures of items that use energy, such as small appliances, furnaces, automobiles, windmills, and so forth. Have them cut these items out and paste them on the poster board. Carefully monitor pupils while they are engaged in this activity. Urge pupils to fill in all areas of the poster board except for the four-inch "reserved" strip at the bottom.

When students have completed this phase, each team should have a poster collage. At this time, pause to lead a discussion centering on the question of what energy sources are used for each of the items depicted on the posters. After this discussion, instruct team members to write labels indicating the various power sources (e.g., electricity, oil, natural gas, solar, wind) across the top of the "reserved" section at the bottom of the posters.

Next, ask members of each group to write the names of items appearing on their posters that use each of these energy sources under the appropriate label. For example, under the heading "natural gas," items such as "stove," "clothes dryer," and "furnace" might be listed. When all students have completed this phase of the activity, display the posters in the classroom or elsewhere in the school building.

KEY IDEAS IN SUMMARY

1. Environmental and energy concerns attract much public attention today. In part, this interest is due to extensive media coverage of events, such as the explosion at the nuclear facility in Chernobyl, that have had a dramatic impact on the environment. Environmental issues are worldwide in scope. Their resolution will require social, political, and personal adjustments. Hence, environmental education plays an important role in the elementary social studies program.

2. Many scientists today are concerned about global warming, which appears to be associated with a carbon dioxide buildup in the lower atmosphere. This buildup results from widespread burning of carbon-based fuels. Global warming may produce many problems. The world's low-lying areas may flood as the polar ice caps melt and sea level rises. There also may be negative effects on kinds of crops that can be grown, threatening the total supply of available food.

3. There is evidence that global acreage occupied by trees is diminishing rapidly. If this trend continues, supplies of oxygen could be threatened. Green leafy surfaces take in carbon dioxide and give off oxygen, and a diminished supply of trees may result in a buildup of carbon dioxide, thus contributing to global warming.

4. Toxic waste pollution is chemical contamination of the environment. Toxic waste problems have already forced populations out of some areas of the world. More and more governments are placing severe restrictions on places authorized for disposal of dangerous chemical wastes.

5. The ozone layer in the upper atmosphere acts as a filter to keep dangerous ultraviolet radiation from reaching the earth's surface. In recent years, some scientists have discovered that the ozone layer is gradually eroding. This destruction is thought to be from release into the atmosphere of chlorofluorocarbons (CFCs). A diminished ozone layer can have serious consequences for animal and plant life. Exposure to ultraviolet radiation may increase the incidence of skin cancer.

6. Use of energy sources such as coal, oil, wood, and natural gas produces carbon dioxide. In addition to their association with the problem of global warming, these energy fuels exist in limited supplies, and in time will be exhausted. Efforts are under way today to expand use of hydro-electric power, solar power, and other renewable energy sources. There is particular interest in using plant derivatives for fuel, such as alcohol made from sugar cane.

7. Classroom lessons focusing on the environment and energy seek to develop learners' sensitivities to these issues. Among other things, these lessons seek to help them (a) develop an appreciation for their immediate environment, (b) note the interrelationships among all living things; (c) suggest what people can do as individuals to maintain healthy environments, (d) appreciate the need to protect certain natural areas, and (e) point out threats to environmental quality and how they might be met.

POSTTEST

Answer each of the following true/false questions.

1. Some scientists believe that damage to the ozone layer could result in more people suffering from skin cancer.

2. Environmental and energy issues are worldwide in scope.

3. One important purpose of environmental and energy education lessons at the elementary school level is to increase learners' sensitivities to these issues.

4. Today, in no country in the world does a fuel source other than gasoline provide more than 10 percent of the automobile fuel used.

5. Scientists today are particularly interested in increasing the availability and use of renewable fuel sources.

QUESTIONS

1. Why have environmental and energy concerns become so widespread in recent years?

2. What do scientists believe to be the major causes of global warming, and why might this trend pose a threat?

3. What are some environmental consequences of deforestation?

4. What evidence is there that problems associated with toxic waste have become serious?

5. What is one of the primary causes of deterioration of ozone in the upper atmosphere?

6. What are some examples of renewable fuels, and why do many experts favor expanding their use?

7. What are some classroom activities that can be used to introduce students to issues associated with the environment and with energy?

8. Suppose the global warming trend were to continue. Consider the impact on plants, especially on food crops. What might some consequences of this trend be for your own local area?

9. Some environmentalists are proposing that broader use be made of renewable fuel sources such as alcohol. Alcohol can be produced from many plant sources, including corn. Describe what might happen were a regulation imposed requiring people to use only fuel from renewable fuels. (This would mean an immediate end to the use of such traditional fuels such as gasoline, diesel oil, other petroleum-based fuels, and coal.)

10. Not everyone agrees with positions espoused by environmentalists. Some people argue that environmentalists take too pessimistic a view of the future. These critics suggest that human beings have always successfully met whatever challenges that confronted them and that there is no reason to fear the future. How receptive are you to these arguments? Why do you take this position?

11. Much has been written about threats to the environment. In your own view, which threat is the most serious? Why do you think so? What might be done to respond to it?

EXTENDING UNDERSTANDING AND SKILL

1. Identify four or five major environmental issues. Prepare a clipping file of news articles related to each. Try to include at least ten articles for each issue you select. Information about environmental issues changes rapidly in the light of new scientific developments, so include only materials published within the past three years. Prepare a table of contents for your file that will enable you to locate individual items quickly.

2. Prepare an environmental/energy education "how-to" idea collection. Include specific suggestions for introducing content related to environmental and energy concerns to learners. Examine such information sources as *Social Education, The Social Studies, Learning* and *The Instructor.* Your course instructor may know of additional source materials. Include at least ten different ideas in your collection.

3. Select a major environmental issue that you might use as a focus for a lesson at a grade level you wish to teach. Develop a complete lesson. After your lesson has been reviewed and approved by your instructor, make copies to share with others in your class.

4. Interview two or three elementary teachers who teach at a grade level that interests you. Ask them how much attention they give to environmental and energy issues in their classrooms. Specifically, what kinds of lessons do these teachers teach in these areas? Find out whether there are any state or local requirements to include content of this kind. Write up results of your interviews in the form of a report. Submit it to your instructor for review.

5. Organize a brainstorming session in your class. For each elementary grade, solicit responses to this question: "What kinds of environmental and energy issues might be appropriate for learners at this grade?" Select someone to write responses on the chalkboard. Your instructor will lead a followup discussion focusing on the appropriateness of the suggestions.

REFERENCES

Brown, L. R., C. Flavin, and S. Postel. "A World at Risk," in Linda Starke, ed., *State of the World, 1989.* New York: W. W. Norton, 1989, pp. 3–20.

Griffin, S. "Conservation Seeds: Pollution Awareness." *Day Care and Early Education* (Fall 1988), pp. 28–29.

Jacobson, J. L. "Abandoning Homelands," in Linda Starke, ed., *State of the World, 1989.* New York: W. W. Norton, 1989, pp. 59–76.

O'Brien, K., and D. K. Stoner. "Increasing Environmental Awareness Through Children's Literature." *Reading Teacher* (October 1987), pp. 14–19.

O'Connor, M. *Living Lightly in the City: An Environmental Education Curriculum for Grades K–3.* Milwaukee, WI: Schlitz Audubon Center, 1983.

Shea, C. P. "Protecting the Ozone Layer," in Linda Starke, ed., *State of the World, 1989.* New York: W. W. Norton, 1989, pp. 62–82.

Shea, C. P. "Shifting to Renewable Energy," in Linda Starke, ed., *State of the World, 1988.* New York: W. W. Norton, 1988, pp. 62–82.

Sisson, E. A. *Nature with Children of All Ages: Activities and Adventures for Exploring, Learning, and Enjoying the World Around Us.* Englewood Cliffs, NJ: Prentice-Hall, 1982.

Sowards, A. *Energy Curriculum Guide for Science, Grades K–6.* Austin, TX: Texas Mid-Continent Oil and Gas Association, 1985.

SUPPLEMENTAL READING

BLUM, A. "Think Globally, Act Locally, Plan (also) Centrally." *Journal of Environmental Education* (Winter 1987–1988), pp. 3–8.

BROWN, L. R. "Feeding Six Billion." *World Watch* (September/October 1989), pp. 32–40.

FLAVIN, C. "How Many Chernobyls?" *World Watch* (January/February 1988), pp. 14–18.

LINGELBACH, J. *Hands-on Nature: Information and Activities for Exploring the Environment with Children*. Woodstock, VT: Vermont Institute of Natural Science, 1986.

SUPPORTING, MANAGING, ASSESSING

COMPUTERS AND TECHNOLOGY

This chapter provides information to help the reader:

1. name several technologies that are commonly used to support instruction in the elementary social studies classroom,
2. describe specific ways computers can be used in the social studies program,
3. identify arguments that support and oppose increased use of technology in school programs,
4. suggest criteria that might be applied in evaluating software for use in elementary social studies programs,
5. point out features of videotape that make it especially well suited to support social studies instruction, and
6. describe potential contributions of emerging optical disc technologies.

PRETEST

Answer each of the following true/false questions.

1. Since the early 1980s, there has been an increase in the quality of software available to support instruction in elementary social studies programs.
2. Computer programs are available that provide pupils with drill and practice experiences, but there are no programs available that seek to develop pupils' thinking skills.
3. The kinds of computers typically used in schools are less expensive today than they were in the early 1980s.
4. One advantage of using videotapes instead of 16 mm films is that videotapes are much less expensive.
5. Today, more schools have equipment for running videotapes than for running optical discs.

INTRODUCTION

Computers, videocassettes, and optical discs are extending the range of teachers' instructional options. These innovations make it possible for teachers to better respond to special needs of their learners. Because of the increasingly pervasive nature of computers and other sophisticated technical equipment in the workplace, there is growing support for the idea that all learners should be "technologically literate." By the time they leave school, young people should be unafraid of technological change, able to use a selection of new technologies, and willing to master new ones as they become available (Armstrong et al. 1990, p. 480.)

In recent years, elementary teachers have been heartened by the growing availability of good computer software to support social studies instruction. The popularity of videocassettes has grown at a tremendous rate over the past five years, rapidly displacing the traditional 16 mm film. Optical disc technologies are only beginning to make their presence felt. The decade of the 1990s may well witness a significant increase in the use of optical discs in elementary social studies programs.

COMPUTERS IN THE SCHOOLS

The numbers of computers in schools have soared over the past ten years. In the early 1980s, few schools had them. By the middle and late 1980s, computers were available in over 90 percent of the nation's schools (Cuban 1986). Early on, teach-

Technology can be a valuable learning tools for even very young pupils.

ers had problems in integrating computer-based instruction into their programs because insufficient machines were available for learner use. Today, many elementary schools have large, well-equipped computer rooms with enough machines for each learner in a class; some schools have one computer in each classroom for every two or three learners; and some have one for each pupil in the class.

This increase in the number of computers has been accompanied by an increased tendency of teachers to use them in their instructional programs (Schug 1988). It appears to have been primarily problems of access that inhibited teachers' interest in the technology.

There are several reasons for this increased availability of computers in the schools. Perhaps the most important is that the public has demanded that they be made available. It has been widely recognized that our economy is becoming more and more dependent on this technology. Consequently, it is assumed that employers in the future will be even more insistent than today that employees be familiar with computers.

The huge demand for computers in this country and throughout the world has resulted in some economies of scale in their manufacture. Prices have come down dramatically. A computer that might have sold for nearly fifteen thousand dollars in the 1970s can be had today for a tenth of that amount. In short, as computers have become more affordable, schools have been able to buy more of them for classroom use.

There have been great recent improvements in the quality of educational software. This has been true in elementary social studies as well as in other areas of the school curriculum. Consequently, teachers today are more inclined to incorporate computer-based lessons into their programs than previously.

Computers today are also much more compact than they used to be. Early word processors were about the size of an upright piano. Today, much more powerful computers take only a modest amount of space on a table or desktop. The physical space required for computer-based instruction is much less today than it was when the first units came on the market.

Despite the increase in numbers of computers in schools, there is by no means universal agreement that computers should be extensively used in educational programs. There continue to be arguments on both sides of this issue.

Some Arguments for More Extensive School Use of Computers

Exposure to computer use provides learners with numerous personal benefits. These skills have high transfer value. Computer expertise gained in a social studies lesson may enable the learner to use word processing skills to increase performance levels in language arts and in other areas where writing is required. Basic computer competence acquired in the elementary grades may facilitate learning when pupils go on to secondary school. Finally, the computer provides a direct link to the "real world" of the employment marketplace. Computers today are a pervasive feature of our national economic life.

Critics of American education point out that in many areas performance levels of our learners do not compare well with those of learners in foreign lands. Increasing use of computers may help remedy this situation. Learners in Europe, for example, are much less likely to have computers at home than are learners in this country (Duff 1986). This suggests that home computers can be used to reinforce computer learning in schools. Instructional programs designed for this possibility might result in enhanced levels of academic performance on the part of learners in American schools.

It is possible to develop computer programs that meet special needs of individual pupils. The technology has the potential to deliver instruction in ways that can help larger numbers of learners succeed. For example, programs may include features that provide learners with immediate feedback to their responses. Immediate feedback helps learners identify their mistakes quickly and contributes to overall learning efficiency. Research has revealed that "computer-assisted instruction can reduce the instructional time necessary for students" (Schug 1988, p. 112). As Schug, an elementary social studies specialist, states (1988), the prospect of increasing instructional efficiency is especially attractive in a content-rich subject such as the social studies.

Some Cautionary Arguments about School Use of Computers

Enthusiasm for school use of computers has grown so widespread, that some school officials may have installed them quickly into their buildings to avert a

---

BOX 13–1   **Are Computers Cost-Effective?**

A teacher recently made these comments to a local school board:

> I am as much in favor of progress as the next person. I *know* the computer revolution is here. I accept the point that we must provide for some measure of computer literacy in our schools. But I wonder whether we are pushing this thing too fast?
>
> I have twenty-eight fifth graders in my class. To make really effective use of the computer, each one of them needs to have a machine to work on. Then, there have to be programs for the machines. These are high priced. The computers also break down occasionally, and repair is expensive.
>
> When I think that we can buy a new textbook for each student at about twenty dollars a book and when I recognize that computers may cost us several thousand dollars a student, I wonder whether our priorities are proper. Wouldn't it be better to have a limited number of computers and invest more money in the most recent and best books available?

Think
About
This

1. Do commitments of scarce educational dollars to purchase computer hardware, software, and maintenance represent an irresponsible expenditure? Why, or why not?
2. How do you think the school board responded to this teacher? Why do you think so?
3. Are there political pressures forcing schools to purchase expensive computer equipment? If so, what is the source of these pressures?
4. Do you think a school board would be inclined to spend savings on new texts if it decided to reduce the number of computers it had originally decided to purchase? Why do you think so?

---

public relations disaster. The tendency of public relations materials of some school districts to emphasize the numbers of computers available for school use suggests that there is political capital to be gained by schools with high-profile computer-based learning programs.

In some cases, computers have been purchased before teachers have been trained adequately in their use. Further, though instructional programs have improved tremendously in recent years, some of the available software is not good. Some simple (if not simplistic) programs are nothing more than electronic versions of pupil workbooks. Little learning difference should be expected when the only change is that pupils type answers into a blank on a computer screen rather than write them on a blank in a printed workbook. This kind of computer use raises serious cost-benefit questions. Cost-conscious critics of school programs might well ask why a five-hundred-dollar computer is needed to replace a five-dollar workbook.

Certain characteristics of computers impose limitations. For example, most of them are not very portable. Even down-sized versions available today are relatively heavy, and they cannot be conveniently moved from place to place. Certainly they do not begin to approach the portability of the typical textbook. Further, they depend on continuous supply of electricity, and they have moving parts that occasionally need attention (disk drives, in particular). Further, only rarely does every pupil have a computer. Contrast this with the common practice of providing every learner with a personal copy of the adopted social studies textbook.

Despite these concerns, computer use in schools is expanding. All signs point to a continuation of this trend in the years ahead. As educators gain more experience with computers, more thoughtful attention is being devoted to the question of how benefits of the technology can be maximized in the classroom.

COMPUTERS IN ELEMENTARY SOCIAL STUDIES CLASSROOMS

Gene Rooze and Terry Northup (1989) have made an extensive study of computer use in social studies programs. They point out that there have traditionally been two views of how computers should be used. On one hand, there are those who believe computer technology as a separate subject should be the focus. On the other hand, some see computer technology as a vehicle for transmitting content from a wide range of other subjects.

It is fair to say that in recent years educators have been increasingly inclined to adopt this second position. Educators today tend to see computer technology as a vehicle to help all young people learn, not as a separate discipline reserved for an enthusiastic few. People have come to see computers much as they view automobiles: many should know how to "drive" them, but only a few need to know how they are put together.

Some excellent books are now available for teachers interested in making more use of computers in their social studies programs. These titles are particularly recommended:

Douglas H. Clements, *Computers in Early and Primary Education* (Englewood Cliffs, NJ: Prentice-Hall, 1985)
Allen Glenn and Don Rawitsch, *Computing in the Social Studies Classroom* (Eugene, OR: International Council for Computers in Education, 1984)
Mario Pagnoni, *Computers and Small Fries* (Garden City Court, NY: Avery Publishing Group, 1987)
Gene E. Rooze and Terry Northup, *Computers, Thinking, and Social Studies* (Englewood, CO: Teacher Ideas Press, 1989)

The subsections that follow suggest three aspects of computer use in the social studies as suggested by Rooze and Northup (1989): (a) computers' role in increasing teachers' instructional options, (b) computers as tools to process information, and (c) computers and teaching specific social studies content. A source list and a procedure for evaluating software quality, and a discussion of ways for integrating computer-based instruction into the instructional program follow.

Increasing Teachers' Instructional Options

Once teachers determine their instructional objectives, they need to consider how to provide pupils with appropriate information. Often this requires what Rooze and Northup refer to as a "mediating device." For example, one teacher might decide to use a videocassette as a mediating device, a second might decide to rely on the course textbook, while a third might work with an overhead projector.

Computers are extremely valuable mediating devices. They have the capability to involve learners in a wide variety of learning experiences. In this respect, they offer many more options than a typical textbook. Computer programs are capable of introducing content in a didactic way, much as a textbook does. But they also can demand active participation in learning, something few textbooks claim to do. Pupils may be asked to respond to questions, speculate about future events, or do other things that demand intense interaction with the content.

Teachers, in response to the particular needs of the lesson they are teaching, can provide learners with computer programs that demand little more than recall of specific information, that challenge them to engage in sophisticated analyses (in the light of data that are, perhaps, provided by the same program), or that prompt them to respond in new and creative ways to novel situations. The computer as a mediating device presents few of the limitations of the textbook or other older technologies, including educational television and audio recordings. Computer technology is liberating. It frees teachers to use one technology as they prepare lessons that incorporate a range of instructional approaches.

A cautionary note needs to be inserted here. There is no intent to suggest that all computer-based programs are superior to those that rely more heavily on

---

BOX 13–2   ARE COMPUTERS ALWAYS BETTER THAN TEXTBOOKS?

A teacher recently made these comments:

> I am weary of hearing the "technology pushers" go on and on about how much more pupils learn from computers than textbooks. I'm not at all hostile to computers. But, I think some of the claims are overblown.
>
> What we continually get are examples of the best computer programs used in eminently responsible ways by superlative teachers. These invariably are contrasted to the worst possible textbooks, used irresponsibly by teachers with mediocre instructional skills.
>
> There are great computer programs, and there are poor ones. There are outstanding textbooks, and there are terrible ones. We should stop pretending that either technology, computer or textbook, is universally "good" or "bad." What we need in our schools are examples of the best of both technologies.

Think
About
This

1. What are your reactions to this point of view?
2. If agreed that computers need to be "sold" in a way that avoids negative comparisons with other technologies, how might you make a case supporting their use?
3. Do you believe that any instructional technology can be so good that it can overcome a lack of proficiency in the teacher?

textbooks and other instructional mediators. The flexibility of the computer suggests that it can also be a vehicle for perfectly terrible instruction. Pupils can be subjected to dreary drill and practice exercises on a computer that are every bit as uninspiring as those found in dusty school workbooks.

The computer does not guarantee imaginative instruction; it simply provides a technology that allows lessons to be organized and delivered by a good teacher. As is true with all instructional mediators, the quality of the lesson delivered derives from the talent of the teacher.

Processing Information

Word processing capabilities of microcomputers are well known. Computers enable learners to develop drafts quickly and to revise easily. Rewriting with a computer using a word processing program removes much of the tedium. In elementary social studies classes, this means that teachers whose pupils have access to computers and good word processing programs may be able to demand more written work and to expect better final versions of learners' papers.

A number of excellent word processing programs are available today. Some pupils may have learned sophisticated programs such as *WordPerfect* or *WordStar* that their parents use on their own computers at home. Other programs have been

designed specifically for school use. Several of these are appropriate for learners in the middle and upper elementary grades. An example of such a program is *Bank Street Writer*. It is available for IBM PC machines and clones, the Apple II family of computers, as well as for some other computers. For information write to: *Bank Street Writer*, Scholastic Incorporated, P.O. Box 7502, Jefferson City, MO 65102.

Databases are enormous collections of data that users can draw upon in response to their specific information needs. Information for some databases is kept at a central location and users may subscribe to these services, accessing the information using a telephone line, a modem (a device that allows computers to communicate over a telephone line), and a personal computer. The Source and CompuServe are examples of database services of this basic type. They make information on a variety of subjects available to their subscribers.

Other databases are self-contained. The information is contained on one or more disks that users insert into their computers when they need to access the data. Sometimes it is possible for users to add information to that initially provided. Rooze and Northup (p. 10) identify several programs of this type that are suitable for use in social studies programs:

One World Countries Data Base and USA Profile
Produced by: Active Learning Systems, 5365 Avenida Encinas, Carlsbad, CA
   92008
Suitable for use on: Apple family computers, Commodore 64, and IBM PC and PC
   clones

MECC Dataquest: The Presidents; MECC Dataquest: The Fifty States; and
   MECC Dataquest: World Communities
Produced by: MECC, 3490 Lexington Avenue North, St. Paul, MN 55126
Suitable for use on: Apple II family of computers

Electronic spreadsheets store information in rows and columns displayed on a computer monitor. Typically, individual rows and columns have their own labels. A teacher might use an electronic spreadsheet instead of a traditional grade book. The rows at the left would have names of pupils in the class. The individual columns would have labels indicating particular assignments, tests, and other bases for grading. Electronic spreadsheets allow users to do more than simply record existing information. They can engage in speculative thinking by engaging in "what if" activities. For example, the impact of a 10 percent improvement on a given pupils' grade on every assignment could be quickly reflected on a spreadsheet. The procedures for adding new information and making calculations are quite simple.

There are many possible applications for using spreadsheet programs in social studies programs. These programs are particularly valuable for engaging learners in lessons designed to develop their skills in making inferences. Rooze and Northup cite an example of using a spreadsheet to calculate the impacts of different rates of population growth in different places. Columns at the top are labeled with each place and its rate of population increase. Rows are labeled with indi-

TABLE 13–1
A completed spreadsheet showing the impact on populations of two countries of differing rates of population increase

	Population Projections	
Year	New Zealand (annual rate of natural increase = 0.08%)	Jordan (annual rate of natural increase = 3.60%)
1989	3,397,000	3,031,000
1990	3,424,000	3,140,116
1991	3,451,392	3,253,160
1992	3,479,003	3,370,273
1993	3,506,835	3,491,603
1994	3,536,890	3,617,301
1995	3,565,185	3,747,524
1996	3,593,706	3,882,435
1997	3,622,456	4,022,203
1998	3,651,436	4,167,002
1999	3,680,647	4,317,014

Note: Data assume that rate of natural increase for each country stays the same for every year cited.

vidual years. Cells in this matrix contain population for each place at each year. Learners can review the displayed data and draw conclusions about the impact of the different growth rates (Table 13–1).

Spreadsheets are widely used in business. Lotus 1-2-3 and VISICALC are two popular programs. For use in schools, many teachers find it convenient to use "integrated software," that includes not only spreadsheet capabilities but word processing and other features. Rooze and Northup suggest two integrated programs as particularly useful for teachers interested in using spreadsheet activities as part of their instruction:

Appleworks
Produced by: Apple Computer, Inc., 20525 Mariana Avenue, Cupertino, California 95014
Suitable for use on Apple family of computers

Microsoft Works
Produced by: Microsoft Corporation, 16011 N.E. 36th Way, Redmond, WA 98073-9719
Suitable for use on: Apple Macintosh, IBM PC and PC clones

Teaching Specific Content

Many programs are available that focus directly on teaching social studies content. Many are closely tied to topics covered in elementary social studies classes. Some programs focus on reinforcing skills and providing learners with skills applications. Others challenge learners to go "beyond the givens" to engage in higher-level thinking skills.

Two examples of programs with a focus on skill development and reinforcement of basic academic content are *Cross Country USA* and *Interviews with History*. One program that engages pupils' higher-level skills is *The Golden Spike: Building America's First Transcontinental Railroad*.

Cross Country USA is suitable for use with children in the upper elementary grades. Pupils' map-reading skills are reinforced as they respond to situations involving truck travel between a large number of U.S. cities. General geographic concepts also receive attention. *Cross Country USA* is available from: Didatech Software Ltd., 3812 William St., Burnaby, B.C. V5C 3H9, Canada.

Interviews with History is suitable for use with elementary pupils in the middle and upper grades. Each learner plays the part of a reporter who interviews important figures from history. There is a provision for learners to be tested on the knowledge they have gained from the interviews and to be provided with remediation on items they miss. *Interviews with History* is available from: Educational Publishing Concepts, P.O. Box 715, St. Charles, IL 60174.

The Golden Spike: Building America's First Transcontinental Railroad is a highly regarded simulation based on circumstances surrounding the building of the first transcontinental rail line. It is a multimedia program that also features filmstrips and some prose materials. Learners work in small groups and engage in problem solving, creative thinking, and decision making. *The Golden Spike: Building America's First Transcontinental Railroad* is available from: National Geographic Society, 17th and M Streets N.W., Washington, D.C. 20077.

These titles represent a tiny fraction of the content-oriented social studies programs available today. Rooze and Northup include a list of such programs in their book (see the complete citation in the "References" section at the end of this chapter).

New social studies-oriented software comes on the market each month. Journals such as *Social Education* (400 Albemarle Street, Washington, DC 20016), *T.H.E. Journal* (Information Synergy, P.O. Box 992, Acton, MA 01720), *Children's Software* (Kendall-Rooney Publishing Company, 90 Lafayette Ave., Sea Cliff, NY 11579) and *Teaching and Computers* (Scholastic, 730 Broadway, New York, NY 10003) often carry articles or advertisements focusing on new software. Many libraries carry these periodicals.

Finding and Evaluating Software

Numerous firms are now selling software suitable for use in elementary social studies classrooms. Rooze and Northup (1989) and the journals listed in the previous subsection are good places to find addresses of firms marketing software of this kind. Ten firms selling software of interest to elementary social studies teachers are listed here. Firms whose addresses have been introduced previously are not included in this list.

Aquarius
P.O. Box 128
Indian Rocks, FL 33535

Broderbund Software
345 Fourth St.
San Francisco, CA 94107

Educational Activities
1937 Grand Ave.
Baldwin, NY 11510

Grolier Electronic Publishing
Sherman Turnpike
Danbury, CT 06816

Learning Arts
P.O. Box 179
Wichita, KS 67201

MicroEd
P.O. Box 24750
Edina, MN 55424

Milliken
1100 Research Boulevard
St. Louis, MO 63132

SVE
1345 Diversey Parkway
Chicago, IL 60614

Tom Snyder Productions
90 Sherman St.
Cambridge, MA 02140

Unicorn Software
2950 E. Flamingo Rd.
Las Vegas, NV 89121

The great increase in the amount of software for elementary social studies classes has given teachers choices from which to select programs, but the increase in volume does not mean that all available software is high quality. As might be expected, the market provides a mix of wonderful, so-so, and downright terrible software. Glenn and Rawitsch (1984) have developed an evaluation checklist that many teachers have found useful when faced with software-purchase decisions. Their software quality checklist is reproduced in Figure 13.1.

Working together to solve problems on a computer helps students accomplish several important social studies goals.

Integrating Computer-Based Instruction

Computer-based instruction works best when it is integrated both with learning in other subject areas and with other instructional techniques used to introduce social studies content. Such integration promotes the development of cumulative learning experiences that have greater impact on learners' development.

Ties with other subjects make especially good sense because computer software in these other areas often is designed to develop competencies relevant to the social studies. For example, many mathematics programs help learners to become more proficient in working with graphically depicted information. An ability to learn from graphical displays of information is also critically important in the social studies.

Integration of computer-based instruction with other methods used to introduce social studies content is also important. If there is no real link between what pupils do when they work with computers and what they do when other instructional techniques are used, they may well view their computer time as a recreational diversion having little real connection to the academic social studies program. Many teachers find it useful to select software that ties closely to academic content also being treated in other ways. For example, when a social studies unit

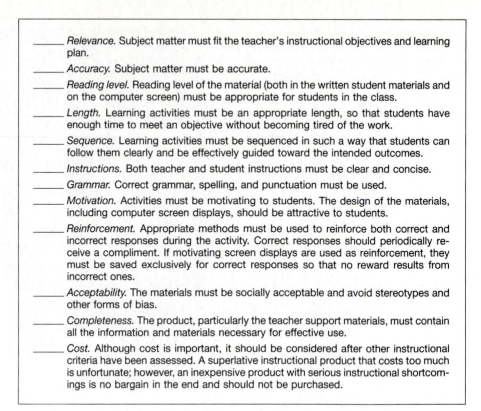

_____ *Relevance.* Subject matter must fit the teacher's instructional objectives and learning plan.

_____ *Accuracy.* Subject matter must be accurate.

_____ *Reading level.* Reading level of the material (both in the written student materials and on the computer screen) must be appropriate for students in the class.

_____ *Length.* Learning activities must be an appropriate length, so that students have enough time to meet an objective without becoming tired of the work.

_____ *Sequence.* Learning activities must be sequenced in such a way that students can follow them clearly and be effectively guided toward the intended outcomes.

_____ *Instructions.* Both teacher and student instructions must be clear and concise.

_____ *Grammar.* Correct grammar, spelling, and punctuation must be used.

_____ *Motivation.* Activities must be motivating to students. The design of the materials, including computer screen displays, should be attractive to students.

_____ *Reinforcement.* Appropriate methods must be used to reinforce both correct and incorrect responses during the activity. Correct responses should periodically receive a compliment. If motivating screen displays are used as reinforcement, they must be saved exclusively for correct responses so that no reward results from incorrect ones.

_____ *Acceptability.* The materials must be socially acceptable and avoid stereotypes and other forms of bias.

_____ *Completeness.* The product, particularly the teacher support materials, must contain all the information and materials necessary for effective use.

_____ *Cost.* Although cost is important, it should be considered after other instructional criteria have been assessed. A superlative instructional product that costs too much is unfortunate; however, an inexpensive product with serious instructional shortcomings is no bargain in the end and should not be purchased.

FIGURE 13-1

Software quality checklist

Reprinted with permission from Allen Glenn and Don Rawitsch, *Computing in the Social Studies Classroom* (Eugene, OR: International Council for Computers in Education, 1984, p. 37).

on the American Revolution is being studied, learning experiences requiring the use of the textbook, learning centers, special library resources, and other materials provide an excellent context for a computer simulation of some aspect of the revolutionary experience.

VIDEOCASSETTES

Videocassette technology as an instructional tool has become tremendously popular in recent years. Nearly all schools now have the necessary playback equipment. Social studies materials' catalogues feature pages of titles appropriate for use in elementary programs.

Videocassettes are rapidly displacing 16 mm films. This is happening for several reasons, one of which is cost. Sixteen millimeter films are very expensive. A half-hour color film may cost more than $500.00; many videocassettes less than a tenth as much. Tight instructional budgets stretch farther when videocassettes are purchased instead of 16 mm films.

Videocassettes are easily stored. A single shelf may hold several dozen. The playback equipment is easier to use than many 16 mm projectors, usually requiring the operator to do little other than turn the power on and insert the cassette. The cassette containers themselves are very durable. These strong containers and a playback system that places little stress on the film make it possible for cassettes to last many years, given reasonable levels of care.

In addition to playing prerecorded videocassettes, many teachers use video equipment to record information of their own choosing. For example, in social studies classes, some teachers make videorecordings of pupils working in groups, engaging in role-playing exercises, and participating in simulations. Portable equipment can be taken on a field trip to make a permanent audio and visual record of the experience.

OPTICAL DISCS

There are two basic kinds of optical discs. The most familiar are audiodiscs, popularly known as compact discs. Videodiscs, which include both audio and visual information, comprise the other major category of optical discs.

Information is retrieved from optical systems using laser technology. As the discs turn, the beam senses stored information and converts it to audio and/or visual signals. Since only the beam strikes the disc surface, no physical wear occurs when the disc plays. Hence, audiodiscs do not wear out as traditional phonograph records do as a result of the abrasion from the playback needle.

Sound reproduction quality of optical discs is superb when signals are played back through a good audio system. This feature makes them much prized in music programs, where faithful reproduction of sound is important. Few audiodiscs have been developed specifically for use in elementary social studies classes. In this part of the elementary curriculum, videodiscs seem to have more potential applications. Today, however, videodisc playback units are not available in many classrooms. The technology certainly is not yet as pervasive as is videocassette technology.

So-called *interactive* videodisc systems hold great promise for social studies instruction. Interactive videodiscs involve a combination of videodisc and computer technology. They allow users to make changes in how information is displayed. For example, sequencing can be varied, specific elements of content can be selected and deleted, and action can be slowed down so pupils can better see how complex situations develop.

An example of a promising interactive videodisc program is GTV. This interactive American history program is designed for use in grades five through twelve. Two full hours of available video are divided into forty short segments of between three to five minutes each. Users can identify which segments they want, and can sequence them. Learners can be involved in sequencing decisions. The program allows them to pursue a common theme across a number of selected segments, to develop short programs to support content in the text, and to otherwise get directly involved in decisions involving selection and organization of information. A word processing feature allows both teacher and pupils to write scripts to accompany the visual stories. GTV runs on the Apple IIGS and Macintosh computers. For information about GTV, write to: National Geographic Society, Department GTV, Washington, DC 20077-9966.

A negative feature of present optical discs, both audio and video, is that the media cannot be erased and rerecorded upon. Teachers' ability to make, erase, and reuse tapes has been one feature that has made videocassette technology so popular. Today, many firms are working to develop optical discs that can be erased and reused. Some early models are already on the market (Tyre 1988). Once this feature becomes widespread, more videodisc units will undoubtedly begin appearing in the nation's classrooms.

CD ROM (compact disc, read-only memory) is an emerging optical disc technology with tremendous educational potential. CD ROM permits users to mix at will existing computer and visual technologies. The storage capacity of CD ROM discs is enormous. Those available today can store 320,000 pages of information each. This is enough data to completely fill a shelf of books four feet wide. Four CD ROM discs could contain the names, addresses, and telephone numbers of every man, woman, and child in the United States (Grotta 1990).

CD ROM Review is a publication that tracks developments relating to this exciting new technology. For subscription information, write to: *CD ROM Review*, IDG/Communications, 80 Elm St., Petersborough, NH 03458.

KEY IDEAS IN SUMMARY

1. Specialized new technologies are providing more instructional options for teachers. Among technologies in use in today's elementary social studies classrooms are computers, videocassettes, and optical discs.

2. There has been a tremendous growth in the number of computers in schools over the past decade. Teachers are using them more and more frequently to support classroom instruction. In recent years, the quality of elementary social studies software has improved tremendously.

3. Not everyone agrees that computers should be used more extensively in school programs. Some people argue that computers have been installed more rapidly than teachers have been trained to use them. It is even argued that certain districts have purchased computers more for cosmetic political reasons than for sound instructional reasons. It is argued, too, that many times individual learners do not have access to a school computer. This situation may put certain learners at a disadvantage.

4. Despite concerns about the expansion of computer use in schools, most evidence supports the view that computer use is increasing. Proponents note that employers demand workers who are familiar with computers. Others argue that computer-based instruction allows pupils to master more content in less time. In a content-dense area of the curriculum such as the social studies, this argument has been particularly appealing.

5. Computer-based instruction needs to be integrated carefully with the rest of the instructional program. It is important that learners recognize ties between activities requiring them to work with computers and other learning activities. If they fail to see this connection, they may see computers as recreational tools that are not linked to the substantive parts of the academic program.

6. Videocassette technology has been widely embraced by elementary social studies teachers. This technology has largely displaced the once-popular 16 mm film. Today, many titles are available that support social studies instruction. Their cost is modest, and individual videocassettes can be easily stored. Playback equipment is easy to operate. Many teachers have access to video recording equipment, and can easily make tapes of their own. The educational possibilities inherent in making audiovisual records of learners' activities have attracted a great deal of interest in this equipment.

7. Optical disc technology is relatively new. Some optical discs, commonly referred to as compact discs, are audio only. Others contain both video and audio information. Videodiscs have great instructional potential. When linked to a computer, they offer teachers the possibility of varying content and sequencing to accommodate their own instructional needs. CD ROM, an advanced optical disc technology, is just beginning to make its impact felt in the schools. This versatile technology has enormous information-storage capabilities. School use of CD ROM promises to increase tremendously over the next decade.

POSTTEST

Answer each of the following true/false questions.

1. Though there are more computers in the schools than there were ten years ago, teachers are using them less today than they did then.

2. Computer skills learned in one instructional setting may help learners in other areas as well.

3. Computers are thought to have more potential than textbooks for actively involving pupils in learning.

4. It is possible for a teacher to use an electronic spreadsheet instead of a traditional grade book.

5. The biggest problem with CD ROM technology is that the CD ROM discs have very little information-storage capacity.

QUESTIONS

1. What is meant by the concept "technological literacy"?

2. What changes have there been in the quality of educational software over the past decade?

3. What are some arguments that support expanded use of computers in schools?

4. What are some arguments that have been made in opposition to expanded use of computers in schools?

5. What are some information sources for teachers who wish to learn more about using computers in their social studies programs?

6. In what ways can computers increase teachers' instructional options?

7. What are some issues to consider when evaluating software?

8. What features of videocassette technology have contributed to its popularity in the school classroom?

9. What are the two basic kinds of optical discs?

10. What are some characteristics of CD ROM that suggest this technology may enjoy many educational applications in the years ahead?

11. Not all pupils have access to computers at home. Some critics of computer use in schools argue that this approach to instruction gives an unfair advantage to learners who have access to computers at home as well as at school. They contend that learners from economically disadvantaged households will not be able to compete academically with these pupils. The push to introduce computers, they say, is just another example of a school policy that will undermine future prospects of the poor. How do you react to this concern? What evidence supports this position? What evidence might be used to refute it?

12. One of the arguments for expanding computer use is that employers increasingly want workers who have basic computer skills. To what extent is it the job of the social studies to respond to wishes of employers? Why do you think so?

13. Some people feel that social studies content often is best taught when groups of learners work together. Yet, when computer-based instruction is used individual pupils often work in isolation at the computer. Is this desirable? Does social studies instruction using computers irresponsibly deny pupils opportunities to learn together?

14. Have elementary learners become so conditioned to thinking of computers as game machines that they are unable to take them seriously as vehicles for dealing with academic subjects? If so, what might you do as a teacher to respond to this situation?

15. Given what you know about computer and optical disc technologies, what changes would you expect to see in school classrooms over the next decade? What factors might act to accelerate these changes? To slow them down?

EXTENDING UNDERSTANDING AND SKILL

1. Interview an elementary social studies teacher on the issue of computer use. How much time do pupils spend working with computers? What specifically do they do in the social studies? How does computer time in the social studies compare with computer time in other areas of the elementary curriculum? Prepare an oral report and share it with your class.

2. With the help of your course instructor, organize several teams from your class to debate this issue: "Resolved that the effort to involve computers in elementary social studies instruction has moved too quickly." You may wish to follow the format for a classroom debate introduced in Chapter 6, "Group Learning."

3. New software for elementary social studies becomes available nearly every month. Read some software reviews in professional journals such as *Social Education*. Begin a file of software titles you would consider for use in your own classroom. Add new entries as you learn about new programs. Take any opportunities you have to review these items personally. This file will prove useful when you begin teaching and are in a position to purchase instructional support materials.

4. Arrange with your instructor or with the director of your campus computer learning center to work directly with some elementary social studies software. Prepare a report for your instructor that focuses on strengths and weaknesses of the program(s) you use. Note the intended ages of learners who typically would use the material and evaluate how suitable the program would be for these pupils.

5. Invite a media specialist from a large, well-equipped school district or a specialist in educational technology from your own campus to talk to your classes on technological innovations that are not yet common in the schools but that seem to be on their way. Ask this person to speculate about changes in school programming, particularly in approaches to teaching social studies, that may result when these technologies become widely available.

REFERENCES

ARMSTRONG, D. G., AND T. V. SAVAGE. *Secondary Education: An Introduction*, 2d ed. New York: Macmillan, 1990.

CUBAN, L. *Teachers and Machines: The Classroom Use of Technology Since 1920*. New York: Teachers College Press, 1986.

DUFF, J. M. "From the Desk of the Editor." *The Engineering Design Graphics Journal* (Autumn 1986), pp. 4, 7.

GROTTA, D. "CD-ROM: A Technology on the Threshold." *Computer Shopper* (January 1990), pp. 235, 237, 259.

Rooze, G. E., and T. Northup. *Computers, Thinking, and Social Studies*. Englewood, CO: Teachers Ideas Press, 1989.

Schug, M. C. "What Do Social Studies Teachers Say About Using Computers?" *The Social Studies* (May/June 1988), pp. 112–15.

Tyre, T. "Erasable Optical Media is Closer to Being Real." *Technological Horizons in Education Journal* (October 1988), pp. 68–72.

SUPPLEMENTAL READING

Budin, H. *Using Computers in the Social Studies*. New York: Teachers College Press, 1986.

Hentrel, B. K. *Computers in Education: A Guide for Educators*. Ann Arbor, MI: University of Michigan Press, 1985.

Johnston, J. *Electronic Learning from Audiotape to Videodisc*. Hillsdale, NJ: Lawrence Erlbaum Associates, 1987.

Lambert, S., and S. Ropiequet. *CD ROM*. Redmond, WA: Microsoft Press, 1986–1988.

Riedesel, C. Alan. *Coping with Computers in the Elementary and Middle Schools*. Englewood Cliffs, NJ: Prentice-Hall, 1985.

14

UNDERSTANDING MAP
AND GLOBE SKILLS

This chapter provides information to help the reader:

1. recognize common problems elementary school pupils experience when they work with maps and globes,
2. identify key map and globe skills,
3. describe map and globe skills appropriate for pupils in different grades,
4. point out basic characteristics of maps and globes,
5. describe approaches that can help learners master certain map and globe skills, and
6. suggest basic concepts pupils must grasp before they can successfully perform map and globe activities.

PRETEST

Answer each of the following true/false questions.

1. It is common for elementary school pupils to underestimate the size of the Pacific Ocean.

2. An analemma indicates longitudes at which the noonday sun is directly overhead on each day of the year.

3. Shapes of countries on conformal maps of the world appear much as they appear on a globe.

4. Coordinates of latitude and longitude are used to pinpoint absolute location.

5. Some younger elementary pupils believe the sun rotates around the earth.

INTRODUCTION

Try to answer the following questions.

1. Reno, Nevada is west of Los Angeles, California.
2. The west coast of South America is in the same time zone as New York City (eastern time zone).
3. If a person flew first from New York to San Francisco and then flew an equivalent distance west from San Francisco, he or she would be more than one-third of the way across the Pacific Ocean.
4. Because Juneau, Alaska, is much farther north, it has colder average January weather than Philadelphia, Pennsylvania.

Here are the answers: Numbers 1 and 2 are true and numbers 3 and 4 are false. Do not feel bad if you missed some of these. Many adults find such questions difficult. They would be even more perplexing to elementary pupils who have little experience in working with map and globe skills. On the other hand, children and adults who are solidly grounded in these skills should be able to respond confidently to questions such as these. Before going on, let us pause a moment to explain the answers.

The question about Los Angeles and Reno is confusing because most people look at flat maps of the United States rather than at globes. Many of these maps distort the shape of the west coast. They make it look like a relatively straight north-south line. Since Los Angeles is on the coast and Reno is inland, it is only natural for people to conclude that Los Angeles must be farther west. In reality, the southern part of the west coast lies in a generally southeasterly direction from the northern part. This is why it is possible for Los Angeles to be east of Reno. The relationship is quite apparent on a globe.

Perhaps because of the names of the two continents—North America and South America—many people assume that South America lies directly south of North

"No, Melissa, the 'International Date Line' is *not* a telephone number reserved for people wanting to contact eligible bachelors and bachelorettes in other countries."

America. It does lie south, but it is also considerably east of most of North America. This is why it is true that the west coast of South America lies in the same time zone as the eastern United States.

Children and adults, too, often greatly underestimate the size of the Pacific Ocean. The Pacific Ocean covers about one-third of the earth's surface. In very rough terms, it is about 10,000 miles (16,090 kilometers) from the west coast of the United States to the western boundaries of the Pacific. This is more than three times the distance from New York to San Francisco.

Many middle-grade children have some understanding of the parts of the globe, such as the equator and the poles. They also recognize that, on the average, the winter temperatures in the northern areas of the northern hemisphere are colder than in the southern areas. Many of these pupils, though, have not grasped that other local conditions, such as elevation, proximity to warm water, and wind

---

BOX 14–1   **Children's Misinformation About World Geography.**

Not long ago, a group of middle-grade pupils was surveyed about selected geographic topics. The following are some of the "facts" about the world many of these young people believed to be true.

1. On any map, the Atlantic always lies to the right.
2. It is impossible for a river ever to flow in a northerly direction.
3. In the northern hemisphere, every place north of location A has colder winters than those at location A.
4. Africa is a country.
5. More Spanish-speaking people in the world live in Spain than in any other Spanish-speaking country.
6. The most northern part of the 48 connected states is the northern tip of the state of Maine.
7. It is about the same distance from New York to London as from Seattle to Tokyo.

Think About This

1. Which of the above misinformation do you believe to be most widespread? Why do you think so?
2. In general, what are the sources of this misinformation?
3. As a teacher, what might you do to help learners correct these mistaken impressions?

---

patterns, also influence temperature. They need this kind of understanding to be able to answer the question about the January temperatures in Juneau and Philadelphia.

Though it is much closer to the equator than Juneau, Philadelphia sits at the eastern edge of a large continental land mass. Because the prevailing winds here blow off the cold continental interior in the winter, the January weather can be very cold. Juneau, by way of contrast, sits on the coast and enjoys moderate winter temperatures because the prevailing west winds blow in off the warm Alaska current.

Map and globe skills taught in elementary social studies classes help pupils to understand the many important physical dimensions of the world. Technological advances draw the peoples of the earth closer together. Map and globe skills provide learners with analytical tools they can use to make sense of the world beyond their local communities. These skills have long received heavy emphasis in social studies programs, and this emphasis will certainly continue.

GLOBES

Globes deserve more attention than they receive in many social studies classrooms. Some of the misunderstandings learners have about the world might be eliminated if they were provided more experience in working with globes and relatively less in working with maps. Globes provide the best representation of our spherical planet. Maps, dealing in only two dimensions, distort shapes and areas; this distortion can lead to serious misconceptions.

For example, many flat world maps use a projection that makes Africa look smaller in area than North America. Surprisingly large numbers of middle grade pupils believe that this is true. Such maps also make Greenland look as large as South America. In fact, South America is nine times larger. Globes avoid these distortions. The relative sizes of the world land masses appear on the globe as they actually exist.

Though the increased use of globes can help pupils gain a better appreciation of size relationships, their use poses problems as well. Globes are bulky. Ideally, there should be enough globes so that no more than three or four pupils at a time need to work with one. In a class of twenty-five, this would mean six or more globes. Often, there is simply not sufficient space to accommodate such a large number.

There are serious problems associated with using globes to teach certain kinds of content. Globes include the entire earth's surface. Consequently, the individual areas of the earth appear to be quite small. If there is an interest in studying only a small part of the earth's surface, a globe might not be as good a choice as a map.

Suppose that a teacher wanted to teach something about Romania. Romania is about 425 miles (684 kilometers) across from east to west. On a standard 16-inch globe, Romania occupies less than one inch of space from east to west. Very little detail can be included in such a small space. A larger globe would involve other difficulties. A globe large enough for Romania to be 36 inches across would be 48 feet in diameter. Such a globe would need to be installed in a special building.

Though they do have limitations when the purpose is to study small parts of the earth's surface, globes are ideally suited to helping learners grasp other kinds of content. As noted previously, they are excellent vehicles for displaying the proper area and location arrangements. They can be used to help develop the locational skills that involve the use of latitude and longitude. The concept of the great circle route is much better taught by using a globe rather than a map. Earth-sun relationships—as they relate to issues such as day and night, the seasons of the year, the 24-hour day, and time zones—are best taught using globes.

Kinds of Globes

Three common globe types found in elementary schools are (1) readiness globes, (2) elementary globes, and (3) intermediate globes.

Readiness Globes. Readiness globes are designed to introduce basic information about globes. They are used mostly in the primary grades. Bright colors are often used to depict the individual countries. The detail does not go much beyond labels for the major countries, the names of capital cities and other large population centers, the names of major oceans and seas, and the labels for the equator and, sometimes, for the Tropic of Cancer and the Tropic of Capricorn. Occasionally, a few additional details are found.

Globes are an essential part of any map and globe skills program.

Even readiness globes sometimes contain a bewildering array of information for very young children. Some pupils in the early primary grades experience great difficulty in distinguishing between the areas of land and water. One teacher reported having a readiness globe that used the color blue to depict certain political areas as well as water areas. One child in the class described Wyoming as a major lake!

Elementary Globes.   Elementary globes are good for use in fourth, fifth, and sixth grades. They include much more detail than readiness globes. This detail may overwhelm children in the primary grades. The additional information often includes the lines of latitude and longitude, the details regarding the scale of the globe, the indications of major world wind patterns, and the depictions of the directions of the major ocean currents. Often, the locations of many more cities and towns than on readiness globes will be included.

Intermediate Globes.   Intermediate globes are best suited for use with older intermediate-grades learners. They include even more detail than elementary globes. Many of them, for example, will include the notations of world time zones.

Many, too, will include an analemma. An *analemma* is the figure-eight-shaped figure that cuts through the Equator. It indicates the locations where the sun is directly overhead at noon on each day of the year.

Some intermediate globes also have a horizon ring. A *horizon ring* is a circular band that surrounds the globe. It has the degrees marked off on its inner surface. The globe can be rotated at will within the ring. By using the degree markers, pupils can engage in relatively sophisticated calculations of degree differences and time differences between pairs of locations on the globe.

Parts of the Globe that Need To Be Emphasized

The information presented on globes is of no use until youngsters understand what it means. There are substantial differences in the types and amounts of information introduced on various kinds of globes. By the end of their elementary social studies experience, youngsters should recognize the functions of features of the globe such as the equator, the Tropic of Cancer, the Tropic of Capricorn, the North Pole, the South Pole, the International Date Line, the Prime Meridian, the horizon ring, the distance scale, the world time zones, and the analemma (Figure 14–1).

They should be able to apply the basic globe skills to solve problems such as finding locations using latitude and longitude, explaining the seasonal changes in

FIGURE 14–1

An **analemma** is used to indicate the latitudes at which the noonday sun is directly overhead on each day of the year. The northern limit of the analemma is the Tropic of Cancer, where the sun is directly overhead on June 21–22. The southern limit is the Tropic of Capricorn, where the sun is directly overhead on December 21–22. The sun is directly overhead at noon at the equator twice each year: once on March 21–22 and again on September 21–22. The apparent movement of the sun is a result of the earth's annual movement around the sun. Because the earth's axis always points to the North Star, at some times of the year the sun's rays strike most directly at points south of the equator, at the equator, or north of the equator. To receive a clearer picture of why this happens, see Table 14.3. Some teachers find that pupils enjoy pointing out where the sun will be overhead at noon on their birthdays.

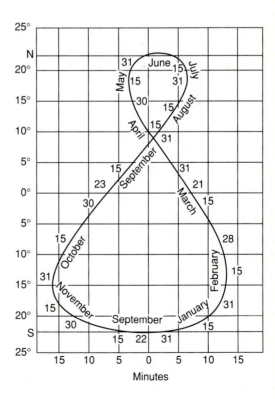

Minutes

terms of the alternating earth-sun relationships, pointing out the function of the international dateline, and explaining the time differences between selected pairs of world locations. Examples of how proficiency in these skills might be built are introduced later in this chapter.

MAPS

Maps are used more frequently than globes in most elementary social studies classrooms. Properly used, maps can be very effective instructional tools. They can be designed to accomplish many purposes; they cost less than globes; and they do not consume much storage space, even in large numbers.

The strengths of the map as a teaching device need to be counterbalanced by an understanding that maps are an imperfect representation of the earth. A three-dimensional surface cannot be transformed to a two-dimensional surface without distortion. To illustrate how this might happen when explaining maps to children, some teachers carefully remove half of the peel from an orange. By pushing down on the peel, the teacher can make a point that something must "give" before the spherical surface can be converted to a flat plane.

Many maps illustrate only a portion of the earth's surface. A survey of the wall maps permanently on display in elementary classrooms in this country would probably reveal more United States maps than anything else. Pupils' continuous exposure to such maps has the potential to lead to false conclusions. The widespread notion among middle-grade pupils that "the Atlantic is always found on the right-hand side of a map" may be a result of years of seeing it so positioned on the U.S. maps attached to classroom walls.

Constant exposure to a large wall map of the United States also has the potential to confuse pupils about the proper size relationships among world places. Elementary school children tend to overestimate the physical size of the United States. This sometimes results in their failure to appreciate the magnitude and importance of the other places in the world.

During World War II, General MacArthur recognized this problem. He was concerned that many incoming officers to the Pacific Theater of the war did not recognize the huge size of the Pacific area. To help the officers grasp this point, he had a special map prepared to illustrate the size of the United States relative to the area of the Western Pacific Ocean. This map is reproduced in Figure 14–2.

World maps are a common wall feature in elementary school classrooms. To some degree, individual maps reflect characteristics of one of these two basic types: conformal maps and equal area maps.

Conformal Maps

Conformal maps are prepared in such a way that the shapes of land areas, for example Australia, are the same on the map as on a globe. An important example

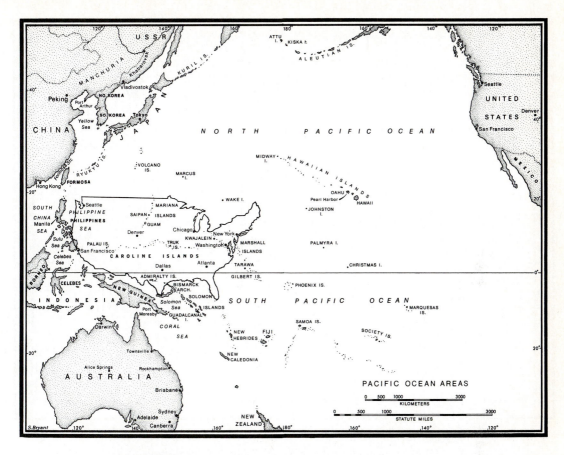

FIGURE 14–2
General Douglas MacArthur's wall map. General MacArthur had this map in his headquarters during World War II, and he used it to illustrate the vast size of the Pacific Region to his incoming officers.

(*Source:* William Manchester, *American Caesar: Douglas MacArthur: 1880–1964.* New York: Dell Publishing Co., copyright © 1978 by William Manchester. Illustration section between pp. 320 and 321. Reprinted with permission.)

of a conformal map is the *Mercator projection* map, named for a famous map-maker who lived in the sixteenth century (Figure 14–3).

To understand how a Mercator projection map is made, imagine a clear glass globe with land areas outlined in dark ink and a tiny light in the center. The globe is placed on a table so a line passing through the North Pole, the light in the center, and the South Pole is perpendicular to the tabletop. A cylinder of paper is slipped over the globe. The light source causes shadows to be cast on the paper cylinder from the boundaries of the land areas. These shadows are carefully traced by the mapmaker. When the cylinder is unwrapped, the result is a Mercator projection map of the world. (In reality, the process is done mathematically. But the principles are as described here.)

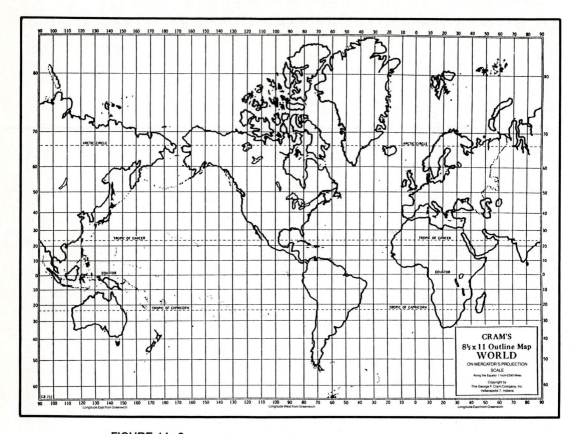

FIGURE 14–3
An example of a conformal world map: Mercator's projection
Copyright George F. Cram Co., Inc., Indianapolis, IN. Reprinted by permission.

   The Mercator projection produces a world map that maintains accurate shapes of land masses. However, relative sizes of places are not accurately portrayed; areas of places more distant from the equator are less accurately displayed than are areas closer to the equator. Places in extreme northern and southern locations are depicted as much larger than they appear on a globe.

   The distortion in land areas on Mercator projection maps can lead to unfortunate misunderstandings. As noted, pupils who do not often work with globes and who see a Mercator map every day often conclude that Greenland is as large as or even larger than South America. In reality, South America is *nine times* larger than Greenland. Greenland's apparent size on a Mercator projection map is a result of its great distance from the Equator. South America, on the other hand, lies across the Equator and hence is relatively undistorted.

   When conformal maps are the only world maps available, it is particularly important to give pupils opportunities to work with globes, and to explain to them why the sizes of land masses in extreme northern and southern regions are distorted on Mercator maps. Learners must have opportunities to compare and contrast globes and world maps so they can appreciate that conformal maps distort sizes of some land masses.

Modifications of the Mercator projection reduce some of these extreme area distortions. In general, though, these modifications give up the Mercator projection's total consistency with the shape of land masses as depicted on the globe as a tradeoff for less distortion in area. Such maps are not truly conformal.

Equal Area Maps

Equal area maps of the world are drawn in such a way that the relative size of land masses, as reflected on the globe, are preserved. As noted previously, Greenland is approximately one-ninth the size of South America. On an equal area map of the world, Greenland and South America are drawn to reflect this true size relationship. Compare areas of Greenland and South America as they appear in the Mercator projection map in Figure 14–3 and in the Robinson's (equal area projection) map in Figure 14–4.

Preserving proper size relationships among land areas requires that some distortion occur in their shapes. It is not possible for an equal area map to be drawn so that all shapes are as they appear on the globe.

There are relatively few equal area world maps hanging in classrooms as compared to conformal world maps. Traditionally, educators (many with little formal training in issues associated with maps and globes) have opted for maps featuring land masses shaped as they appear on globes.

Because of the enormous distortions of areas of some important world land masses on conformal maps, equal area maps should be available in every elemen-

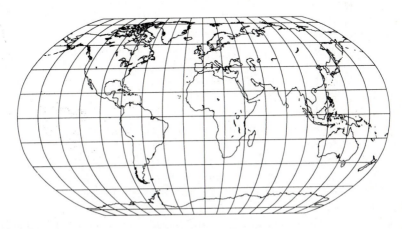

FIGURE 14–4
An example of an equal area world map: Robinson's projection.

Reprinted with permission from Edward B. Espenshade, Jr., ed., *Goode's World Atlas*. 18th ed., p. xi. Chicago: Rand McNally, 1990.

tary classroom. Ideally, each classroom should have one world map of each type. Exposure to both conformal and equal area maps *and* to globes provides children with a solid grounding in relative sizes and areas of land masses. Such lessons, too, reinforce the idea that all renderings of a sphere onto a flat surface result in important distortions.

BASIC MAP AND GLOBE SKILLS

Eight basic map and globe skills are of interest to the elementary social studies teacher. These skills are the following:

1. recognizing shapes
2. utilizing scale
3. recognizing symbols
4. utilizing direction
5. determining absolute location
6. pointing out relative location
7. describing earth-sun relationships
8. interpreting the information on maps and globes

Each of these skills can be understood at many levels of sophistication. In well-planned programs, they tend to be introduced so that pupils in the early grades deal with only the very basic skills. In the middle and upper grades, learners are exposed to the more sophisticated skills.

Some specialists in geographic education have gone so far as to suggest that specific kinds of map and globe skills should be taught at each elementary grade level. This practice has often resulted in long lists of grade-level-specific learning activities. There is a danger of cutting the content into "bites" that may be too small. The learning outcomes may focus on trivial content.

Another argument against the practice of developing unique skills activities for each grade is that youngsters *within* a given grade level vary tremendously. Some second graders can handle fairly sophisticated content; on the other hand, some sixth graders experience difficulty with skills activities that are supposed to provide few serious challenges to second graders.

When thinking about sequencing skills, it makes more sense to think in terms of simple to complex. It is useful to consider the sorts of skills activities that, *in general,* might be appropriate for children in the early grades (kindergarten to second grade), middle grades (third to fourth grade), and upper grades (fifth to sixth grade).

Even this kind of a three-stage sequence of skill development must be approached cautiously because of the individual differences among pupils. The most important point about skills development is that the more basic information should be introduced before the more complex.

In the subsections that follow, basic information about each basic skill is introduced. In addition, ideas about sequencing instruction from the early grades, through the middle grades, and into the upper grades are provided.

Recognizing Shapes

Recognizing shapes is one of the most fundamental map and globe skills. Though the skill may appear to be simple or even simplistic, many sophisticated analyses in geography require a grasp of the importance of physical shapes, particularly those of land masses. For example, to appreciate that a narrow peninsula may have a climate that varies dramatically from the climate of a central location at the heart of a continent, a person must know what a peninsula is. The kinds of learning associated with recognizing shapes increase in complexity as children move through the elementary program.

Utilizing Scale

Scale is an abstract and very difficult concept. Teachers find teaching the utilization of scale to be one of their most challenging assignments. (See the following boxed essay for a suggested method to help pupils understand the concept of scale.) Scale is difficult because it requires the concurrent understanding of two subordinate understandings. Each of these can frustrate pupils, especially those in the early elementary grades.

BOX 14–2   **Helping Young Children Learn About Scale.**

Scale is a challenging concept for children in the early grades. Some teachers have found it useful to take pictures of familiar objects in the classroom using a camera that produces instant prints. Then pupils are asked to measure the object as it exists in "real life" and the object as it is depicted in the photograph. They can be asked how many heights of the object in the photograph would be required to reach the same height as the real object.

This exercise can help learners grasp the idea that multiples of units on a scale can be used to determine how large something is in reality. It is often useful to take pictures of similar objects at different distances. This helps develop the idea that scales can change.

Think About This

1. What major misconceptions do you think children in the early grades might have at the beginning of this exercise? Why do you think so?
2. What kinds of objects in the classroom might be best suited as subjects for a photograph to be used to introduce the idea of scale?
3. What difficulties might you expect learners to have in understanding the scale differences revealed by photographs of the same object taken at different distances? How might these difficulties be overcome?

First, to appreciate scale, a person needs to know that geographical features (mountains, rivers, oceans, and so forth) can be visually depicted in a convenient way. For example, it is possible to represent a mountain by taking a photograph of the mountain. Learners need to grasp that the mountain is real; they need to know the photograph is real; and, most importantly, they need to understand that there is a connection between the mountain as depicted in the photograph and the actual mountain itself.

Second, a child looking at a photograph of a mountain needs to recognize that there is a knowable physical size relationship between the size of the mountain as it exists on the earth's surface and the size as it is depicted in the photograph. A sound understanding of the principle of using small, convenient representations as reliable indicators of the size of large phenomena is fundamental to an appreciation of scale. Pupils who lack this basic knowledge have a very difficult time grasping the idea that the scales on maps and globes can be used to make accurate statements about the actual sizes of the physical features of the earth.

Recognizing Symbols

Both maps and globes feature many symbols. These symbols represent a convenient shorthand for the kinds of phenomena that exist in the world. For people who understand them, they efficiently communicate a tremendous amount of information. But for individuals who do not know what they mean, they are

Simple maps, such as this one constructed by a primary grade class, helps pupils learn important map skills such as symbols, direction, and relative location.

confusing marks that can lead to serious misunderstandings. Because symbols are so basic to an understanding of maps and globes, recognizing symbols has long been recognized as one of the most important map and globe skills.

Pupils must recognize that symbols represent real objects. Maps and globes in their entireties are symbols. They are representations of part of or all of the earth's surface. It is important that pupils understand that even the colors on maps and globes function as symbols. Younger pupils are sometimes confused about this. When they see Kansas depicted in orange, they may receive the impression that everything in Kansas literally *is* orange. Teachers, then, need to be careful to explain the symbolic nature of maps as a whole as well as the meaning of the more specific symbols indicating things such as airports, highways, boundary lines, and large cities.

LESSON
▪ IDEA ▪

Learning about Map Symbols

Grade Level: 1–3. *Objective:* Learners can create symbols to represent real objects. *Suggested Procedure:* Six ideas for helping beginning learners understand map symbols follow.

1. Cut out well-known symbols for businesses and other organizations from newspapers and magazines. For example, symbols representing the Olympics, the United Nations, Volkswagen, Texaco, and many other organizations, firms, and groups might be selected. Ask how many youngsters recognize each symbol. Explain why symbols are used (to save time, to provide for ready recognition, and so forth). Does the school have a mascot? Is there a symbol that represents a favorite sports team? Lead into the idea that mapmakers and globe makers use many symbols.

2. Let pupils decide on five new clubs that should be started in the school. Once they have identified these groups, set them to work developing a symbol for each club. Sometimes it works well to organize learners into teams for this activity. Follow up with a discussion about what goes into a good symbol. (It is easy to remember, and quickly communicates a great deal of information about the group or thing for which it stands.)

3. To prepare children to work comfortably with the symbols that will appear on the maps or globe they will use, develop sets of flashcards. On one side will be the symbol. On the other side will be the thing for which the symbol stands. These cards can help youngsters grasp the meaning of symbols.

4. Another technique to help pupils learn the meanings of symbols used on maps involves the use of simple two-part puzzles. These can be made from construction paper. From sources such as *National Geographic*, find pictures of things that are depicted by symbols on maps. Paste a picture on the top half of a sheet of construction paper. On the bottom half, draw the symbol used for the thing depicted. Then cut the sheet into two parts. Give pupils a mixed group of top and bottom sheets, and have them try to fit the sheets together by using their knowledge of symbols. When the sheets fit properly, they know they have matched the symbol to the thing it depicts. See the figure on page 358.

Photo of church

Symbol of church

5. Ask pupils to develop symbols for the school desks or tables, for the teacher's desk, for the doors, and for the chalkboards. Then give them a blank outline map of the classroom. Ask them to use their symbols to indicate the locations of the school desks or tables, the teacher's desk, the doors, and the chalkboards. Display the finished products, and ask several volunteers to explain their maps.

6. Provide pupils with a simple map featuring a key that explains the symbols. Ask them to explain what they might see if they took a trip along a specified route depicted on the map. Remind them to refer to the meanings of the symbols provided in the key. An example of such an exercise is provided in the figure on page 359.

   Directions: Describe a trip a person might make along this route, starting at point *A* and finishing at point *B*. Use the key below to interpret the symbols on the map.

Recognizing shapes, utilizing scale, and recognizing symbols all have different educational emphases at different grade levels. These emphases are summarized in Table 14–1.

Utilizing Direction

The proper use of globes and maps depends on an ability to become properly oriented to direction. A sound understanding of the major and intermediate compass directions is basic to pinpointing locations. It is particularly important that learners master and use the concepts of directions before working with wall maps.

Otherwise, they tend to use terms such as "up" and "down" when referring to "north" and "south," and "right" and "left" when referring to "east" and "west." These inappropriate terms can contribute to the development of inaccurate information (the Pacific Ocean always lies to the left).

Determining Absolute Location

Determining absolute location requires pupils to locate any point on the earth's surface. To adequately perform the skill, learners must be familiar with the lines of latitude and longitude. Specifically, they must understand how a longitude-latitude grid system can be used to identify the "address" of every location on earth. Generally, teachers have pupils work with very simple grids before they introduce the global system of latitude and longitude (Figure 14–5).

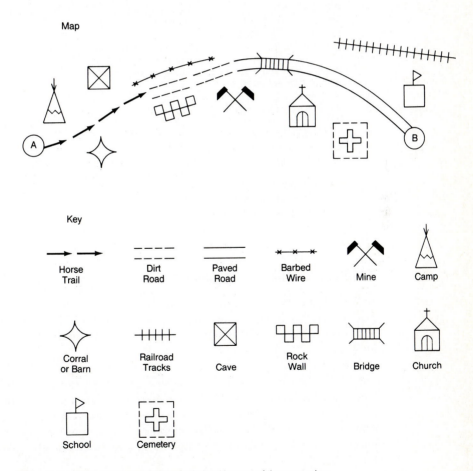

The authors wish to thank Judy Harber for help with some of these exercises.

TABLE 14–1
The Grade-Level Emphases for (1) Recognizing Shapes, (2) Utilizing Scale, and
(3) Recognizing Symbols.

	Kindergarten to Second Grade Emphases	Third to Fourth Grade Emphases	Fifth to Sixth Grade Emphases
Recognizing Shapes	Introduction to basic information about shape. Recognition that the earth is basically round. Recognition of the basic shapes of the continents and oceans (near end of second grade).	Recognition of the shapes of smaller land masses, such as islands, peninsulas, and isthmuses. Recognition of the shapes of smaller bodies of water, such as lakes, bays, and sounds.	Recognition of certain kinds of map distortion. Identification of the patterns of flow of the major rivers. Identification of the shapes of the major physical regions.
Utilizing Scale	Introduction of the basic concepts such as "larger" and "smaller." Recognition of the simple increments of measure (city blocks, for example). Identification of the objects of different sizes in pictures.	Utilization of the scale on simple maps. Solution of simple distance problems using scale. Recognition that scale may vary from map to map and globe to globe.	Utilization of the many kinds of scales. Recognition that the amount of detail on a map varies with its scale.
Recognizing Symbols	Recognition of the meanings of common signs (stop signs, for example). Recognition that some colors on maps are regularly used to represent land and water. Recognition that symbols stand for things in the real world.	Utilization of symbols for the major landscape features on maps and globes. Recognition of the traditional symbols for cities, railroads, rivers, and highways.	Utilization of the symbols on special purpose maps. Recognition that the same symbol may mean different things on different maps and globes.

Pointing Out Relative Location

Relative location refers to the location of one place in terms of one or more other places. When Chicago is described as being north of Houston, east of Omaha, and west of New York, the description is making reference to Chicago's relative location.

Many elementary social studies programs begin building the skill of pointing out relative location by helping youngsters to first recognize their relative location with regard to familiar places. The school's relative location might be described by pointing out its position in terms of the nearby parks and homes. Often, the local community is pinpointed first by reference to places in the state, later by reference to places in the nation, and still later by reference to other locations around the globe.

FIGURE 14–5
An example of a grid activity to help pupils learn how to find places when given the coordinates of latitude and longitude.
Directions: Find the secret word by placing an X in each of these squares: C2, C5, C8; D2, D5, D8; E2, E3, E4, E5, E8; F2, F5, F8; G2, G5, G8.

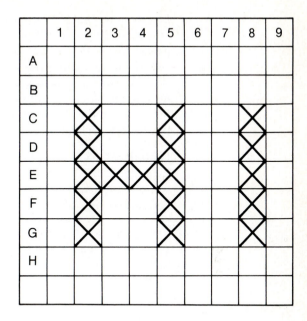

	1	2	3	4	5	6	7	8	9
A									
B									
C		X			X			X	
D		X			X			X	
E		X	X	X	X			X	
F		X			X			X	
G		X			X			X	
H									

LESSON
• *IDEA* •

Learning about Absolute Location

Grade Level: 2–4. *Objective:* Learners can apply knowledge of the grid system to locating places on maps. *Suggested Procedure:* Five ideas for helping beginners learn about relative location follow.

1. Prepare a simple grid with squares along the top identified by numbers and squares along the side identified by letters. In advance, determine which squares, when colored in, will spell a word. Give learners the directions to shade in squares that are identified by coordinates. (Shade in these squares: A-1, A-3, B-2, B-3, B-4, B-5, C-1, C-5, C-6 . . . and so forth.) When pupils have completed the exercise, they should be able to see the secret word. See the sample provided in Figure 14.5.

2. Provide children with a simple outline map of the world. The map should include the lines of latitude and longitude, and a simple compass rose. Play a Find the Continent game with the members of the class. Give map coordinates. Then ask pupils to name the nearest continent. (What is the nearest continent to 30° south latitude and 150° east longitude? [Australia])

3. In a learning center, provide several short books about various countries of the world. Inside each book neatly print a coordinate of latitude and longitude that would fall within the boundaries of the country about which the book is written. Provide pupils with an outline map of the world featuring the political boundaries of the nations. Ask them to use the coordinate of latitude and longitude to identify the location of the country the book describes, then shade in or color this country on the outline map.

4. In a learning center, place several newspaper articles with datelines from a number of cities around the world. Attach each article to a sturdy piece of paper. Above the article, write the latitude and longitude of the dateline city. Then have pupils use a globe or an atlas to locate the city.

5. Write an itinerary about a journey to various cities in the world. Instead of naming the cities, identify them only by coordinates of latitude and longitude. Give these to pupils. Ask them to name the cities and plot the route the traveler took on a world outline map. Here are some possibilities:

Latitude 22° 53′ 43″ S, Longitude 43° 13′ 22″ W (Rio de Janeiro, Brazil)
Latitude 62° 28′ 15″ N, Longitude 114° 22′ 00″ W (Yellowknife, Northwest Territories, Canada)
Latitude 48° 50′ 14″ N, Longitude 2° 20′ 14″ E (Paris, France)

Different aspects of utilizing direction and of determining absolute location and relative location are emphasized when these concepts are taught at different grade levels. These emphases are summarized in Table 14–2.

TABLE 14–2
The Grade-Level Emphases for (1) Utilizing Direction, (2) Determining Absolute Location, and (3) Pointing Out Relative Location.

	Kindergarten to Second Grade Emphases	Third to Fourth Grade Emphases	Fifth to Sixth Grade Emphases
Utilizing direction	Introduction to the four cardinal compass directions. Introduction, very basic, to latitude and longitude (referred to at this level as north-to-south lines and east-to-west lines).	Description of the locations of continents in terms of their directional locations from one another. Location of the Prime Meridian. Utilization of a compass to orient a map, and of the compass rose on a map. Introduction to the intermediate directions.	Recognition of the difference between true and magnetic North Utilization of intermediate direction to provide precise information about locations and paths of travel.
Determining absolute location	Utilization of relative terms such as "right," "left," "near," "far," "up," "down," "back," "front." Location of the places on a globe as being north or south of the equator.	Introduction to the use of grid systems. Location of the places on maps and globes using simple grid systems.	Location of places using the coordinates of latitude and longitude. Identification of the degree position of important lines of latitude including the equator, the Arctic and Antarctic circles, and the Tropics of Cancer and Capricorn.
Pointing out relative location	Description of one place in a room in terms of the other places in the room. Identification of the location of the school in terms of the other parts of the community.	Description of the location of the state within the nation. Identification of the local community in terms of its location in the state and nation.	Location of the local community relative to any other place on the globe. Description of the relative location of any two points on the globe.

Describing Earth-Sun Relationships

Proper understanding of earth-sun relationships is an essential ingredient of knowledge regarding diverse topics such as global time, the seasons, and the changing annual wind patterns. Many elementary youngsters find content related to earth-sun relationships to be difficult.

Part of the problem is our language. We speak of the sun "rising" and "setting." This terminology is based on an illusion that makes sense. As residents of the earth's surface, we are not physically aware that the globe is spinning on its axis. Hence, the "rising" and "setting" terminology does accurately describe what we see, but this language does not properly describe what is going on. Adults (most of them, at least) know that the sun does not move, but rather that the earth's spinning only makes it appear to do so. Younger elementary children lack this understanding. Many of them really believe that it is the sun that does the moving.

As they progress through the elementary program, learners are exposed to the concepts of the "seasons." They are taught that the seasons change because the angle of the sun's rays strikes some parts of the earth's surface more directly at certain times of the year than at others (Figure 14–6). Many children who grasp this basic idea have trouble understanding exactly how this happens. Some conclude erroneously that the earth wobbles back and forth on its axis, thus causing a change in where the sun's rays strike most directly. Teachers find they must work very hard if pupils are to grasp exactly how the seasonal change can occur without "global wobble."

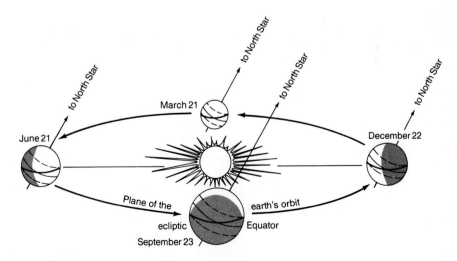

FIGURE 14–6
The location of the earth in relation to the sun on key dates. Many elementary pupils have difficulty accepting the idea that the earth does not swing back and forth or wobble on its axis. A figure such as this can help to explain what actually happens. The earth's axis always points toward the North Star. Note that the sun directly strikes its surface at different points at different times of the year.

Molded relief maps are fascinating to pupils and are useful in teaching a wide variety of map skills.

Interpreting Information on Maps and Globes

The skill of interpreting information on maps and globes is the broadest of them all. It is perhaps the most important for elementary social studies programs because it establishes a purpose for many of the other map and globe skills. Unless programs involve pupils in using the other skills, they may see the instruction that focuses on these skills as boring and directed toward no useful end. But when these skills are used to produce new information, pupils tend to appreciate their importance. Table 14–3 summarizes the different grade-level emphases used when teaching pupils how to describe earth-sun relationships and when teaching them how to interpret map and globe information.

TEACHING ALL OF THE SKILLS AT EACH GRADE LEVEL

Sometimes, new teachers assume that the more basic skills (such as, perhaps, symbol recognition) should be taught to younger children and that these learners should not be exposed to the more advanced skills. There are two difficulties with this approach.

First, there is nothing inherently either easy or difficult about any of these skills. Each can be taught at varying levels of complexity. A teacher would not

TABLE 14–3

The Grade-Level Emphases for (1) Describing Earth-Sun Relationships and (2) Interpreting the Information on Maps and Globes

	Kindergarten to Second Grade Emphases	Third to Fourth Grade Emphases	Fifth to Sixth Grade Emphases
Describing earth-sun relationships	Recognition of the terms "summer," "fall," "winter," "spring," "day," and "night." Identification of the direction of sunrise and sunset. Description of how the turning of the earth causes night and day.	Description of how the earth moves around the sun. Description of the inclination of the earth on its axis.	Description of the relationship of the sun to the equator, Tropic of Cancer, Tropic of Capricorn, Arctic Circle, and Antarctic Circle. Recognition that the globe is divided into 360 degrees. Recognition that the earth has twenty-four time zones that are each fifteen degrees wide. Utilization of the analemma to determine where the sun's rays strike the earth most directly on each day of the year.
Interpreting the information on maps and globes	Interpretation of the information from pictures and simple maps. Recognition that no one, not even an astronaut in space, can see the whole earth at one time. Construction and interpretation of simple local neighborhood and community maps.	Preparation of more complex local community maps and the interpretation of information contained on these maps. Description of the population distributions and terrain features on maps. Explanation of the basic causes of climate by referring to the information on maps.	Prediction about the probable climate of a place by viewing maps to determine its elevation, proximity to ocean currents, latitude, and continental or coastal position. Explanation of the geographical constraints on historical or current events through reference to maps. Prediction of elevation change by examining river flow direction on maps.

expect kindergarten children and sixth graders to engage in similar learning activities nor to develop similar depths of understanding about a given skill. Yet each group should be exposed to appropriate learning experiences for each skill.

Second, when teachers of younger children decide to omit the teaching of a "difficult" skill, they often eliminate that of interpreting information. This is a serious mistake. This skill allows pupils to put to work the other skills they have learned as they try to solve problems.

Interpreting exercises help pupils see a purpose for lessons that require them to master map and globe skills. These activities extend their abilities to make sense out of their world. If such activities are eliminated in the early grades, many pupils will see little use in learning the other basic map and globe skills. As a result, teachers may face serious motivational problems, which can inhibit learning.

KEY IDEAS IN SUMMARY

1. Many adults have confused ideas about locations of places on the globe. Elementary pupils are even more likely to insufficiently grasp the map and globe skills needed for the proper understanding of geographical location. Some misunderstandings result from a lack of any information at all, others from inadequate information. For example, large wall maps sometimes distort shapes and sizes of land masses.

2. Globes should receive more attention in elementary social studies classrooms. Only the globe shows places on earth with a minimum of shape and size distortion and with accurate relative placement of water and land areas. To be useful as teaching tools, there should be at least one globe available for every three or four pupils.

3. Globes have disadvantages. They are bulky. They are rather expensive. They do not lend themselves well to teaching certain kinds of content. For example, if a teacher wanted to teach about a relatively small area, perhaps the state of South Carolina, the area of interest would be too small on a globe to be of any practical value. A globe large enough to display South Carolina at a size sufficient for learners to see easily might be too large to fit in the classroom.

4. There are three common types of globes found in elementary schools. These are (a) readiness globes, (b) elementary globes, and (c) intermediate globes. Readiness globes include only basic information. Elementary globes include latitude, longitude, and other details not included on readiness globes. Intermediate globes include even more information.

5. Maps are useful for teaching certain kinds of content, such as the study of relatively small areas. Typically they are less expensive than globes, and are much easier to store.

6. Because they attempt to represent a sphere on a flat surface, all maps include distortions. On conformal world maps, shapes of land areas are as they are on the globe, but the areas of land masses distant from the equator are greatly distorted. On equal area world maps, areas of land masses are consistent with areas as they appear on the globe, but shapes may be distorted. Teachers need to instruct students about the problem of distortion. Ideally, students should have opportunities to compare and contrast depictions of places in the world as they appear on the globe, on a conformal world map, and on an equal area world map.

7. There are eight basic map and globe skills. They are (a) recognizing shapes, (b) utilizing scale, (c) recognizing symbols, (d) utilizing direction, (e) determining absolute location, (f) pointing out relative location, (g) describing earth-sun relationships, and (h) interpreting information on maps and globes.

8. It is desirable to introduce all eight map and globe skills at each level of the elementary school program. The skills remain common throughout the pro-

gram, but the activities used to introduce and reinforce them change with grade levels.

9. It is especially important that pupils have opportunities to use map and globe skills to solve problems. Such experiences help establish the importance of these skills. Additionally, they can extend learners' sense of understanding of the world and, by so doing, build interest in other aspects of the social studies program.

POSTTEST

Answer each of the following true/false questions.

1. It is possible to produce a map in which there is no distortion whatever.
2. Sometimes, very young elementary school children have difficulty differentiating between land areas and water areas on a globe.
3. It is recommended that conformal world maps but not equal area world maps be available in every classroom.
4. Some elementary school pupils believe the seasons occur because, from time to time, the earth wobbles on its axis.
5. Of the eight basic map and globe skills, only the simplest one or two should be taught to children in kindergarten and grade one.

QUESTIONS

1. What factors contribute to misunderstandings many pupils have about the relative locations of places on the earth's surface?
2. What are some advantages of using globes when providing learners with basic understandings about shapes and sizes of different lands?
3. What are the characteristics of readiness globes, elementary globes, and intermediate globes?
4. What are general characteristics of conformal world maps and equal area world maps?
5. What are the eight basic maps skills?
6. Suppose you were challenged to defend the inclusion of map and globe skills instruction in the elementary social studies program. How would you respond?
7. In the past, some people have said that the skill of interpreting information on maps and globes is too sophisticated for pupils in kindergarten to second

grade. How do you feel about the suggestion that this skill be reserved for older learners? Why do you take this position?

8. Many pupils have a difficult time understanding that the earth does not wobble back and forth on its axis. The axis always points to the North Star, regardless of the time of year. What might you do to help learners grasp this point?

9. Suppose you were assigned to teach map and globe skills to a group of third graders. What would you use maps for? What would you use globes for?

10. Children in the elementary grades often greatly underestimate the size of the continent of Africa. What might you do to help them understand the size of this continent relative to the size of North America? Relative to the size of the United States?

EXTENDING UNDERSTANDING AND SKILL

1. Interview four or five pupils who are at a grade level you would like to teach. Ask questions to determine the accuracy of their information about subjects such as (a) the relative locations of major U.S. cities, (b) the directions of flow of major U.S. rivers, and (c) the relative sizes of the continents. Share your findings with others in your class.

2. For each of the eight basic map and globe skills, prepare a lesson directed at the age group you would like to teach. Discuss your suggestions with others in your class and with your instructor.

3. Look at several elementary social studies textbooks. Do a content analysis of each to determine how much attention is paid to developing pupils' understandings of the eight basic map and globe skills. Prepare a short paper in which you describe the relative attention paid to each skill.

4. Develop a series of five or six activities focusing on the skill of interpreting information on maps and globes, designed for use by children in kindergarten, grade one, and grade two. Make copies of your activities to share with others in your class.

5. Prepare a complete plan for a field trip designed to strengthen learners' grasp of basic map and globe skills. Identify the preplanning procedures, learning objectives, teacher activities, pupil activities, and evaluation procedures. Turn your plan into your instructor for review.

REFERENCES

ESPENSHADE, E. B., JR. *Goode's World Atlas*, 18th ed. Chicago: Rand McNally, 1990.
MANCHESTER, W. *American Caesar: Douglas MacArthur: 1880–1964*. New York: Dell, 1978.

SUPPLEMENTAL READING

DAVID, D. W. "Big Maps—Little People." *Journal of Geography* (March/April 1990), pp. 58–62.

FORSYTH, A. S. "How We Learn Place Location: Bringing Theory and Practice Together." *The Social Studies* (November/December 1988), pp. 500–503.

GREENHOOD, D. *Mapping*. Chicago: The University of Chicago Press, 1971.

HASS, M. E., AND B. G. WARASH. "Adventures with the Globe: Early Childhood Geography." *Day Care and Early Childhood* (Winter 1989), pp. 10–13.

HATCHER, B. "Putting Young Cartographers on the Map." *Childhood Education* (May/June 1983), pp. 311–15.

MARTIN, K. D. "Creating an Interactive Globe." *Journal of Geography* (July/August 1989), pp. 140–42.

MELAHN, D. "Putting it in Perspective: Geography Activities for Primary Children." *Journal of Geography* (July/August 1989), pp. 137–39.

15

READING, WRITING, AND SOCIAL STUDIES LESSONS

This chapter provides information to help the reader:

1. develop strategies appropriate for each stage of the reading process,
2. determine the approximate grade-level reading difficulty of individual prose selections by using the Fry Readability Graph,
3. recognize characteristics that contribute to the difficulty level of an individual prose selection,
4. describe vocabulary problems that may interfere with learners' abilities to learn from prose material,
5. point out how pupils may be taught to work more effectively with selected parts of a textbook, and
6. identify writing functions that can be developed through social studies lessons.

PRETEST

Answer each of the following true/false questions.

1. A primary purpose of prereading strategies is to provide a frame of reference for pupils to use when they read.
2. Structured overviews are basically summaries of material to be read that are presented by the teacher prior to reading.
3. The major purpose of during-reading strategies is to help pupils learn word-attack skills.
4. The postreading stage facilitates learners' comprehension of what they have read.
5. The Cloze Procedure helps the teacher to identify the general appropriateness of a reading selection for an individual learner.

INTRODUCTION

Though today's teachers employ many kinds of information sources, the social studies textbook continues to be widely used. Other reading materials also feature prominently in social studies lessons, including encyclopedias, almanacs, magazines, and newspapers. Because of the heavy reliance teachers place on printed materials, in many classrooms pupils' abilities to learn are strongly influenced by their reading abilities.

Reading competence associates with success in many academic areas. Increasingly, schools are challenging teachers to provide reading instruction throughout the school day, not just during the prescribed reading period. Hence, it has become common for teachers to devote attention to reading during the social studies period.

Concern for developing pupils' literacy is also reflected in the current emphasis on improved writing skills. Social studies lessons provide numerous opportunities for teachers to support the development of learners' writing abilities. This chapter introduces general approaches to helping pupils become more proficient readers and writers while learning social studies content.

DEVELOPING READING STUDY SKILLS

The human brain does not act as a camera that passively records its exposure to reality. Instead, the brain actively organizes and transforms information. The way a person's brain does this has an important bearing on how well he or she retrieves

BOX 15–1 **Third Graders' Abilities to Think and Write about What They Read: Some Disappointing Statistics**

In 1989, the National Center for Education Statistics reported on third graders' higher-level thinking abilities as reflected in their written responses to questions about a social studies reading assignment. It was hoped that, at a minimum, pupils would be able to make some comparisons. This is what the researchers found.*

69.6 percent of the pupils made no comparisons at all in their written responses.
29.9 percent of the pupils made unsatisfactory comparisons.
0.5 percent of the pupils made only minimal comparisons.
None of the pupils made satisfactory comparisons.
None of the pupils made elaborate comparisons.

Think About This

1. What are your general reactions to this information?
2. Should third graders be able to make comparisons and contrasts based on their reading?
3. Do these results suggest more attention to reading and writing processes in social studies lessons is in order?

*Data are from Curtis O. Baker, ed., and Laurence T. Ogle, assoc. ed., *The Condition of Education, 1989: Volume One—Elementary and Secondary Education.* Washington, DC: National Center for Education Statistics, 1989, p. 75.

information and uses it later. Pupils can be taught to monitor the way they organize and store information and thus improve their learning from printed material. They need special help during three important reading stages. These are (1) prereading, (2) reading, and (3) postreading.

Instruction during the *prereading* stage is designed to help pupils discover a personal purpose for reading and establish a scheme to organize information they will be learning as they read. Teachers assist in this process by relating new information from the reading assignment to previously mastered material. Teachers also tell learners what they will be expected to do after completing reading to demonstrate that they understand what they have read.

During the *reading* stage learners read the assigned material. The teacher monitors them carefully to spot individuals who may have difficulty understanding what they are reading. This monitoring involves questioning pupils about what they are reading and encouraging them to think about the content. The teacher sometimes asks pupils to develop questions of their own that can be answered using the content from the reading assignment, and encourages learners to take notes focusing on major points.

During the *postreading* stage the teacher encourages pupils to reflect upon and evaluate what they have read, often by discussing one or more of the major ideas introduced in the reading assignment. The teacher attempts to involve the entire class in the postreading discussion, which allows him or her to identify and help individuals who may still be experiencing difficulty.

Developing reading study skills is an important part of any social studies program.

Prereading Techniques

Prior experiences help readers fit what they read into meaningful patterns. When people are lacking any experiential base related to what they read, they may find the information difficult to understand, and they may fail to grasp certain important ideas.

In elementary social studies classes, pupils often become frustrated when asked to read about people and places that are totally unfamiliar. Prereading techniques seek to provide a frame of reference for pupils that will help them better grasp information introduced in prose materials. The teacher must help pupils establish a tie between what they already know and what they will be reading as part of a learning assignment. Three techniques that teachers have found useful are (1) the structured overview (2) ReQuest, and (3) reading guides: prereading stage.

The Structured Overview

A structured overview provides pupils with a graphic or pictorial display that illustrates relationships among concepts that will be featured in a reading assignment. Pupils should be involved in developing the overview. The teacher may ask them to brainstorm what they know or think they know about the topic to be read. The teacher may also ask learners to think about experiences they have had that might help them understand the subject to be studied.

Suppose a group of fifth graders were going to be assigned to read material on "The Westward Movement." The teacher might begin by asking them to think about the general issue of moving. What are things people have to think about when deciding whether to move or to stay where they are? What must they think about after the decision to move has been made? Responses to such questions can be graphically organized into a structured overview. An example is provided in Figure 15–1.

The structured overview diagram is used by pupils as they begin their reading. They are invited to add components to it as needed. The overview suggests things for them to think about as they read. It gives purpose to the activity. It helps them to fit new information into an orderly pattern, and to make sense out of what they read.

The structured overview can also play a role during postreading. Its categories provide a framework the teacher can use to discuss and debrief content with learners.

ReQuest

ReQuest is an acronym for "reciprocal questioning" (Manzo 1969). It involves both teacher and pupils in asking and answering questions related to a prose selection. Learners' active participation in framing questions helps them draw on prior knowledge related to new content to be introduced in the reading assignment. It also helps them to see relationships between their own interests and topics to be covered in the reading. Questions guide pupils toward appropriate content once they begin working on the assignment.

These steps are followed in the ReQuest technique:

1. The teacher and pupils read together the first sentence of a reading assignment.
2. The teacher closes his or her book while pupils keep theirs open. Pupils are

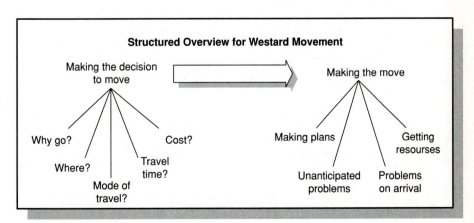

FIGURE 15–1
Sample structured overview diagram.

invited to ask the teacher any question they wish that relates to the sentence that has been read. The teacher answers the questions as accurately as possible. If one sentence is not enough to stimulate questions, another sentence or two may be read. During this phase the teacher may guide the general direction of learners' questions.

3. The pupils close their books. The teacher asks questions. These questions are designed to help pupils recall information from their own experience that may help them understand content introduced in the reading material.

4. Procedures outlined in steps one, two, and three may be repeated several times. When the teacher senses pupils are ready, he or she asks, "What do you think you will be reading about in the rest of this material?" This question helps learners develop expectations that can help them better understand what they will be reading.

Reading Study Guides: Prereading Stage

Reading study guides are used during all stages of the reading process. They are designed to help pupils monitor their own comprehension. These guides are prepared by the teacher. Development begins by the teacher scanning reading material to identify *pausing points,* places where readers might logically be asked to stop and assess their understanding of what they have read.

The reading study guide takes the form of sheets of paper containing questions or points for learners to consider. The guide tells pupils how far to read before stopping to think about questions or consider points.

The reading study guide for prereading helps learners organize material they will be reading. It prompts them to think about what they already know, and to speculate about what they might do to demonstrate their learning after they have completed reading. Questions such as these often are found in a prereading stage reading study guide.

1. *Establishing familiarity with the content*
   (a) How does the material relate to what I already know? (Pupils are encouraged to skim content quickly to answer this question.)
   (b) How interesting does the material appear to be?
   (c) What are some new ideas I will be expected to learn?
   (d) How is the material organized?
   (e) What would be the best way for me to read this material?
2. *Establishing a purpose for reading*
   (a) What will I be expected to know and do after I have finished reading?
   (b) Why is this material important?

During-Reading Techniques

As they read, pupils need to know how to recognize important information and to make connections among ideas that are presented. Many elementary school learners have difficulty distinguishing between important and unimportant content.

Many also have problems identifying relationships among important content elements. Three techniques that are widely used to help learners are (1) visual frameworks, (2) multipass reading, and (3) reading study guides: during-reading stage.

Visual Frameworks

Visual frameworks help pupils to organize content from the materials they read. Many teachers have traditionally responded to the need to help learners organize material by teaching them to outline what they have read. Some pupils find outlining to be very tedious and fail to appreciate its value in helping them grasp new content. Younger elementary pupils often lack outlining skills. The visual frameworks approach overcomes some of the difficulties with content outlining.

The number of reading purposes that might be established for a prose selection of only two or three paragraphs is enormous. Assignments that require learners to focus on a specific category of fact might be made. Others might require them to identify certain cause and effect relationships. Still others might ask pupils to make predictions of future trends based on the information introduced in the reading assignment.

It is clear that an assignment asking learners to focus on certain kinds of facts requires them to look differently at the reading content than when they are asked to identify cause and effect relationships. To assist pupils in developing an appropriate approach to their reading assignments, it makes sense for teachers to explain the nature of the task clearly. Then additional assistance can be provided through visual frameworks. These are devices that will help learners "see" on which elements of content they should focus. They also provide a means for taking good notes on the reading.

LESSON • IDEA •

Using Visual Frameworks: Spanish Colonizers and the Caribbean

Grade Level: 5. *Objective:* Learners can identify information from a reading passage by completing a visual framework. *Suggested Procedure:* To see how this approach might work, suppose that two teachers have different purposes in mind when they assign learners in their classes to read the same short selection. Following the selection itself, there will be a brief description of the "purpose" established by each teacher and a related visual framework. Here is the selection:

> Christopher Columbus first landed on San Salvador Island. This happened in 1492. San Salvador is part of those islands that today we call the Bahamas. Later, Columbus went on to discover many Caribbean islands. He set up a fort on one of the biggest islands. This island is called Hispaniola.
>
> Another famous Spanish sailor was Nicolas de Ovando. In 1502, he was sent to become the governor of Hispaniola. He brought many colonists with him. The colonists tried to make money in two ways. Some of them tried farming. Some of them tried mining. One of their big problems was finding people to do the hard work.
>
> One thing the early Spanish colonists tried to do was to make slaves of the Indians. This did not work. The Indians died when they were forced into slavery. At

first, the Spanish tried to solve the problem by capturing the Indians from other Islands. But many of these Indians died, too. Later, slaves were brought from Africa.

Even after all of these things were tried, there were still not enough people to do the work. Many of the original colonists from Spain gave up on Hispaniola. They moved to other islands in the Caribbean. Some of these colonists were led to island of Puerto Rico. This happened in 1508. The Spanish leader who led them there was Ponce de Leon. Another leader, Juan de Esquivel, took another group to Jamaica in 1509. The largest Caribbean island, Cuba, was reached by Spanish settlers in 1514.

The Purpose of Teacher 1:   What islands were discovered by Spain between 1492 and 1509, and who were the four famous Spanish explorers who took part in these discoveries?

To help pupils draw this information out of their reading, a visual framework like the following might be developed:

The Islands and Leaders

Islands   **Leaders**

_____   _____

_____   _____

_____   _____

_____   _____

This framework could help a learner read the material to find the information the teacher has established as a priority. Pupils may choose to write the information they find on the appropriate line.

The Purpose of Teacher 2:   How did the early Spanish settlers try to meet their need for workers, and what happened as a result?

To help learners draw this information out of their reading, a teacher might develop a visual framework such as the following for them to use:

Why Workers Were Needed

_____

_____

_____

_____

This Was Tried First   **This Was Tried Second**

_____   _____

_____   _____

Results   **Results**

_____   _____

_____   _____

Final Outcome

_____

_____

_____

Recall that both Teacher 1 and Teacher 2 are having their pupils read exactly the same material. But their purposes are very different. For this reason, the visual framework developed by Teacher 2 looks quite different from the one developed by Teacher 1. Teacher 2's framework helps learners focus on content they will need to respond to the cause-and-effect kind of question that this teacher sees as the major purpose of the reading assignment. The framework of Teacher 1, while very appropriate for that teacher's purpose, would not be appropriate at all for Teacher 2's purpose.

Visual frameworks can take many shapes. Some teachers help their pupils to work out their own frameworks. Whether developed by the teacher alone or with some active pupil participation, visual frameworks help learners master content assigned in required reading.

Multipass Reading

Multipass reading encourages readers to go over the same material several times, approaching the reading with a different purpose each time. The purpose of the first pass is to help learners develop a framework for the content and to relate it to what they already know. This is accomplished quickly. Learners are encouraged to skim the content, note major chapter divisions, and glance at the illustrations.

Once pupils have completed the first pass, the teacher asks general questions, such as the following.

- What is this chapter or section about?
- What do we already know about these events?
- How is the chapter organized? What comes first, second, third, and so forth?
- What kinds of photos or illustrations did you see? Why do you think they might have been included?

The second pass through the material helps pupils to identify major ideas. During this pass, learners read major headings, subsection headings, and the first sentences of paragraphs.

Most writers include the major ideas of their paragraphs in the first one or two sentences. When pupils read only the first sentence of each paragraph, they are able to pick up a surprising amount of key information. Even slow readers find they can learn a good deal about the content when they follow this procedure.

After learners have completed the second pass, the teacher again asks questions, such as:

- What are the main ideas you found?
- Are these ideas similar or different from those you already knew?
- What additional information do you need to find out whether the ideas you read about are true or false?

During the third pass, learners look for specific details. At this point they typically have a good idea about how the content is organized. This allows them to find needed details relatively quickly. Often this phase concludes with questions from the teacher, such as the following.

- What do people in Ethiopia eat?
- How are their houses different from ours?
- Is the climate there in summer different from ours?
- What different things are taught in school to boys and girls?

The final pass is for review. Pupils quickly read the entire assignment from beginning to end. This last pass helps individuals who may have missed important information to fill in the gaps.

Teachers who have not used multipass reading sometimes wonder about how much time it takes. The technique is not so time consuming as one might suppose. Some of the passes are completed very quickly. Once pupils have developed a general feel for how content is organized, even reading for details does not require a great deal of time. The higher rates of comprehension that often result with this technique save time later. Less time is needed for reteaching and review.

Reading Study Guides: During-Reading Stage

Reading study guides during this part of the reading activity help learners monitor their understanding as they read. The guide tells them when to stop and answer questions. The following questions are typical. Note the different purposes of questions in this example.

1. *Monitoring understanding*
   (a) Do I understand what I just read?
   (b) What are the important ideas in what I just read?
   (c) How does what I read relate to what I already know and believe?
   (d) What kinds of pictures came to mind as I read this material?
2. *Predicting and hypothesizing*
   (a) What do I expect to read about next?
   (b) Were the earlier ideas I had about what was going to happen correct?
   (c) What might be on a test over this material?
3. *Expanding and integrating*
   (a) How do all of the ideas I read about fit together?
   (b) If I could talk to the author about some of the things I read, what would I ask?

      (c) If I were to tell somebody about what I read, what would I say?
4. *Dealing with comprehension failure* (for pupils who have difficulty understanding some of the content)
      (a) Will it help if I reread the material?
      (b) Can I ignore the problem and hope I will understand the content better once I read on?
      (c) What might I ask the teacher that would help?
      (d) Where else could I turn for help about this content?

Postreading Techniques

What teachers do after learners have completed reading assigned material has an important influence on pupils' comprehension of the information. Learners need help relating new information to what they have learned previously.

    Small-group activities are particularly useful during the postreading stage. Sharing information with other learners stimulates pupils to reflect upon and react to what they have read. Also, the setting allows group members to benefit from the thinking processes of pupils who have successfully grasped the new content. This experience often helps pupils who are not well informed about what they have read to recognize and use approaches employed by more successful pupils. Approaches teachers use during postreading include (1) graphic post-organizers, (2) interaction frames, and (3) reading guides: postreading stage.

Graphic Post-Organizers

Graphic post-organizers represent an extension of the structured overview approach introduced earlier. The basic differences center on timing and on who is responsible for preparing the material. Structured overviews are prepared before reading takes place, and they are prepared jointly by pupils and their teacher. Graphic post-organizers are developed by pupils alone after they have completed reading the assigned material.

    In preparing learners to develop graphic organizers, the teacher divides the class into groups of four to six members each. The teacher provides each group with two packs of index cards, each of a different color.

    To begin the activity, the teacher tells class members that they are first to use note cards in only one of the packs. ("When we start, use only the *pink* cards. We will use the green ones later.") The teacher tells pupils that they should identify as many different major ideas (concepts) from the reading as they can. ("Let's think about what we read. First of all, take several pink cards. Quietly, write on the cards as many major ideas from the reading as you can recall. Write only one idea on each card. If you need more cards, raise your hand. I will bring you some. Are there questions? [Teacher responds to questions.] All right. Let's start.")

    The teacher monitors individual groups. After pupils have completed writing on their cards, the teacher moves on to the next phase of the activity. This requires members of each group to talk about their main ideas. Each group develops a master set of pink cards containing all of the major ideas the group has identified.

("Now, we will begin talking about the ideas we remembered. When I tell you to begin, I want you to take turns sharing with others in your group the major ideas you wrote on your cards. When everyone has had a turn, I want you to organize a large pile of pink cards that contains every major idea someone in your group identified. Kevin, can you tell me what I want the groups to do next? [Kevin responds. Teacher clarifies any misunderstandings.] Let's begin.")

As this phase unfolds, the teacher may need to establish a ground rule about the maximum number of major ideas each group will be allowed to have. The purpose of the exercise is for learners to identify the truly important ideas. Pupils sometimes indiscriminantly identify both important and unimportant ideas. If a teacher senses this happening, he or she might require each group to agree on no more than five or six major ideas. ("Some ideas you have identified probably are more important than others. As a group, I want you to identify no more than *six* major ideas. If you have more than six, discuss the ideas in your group. Then, decide which six are the most important.")

Next, the teacher asks pupils to lay their cards face up on the table. If there are important relationships among some of the major ideas, they should place these cards side by side. ("Now, put the cards with your major ideas on the table. Lay them so they are facing up. If some of these ideas are closely related, put those cards close together.")

At this point, pupils are directed to take cards from the second packet. ("All right, now I want each of you to take several of the *green* cards.") They are directed to look at the cards with the major ideas (the pink cards) and think about as many facts and other pieces of information from the reading that are related to the main ideas. They should write one fact or one item of information on each green card. ("Look at your major ideas. Your reading presented quite a bit of information about each one. I want you each to write down some information about the major ideas on the green cards. Write only one idea on each green card. Also, you might make a note about the specific major idea it relates to. Any questions? [Teacher responds to questions.] Let's begin.")

When this phase concludes, pupils are given time to discuss what they wrote as a group. The teacher then asks each group to arrange the cards with the specific information under the main ideas to which they refer (under the pink cards). ("Take a minute or two to talk about what you wrote. [Three or four minutes will suffice.] Now, I want you to arrange your green cards under the pink cards containing the major ideas. Be sure each green card goes under the pink card that contains the major idea to which it refers." [Pupils do this.])

A graphic layout of major ideas and supporting information results from this activity, with one set of cards representing major ideas and the other representing supporting information. All groups are asked to make chart displays of this information. They might use a large piece of paper or an overhead transparency. ("I want each group to draw a chart identifying the major ideas and related information. I am going to give each table a large piece of paper and some markers. Make a nice drawing that we can put up on the wall." [Teacher monitors this activity.])

The activity concludes with each group displaying its chart. A final discussion focuses on similarities and differences in major ideas and supporting information on each chart. The teacher may also wish to comment on any ideas that were missed by all groups.

Interaction Frames

Interaction frames help learners work with social studies content that refers to interactions among individuals or groups. For example, many fifth-grade classrooms read about the conflict between Roger Williams and the Puritan leaders of the Massachusetts Bay Colony. The interaction frame procedure is particularly useful for helping learners grasp positions of contending parties in such situations. Interaction frames are organized around these four key questions:

1. What were the goals of the various individuals or groups?
2. What actions did they take to accomplish these goals?
3. How did the individuals or groups get along?
4. What happened as a result of contacts between and among these individuals or groups?

Pupils are asked to think about what they have read as they respond to these questions. The teacher begins an interaction frame lesson by identifying the specific people or groups that will be the focus of the activity. Pupils are organized into groups, and each group develops answers to the four key questions. Each group shares its responses as part of a general class discussion. Pupils may construct a summary interaction frame chart based on the discussion. A model for such a chart is provided in Figure 15–2. Teachers may find it useful to provide copies of this chart to the class to reinforce understanding.

Reading Study Guides: Postreading Stage

Reading study guides during postreading help learners evaluate their content understanding. They also help them determine whether they need assistance with new information. Questions such as these are typical of those found in postreading stage reading study guides.

1. *Reflecting on what was read*
   (a) How interesting was the material?
   (b) How difficult did I find it?
   (c) What pictures come to mind as I think about what I read?
2. *Evaluating learning*
   (a) Am I able to write or state a summary of what I read?
   (b) Does my summary include all of the major ideas?
   (c) How do the ideas I read about compare to what I thought the material was about before I read it?
   (d) What parts did I find the most difficult?
3. *Anticipating the test*
   (a) What questions are likely to be on the test?

Individual or Group A	Individual or Group B
Goals of A	Goals of B
1.	1.
2.	2.
etc.	etc.
Actions taken by A	Actions taken by B
1.	1.
2.	2.
etc.	etc.

How did A and B get along? Conflicts (if any):
1.
2.
etc.
Compromises (if any):
1.
2.
etc.

What happened to A	What happened to B
1.	1.
2.	2.
etc.	etc.

Summary

_____

_____

_____

FIGURE 15-2
Sample format for an interaction frame chart

    (b) How can I review for the test?
    (c) How can I remember the information I will need to know for the test?
4. *Recording the products of reading* (Pupils write the answers to these questions.)
    (a) What key words and ideas did I learn?
    (b) What questions did I have about the material?
    (c) How could I summarize the material?
    (d) What kind of diagram might I construct that would help me organize and remember key points? (Pupils are encouraged to develop diagrams of their own design.)

    In summary, the postreading phase includes techniques designed to help learners better understand what they have read. Many of these techniques feature group interaction techniques that allow learners opportunities to work actively with new content and to benefit from insights of others. Postreading activities also provide teachers with opportunities to identify specific pupils who need more assistance with content introduced in reading assignments.

READABILITY ISSUES

Learners may face two general problems when they try to read the assigned materials in their social studies classes. First, the reading difficulty of the materials may be too high. Sentences may be long and complex. Second, the vocabulary used may contain many unfamiliar or difficult terms. The material that follows suggests several approaches to the general issue of reading comprehension focusing on these two general problems.

The Kinds of Vocabulary Difficulties

As we might expect in the elementary school, there are tremendous differences from grade level to grade level in the kinds of words that the mythical "average pupil" might be expected to know. Certainly it comes as no surprise that the vocabularies of average first graders are much more limited than those of average sixth graders. These differences are to be expected given the differences in physical maturity and in the extent of the life experiences of these pupils. Even with these grade-to-grade differences, there are some common patterns of difficulty.

Many pupils encounter difficulty with the readability of social studies texts.

Unfamiliar Vocabulary.   From time to time, nearly every learner will encounter words he or she does not recognize. Since this very same thing happens to adult readers who have much larger vocabularies, it is not surprising at all that it is a problem for pupils in the elementary grades.

Teachers, particularly beginners, sometimes are not prepared for the very limited vocabularies of many of the pupils in their classrooms. Sometimes these problems are difficult for teachers to spot as the causes of learners' reading difficulties. Teachers' eyes tend to skim over "simple" explanatory vocabulary to look for new, specialized terms that they do not expect learners to know. For example, when looking over material on election trends, an inexperienced teacher might fail to recognize that some members of the class might not know what a trend is. Without an adequate grasp of this term, pupils would have a high probability of experiencing difficulty with the content.

Out-of-date Words or Phrases.   Out-of-date expressions are really a category of unfamiliar terms, but of a particular kind: they are words or phrases that are no longer in common use. Such words pose a particular problem for learners when the prose material was written many years ago. Vocabulary changes over time. Some words that were very common years ago are used rarely today. For example,

---

BOX 15–2   **Is School Reading Being Made Too Easy?**

Recently, a concerned parent made the following comments at a meeting of a local school board.

> This past week, I had a chance to visit my son's third-grade classroom. While I was there, I looked over the textbooks that are being used. I am absolutely appalled by the extremely limited vocabularies used in these books. It appears to me that the publishers are pandering to the lowest common denominator. They have simplified these materials to the point that average and bright youngsters are not being challenged. In fact, I am very much concerned that my son will become terribly bored with this kind of material. It could affect his attitude toward school and toward learning. That concerns me.
>
> I would urge members of the board to look at some of the textbooks that were in the schools in Abe Lincoln's day. There was nothing simple or insulting about the vocabulary in those books. Of course, many youngsters didn't know all of the words when they had to begin reading them. But these books challenged the children. They made them stretch. They sought to *educate*. Can we say the same about the pap-filled textbooks we use now? I don't think so.

Think About This

1. Do educators today worry too much about the levels of difficulty of textbooks?
2. Do you think that textbooks are too easy, about right, or too difficult? Why do you think so?
3. If this parent is right in asserting that textbooks in Lincoln's day were more difficult to read, why might this have been true?
4. If this parent came to speak to you about this issue, how would you respond?
5. What do you think the members of the school board would say to this parent? Why do you think so?

at the turn of the century, children often wore arctics to school on rainy days. *Arctic*, a word meaning a high rubber overshoe, is almost never used today. Similarly, the word *lizzy* (sometimes *tin lizzie*) was applied endearingly by the Americans of the 1920s to their Model T Fords. Few pupils in the schools today know this term.

Outdated words and phrases are somewhat easier than the general unfamiliar vocabulary for teachers to deal with. These words tend to strike teachers as unusual when they encounter them in materials they look over in preparation for providing them as reading assignments. When teachers spot such terms, they can explain their meanings to pupils at the time the reading assignments are made.

Specialized Vocabulary.   Specialized vocabulary terms are generally closely tied to an academic subject area. For example, in geography, terms such as *latitude* and *longitude* might be regarded as tied to the content of this subject. Most teachers do not expect learners to be familiar with specialized vocabulary when they begin their study of a subject, and will often thoroughly explain the meaning of these specialized terms before asking pupils to read content in which they appear.

Vocabulary difficulties pose a very real problem for elementary learners in social studies classrooms. In attempting to respond to these difficulties, teachers have tried a number of approaches. Some teachers have pupils read short selections aloud and then ask questions about the meanings of words. Sometimes, they ask them to stop reading every time they encounter a word they do not know and take the time to look it up in a dictionary.

Asking learners to look up unfamiliar vocabulary in the dictionary poses several problems. The first of these has to do with the nature of dictionary definitions. Some definitions themselves contain words that are unfamiliar. Suppose, for example, that a given child did not know the meaning of the word *measles*. He or she might find something like this in a dictionary:

- *measles:* An acute contagious viral disease characterized by eruptive red

   blotching of the skin.

A learner who did not know the word *measles* would probably not know such words as *acute, contagious, viral,* or *blotching.*

It is true that some school dictionaries do a marvelous job of defining words in language pupils can understand. But there continue to be many classroom dictionaries that do not do this. In response to the problems their learners have experienced when working with such dictionaries, some teachers take the time to construct glossaries of their own. These glossaries contain the definitions of words that, over time, the teachers have found to pose problems for pupils. Words are defined in very simple terms. For example, a teacher-made glossary might define measles like this:

- *measles:* A common disease in children. It is a contagious disease. This means

    that someone who has it can pass it on to someone else. People with

    measles have skin that is covered with lots of red spots.

Most learners find it much easier to work with this kind of a definition than with a formal dictionary definition.

Some reading authorities express concern that many attempts to broaden pupils' vocabularies by having them look up words interrupt the reading process. This delays the completion of the assigned reading, and has the potential to make even a relatively short reading assignment appear to be a long and tedious undertaking.

An approach to helping learners broaden their vocabularies that does not interrupt the completion of the entire reading task is the *Language-Based Vocabulary and Reading Strategy* (Stansell 1984) (Figures 15.3 and 15.4). This procedure is designed to help learners identify the problem words while they are engaged in reading the text. It does not require them to stop reading. The Language-Based Vocabulary and Reading Strategy assumes that many problem words may "make sense" if pupils continue to read and come to understand how the problem words are used. Learners may infer the meanings of many initially troubling terms from the contexts in which they appear throughout the assigned selection.

The Fry Readability Graph

The general grade-level difficulty of a given prose selection is an item of interest to elementary social studies teachers. This is particularly true when new materials

---

1. If you find a new word or expression you do not know, mark it and *keep reading.* ("Marks" might be very light pencil checks, bookmarks indicating the page in the text with the problem word, a written list of words jotted down by the pupil, or some other means acceptable to the teacher.)
2. At the end of the reading time, look back over the list of words or expressions you have marked. List each one in the appropriate column of the handout sheet (see Figure 15–4).
3. For the words you are not sure of, write your "best-guess" meaning in the appropriate column. Next, check your guess. Look in your glossary first. (This assumes that a glossary is available. If not, skip this step.) If you do not find the word, look in a dictionary.
4. If your guess was correct, place an *X* in the *Glossary/Dictionary* column of the handout. If your guess was not correct, then write the definition in this same column.
5. Choose one of the words you learned without the help of the glossary or the dictionary. This will be one of the words for which you provided an *X* in step 4. Be prepared to tell others how you learned the meaning of the word from your reading.
6. Turn in the completed handout to your teacher.

FIGURE 15–3

Language-based vocabulary and reading strategy: instructions for pupils*

*These instructions are adapted from those developed by John C. Stansell, Department of Educational Curriculum and Instruction, Texas A&M University, College Station, TX (Stansell 1984).

Name: _____			
Words I learned from reading the material (ones I did not have to look up)	**Words I am still not sure about**	**My best guess**	**Glossary/ dictionary meaning**

FIGURE 15–4
Learning words through reading worksheet

are being examined. It makes sense for teachers to have some way of determining how difficult, on average, a given prose selection might be. The Fry Readability Graph, developed by Edgar Fry, is a tool that many teachers have found useful. It provides estimates of reading difficulty by grade level. That is, it suggests whether a given item might be approximately at a first-, second-, third-, fourth-, or some other grade level in terms of its general "readability."

It should be understood that the Fry Readability Graph provides information about *average* grade-level readability. It does not provide information about how an individual child might fare when asked to read a particular prose selection. Recall that the term *average* suggests a middle score. Even in a hypothetical classroom where pupils have all of the intellectual characteristics of the total national population of fourth graders, about half of the pupils would have reading skills below the average and about half would be above the average. Thus, simply because a teacher might know that a given story is at the fourth-grade reading level does not assure that all learners in a particular fourth-grade classroom will be able to read and learn from the material.

Note the directions for using the Fry Readability Graph that follow Figure 15.5. The Fry Readability Graph presumes that reading difficulty is associated with two major factors: the sentence length and the number of syllables in the individual words. In general, material is less difficult to read when the sentences are shorter and when the numbers of words with many syllables are small. This information is useful to elementary social studies teachers when they prepare prose materials of their own for learners. Also, Fry's information can be helpful to teachers when they decide to rewrite some material from a textbook or another source so that the reading difficulty is reduced.

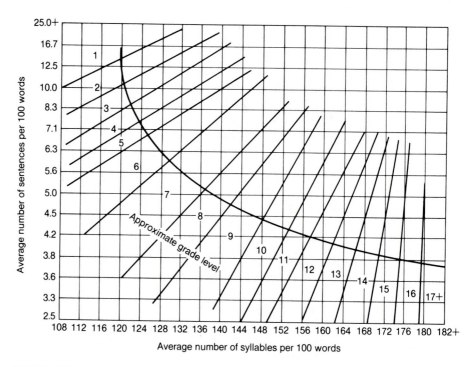

FIGURE 15–5

Fry readability graph.

(*Source:* Edward Fry, "Fry's Readability Graph: Clarifications, Validity, and Extension to Level 17." *Journal of Reading* [December 1977], p. 249. Reprinted with permission.)

Expanded Directions for Working Readability Graph

1. Randomly select three sample passages and count out exactly 100 words each, beginning with the beginning of a sentence. Count proper nouns, initializations, and numerals.

2. Count the number of sentences in 100 words, estimating length of the fraction of the last sentence to the nearest one tenth. Do this for each of the three samples. Then compute an *average* for the three samples.

3. Count the total number of syllables in the 100-word passage. If you do not have a hand counter available, simply put a mark above every syllable over one in each word; then when you get to the end of the passage, count the number of marks and add 100. Small calculators can also be used as counters by pushing numeral 1, then push the + sign for each word or syllable when counting. Do this for each of the three samples. Then compute an *average* for the three samples.

4. Enter graph with *average* sentence length and *average* number of syllables; plot dot where the two lines intersect. The area where dot is plotted will give you the approximate grade level.

5. If a great deal of variability is found in syllable count or sentence count, putting more samples into the average is desirable.

6. A word is defined as a group of symbols with a space on either side; thus, *Joe, IRA, 1945,* and *&* are each one word.

7. A syllable is defined as a phonetic syllable. Generally, there are as many syllables as vowel sounds. For example, *stopped* is one syllable and *wanted* is two syllables. When counting syllables for numerals and initializations, count one syllable for each symbol. For example, *1945* is four syllables, *IRA* is three syllables, and *&* is one syllable.

Consider this situation. Suppose that a sixth-grade teacher is about to assign pupils to read some material about the patterns of living in the cities of Brazil. This teacher knows that the textbook authors did a reasonably good job of keeping the material at about the sixth-grade level of reading difficulty. But, in this class, a few pupils have reading skills that are far below the grade level. This teacher might decide to rewrite some of the material to reduce its grade-level difficulty.

This is the version of the material as it appeared in the textbook. It is at about a sixth-grade level of reading difficulty.

> In our country, the neighborhoods with expensive houses most often are not found close to the downtown areas of big cities. They tend to be located at some distance away. Frequently, these neighborhoods are in the suburbs, areas outside of the city itself, where people live in houses. People who live in these houses have cars. They drive to work and to stores. When they drive to work, they are usually gone from the house all day.
>
> In Brazil, the high-priced neighborhoods are often very close to the downtown areas. Here, many people do not own cars. They like to live close to their work.

This is how the material looked after the teacher reworked it:

In our country, the neighborhoods with costly homes are not usually close to the downtown part of big cities. They tend to be some distance away. Often, they are in suburbs. Suburbs are areas outside of the city itself where people live in houses. People living in these houses have cars. They drive to work. Once at work, they stay all day.

In Brazil, the costly homes are often close to the downtown areas. Many people don't own cars. They like to live close to their work. Even car owners like to live close to downtown. They like to go home for lunch. They think that's nice.

The teacher might decide to give the second version to the less-able readers in the class. Note that much of the information has remained intact from the original. But the sentences are shorter, and some of the words have been simplified. In general, it is easier to reduce the grade-level reading difficulty by writing shorter sentences than by finding shorter vocabulary words.

The second version has a measured level of reading difficulty of about grade three. This represents a significant reduction in reading difficulty. It suggests that, when time permits, teachers can convey information in a simpler form by rewriting selected passages from more difficult prose materials. The Fry Readability Graph can be used to determine the approximate grade-level reading difficulty of the rewritten material.

The Cloze Procedure

While the Fry Readability Graph can provide useful information about the general level of reading difficulty of a given prose selection, it cannot predict how a given learner will fare with this material. To get this kind of information, many elementary social studies teachers have found the Cloze Procedure (Taylor 1953) to be a useful tool.

The Cloze Procedure can provide some indication of the appropriateness of a particular prose item for an individual pupil. The Cloze Procedure consists of a simple teacher-made test constructed from a part of the textbook (or other prose selection) that learners will be asked to read. The teacher should select a passage that is at least 250 words long. Somewhat longer passages are even better. They represent a broader sample of the content. Hence, the resulting pupil scores will be more reliable.

The following directions should be followed in preparing, administering, and scoring a Cloze Procedure. See Figure 15.6 for a sample Cloze Procedure test.

1. Identify a sample from some reading material to be assigned to the class.
2. Type this passage, using *triple* spacing, so that every *fifth* word is omitted. Leave a blank long enough for learners to write on wherever a word is omitted.
3. Follow the pattern of deleting every fifth word, except when the fifth word falls at the beginning of a sentence. When this happens, retain the first

People have come to _____ from many parts of _____ world. Many European settlers
              1   2

_____ from Portugal. Portuguese, Portugal's _____ , is Brazil's official language. Settlers
  3   4

_____ from other parts of _____ , from Africa, from Asia, _____ , from other parts of
  5   6   7

_____ world. Today, there are _____ from many racial and _____ backgrounds in Brazil.
  8   9   10

    Brazil's _____ is not evenly distributed. Most _____ the people live close _____ the
           11   12   13

Atlantic Ocean. Inland _____ the Atlantic, the population _____ to be much less _____ . In
                  14   15   16

some parts of _____ country, there are almost _____ people at all.
          17   18

    Brazil_____ second to the United _____ in population among the _____ of the Western
         19   20   21

Hemisphere. Brazil's _____ is growing much faster _____ that of the United _____ . Some
                22   23   24

people believe that _____ in the future may _____ a larger population than _____ United
                 25   26   27

States.

    Brazil's largest_____ are located in the _____ part of the country _____ too far from the
                 28   29   30

_____ coast. São Paulo is the _____ largest city. Rio de Janeiro is _____ so large, but it
  31   32   33

_____ be Brazil's best known _____ . Its famous carnival and _____ beaches are known
  34   35   36

throughout _____ world. Brasilia, the capital _____ of Brazil, is located _____ miles inland. It
        37   38   39

was _____ planned city built in _____ empty interior of the _____ . The capital of the
    40   41   42

_____ States, Washington, was also_____ planned city. Manaus is _____ unusual city. It is
  43   44   45

_____ miles up the famous _____ River. It was originally _____ by people hoping to
  46   47   48

_____ a fortune in Amazon _____ .
  49   50

Key

1. Brazil	11. population	21. countries	31. Atlantic	41. the
2. the	12. of	22. population	32. nation's	42. nation
3. came	13. to	23. than	33. not	43. United
4. language	14. from	24. States	34. may	44. a
5. came	15. tends	25. Brazil	35. city	45. an
6. Europe	16. dense	26. have	36. splendid	46. located
7. and	17. the	27. the	37. the	47. Amazon
8. the	18. no	28. cities	38. city	48. settled
9. people	19. ranks	29. eastern	39. many	49. make
10. cultural	20. States	30. not	40. a	50. rubber

FIGURE 15–6
A sample cloze procedure test

word, delete the second, and resume the practice of omitting every fifth word from this point.

4. Place numbers under each blank. Begin with "1" and continue on with consecutive numbers until the last blank has been numbered. (For example, in a 250-word passage, there would be fifty blanks.)

5. Prepare a teacher key. This will consist of a list of the words deleted and the numbers of the blanks indicating the location in the passage from which each word was taken.

6. Provide pupils with these tests once copies have been made. Ask them to look at the test as a puzzle. Challenge them to fill in the blanks with words that will result in a passage that reads well and makes good logical sense. Tell them to look for clues that might help identify the missing words throughout the entire passage.

7. In scoring the tests, count as correct only words that are *identical* to those in the original passage. Accept misspellings. Do not accept synonyms.

8. Compute the percentage of the correct words. For example, if there were fifty blanks in the test and a given pupil had thirty-eight correct responses, the score would be 76 percent ($38/50 = 0.76$).

The following guidelines should be used to interpret pupil Cloze Procedure test scores.

1. A pupil who receives a score of 58 percent or higher is said to be operating at the *independent level* with regard to this reading material. This means that the youngster should be able to read and learn the material with minimal teacher assistance.

2. A pupil with a score falling between 44 and 57 percent correct is said to be operating at the *instructional level*. This means that the person should be able to read and learn from this material if teacher help is available.

3. A pupil who receives a score of 43 percent or lower correct is said to be operating at the *frustrational level*. Such a youngster might be expected to experience great difficulty in reading and learning from the material on which the test was based.

The percentage-correct figures that define each of the levels are those recommended by a leader in reading research. John Bormuth (Bormuth 1968). The message to the teacher when youngsters score at the instructional or frustrational levels is simple. Considerable help must be provided if they are to profit from reading the material on which the test was based. Those youngsters scoring at the frustrational level are particularly probable to experience great difficulty.

When working with pupils who score at the frustrational level, two alternatives are to find another source of information that is written at a less challenging level of difficulty or to rewrite some of the material so that it demands less-sophisticated reading skills. A teacher who took the latter option might check his or her work by comparing the grade-level reading difficulty of the original to the rewritten version using the Fry Readability Graph. Still another alternative might be to abandon the prose material entirely as an information source for some individuals. It might be possible to find cassette recordings, films, photographs, or other means of conveying the information that will not require the youngster to read.

The Fry Readability Graph and the Cloze Procedure can be used in tandem. If a teacher has used the Fry Readability Graph to determine the approximate grade-level reading difficulties of the prose materials that he or she has available, then he or she may have a good feel for some alternative prose materials that might be more suitable for a youngster who gets a low score on a Cloze Procedure test.

Suppose that the Cloze test had been built on material on Latin America from a textbook that the teacher had identified as being at about the sixth-grade level of reading difficulty by using the Fry Readability Graph. If the teacher also had on hand some other material dealing with Latin America that had been identified as being at a third- or fourth-grade level of reading difficulty, then it would make sense to provide some of these materials to learners who received low Cloze test scores on the sixth-grade level material. Using the Fry Graph and the Cloze Procedure together can help the teacher achieve a good "fit" between individual pupils and the materials they are assigned to read.

WORKING WITH THE PARTS OF THE TEXTBOOK

Learners in elementary social studies classes work with many different kinds of prose materials. Most spend at least some of the time reading the material in social studies textbooks. Particularly at the middle- and upper-grade levels, there is a tendency for some of these books to be quite large and intimidating. The problem is not that they do not contain useful information, but rather that they contain so much material that pupils often cannot find what they need. Time spent preparing learners to work with textbooks can result in much more effective use of this important information tool.

Textbooks have predictable organizational patterns. This statement is hardly startling news to adults, but many learners in the elementary grades have never thought about how textbook content is arranged. Lessons designed to help them recognize the organizational patterns can remedy this situation.

The Table of Contents
Simple lessons can be built around the table of contents. These can help learners grasp the nature of the content covered, the organization of the content, and the relative importance assigned to each element of content. Figure 15.7 illustrates part of a typical table of contents from an elementary social studies text.

The teacher can lead a class discussion based on information contained in a book's table of contents. Questions such as these could help pupils learn something about the organization and emphasis of the book in Figure 15–7.

Contents

Using Your Textbook   2
Reviewing Maps and Globes   4
    Using Globes   4
    Using Maps   6

UNIT 1   Learning About Communities   12
CHAPTER 1   What Is a Community?   14
   Lesson 1   Communities Are People   15
   Lesson 2   Communities Bring People Together   19
   Building Citizenship   People Who Make a Difference   Helping a School   23
   Lesson 3   Meeting Needs in Communities   24
   Building Thinking Skills   Asking Questions   28
   Chapter 1 • Summary and Review   30

CHAPTER 2   Communities and Geography   32
   Lesson 1   Landforms and Bodies of Water   33
   Building Geography Skills   Using Map Scales   38
   Building Geography Skills   Understanding Hemispheres and Intermediate Directions   40
   Lesson 2   Climate and Natural Resources   43
   Lesson 3   Geography Makes a Difference   48
   Chapter 2 • Summary and Review   52
   Unit 1 Review   54

CHAPTER 3   The Indians Build a Community   58
   Lesson 1   The First Americans   59
   Lesson 2   The Geography of the Southwest   64
   Lesson 3   Mesa Verde, an Indian Community   67
   Lesson 4   A Visit to Mesa Verde Today   71
   Building Citizenship   People Who Make a Difference   Keeping Customs Alive   75
   Building Thinking Skills   Comparing and Contrasting   76
   Chapter 3 • Summary and Review   78

CHAPTER 4   The Spanish Build a Community   80
   Lesson 1   The Geography of St. Augustine   81
   Lesson 2   St. Augustine Begins   84
   Building Time Skills   Reading Time Lines   88
   Lesson 3   A Visit to St. Augustine Today   90
   Chapter 4 • Summary and Review   94

CHAPTER 5   The Pilgrims Build a Community   96
   Lesson 1   The Geography of Plymouth   97
   BUILDING STUDY AND RESEARCH SKILLS   Using the Library   100
   Lesson 2   Building Plymouth Community   102

FIGURE 15–7
Sample table of contents.

Source: From *Communities Near and Far* by Barry K. Beyer, Jean Craven, Mary A. McFarland, and Walter C. Parker, pp. iii–viii. Copyright © 1990 by Macmillan Publishing Company. Reprinted with permission from Macmillan/McGraw Hill School Publishing Company.

Lesson 3 A Visit to Plymouth Today   108
Chapter 5 • Summary and Review   112
Unit 2 Review   114

CHAPTER 6   Communities Have Differences   118
Lesson 1   Living in Small Communities   119

BUILDING THINKING SKILLS Sequencing   122
Lesson 2   Living in Large Communities   124
Chapter 6 • Summary and Review   128

CHAPTER 7   Rural Communities   130
Lesson 1   Farming Communities   131
Lesson 2   A Dairy Farm   134
Lesson 3   From Farm to You   139
Building Bridges   A Rural Community in Canada   143
BUILDING STUDY AND RESEARCH SKILLS   Reading Flow Charts   146
Chapter 7 • Summary and Review   148

CHAPTER 8   Urban Communities   150
Lesson 1   Urban Communities and Resources   151
Building Citizenship   People Who Make a Difference   Saving Pigeon Creek 155
Building Study and Research Skills   Reading Bar Graphs   156
Lesson 2   Seattle, an Urban Community   158
Lesson 3   Manufacturing in Seattle   162
Building Bridges   An Urban Community in Mexico   165
Chapter 8 • Summary and Review   168

CHAPTER 9   Suburban Communities   170
Lesson 1   Suburban Communities   171
Lesson 2   A Suburb in Georgia   174
Lesson 3   Transportation and Suburbs   177
Building Geography Skills   Reading Transportation Maps   180
Building Bridges   A Suburb in England   182
Chapter 9 • Summary and Review   186
Unit 3 Review   188

CHAPTER 10   A Community Grows   192
Lesson 1   The Geography of San Francisco   193
Lesson 2   San Francisco Grows   196
Lesson 3   San Francisco Today   200
Building Bridges   A Growing Community in Kenya   203
Building Thinking Skills   Predicting   206
Chapter 10 • Summary and Review   208

CHAPTER 11   A Community Changes   210
Lesson 1   The Geography of Pittsburgh   211

Building Geography Skills   Reading Product Maps 214
Lesson 2   Pittsburgh Changes 216
Building Citizenship   People Who Make a Difference   Cleaning Up Pollution 219
Lesson 3   Pittsburgh Today 220
Building Bridges   A Changing Community   in China 224
Chapter 11 • Summary and Review 228
Unit 4 Review 230

CHAPTER 12   Community Government 234
Lesson 1   Communities and Rules 235
BUILDING THINKING SKILLS Making Decisions 238
Lesson 2   A Community's Government 240
Lesson 3   Being a Good Citizen 243
BUILDING CITIZENSHIP   Point/Counterpoint Should Girls Play Little League Baseball? 246
Chapter 12 • Summary and Review 248

CHAPTER 13   Our Country's Capital 250
Lesson 1   A New Country 251
Lesson 2   Governing Our Country 256
Lesson 3   A Capital for a New Country 259
BUILDING CITIZENSHIP   Point/Counterpoint   Where Should Our Capital Be Located? 262
Building Geography Skills   Reading Grid Maps 264
Lesson 4   A Tour of Washington, D.C. 266
Chapter 13 • Summary and Review 274
Unit 5 Review 276

Special Section 278
Exploring Your Community 278
Part 1   A Guidebook to Your Community 279
Building Citizenship   People Who Make a Difference   You Can Make a Difference 289
Part 2   A Play About Detroit's History   *By Wendy Vierow* 290

Reference Section 297
Atlas 298
Dictionary of Geographic Terms 306
Gazetteer 307
Biographical Dictionary 312
Glossary 314
Index 322
Credits 328
People Who Make a Difference
Helping a School 23
Keeping Customs Alive 75
Saving Pigeon Creek 155
Cleaning Up Pollution 219
You Can Make a Difference 289

FIGURE 15–7
Continued

Point/Counterpoint

Should Girls Play Little League Baseball? 246

Where Should Our Capital Be Located? 262

Building Skills

THINKING READING

Asking Questions	28	
Comparing and Contrasting	76	
Sequencing	122	
Predicting	206	
Making Decisions	238	

STUDY TIME

Reading Time Lines	88
Using the Library	100
Reading Flow Charts	146
Reading Bar Graphs	156

GEOGRAPHY

Using Map Scales 38

Understanding Hemispheres and Intermediate Directions 40

Reading Transportation Maps 180

Reading Product Maps 214

Reading Grid Maps 264

Compass Rose	8	Making an Airplane	164
Sarah's Time Line	88	Reviewing San Francisco Time Line	208
St. Augustine Time Line	89	Reviewing Pittsburgh Time Line	228
Plymouth Time Line	115	Reviewing Washington, D.C., Time Line	274
Dairy Products	140	Detroit Time Line	281
Getting Ready for School	146	Transportation in Detroit	284
Making Cheese	147		
Population of U.S. Rural and Urban Areas	156		
Population of the Four Largest U.S. Cities	157		

1. How many units are there in the book? How many chapters? Why are there more chapters than units?
2. Some units seem to have more chapters than others. Why do you think this is so?
3. If you were to tell a friend about topics covered in this book, what would you say?
4. The chapter "What is a Community?" comes before the chapter "Suburban Communities." Why do you think the authors decided on this order?
5. Do you think these authors are interested in geography? How can you tell?
6. Are these things in this book: an atlas, a glossary, an index, a gazetteer? If so, where are they? Just what is a *gazetteer?*
7. What kinds of skills are important to these authors? Where would you find information about them?
8. What kinds of time lines are featured in this book? Where would you find them? Look at several examples. What special kinds of information do they give you?

The level of difficulty of table of contents questions needs to conform to the age and sophistication of learners in a particular class. When pupils succeed in finding answers to well-designed questions, they tend to develop a good mental picture of their textbook's organizational scheme. This helps them use the book more efficiently.

Characteristics of Individual Chapters

Social studies textbooks tend to feature a repetitive chapter organization that remains consistent throughout the book. Often, certain chapter design characteristics have been included to help pupils master the content. Familiarizing learners with the particular chapter structure of their text helps them when they begin using the books.

The chapter structure in *Communities Near and Far* (Figure 15.7) is typical of that found in many social studies texts designed for use in the lower grades. In orienting a class to this book's format, the teacher might call attention to several notable characteristics. First of all, the chapters are quite short. Each includes three content-related lessons. Each includes special lessons devoted to improvement of skills or to helping pupils extend what they have learned to other settings. Each concludes with a "summary and review" section.

The Index

Exercises that focus on the index can help learners recognize that authors have decided to emphasize some kinds of content more than others. They also reinforce important alphabetizing skills and familiarize pupils with the process of using the index to find specific information.

Before having pupils work with the index, teachers often have them perform a few simple alphabetizing exercises. These can be scaled in terms of their difficulty. Note the differences in the three lists of words in the sample exercise in Figure 15.8. Note that words in the "least difficult" list all begin with a different letter. Those in the "more difficult" list begin with the same letter, but the second letter

Least Difficult	More Difficult	Most Difficult
_____ cat	_____ gill	_____ hood
_____ tent	_____ gaze	_____ hook
_____ wasp	_____ greet	_____ hoe
_____ log	_____ gun	_____ honey
_____ ant	_____ gob	_____ hoot

Directions: Tell the class members to put a "1" in front of the word that comes first, a "2" in front of the word that comes second, and so on through the fifth word for each list. Have them order each list separately.

FIGURE 15–8
Placing words in alphabetical order

in each word is different. The words in the "most difficult" list have identical first and second letters, and some have identical third letters.

After learners have worked with alphabetizing exercises, the teacher can direct their attention to the textbook index. Figure 15.9 illustrates a portion of the index in *Communities Near and Far* (Beyer et al. 1990).

The teacher may ask pupils questions about the index. The following sample questions are based on the index page illustrated in Figure 15.9.

1. Why is "Jail" listed in the index ahead of "Judges"?
2. On what pages would you find information about the Gulf of Mexico?
3. How many pages are devoted to Houston, Texas?
4. How many pages are devoted to Georgia?
5. Why do you think more pages deal with Georgia than with Houston?

INTEGRATING WRITING INTO SOCIAL STUDIES LESSONS

In recent years, concerns about pupils' writing skills have paralleled worries about their reading abilities. As with reading, teachers have been encouraged to provide opportunities for pupils to write in all of their major elementary school subjects. Social studies lessons often present an excellent context for learners to develop and refine their writing abilities.

Researchers report that languages reflect and reinforce the cultures of their speakers (Halliday 1973; Halliday and Hasan 1989). One implication of this finding is that language instruction should tie clearly to pupils' use of language in natural settings (Halliday 1973). There are many opportunities to do this in the context of social studies instruction. Michael A. K. Halliday (1973) has identified these seven basic functions of language: (1) instrumental, (2) regulatory, (3) interactional, (4) personal, (5) heuristic, (6) representational, and (7) imaginative. These functions suggest a framework for planning writing activities that are closely tied to social studies lessons.

Instrumental Function

The instrumental function of language, sometimes referred to as the "I want" function, concerns how people use language to meet their needs. For example, people write to apply for jobs, to place orders for goods and services, and to invite people to visit. Pupils might engage in social studies-related, instrumental function writing by doing such things as the following:

1. writing letters requesting information from government agencies
2. writing to invite special guests to the classroom
3. writing a class request to the principal
4. completing mock job applications or loan applications
5. writing captions to accompany collages of pupil-assembled pictures illustrating personal "wants and needs"

Geography

Geography
 bodies of water, 47–49
 choice of living place, 51
 climate in, 47–48
 of Florida, 82–83
 of Great Plains, 62–63
 landforms in, 47–49
 meaning of, 47
 natural resources in, 45–46
 of Pittsburgh, Pennsylvania, 211–213
 of Plymouth, Massachusetts, 97–99
 of St. Augustine, Florida, 81–83
 San Francisco, California, 193–195
 of Southwest, 64–66
 studying, 48
Georgia, 126, 173–179
Globe, 4, 5, *p5*
Gold, 84, 153, 196–197, 199
Golden Gate, 194
Golden Gate Bridge, 193–194, *p193, p195*
Gold rush, 196–197, 199, *p196, p197*
Goods, 26, 45, 120, 125
Government, 237, 240–245, 252, 256–258,
 260, 282
Graph. *See* Bar graph
Great Hall of the People, 226
Great Lakes, 34–35, 37
Great Plains, 64, 132
Grid map, 264–265, *m265, m268–269,*
 m277
Guide words, 101
Gulf of Mexico, 34–35, 49

H

Harbor, 82–83, 98, 194
Harvest, 105–106
Hawaii, 44, *p44*
Hay-stacking, 138
Hemisphere, 40–41, *m41*
Hills, 36, 195, 221, *p36, p195*
History
 of Detroit, Michigan, 281
 meaning of, 74
 of Pittsburgh, Pennsylvania, 216–218
 of Plymouth, Massachusetts, 97–107
 of St. Augustine, Florida, 84–87
 of San Francisco, California, 196–199
 of Washington, D.C., 251–263

Holiday, 20–22
Holsteins, 131
Honolulu, Hawaii, 44, *p44*
Hopi Indians, 70, 75
Houston, Texas, 157

I

Illinois, 50, 172
Immigrant, 201, 216, *p216*
Independence Day, 21, 255
Indiana, 234, 240–245
Indian Ocean, 204
Indians, 59–73, 103–104, 106–107,
 290–296, *m61, p59, p60, p62, p63,*
 p67–70, p103
Industries, 154, 162
Intermediate directions, 42
Island, 82

J

Jail, 236
Jefferson Memorial, 270, *p270*
Jefferson, Thomas, 254, 270
Joe Louis Arena, 287, *p286*
Judges, 258
Juneau, Alaska, 44, *p44*

K

Kenya, 203–205, *m204, p203, p205*
Kiva, 69, *p69*

L

Lakes, 37, 46, 152
Landform, 36, 47–49, 65–66, *p36*
Law, 236–237, 241, 252, 257–258
L'Enfant, Pierre, 260
Lexington, Massachusetts, 254, *p254*
Library, 100–101
Lincoln, Abraham, 271
Lincoln Memorial, 271, *p271*
London, England, 183–185, *m183, p184*
Los Angeles, California, 157

M

Manufacturing, 162–164
Maps, 6–11

FIGURE 15–9

Example of an index page.

Source: From *Communities Near and Far* by Barry K. Beyer, Jean Craven, Mary A. McFarland, and Walter Parker, p. 324. Copyright © 1990 by Macmillan Publishing Company. Reprinted with permission from Macmillan/McGraw Hill School Publishing Company.

Teachers need to incorporate the various writing functions in social studies lessons.

Regulatory Function

This function concerns tasks that control behavior or that provide information about how a task should be performed. It is sometimes called the "do as I tell you" function. Road signs, directions for repairing or constructing something, and printed collections of traffic laws illustrate the regulatory function of written language. Pupils might perform regulatory function writing activities such as these:

1. writing to friends out of town inviting them to visit and giving them directions to the pupil's home
2. pretending that a trek over the Oregon Trail has just been completed, pupils can write to friends in the East telling them what they should bring and providing them with other directions about "moving West"
3. writing rules for the classroom, the school, or for care of pets or materials
4. writing suggestions to the principal about needed new rules
5. preparing written directions for such things as building a log cabin, making candles, or engaging in a traditional craft

Interactional Function

This function, sometimes labeled the "me and you" function, includes communications that seek to improve the quality of interpersonal relations. Social studies activities consistent with this function include the following:

1. writing to a friend to visit the classroom
2. preparing and sending thank you notes to special guests
3. creating personal holiday greeting cards to be sent to specific people
4. writing regularly to a pen pal in another state or country
5. playing the role of an explorer and writing an imaginary letter back home to a member of the explorer's immediate family

Personal Function

This communication type is used by people to express their personal feelings or ideas and to explore the personal meaning of something. Letters to the editor, reaction statements, and poetry are examples of writing in this general category. The personal function is sometimes called the "here I come" function. The following examples illustrate ways of involving pupils in personal function writing.

1. writing letters to the editor in reaction to something printed in a news or editorial column
2. writing an account of a personally experienced event
3. preparing and sending a letter to a public official expressing personal opinions about a controversial issue
4. writing a poem to express feelings about something studied in a social studies lesson
5. keeping a personal diary
6. preparing a time capsule that includes items of interest to class members along with explanations of some of their personal beliefs

Heuristic Function

Sometimes referred to as the "tell me why" function, the heuristic function of language has to do with information seeking or gathering activities. People exercise this function when they take notes or develop questions they want to have answered. The following examples illustrate possible applications of heuristic function writing in the elementary social studies classroom.

1. writing down questions to be asked after study of a particular social studies topic or to be asked to a guest speaker
2. keeping note cards with information about a topic that is being studied
3. taking notes while listening to a speaker
4. keeping minutes at a meeting
5. writing down hypotheses to explain a puzzling situation after considering relevant data have been considered

Representational Function

The representational function of language concerns the use of language to transmit information, and is sometimes referred to as the "I've got something to tell you" function. The following examples suggest possible uses of representational function writing in elementary social studies classes.

1. maintaining an imaginary diary for someone who was present at an important historical event
2. writing a short history of the local community
3. preparing a classroom newspaper or newsletter
4. labeling items on a map and writing accompanying explanations
5. developing lists of major ideas to be included in oral reports
6. writing an account of a past event based on an oral history interview
7. writing a report of information learned on a field trip

"If I pass your grade, Ms. Johnson, I promise I won't write one of those 'kiss and tell' books."

Imaginative Function

This is a creative, "let's pretend" function of language. When using it, individuals allow their minds to wander in unpredictable ways. Possibilities for including imaginative function writing in social studies lessons include the following:

1. writing stories to complete a "what would happen if . . .?" statement
2. writing a play or television script about something studied in a social studies lesson
3. writing song lyrics about a topic studied in a social studies lesson
4. inventing and writing novel solutions to important social problems such as drug abuse and air pollution
5. preparing a written account describing what life might be like fifty years from now
6. preparing political cartoons referring to current topics and issues

These seven functions are all part of a comprehensive writing program. Teachers tend to restrict social studies writing activities to those related to the representation function. Other kinds of writing must also be encouraged. Over time, this kind of training improves the sophistication of pupils' writing skills. This makes them more effective communicators not only in their social studies classes but in other settings as well.

KEY IDEAS IN SUMMARY

1. Reading materials are widely used as information sources in elementary social studies classes. This suggests a need for social studies teachers to be concerned about learner's reading abilities. It makes sense to integrate some reading development activities in social studies lessons.

2. Specific plans for assisting pupils to learn from prose materials can be developed for each of the three major stages of the reading process. These stages are prereading, during reading, and postreading.

3. Prereading activities are designed to help pupils establish connections between what they presently know and new content to be introduced in reading assignments. Three widely used prereading techniques are the structured overview, ReQuest, and the prereading stage reading guide.

4. As their name implies, during-reading techniques seek to maximize learners' understanding while they read. Three techniques often used for this purpose are visual frameworks, multipass reading, and during-reading stage reading guides.

5. Actions teachers take once pupils have completed a reading assignment can strongly influence what they learn. Among techniques often used during the postreading stage are graphic post-organizers, interaction frames, and postreading stage reading guides.

6. Elementary social studies teachers are concerned with the general level of reading difficulty of particular prose selections. The Fry Readability Graph is often used for determining the approximate grade-level reading difficulty of a given item. Teachers also are interested in knowing how well an individual pupil might be expected to fare when assigned to read a specific prose selection. The Cloze Procedure is a technique often used to gather this kind of information.

7. The textbook continues to be widely used as an information source in elementary social studies classroom. Pupils' learning from textbooks can be enhanced when the teacher thoroughly familiarizes them with their texts. Such lessons often focus on textbook features such as the table of contents, the organization of units and chapters, and the index.

8. There are concerns for developing writing as well as reading skills in social studies lessons. Writing activities can be organized under seven major language functions: (a) instrumental, (b) regulatory, (c) interactional, (d) personal, (e) heuristic, (f) representational, and (g) imaginative.

POSTTEST

Answer each of the following true/false questions.

1. The Fry Readability Graph yields a score that tells how well an individual pupil is likely to do when asked to read a particular assignment.

2. Graphic post-organizers help learners recall major ideas introduced in a reading assignment and specific information related to those ideas.

3. Multipass reading requires pupils to read the same material several times, looking for somewhat different things every time.

4. Social studies lessons provide few opportunities for teachers to help learners improve their writing skills.

5. The representational function of language focuses on the use of language to transmit information.

QUESTIONS

1. What are the three stages of the reading process?
2. How is a structured overview developed, and what is it used for?
3. How do reading study guides for each stage of the reading process differ?

4. What is the purpose of a visual framework?

5. What are the steps in multipass reading?

6. How can interaction frames help learners master content from reading assignments?

7. How is a Cloze test prepared?

8. How might a teacher introduce learners to a new social studies textbook?

9. What is the interactional function of language?

10. What writing activities might be assigned to pupils to give them practice with the imaginative function of language?

11. Some people have suggested that, in the future, pupils will read less in their social studies classes than they do now. In part, this will result from new technologies such as microcomputers. Do you agree with this view? If so, should teachers place less emphasis on development of reading skills in their social studies lessons?

12. "Reading problems should be taken care of during the *reading* period. During our *social studies time*, we should just do social studies." Do you agree? Why?

13. "A good fourth grade teacher will see to it that every child in the class is reading at the fourth-grade level." Do you agree with this statement? Why?

14. "When I have my class reading social studies materials, I always make sure that every child reads some material containing very difficult new vocabulary. This is the only way to intellectually 'stretch' each pupil." Explain why you support or oppose this view.

15. "There is a danger that teachers who emphasize development of pupils' writing skills in their social studies classes will rob time from social studies content and turn these classes into additional language arts sessions." How do you react to this comment?

EXTENDING UNDERSTANDING AND SKILL

1. Survey some elementary teachers about the reading problems their learners typically experience with social studies materials. Share your findings with the class, or prepare a short paper summarizing the results.

2. Complete the following activities using a social studies textbook designed for a grade level you would like to teach.
   (a) Prepare a list of outdated terms contained in the text.
   (b) Prepare a list of specialized terms used in the text.
   (c) Prepare a list of other terms in the text that may be unfamiliar to pupils.
   (d) Using a total of ten terms from lists prepared in (a), (b), and (c) above, prepare a teacher glossary. Be sure your glossary defines these terms in language learners at this grade level might be expected to understand.

3. Select a social studies textbook designed for a grade level you would like to teach. Then do the following:
   (a) Use a Fry Readability Graph to determine its approximate grade-level readability.
   (b) Select a 500-word passage from the book, and prepare a Cloze Procedure test based on this material.

4. Examine a page in an elementary social studies textbook that might be assigned as required reading. Prepare three different sets of purposes or focus questions. For each set, develop a visual framework to focus pupil's attention on pertinent content elements.

5. Identify a topic you might teach to learners in the middle or upper grades. Identify appropriate writing activities consistent with each of these language functions: (a) representational, (b) heuristic, and (c) imaginative.

REFERENCES

BAKER, C. O., AND L. T. OGLE, eds. *The Condition of Education, 1989: Volume 1 — Elementary and Secondary Education.* Washington, DC: National Center for Education Statistics, 1989.

BEYER, B. K., J. CRAVEN, M. A. McFARLAND, AND W. A. PARKER. *Communities Near and Far.* New York: Macmillan, 1990.

BORMUTH, J. R. "The Cloze Readability Procedure." *Elementary English* (April 1968), pp. 429–36.

FRY, E. "Fry's Readability Graph: Clarifications, Validity, and Extension to Level 17." *Journal of Reading* (December 1977), pp. 242–52.

HALLIDAY, M. A. K. *Explorations in the Functions of Language.* London: Edward Arnold, 1973.

HALLIDAY, M. A. K., AND R. HASAN. *Language, Context, and Text: Aspects of Language in a Social-Semiotic Perspective,* 2d ed. New York: Oxford University Press, 1989.

MANZO, A. V. "ReQuest: A Method for Improving Reading Comprehension through Reciprocal Questioning." *Journal of Reading* (November 1969), pp. 123–26, 163.

STANSELL, J. C. "Getting More Mileage from Sustained Silent Reading." Unpublished paper presented at the Sam Houston Area Reading Conference. College Station, Texas, February 1984.

TAYLOR, WILSON L. "Cloze Procedure: A New Tool for Measuring Readability." *Journalism Quarterly* (Fall 1953), pp. 415–33.

SUPPLEMENTAL READING

BEYER, B. K., AND R. GILSTRIP. *Writing in Elementary Social Studies.* Boulder, CO: Social Science Education Consortium, 1982.

POOSTAY, EDWARD J. "Show Me Your Underlines: A Strategy to Teach Comprehension." *The Reading Teacher* (May 1984), pp. 828–30.

STEFFENS, H. "Designing History Writing Assignments for Student Success." *The Social Studies* (March/April 1989), pp. 59–63.

TALBOT, B., "Writing for Learning in School: Is it Possible?" *Language Arts* (January/February 1990), pp. 47–56.

WALTON, S., AND R. HOBLITT. "Using Story Frames in Content-Area Classes." *The Social Studies* (May/June 1989), pp. 103–6.

ZABRUCKY, K., AND D. MOORE. "Children's Ability to Use Three Standards to Evaluate Their Comprehension of Text." *Reading Research Quarterly* (Summer 1989), pp. 336–52.

16

MANAGING THE SOCIAL STUDIES CLASSROOM

This chapter provides information to help the reader:

1. identify the relationship between instruction and classroom management,
2. list aspects of space management to consider when arranging the classroom and point out ways to organize and manage materials efficiently,
3. identify routines that characterize a smoothly functioning elementary classroom,
4. recognize the importance of planning transitions that connect parts of social studies lessons,
5. describe characteristics of teachers who respond effectively to episodes of learner misbehavior, and
6. state basic principles that should be included in a responsible plan for discipline.

PRETEST

Answer each of the following true/false questions.

1. Good classroom managers typically respond harshly to a learner who gives even a hint of potential misbehavior.
2. To facilitate good classroom management, authorities agree that the teacher's desk should be placed in the front and center of the classroom.
3. Private correction of behavior is generally preferable to public correction.
4. Helping pupils to learn self-control is a major purpose of classroom discipline.
5. All pupils who break a given classroom rule, should receive the same kind of punishment.

INTRODUCTION

Ms. Lien slumped wearily in the chair behind her desk at the end of the school day. She was discouraged. Today she had tried a variety of activities during her social studies lessons. She had done some group work, devised some role-playing exercises, and had done other things designed to get her pupils actively involved. Despite her high hopes, the lesson had been a disaster.

Her children saw the change in routine as a chance to talk and play. When she had worked with one group, pupils in others had jumped up and run around the room. She had been so busy trying to keep the groups on task that she was sure she had missed seeing other glaring incidents of misbehavior. To top it off, the principal walked in just as the situation approached its chaotic peak. The principal did not look pleased.

Out of frustration, she had stopped the lesson in midstream. She directed pupils back to their original seats, and reorganized the room into traditional rows. For the last ten minutes, she had them answer questions from the textbook. Ms. Lien was not happy about this decision, but at least they had quieted down and done the work.

"Why had all this happened?" she wondered. "What is wrong with these children? Can they really prefer to do the same boring textbook work day after day?"

Beginning elementary social studies teachers often face similar problems. A cycle of unhappy events sometimes reinforces instruction patterns that are not particularly innovative. Typically, this cycle begins when an enthusiastic new teacher tries to implement a novel approach, often one requiring learners to function in small groups rather than as a class. The learners, unfamiliar with the procedure, frequently do not know how to act, and sometimes adopt unacceptable behavior patterns. The eager new teacher suddenly is confronted with classroom control problems. The cycle concludes when the new teacher abandons the novel instructional approaches, believing they "caused" the problems.

In and of themselves, individual techniques do not cause classroom control difficulties. Problems result because of deficient management. Different techniques require different approaches to management, and there exist management techniques that are suited to each type of instructional method. For example, if a teacher uses a technique requiring learners to work in groups, there are specific management actions available that will, when sensitively applied, ensure a productive exercise. Among other things, the teacher must carefully instruct pupils about what their groups are to do and what their specific responsibilities within each group are. Effective social studies teaching demands teachers who know effective instructional and management techniques.

Most control problems teachers experience are relatively minor, involving pupils who are inattentive, talking, briefly out of their seats, or something similar. Relatively few elementary teachers confront the kinds of classroom disasters featured in media reports about exceptionally poor teaching environments. Many teachers find that they are able to implement interesting, innovative techniques in classrooms where learners' behaviors continue to be exemplary. These successful teachers have mastered management procedures that support their instructional activities.

It is common for prospective teachers to worry about their abilities to control learners in the classrooms. Many of these concerns reflect their inexperience at preventing discipline problems and at dealing with them when they do occur. This chapter introduces specific approaches for preventing and responding to management and discipline problems. The first section, focusing on classroom management, outlines techniques for preventing discipline problems. The second suggests ways teachers can respond to pupil misbehavior.

DIMENSIONS OF CLASSROOM MANAGEMENT

Classroom management refers to the way a teacher organizes time, materials, and space to facilitate smooth and efficient operation of the classroom. Kounin (1970) found that the basic difference between effective and ineffective classroom managers was not their method of responding to inappropriate behaviors, but rather their approach to organizing the classroom. A later investigation (Emmer et al. 1980) determined that smoothly functioning classrooms were not accidents. Neither were they the result of "good" learners who just happened to be enrolled. Rather, they came about because of systematic management planning by teachers that started before the school year began. These teachers had a clear vision of how they wished their learners to behave and communicated these expectations to their pupils. They thought about issues associated with space management, time management, and establishing routines and procedures.

Space Management

Careful arrangement of instructional space helps teachers minimize control problems and provides an environment that is supportive of certain instructional ap-

Resolving problems of misbehavior is one of the important tasks of all teachers.

proaches. For example, pupils seated in rows may have difficulty working together in groups. If they can be seated in chairs arranged around small tables, they will find it much easier to work on group projects.

The physical arrangement of the room sends a message to all who enter. Placement of furniture, learning materials, bulletin boards, and other classroom features communicates a teacher's values and enthusiasm to pupils. Some arrangements communicate excitement and a sense of welcome. Others suggest rigidity, boredom, and are perhaps even threatening.

Physical organization gives each room its own ambience. *Ambience* refers to the sense of "character" a learner gets from his or her general impression of the environment. Weinstein (1979) identifies characteristics associated with a negative classroom ambience. She notes that, as the quality of the ambience decreases, there is an increase in teacher control statements, teacher behavior becomes less friendly and less sensitive, pupils become less involved in lessons, and conflicts among learners become more frequent. In other words, classrooms that communicate to learners a sense of boredom, coldness, threat, and general unpleasantness are classrooms where behavioral problems might be expected.

Teachers need to consider several aspects of the environment when organizing classroom space to provide a more positive ambience. Among these are seating arrangements, placement of the teacher's desk, use of wall space, identifying places to store equipment, and selecting spaces for books and other materials.

Floor Space.   The floor space of the classroom needs to be arranged to accommodate the activities that are to take place. This kind of organization can communicate to pupils the types of behaviors that are expected.

In social studies classrooms different activities clearly require different floor space arrangements. If pupils are to work in a single large group, the room must be arranged to facilitate large-group work. Chairs must be arranged so that the teacher can maintain good eye contact with pupils. Furthermore, individual pupil desks should be arranged so that opportunities for youngsters to interact with one another are minimized. If the teacher plans to make an assignment that will require learners to do some seat work, enough space around the desks should be left to allow the teacher to move easily throughout the classroom to check on individual pupil progress.

BOX 16–1   **Let's Shape the Learner to the Room, *Not* the Room to the Learner.**

A parent recently made the following comments when the local elementary school parents' group was asked to raise money to buy screens so that groups of pupils operating in different parts of the classroom would not interfere with one another's work.

> I think we're making a mistake. Aren't we making life too easy for our kids? Certainly they won't be able to talk to one another if we "cage" them in with visual screens. But is that our purpose? Shouldn't children learn how to be quiet regardless of their physical settings? Shouldn't the teachers teach this as part of the school program? I think they should. Our children will miss something valuable in their elementary school experience if we take the easy way out and make it physically impossible for them to behave in an irresponsible manner. In the real world they will be faced with many opportunities to misbehave. They need to learn how to deal with these temptations. A plan that will help them to avoid their responsibilities is a mistake.

Think About This

1. How do you think other parents at the meeting responded? Why do you think they responded in this way?
2. How much logic is there in the argument that schools should teach pupils to deal with temptation by making it possible to misbehave?
3. If you were a teacher of a classroom in which these visual screens were to be installed, how would you respond to the concerns of this parent?

If the chalkboard is to be used, the desks must be positioned so that learners can see it. The teacher must consider such limitations as the positions of windows and unique lighting patterns. Pupils who cannot see what the teacher is doing may develop inappropriate patterns of behavior.

Many social studies teachers will find a need for at least one small-group meeting area. Small-group areas need to be arranged so that when the teacher works with one group he or she can maintain good visual contact with the other pupils in the class. There should be sufficient space between the members of a single group and the others in the class so that the activities of the group do not interfere with those of the others.

Some teachers may wish to use learning centers in their instructional programs. These centers need to be accessible to all the pupils in the class. They need to be designed so that the activities of learners working at a given center do not attract the attention of other pupils. If special equipment, such as filmstrip projectors or tape recorders, are to be used at a given center, arrangements must be made so that the sound does not interfere with the work of others. The teacher may need to provide earphones for pupils rather than allowing them to use the built-in speakers.

As noted, traffic patterns are an important consideration for teachers as they prepare floor plans of their classrooms. The areas of high traffic must be identified. Typical "high traffic" areas include the entrances to the classroom, the places where pupils store personal belongings, the drinking fountains, book and equipment storage areas, and the area around the teacher's desk.

Each of these areas needs to be kept free from obstructions. Part of the strategy here is to remove anything that might slow a youngster down or attract his or her attention. For example, no pupil desk should be too close to the main entrance of the classroom. A learner seated at such a desk may well find his or her attention diverted every time someone enters or leaves. It is especially important to keep pupil desks well away from drinking fountains and pencil sharpeners.

The Teacher's Desk.   The specific placement of the teacher's desk is an important issue. Many times the desk is situated at the front and center of the classroom. This may not be the best choice. A better option might be to place the desk in an unobtrusive place at the rear of the classroom. There are several advantages to this placement decision.

A teacher desk at the rear of the classroom cannot be used as a teaching station. This kind of placement assures that the teacher will not fall into the undesirable pattern of sitting down and attempting to teach from his or her desk chair. Teaching in that manner communicates a lack of enthusiasm, and it can result in control problems. Teachers who move about the classroom are perceived to be more interested in their pupils and also to be "warmer" people.

Placing the teacher's desk at the back of the room allows the teacher to better monitor independent work. Learners tend to stay at their assigned tasks because they are unable to see whether the teacher is looking at them. (Many will conclude, "I'd better get busy, because the teacher may be watching me.")

A final consideration related to the teacher's desk has to do with its use as an instructional location. In general, it is better for teachers to go to the desk of a pupil who is having a problem than for the pupil to move to the teacher's desk. Pupils who must get out of their seats and walk to the teacher's desk may have to pass close to many others in the class. This may result in a disruption of the work patterns of several pupils. When the teacher walks through the class to assist a given individual, there is a tendency for learners to increase their attention to the assigned task.

Wall Space.   The constructive use of wall space can contribute to a healthy classroom learning environment. Walls can be used for diverse purposes. For example, they might be used to display materials designed to spark pupils' interest in social studies materials, the pupils' work, the classroom rules and regulations, and the good models learners are to follow in completing certain assignments.

Planning for wall space use should be done before the beginning of the school year. Attractive and interesting walls can motivate and excite children when they come into the classroom for the first time. Basic "classroom rules" should also be displayed where pupils can see them. These rules should be discussed with learners on the first day of school. As needed, the rules can be amended throughout the school year.

On the first day of school, one bulletin board should feature a display of materials designed to spark interest in the initial social studies unit. Some teachers attempt to prompt pupils' curiosity by posing a puzzling question that they should be able to answer once the unit has been completed. As work on the unit progresses, teachers can modify the initial display to include materials developed by pupils as they study the unit content.

A place for the display of the daily schedule and for special assignments should be provided on one wall in the classroom. Elementary pupils do better when they feel secure about what they are doing and about what is expected of them, so this kind of display can be very helpful. A daily schedule also communicates to learners that their teacher is well organized. Abundant research points out that most successful teachers operate in an organized, businesslike fashion (Good and Brophy 1986).

Equipment Storage.   Good elementary social studies programs utilize many support materials. Among these are films, filmstrips, cassette tapes, videotapes, and computer software. The machines required to use these materials are bulky. Special arrangements must be made to store this equipment. The individual machines should be easily accessible, but they should be stored in places that do not subject them to a risk of being damaged. This kind of equipment is very expensive, and professional teachers work hard to keep it in good working order.

Materials Storage.   Social studies teachers use a wide variety of materials. These include textbooks, supplementary books, artifacts, pictures, recordings of all kinds, computer software, documents, charts, and many other items. The plans for storing these items must be included in the classroom-utilization scheme. Pupil projects, duplication masters, reams of duplication paper, and the other materials teachers use to support instructional activities will also require space. These items need to be stored with a view both to safety and to accessibility.

Personal Belongings Storage.   Many elementary teachers designate places in the classroom for pupils to store personal items. Sometimes the individual desk tops have adequate storage space. Some teachers devise racks of empty plastic dish pans, stacked boxes, or other storage areas. Areas for personal belongings should be designated before pupils arrive. This allows teachers to give pupils explicit instructions regarding what they are to do with their personal items.

See Figure 16–1 for a checklist on space management.

Time Management

The responsible allocation of class time is a hallmark of the effective teacher. Time-management planning considers the ways to minimize time spent on non-instructional tasks, to keep pupils' attention engaged when formal instruction is

	Yes	No
1. Traffic patterns are free from distractions.		
2. Seating is arranged so that the teacher can easily get to each pupil.		
3. All pupils have an unobstructed view of the main instructional area.		
4. Materials are stored in secure, yet accessible, places.		
5. Small-group areas and learning centers are arranged so that they will not interfere with other instructional activities.		
6. Rules are posted in a prominent place.		
7. The daily schedule is posted.		
8. The teacher's desk is placed unobtrusively.		

Potential Problem Areas: _____

_____

_____

_____

Possible Solutions: _____

_____

_____

_____

FIGURE 16–1
Space-management checklist.

being presented or when they are working on assignments, and, in general, to reduce the total amount of time spent on nonproductive sorts of activities.

Transitions.   Smooth and efficient movement from one aspect of a lesson to another is one aspect of effective time management. Unless there is careful planning for transitions, a good deal of time can be wasted. Such "slack time" also presents pupils with opportunities to behave inappropriately. Thus, transitions planning has the twin advantages of making lessons flow more smoothly and of reducing the probability that classroom control problems will develop.

To deal with the issue of transitions, lesson planning has to go beyond the thought about what kinds of content and what kinds of activities will be featured. The "boundaries" between the activity types need to be identified clearly, and specific plans must be made to move learners quickly out of one phase of a lesson and into another phase.

This kind of planning does not need to be complex. For example, if papers will be returned, designated pupils can distribute them quickly. The papers can be presorted so that each "teacher helper" gets only the papers for those few pupils for whom he or she is responsible. Such procedures can greatly speed up the process of returning papers and can save scarce classroom time for the important instructional tasks.

Activity changes that call for pupils to move from one place to another can cause difficulties. Learners should be provided with instructions that specify exactly how they should change seats, enter and leave the room, and move through the hallways to the library, gymnasium, or other designated areas.

Beginning Class.   Every effort should be made to promptly start the instructional phase of the class period. Roll-taking, materials-development, and announcement-making procedures should be planned with a view to time efficiency. Without good planning in these areas, many beginning teachers find themselves using a substantial part of the class period taking care of noninstructional matters. When this happens, there often is not sufficient time left for youngsters to derive as much from lessons as they might.

Distraction from the assigned tasks cuts into pupils' learning efficiency and may result in classroom control problems. Before a lesson begins, pupil work areas should be cleared of all items not specifically needed for the day's lesson. When the learning areas contain only the materials closely tied to the central focus of the lesson, pupils find it much easier to stay on the task.

Some teachers find it useful to teach pupils to look for a specific signal indicating that the administrative procedures have been completed and the instructional activities are about to commence. For example, pupils might be taught to look for a movement by the teacher to the front and center of the classroom, followed by a quiet gaze over the class. When this occurs, they should understand that the instruction is about to begin, and should quiet down and look up at the teacher.

When the teacher gives the instruction signal, he or she should refrain from beginning until *all* members of the class are quiet and paying attention. It may be necessary to have a word with one or two pupils before all are paying attention.

When the teacher refuses to begin until all are paying attention, he or she communicates to pupils that it is important for them to hear what will be said. A quiet, attentive class assures that all learners will be able to hear the teacher's instructions. This may not happen if some pupils continue to talk. A failure to hear can lead to misunderstandings, and misunderstandings can lead to time-wasting confusion and potential control problems.

Pacing the Lesson.   The lesson pacing, the rate at which a teacher helps pupils move through their daily work, needs to be brisk enough to provide a sense of productive movement, but not so quick that individuals become lost. Repetition of the key points is important, but the teacher needs to avoid overdwelling on items that learners have already mastered. When this happens, boredom sets in. Boredom is a painful form of sensory deprivation. Some pupils may seek relief by engaging in unacceptable behaviors.

To determine an appropriate pace, some teachers consciously identify a few representative pupils to serve as a reference group. The teacher carefully monitors the understandings of these pupils to determine whether the pace is too slow, too fast, or about right.

Different pupils in the class will finish their work at different times. Activities must be designed for those who are early finishers. These need to be selected with care. It is important that these activities are not viewed as "punishment" for completing work quickly, accurately, and efficiently. If these activities are something to which pupils look forward, they will act as stimuli to the others in the class to work quickly and productively on the assigned tasks.

Providing Assistance.   Developing procedures for responding to pupils who need help is another important dimension of time management. Sometimes, several learners will indicate that they need help. When the teacher spends too much time with a single pupil, the others in the class may become frustrated. Furthermore, because the teacher's attention may be concentrated on one person, the others in the class may be tempted to misbehave. Developing a system for responding to learners who need help can result in better assistance for the pupils and can reduce the possibility of classroom control problems.

As noted, organizing pupils' seats so that the teacher has free and easy movement is important. Ease of access by the teacher to each youngster in the classroom saves time and makes it easier for the teacher to work with larger numbers of learners.

A basic consideration when responding to pupils' appeals for help has to do with the issue of how much help ought to be provided. The teacher clearly has an obligation to assist learners who find themselves "blocked" because of some critical misunderstanding. On the other hand, the teacher does not want to do the work for individuals who are perfectly capable of doing it themselves. We do not want to reinforce pupils who are not applying themselves to the assigned task.

F. Jones (1979) provides suggestions to encourage pupils to do as much of their own work as possible. His research reveals that the average teacher spends much more time working with individual pupils than is really necessary. To remedy this, he proposes that the teacher, when working with a learner seeking help, begin by finding something that the pupil has done well. The youngster should be complimented on what he or she has done. This helps build self-confidence.

The teacher should give the pupil a very direct suggestion regarding what he or she should do next. For example, the teacher might say something about how the very next step in a process should be begun. It is important that the teacher should not actually do the pupil's work. Once the suggestion is made, the teacher should move on to the next person. Jones suggests that the teacher should not spend more than about twenty seconds with each pupil. If this time schedule can be maintained, the teacher can get to each individual in the class. Once all pupils have been visited, then individuals can be rechecked to assure that they are back on track.

Some teachers have found that "peer helpers" can work effectively with individuals in the class who experience difficulty. Peer helpers are other pupils in the class who have a good grasp of the material. Some teachers provide peer helpers with special badges to provide them with some valuable recognition for their own good work.

Establishing Routines and Procedures

Routines need to be developed for managing recurring and predictable events. This general management principle is very much applicable to elementary teaching. Teaching is a very people-intensive occupation. During a typical day, teachers have more numerous and more intensive interpersonal contacts than do many other professionals. Unless there is a system to manage these interactions, a severe emotional strain can result. To assure that the reservoirs of energy remain sufficiently high to deal with the many incidences of interpersonal interaction, teachers need systems that will impose some pattern on their work day (Figure 16–2).

Some routines should relate to administrative matters. For example, the teacher should think through how tasks such as taking attendance, collecting assignments, and returning corrected work can be best accomplished.

Other routines apply to pupils' behavior. For example, what should pupils do and how should they behave when entering and leaving the classroom? What are the expectations the teacher has for them when they are using the drinking fountains or the pencil sharpeners? How should they move from one part of the room to another?

The routines for pupils can also relate to the special information they will need when certain learning activities are taking place. Suppose, for example, that a teacher is interested in having pupils do some work in small groups. Learners in the elementary school do not, as a matter of course, know how to function as

1. What should pupils do upon entering the classroom?
2. What procedures will be used to take attendance and to handle the other routine administrative matters?
3. What signal will be used to capture pupils' attention?
4. How will materials be distributed?
5. How will materials be collected?
6. Where will books and supplies be stored?
7. How will assistance be provided to pupils who need help?
8. What will be the rules for using the pencil sharpener, the drinking fountain, and the restrooms?
9. What will be the policy regarding out-of-seat behavior?
10. How will pupils' participation be managed during classroom discussions?
11. How will pupils move from one part of the classroom to the other?
12. What will be the routine for bringing an activity to a close?
13. What procedure will be established to provide guidelines for those who finish work early?
14. What procedures will govern dismissal and leaving the room?

FIGURE 16–2
Questions to consider when planning needed routines and procedures.

members of small groups, and need directions that will help them to work productively.

Once the teacher has decided upon his or her expectations for pupils in a variety of recurring classroom situations, these expectations need to be explained to learners. Such information should be treated with the same level of attention as content related more clearly to the academic subjects. The routines should be explained, demonstrated, and practiced until all members of the class clearly understand the teacher's expectations.

When pupils master these routines, the teacher will be free to deal with situations that are exceptional or out of the ordinary. Without the worries associated with routine matters, such as using the pencil sharpener, the teacher will have more time to devote to serious matters that deserve his or her undivided attention. A result can be more the effective use of the teacher's time and a reduction in the teacher's level of stress.

RESPONDING TO INCIDENTS OF MISBEHAVIOR

Every teacher from time to time faces misbehavior problems. Almost every child at some time or other during his or her years in school will misbehave. The objective of classroom management is not to eliminate inappropriate behaviors but to reduce their frequency.

The purpose of good classroom discipline is not simply to make the job of the teacher easier. There are also important educational goals for pupils. Discipline programs should help pupils develop self-control and accept responsibility. These are socially useful patterns; they will have a broad application throughout the lives of learners presently in the schools (Figure 16–3).

The goals of discipline are compatible with the academic goals of the elementary social studies program. A self-controlled and responsible citizenry is a keystone to the survival of a democracy. Given this reality, an episode of misbehavior does not need to be viewed as requiring a teacher response that has little to do with the academic program. Rather, it might be looked at as an opportunity to teach pupils the socially desirable patterns of behavior, an outcome clearly consistent with the aims of the social studies.

The methods used to confront discipline problems need to be evaluated in terms of how well they help promote the goals of self-control and personal responsibility. For example, coercion and fear may be used to get a pupil to refrain from an unacceptable behavior pattern, but they may do little by way of advancing the individual toward the goal of more self-controlled behavior. There need to be incentives for the pupil to change his or behavior in the desired direction. Skilled teachers vary these incentives in light of their understandings of the personal characteristics of the pupils in their classrooms.

The "Flow" of Discipline Problems Through the School Year

There should be a somewhat predictable pattern to the frequency of discipline problems a teacher faces throughout the school year. If the teacher is succeeding in his or her goal to have pupils develop more self-control and behave responsibly, there should be a general decline in the number of discipline problems as the year progresses.

This does not suggest, however, that there will not be flareups and problem spots during the year. For example, children in elementary schools tend to get very excited before the major holidays or before the end of the school year. A break of warm sunny weather in early spring after weeks of snow or dreary rain will sometimes divert their attention from their school tasks and make them more difficult to work with.

Despite the inevitable "challenging days" that all teachers face, the general trend should be in the direction of fewer discipline problems as the year progresses. If this is not the observed pattern, the teacher needs to reassess his or her responses to discipline problems, and perhaps change what is being done to promote self-controlled, responsible behavior.

Characteristics of Teachers Who Are Good Discipline Managers

Teachers who have established effective discipline-management procedures share certain characteristics. First, they tend to be individuals who are willing to assume personal responsibility for dealing with discipline management. They accept discipline management as an integral part of their roles as teachers, and reject the idea that such problems result from factors beyond their control.

Approach 1: Punishment/Coercion

In general, coercion and punishment are not very effective means of moving individuals toward self-control. This is true because control remains external to the individual. Once the fear of punishment is removed, the individual may return to an unacceptable pattern of behavior.

Advantages
Punishment is better than no control at all. It might be an appropriate "last resort" response for pupils under certain sets of circumstances. Punishment is almost never a good "first choice" response to a pupil's misbehavior.

Disadvantages
Punishment can lead to a breakdown of communication. Resentment often results. Many times pupils will not see the connection between their misbehavior and the punishment. Rather, they will view the punishment as a capricious act on the part of the person administering it. Finally, punishment, in and of itself, fails to teach the pupil an appropriate substitute behavior.

Approach 2: Affection/Praise

This approach depends for its effectiveness on the existence of a positive relationship between the pupil and his or her teacher. This approach does not foster growth in self-control. "Good" pupil behavior is a result not of self-control, but rather of a pupil's expectation that his or her behavior will be rewarded by praise from the teacher.

Advantages
This approach does tend to create warm working relationships between pupils and teachers. Thus, it can change pupil behaviors in a positive direction in a way that does not create an atmosphere of disharmony.

Disadvantages
This approach can cause a pupil to develop an overly dependent relationship with his or her teacher. This kind of a relationship is not conducive to helping pupils develop internal mechanisms to control their behaviors.

Approach 3: Tangible Reinforcers

The use of reinforcers to shape pupils' behaviors is a powerful tool. It has proved particularly effective in small-group settings. The approach is sometimes difficult to apply in large-group arrangements.

FIGURE 16–3
Approaches to promoting pupil growth in self-control.

Additionally, they tend, as much as possible, to deal with discipline problems themselves rather than referring them to the principal or other school authorities.

Second, these teachers favor long-term approaches to solving discipline problems. They are not interested in simply stopping an immediate undesirable behavior. Their concern is for long-term strategies than can be used to diminish the likelihood that the undesirable behavior will occur again.

The third characteristic bears some relationship to the second. These teachers are very much interested in determining whether the observable misbehavior is a manifestation of a deeper, but unseen, cause. They recognize that pupils' home lives, nutritional problems, and personal difficulties may play a part in unacceptable behavior patterns that manifest themselves in the classroom. When feasible, these teachers attempt to deal with underlying causes of misbehavior, not just with the misbehavior itself (Brophy 1983).

Advantages
This approach does have the potential to help pupils internalize appropriate behavior patterns.

Disadvantages
The teacher must find out what a "problem" pupil considers to be reinforcing. This is a very difficult task. For example, those things that might reinforce a learner may be unavailable to the teacher or inappropriate for use in the classroom. Also, the pupil may become too dependent on the expectation of a reward.

Approach 4: Rules and Regulations

Children learn responsibility as they become familiar with the application of rules in many social settings. Effective rules must be reasonable. Pupils need to understand the reasons for rules before they will accept them.

Advantages
Pupils gain an initial security by learning what behaviors are expected of them. By learning that they personally choose the consequences that follow from either obeying or disobeying the rules, pupils are encouraged to develop personal responsibility for their actions.

Disadvantages
If for some reason pupils who have been used to operating where a set of formal rules is available find themselves in a situation where there are no formal rules, they may be at a loss as to how they should behave. If teachers do not enforce rules, these rules will have little influence on learners' behaviors.

Approach 5: Behavior Based on Values or Self-chosen Principles

This is a goal toward which teachers should strive. At this point, pupils "choose" good behavior on their own, not because of external pressures.

Advantages
Pupils learn how to adjust to a variety of situations. They tend not to depend on others when they have to make values choices. Independent decision making improves self-concepts.

Disadvantages
A high degree of maturity is required of pupils who base personal decisions based on their own values or self-chosen principles. Much adult guidance is required before most pupils can begin to operate at this level.

Basic Principles of Discipline

1. *The dignity of the pupil must be preserved when the teacher responds to a behavior problem.* One of the basic purposes of the social studies is to help bolster learners' beliefs in their individual worth and importance. This purpose must be kept clearly in focus when teachers respond to misbehavior problems. Teacher responses that pupils see as undercutting their personal dignity are counterproductive. They can give rise to additional behavior problems as pupils feel compelled to assert themselves. Teacher comments should be directed toward a specific behavior and never to the general character or worth of the individual child.

2. *Private correction is preferable to public correction.* This admonition is consistent with the intent of the first principle. When pupils are corrected in private, they are not faced with the sometimes difficult task of "saving face" in front of their peers. Furthermore, a private conversation enables the teacher to

One-to-one conferences to deal with discipline problems in private are preferable to public correction.

deal with the problem on a much more personal basis than is possible when a large audience of pupils is privy to the exchange between the teacher and the misbehaving child.

3. *The causes of the misbehavior, not just the misbehavior itself, need to be addressed.* If there is to be a long-term revision of behavior, the conditions causing the unacceptable behavior need to be identified and changed. Learners who misbehave often are seeking help through behavior that draws the teacher's attention (even unfavorable attention). Professional social studies teachers work to determine the basic source of the difficulty.

Looking for the source of misbehavior problems calls for a strong and personally secure teacher. The teacher must be prepared to consider the possibility that his or her own behavior has contributed to the pupil's difficulty. For example, a teacher who yells at children who are misbehaving may be reinforcing misbehavior on the part of learners who crave attention. The teacher must be strong enough to consider a change in his or her own patterns in the classroom if an investigation reveals that the existing patterns are contributing to a pupil's problem.

4. *Trivial and serious problems must be distinguished.* Many of the incidents that occur in elementary social studies classes reflect little more than childish irresponsibility. Teachers do need to respond to these problems, but they should not overreact to the point that these minor episodes take on crisis-level dimensions. Teachers who react too harshly to relatively minor lapses in behavior may find that they have an increasingly difficult time establishing warm and productive working relationships with pupils in their classes.

5. *The responses to misbehavior must be consistent and fair.* A first "rule" associated with this principle is that all misbehavior should be responded to by the teacher. Few classroom problems disappear when the teacher pretends they do not exist. More commonly, these problems escalate to become more serious.

In the social studies, we are interested in helping pupils respect one another's rights to follow certain social rules. For example, many teachers in the early grades emphasize the importance of seeking recognition and taking turns during a class discussion. If this is an expectation, the teacher should think through how he or she will respond to individuals who fail to behave in this way. Consequences of misbehaving in this way should be made clear to learners, and should be applied consistently when different learners misbehave in the same way at different times. Clear behavior expectations, a planned set of responses, and consistent application of responses go together to reduce the incidence of behavior problems.

6. *Pupils should be taught to recognize the link between misbehavior and the consequences of misbehavior.* Citizenship education, a major theme in the elementary social studies program, places heavy emphasis on learners' developing responsibility for their own actions. In the area of discipline, this means that teachers should work to teach their pupils that the consequences for misbehaviors are not random or chance events. They do not fall on someone because he or she is "unlucky." Rather, they are the direct result of an unacceptable behavior pattern. Furthermore, pupils must come to understand that they have chosen this unacceptable pattern and, having done so, must be prepared to bear the consequences.

Effective elementary social studies teachers incorporate these basic principles in many ways. More experienced teachers tend to use a much broader variety of responses to discipline problems than do beginning teachers. One of the tasks of the newcomer to elementary social studies teaching is to expand the repertoire of responses to discipline problems and to think through how a decision to use a given response should be made. Categories of responses that experienced teachers have found to be effective are introduced here.

Selecting Responses to Misbehavior

A general guideline to follow in selecting a response to misbehavior is that the response should vary in terms of the seriousness and duration of the misbehavior. With regard to the question of duration, the teacher must consider whether this is a first-time misbehavior or whether it is one in a recurring series. Some teachers have found it useful to think through a series of responses that they might make, given the various levels of seriousness of the problem behavior. Less severe responses are planned for minor problems, and more severe responses are planned for serious misbehavior difficulties.

The sections that follow suggest four general categories of teacher responses: (1) supporting self-control, (2) providing situational assistance, (3) implementing punishment, and (4) involving others. The suggested responses for less severe difficulties should be drawn from those described for the first two categories. The suggestions for more severe misbehavior problems are found under the third and fourth category headings.

The suggestions under each category heading are scaled in terms of their severity, from least severe to most severe. These lists are not meant to be definitive guidelines. They are intended to suggest the wisdom of planning in advance to respond differently to different types of misbehavior problems in the classroom. Such

---

BOX 16–2   A Discipline Observation Form.

This form might be useful to note how teachers deal with problems of misbehavior. The responses might be compared to the principles of discipline and classified according to the range of responses.

Directions   In the first column, identify the time when the misbehavior occurred. Next, write the misbehavior and, in the third column, note the response of the teacher.

Time	Behavioral Incident	Teacher Response
1.		
2.		
3.		
4.		
5.		

Think About This

1. When do most problems seem to occur in classrooms?
2. What type of problems seems to be most common?
3. What conclusions could you draw about the type of responses generally used by the teachers you observed?

advance planning, particularly for teachers new to the profession, can provide a much-needed sense of confidence in the important area of classroom management.

Category 1: Supporting Self-Control

The responses in the first category, as its name suggests, focus on helping pupils reassert personal control over their own behavior. Many of these techniques can be accomplished with minimum disruption of the other pupils in the class.

Reinforcing Productive Behavior.   Pupils grow in self-control when teachers reinforce them for self-controlled behavior. When individual learners do a good job of following directions and obeying discussion rules during a social studies discussion, the teacher can single out individuals for praise. Sometimes, a whole class can be awarded if all pupils have done well. The prospect of seeing a good social studies film sometimes works well to reinforce good self-control behavior of an entire class.

Using Nonverbal Signals.   Minor problems should be handled so that they do not interrupt the flow of a lesson. Nonverbal teacher responses communicate to misbehaving learners that their actions have been noted. Common nonverbal signals include eye contact (known in the trade as the "cold, hard stare"), hand movements, and facial expressions.

Nonverbal communication does not disrupt the ongoing lesson. At the same time, the teacher's actions do let pupils who are misbehaving know that a change in their behavior is expected. In essence, the teacher is giving them time to adjust their behavior before imposing more serious consequences.

Using Proximity Control.   Experienced teachers have long known that minor behavior problems often disappear when they quietly move to the area of the classroom where the behavior is occurring. Many pupils find it difficult to misbehave when the teacher is nearby. Alert teachers frequently manage to walk to a potential trouble spot in the classroom while maintaining the flow of the lesson. When this happens, they are able to influence learners' behavior in a way that does not disrupt the learning process.

Using the Pupil's Name.   Using the pupil's name is somewhat more obtrusive than the options discussed above. It simply involves the teacher mentioning the name of the misbehaving student as an integral part of the lesson. Suppose that a teacher and a class were discussing the exploration of the New World. The teacher might say something like this to alert a misbehaving pupil that his or her inappropriate actions had been noted: "Now, if John were a member of the crew sailing for the New World, he would have to. . . ." This technique is guaranteed to attract John's attention. Often, this is all that is required to help a pupil change from an unacceptable to an acceptable pattern.

Redirecting Pupil Activity.   Teachers who work with very young elementary children especially like this technique. It simply involves focusing pupil attention away from an inappropriate activity. This is done by drawing their interest to an acceptable substitute activity. "Jill, have you seen the new state flags in this box? Would you like to look at them? Do you think you could tell me how many have the colors blue and red?"

Self-monitoring Study Behavior.   This approach can take several forms. Some teachers specify a specific behavior pupils are to engage in when they feel themselves losing their self-control. For example, they might be taught to put their heads on their desks or to clench their fists and count to ten before doing anything else. This substitute behavior, one that is not disruptive to the learning of the others in the class, provides some emotional release. It also gives pupils time to think about the alternatives to behaving in a way that the teacher will find distressing (Brophy 1983).

   In another and quite different version of this general approach, the teacher asks the misbehaving child to move to another part of the classroom. The teacher quietly talks to the child and asks him or her to think out loud about the problem, to consider the possible causes, and to suggest the possible solutions. This version works especially well in social studies classes where the teacher has helped pupils learn the problem-solving techniques by thinking through the processes of problem solution with the whole class (Camp and Bash 1981).

Category 2: Providing Situational Assistance
The second category contains approaches teachers can take to change environments or situations that might be supporting inappropriate behavior patterns. In

"Our fire drills present no problem in getting students out of the building. I'm open to suggestions on getting them back in."

general, these responses are somewhat more disruptive of the learning process than those introduced in the first category.

Giving a Quiet Word. The teacher simply moves close to the misbehaving pupil and quietly reminds him or her of what he or she needs to do to behave properly. This should be accomplished quickly. The idea is to communicate with the child without drawing the attention of the entire class to the situation. A gentle verbal reminder of this type will often suffice to prompt a positive change in a pupil's behavior.

Providing a Rule Reminder. This approach is used when one or more youngsters are in violation of the adopted classroom rules. When this happens, the teacher acts quickly to remind the misbehaving students about what the rule says. Often, this is done in the form of a question. "Bill's group, what is rule number three?" Once an acceptable response is forthcoming and the undesirable behavior ceases, the work on the ongoing lesson continues.

Removing the Pupil from the Situation. The teacher may ask a misbehaving pupil to move temporarily to another area of the classroom and to resume his or her work in the new location. The directions to the youngster should not take the form of an angry confrontation. The idea is to politely and calmly direct the youngster to change his or her location. "Manuela, please take your material and move to the empty table. Continue working there."

Responding to Misbehavior with Clarity and Firmness. If the above responses fail to bring about a change in behavior, the teacher will need to take stronger measures. A number of options are available to reinforce the teacher's displeasure with the present pattern of behavior.

The teacher might decide to use an oral response. This could involve a very firm and clear statement from the teacher that identifies the misbehaving pupil by name, describes exactly what behavior is unacceptable, and suggests an appropriate alternative behavior. "Joanne, you cannot talk when someone else has been recognized. You must wait your turn. Raise your hand, and I will give you a chance to speak."

Other options for the teacher include making strong eye contact with the misbehaving pupil, moving in his or her direction, and placing a hand on his or her shoulder. These physical actions are designed to underscore the teacher's displeasure with a pupil's present behavior. They will often result in a change to a pattern the teacher finds more acceptable.

Holding a Conference with the Pupil. If a learner's misbehavior persists, a teacher-pupil conference is in order. The teacher might begin by identifying the problem, sharing his or her feelings about it, and asking the pupil to suggest how the problem might be remedied.

Some teachers find it useful to conclude a conference of this type with a *behavior contract,* which should specify actions the pupil might take to improve the situation. The contract should suggest some benefits for the pupil when he or she succeeds in changing the undesirable behavior pattern. It might also mention the consequences that might follow if unacceptable behavior patterns persist.

Soliciting Parental Assistance.   Parents of children with undesirable behavior patterns can be important allies of teachers. Telephone calls to parents need to be conducted in a professional manner. The emphasis should be a positive one, focusing on the nature of the problem and the possible approaches to solving it. If parents are approached in this manner, most are very willing to help. Sometimes, they are not even aware that their son or daughter has problems behaving in class. A call to parents affirms the teacher's sincere interest in their child's welfare. Parents will often eagerly join hands with the teacher to help resolve the difficulty (Figure 16–4). Most parents sincerely want their children to do well in school.

Parents can be the teacher's best allies. However, good parental relationships do not happen by chance. They result from good planning and hard work. Most parents want what is best for their children and are concerned about their progress. Many are uncertain as to how they might help. Some of the following ideas can be useful to teachers interested in building positive relationships with parents.

I. Building a Foundation for Positive Parent-Teacher Relations

A. An introductory letter to parents the first week of school. The letter should be positive in tone, giving a time and a phone number for reaching the teacher. A brief overview of the class rules should also be included.
B. Regular communication to parents, informing them of the objectives and the future projects that will be required of the pupils.
C. Positive notes sent home when the child has done what is expected.
D. Sending home examples of pupil work.
E. Making homework clear, meaningful, and free from errors.
F. Telephoning parents about good things their children have done.

II. Expanding Parent-Teacher Contact

A. Inviting parents to visit school. These should be in addition to regular parent organization meetings.
B. Visiting parents at their homes.
C. Providing suggestions to parents concerning the activities that may help their children achieve.
D. Setting up parent-pupil-teacher conferences.

III. Parental Assistance

A. Involving parents as classroom aides.
B. Securing parental assistance on field trips.
C. Asking parents to share an interest with the class.
D. Involving parents in tutoring.

FIGURE 16–4
Working with parents.

Category 3: Implementing Punishment

Punishment is an option that should be used only after all of the alternatives discussed in the first two categories have been exhausted. Punishment that is administered capriciously for minor lapses from appropriate behavior patterns is counterproductive. If punishment is meted out frequently, it loses its potency. For example, teachers who regularly punish pupils for unimportant incidents that reflect childish irresponsibility more than serious behavior problems have little left in their repertoire of responses when something truly serious occurs.

There are a number of punishment options. Those that are described in the following subsections are scaled from least severe to most severe.

Loss of a Privilege. The loss of a privilege is a very effective punishment for elementary pupils. Its effectiveness depends on each pupil having a privilege he or she is loath to lose. Part of the citizenship training in elementary social studies classes often involves assigning each child some job or responsibility. These small duties give learners a sense of importance and help build a commitment to the idea that contributing adults in our society assume certain civic obligations. Pupils often become quite personally committed to the duties to which they are assigned. Many of them will view the loss of the right to perform these assigned responsibilities as punishment.

Many teachers introduce high-interest activities as rewards for doing well on assigned work. In one school, the fourth and fifth graders are allowed to play chess once or twice a week, provided that the class has done well on the assigned tasks. Many pupils have become very interested in the game. The loss of the right to play chess certainly would be regarded as punishment by many of these pupils.

To be effective, punishment that involves the loss of a privilege should be arranged so that the privilege is not lost for too long a period of time. When the punishment is administered, the teacher must let the child know that if he or she improves the inappropriate behavior, the privilege will be reinstated.

In-Class Isolation. Some teachers have an isolation area in their classrooms. This is simply a part of the classroom where a pupil can be sent so that he or she will be unable to interact with the other children in the classroom. Because most children enjoy being with their peers, this kind of isolation is often viewed as punishment.

Under some circumstances, the teacher may allow a misbehaving child to continue working on the assigned tasks while he or she is in the isolation area. Under others, the teacher may ask the pupil to reflect on what he or she has done and write down some ideas about how the behavior might be changed. The ideas produced by the pupil can be used as a basis for a teacher-pupil conference. Under still other conditions, the teacher may not allow the pupil to do anything in the isolation area. This latter option is often reserved for situations when the child's offense has been particularly serious. The boredom resulting from this situation is regarded by many pupils as an especially severe punishment.

Removal from Class. When very serious misbehavior persists, it is sometimes necessary to remove a pupil from the classroom. This might mean sending him or her to the principal's or to the counselor's office for a conference. The teacher should never send a pupil to an unsupervised area such as the hall. If something happened to the child while he or she was in this unsupervised setting, the teacher might be legally liable.

A decision to send a learner to a principal or to another school official should be done only after this individual has been informed about the situation. If a teacher becomes convinced that a child's behavior over time is not improving, the appropriate school officials should be briefed about what the teacher has tried to do to resolve the problem. This information provides a context these professionals can use as they attempt to work with the misbehaving child.

Occasionally, disruptive children are sent to the room of another teacher. This option depends on previous communication with another teacher who agrees to cooperate. When this happens, the misbehaving child should not be allowed to participate in fun-type activities in the other teacher's room. Part of the punishment involves the denial of the right to participate in the ongoing instructional experiences of the other pupils.

Makeup of Time Wasted in Class. Some pupils waste a good deal of time when they are misbehaving. Consequently, they fail to complete their assigned work. One response to this situation is for the teacher to punish these pupils by asking them to remain in the classroom at recess time or after the end of the regular school day. If this is done, the teacher must take care not to give them special attention or privileges, otherwise the so-called "punishment" could be viewed as a reward. This might encourage rather than discourage the inappropriate patterns of behavior.

All attempts to implement punishment should go forward with the understanding that punishment is not an end in itself. It is something implemented as a step in a larger effort to teach pupils to behave in an acceptable manner. Every effort must be made to suggest appropriate patterns to pupils and to help them commit to these patterns.

In this section, no mention has been made of corporal punishment. This is not an accidental omission. Corporal punishment of any kind is illegal in some states. Even where it is legal, the authors believe that the other alternatives are much better. Corporal punishment may sometimes stop an undesirable behavior, but—in general—the physical, emotional, and even legal risks associated with the practice are too great to justify its use.

Category 4: Involving Others
The fourth category is of last resort. When all the other measures have failed, the teacher must seek outside assistance. Assistance can be sought from several sources.

A Face-to-Face Conference with Parents. With a problem this serious, there should already have been phone or letter contact with parents. The teacher needs to prepare for a face-to-face meeting by organizing all the available records relating to the pupil's misbehaviors. The teacher should have begun documenting the instances of misbehavior and his or her attempts to change it long before a decision is taken to call in the parents. These records should be dated, and they should describe the misbehavior and the teacher's responses in very specific

A discipline plan prepared before the beginning of the school year can eliminate many problems associated with classroom control. This form identifies areas that frequently are included in such a plan.

I. Positive Reinforcement

The following rewards will be given to individuals who follow class rules.

1. _____

2. _____

3. _____

The following group reinforcers will be given to the entire class when the group follows class standards.

1. _____

2. _____

3. _____

II. Class Rules

The following basic rules are needed in my classroom.

1. _____

2. _____

3. _____

4. _____

5. _____

III. Consequences

When the rules are not followed, the following range of consequences will be applied.

First violation: _____

Second violation: _____

Third violation: _____

Serious violation: _____

FIGURE 16–5
A teacher's personal discipline plan.

terms. When this information is available, it is much easier to make a convincing case to parents.

The teacher should strive to maintain a positive tone throughout the conference. The idea is for the parents and the teacher to agree cooperatively on the steps to resolve the situation. When a spirit of cooperation rather than confrontation guides the meeting, there is a good chance that both the teacher and the parents will dedicate their best good-faith efforts to helping the misbehaving child.

Problem-Solving Conference with Other Professionals. In especially difficult cases, a team of professionals who have worked with a pupil may need to be brought together. This group might include the teacher, the school principal, the counselors, the psychologist, and other school and outside agency people who have worked with the child. The purpose of a meeting of this kind is to decide upon a course of action. The possibilities include permanent placement in another classroom, assignment to another school, recommendations for additional counseling, suspension, or other options. Many of these decisions call for administrative concurrence. The decisions of the group must be reported to administrators who will be responsible for accepting and implementing recommendations.

See Figure 16–5 for an example of a personal discipline plan.

KEY IDEAS IN SUMMARY

1. Some teachers have difficulty managing pupils' behavior in the classroom. Experienced teachers recognize that they must plan their management procedures as carefully as they plan for other parts of their lessons.

2. The term *classroom management* refers to the way a teacher organizes time, materials, and space to facilitate smooth and efficient operation of the classroom. Good organization requires careful planning and clear communication of behavioral expectations to pupils.

3. Space management helps teachers prevent control problems. Room organization gives the individual classroom its own ambience, or character. The ambience of a given classroom affects how pupils perceive it and how they behave when they are in it.

4. Aspects of the classroom environment associated with learners' propensities to behave properly or improperly include arrangement of floor space, identification of places to store equipment, placement of the teacher's desk and selection of spaces for book and other materials.

5. Teachers who manage classroom behavior successfully tend to be good time managers. It is particularly important that time be well managed (a) during transitions, (b) when pacing lessons, and (c) when assisting individual pupils.

6. Classroom discipline problems tend to be less frequent when the teacher has established, well-understood routines and procedures for such issues as moving from place to place, obtaining permission to speak during a discussion, and turning in assigned work.

7. All teachers from time to time experience discipline problems. Some of these occur at relatively predictable times during the school year, for example immediately preceding holidays. In cold climates, the first warm sunny days of spring sometimes prompt some learners to misbehave.

8. Basic principles of successful discipline include (a) the need to preserve the dignity of the offending child when responding to an episode of misbehavior, (b) the idea that private correction is generally preferred over public correction, (c) the notion that the cause of the misbehavior needs to be addressed, not just the misbehavior itself, (d) the need to distinguish between trivial and serious problems, (e) the need to respond to misbehavior fairly and consistently, and (f) the obligation to help pupils recognize links between misbehaviors and attendant consequences.

9. In responding to episodes of misbehavior, it is wise to have in mind responses that vary in their severity depending on the seriousness of the problem. Teacher responses can be categorized as (a) designed to promote and support self-control, (b) designed to provide situational assistance, (c) designed to implement punishment, and (d) involving others.

POSTTEST

Answer each of the following true/false questions.

1. Certain instructional techniques have been found to cause classroom control problems.

2. Most classroom control problems teachers face are relatively minor.

3. It is common for control problems to occur at transition points within lessons.

4. Public correction of a pupil is almost always preferred over private correction.

5. *Proximity control* assumes that pupils will behave better when the teacher is nearby.

QUESTIONS

1. What kind of classroom-management planning should take place before the school year begins?

2. What characteristics have researchers found to typify teachers who experience few classroom control problems?

3. How can classroom space be organized to support good classroom control?

4. What kinds of time-management decisions can reduce the incidence of control difficulties?

5. How can establishing routines serve to prevent discipline problems?

6. What are some of the basic principles of discipline?

7. During which kinds of social studies lessons would you expect control problems to occur? Why?

8. Describe your ideal space arrangement for teaching social studies lessons at a grade level of your choice. Give your reasons.

9. Should the teacher, alone, establish classroom rules? Should they be established by the pupils? Should they be jointly planned by the teacher and pupils? Explain.

10. Describe ways time might be wasted during social studies lessons. What might a teacher do to prevent this?

11. Which two of the basic principles of discipline do you think are most often overlooked by teachers? Why?

12. Consider the available alternatives for responding to discipline problems. Which approach to you feel most comfortable with? Least comfortable? Explain.

EXTENDING UNDERSTANDING AND SKILL

1. Visit a class in a nearby school. Make a sketch of the physical arrangement of the room. Report to your class, commenting on what you observed. Suggest changes you might make if this were your own classroom, and include your reasons.

2. List routines and procedures you might introduce to pupils on the first day of school. Share these with others in your class, and ask for comments.

3. Interview several teachers about special rules they have for learners during social studies lessons. Produce a master list in your class, and ask your instructor to comment. Distribute copies of an edited version, prepared in light of the instructor's comments, to all class members.

4. With other members of your class, role play a parent conference about a misbehaving child.

5. Visit a class and observe how the teacher handles discipline problems. Report on how the teacher's responses reflect one or more basic principles of discipline.

6. Prepare a written plan describing how you would approach misbehavior problems arising during social studies lessons. Turn this plan in to your instructor for comments.

REFERENCES

BROPHY, J. "Classroom Organization and Management." *The Elementary School Journal* (March 1983), pp. 265–85.

CAMP, B., AND M. BASH. *Think Aloud: Increasing Social and Cognitive Skills—A Problem-Solving Program for Children, Primary Level.* Champaign, IL: Research Press, 1981.

EMMER, E. T., C. M. EVERTSON, AND L. ANDERSON. "Effective Classroom Management at the Beginning of the School Year." *The Elementary School Journal* (May 1980), pp. 219–31.

GOOD, T., AND J. BROPHY. "School Effects." In M. Wittrock, ed., *Handbook of Research on Teaching.* New York: Macmillan, 1986, pp. 570–602.

JONES, F. "The Gentle Art of Classroom Discipline." *National Elementary Principal* (June 1979), pp. 26–32.

KOUNIN, J. *Discipline and Group Management in Classrooms.* New York: Holt, Rinehart and Winston, 1970.

WEINSTEIN, C. "The Physical Environment of the School: A Review of the Research." *Review of Educational Research* (Winter 1979), pp. 577–610.

SUPPLEMENTAL READING

ARONSON, E., N. BLANEY, C. STEFAN, J. SIKES, AND M. SNAPP. *The Jigsaw Classroom.* Beverly Hills, CA: Sage, 1978.

CHARLES, C. M. *Building Classroom Discipline: From Models to Practice.* New York: Longman, 1985.

CHARLES, C. M. *Elementary Classroom Management.* New York: Longman, 1983.

DOYLE, W. "Classroom Organization and Management." In M. Wittrock, ed., *Handbook of Research on Teaching.* New York: Macmillan, 1986, pp. 392–431.

DUKE, D. L., AND A.M. MECKEL. *Teacher's Guide to Classroom Management.* New York: Random House, 1984.

EVERTSON, C. M., E. T. EMMER, B. S. CLEMENTS, J. P. SANFORD, AND M. E. WORSHAM. *Classroom Management for Teachers,* 2d ed. Englewood Cliffs, NJ: Prentice-Hall, 1989.

JONES, V., AND L. JONES. *Comprehensive Classroom Management,* 2d ed. Boston: Allyn and Bacon, 1986.

SAVAGE, T. *Discipline for Self-Control.* Englewood Cliffs, NJ: Prentice-Hall, 1991.

CHAPTER

17

EVALUATING LEARNING

This chapter provides information to help the reader:

1. distinguish between formal and informal evaluation procedures,
2. describe procedures for using selected informal evaluation techniques,
3. point out strengths and weaknesses of selected formal evaluation techniques,
4. distinguish between norm-referenced and criterion-referenced assessment,
5. suggest ways records can be kept to indicate pupil progress in elementary social studies classrooms, and
6. explain how evaluation data can be used to assess an instructional program's effectiveness.

PRETEST

Answer each of the following true/false questions.

1. In general, teachers of pupils in grades five and six tend to use formal evaluation techniques more frequently than teachers of pupils in grades one and two.

2. Nearly all informal evaluation techniques take longer to administer than formal evaluation techniques.

3. It is not necessary for teachers to keep records of pupils' performance when informal evaluation techniques are used.

4. Essay tests can be used to assess learners' abilities to interpret, compare and contrast, and generalize.

5. A matching test is a reasonable choice if the teacher's purpose is to test pupils' understanding of new terms.

INTRODUCTION

Evaluating learning is a two-part process. First, measurements of some kind must be taken of pupils' individual performances. The teacher may take these measurements using informal techniques (relatively open-ended exercises that can be completed successfully by pupils who have mastered the relevant content) or formal techniques (typically structured examinations that feature multiple-choice, true/false, matching, completion, and essay items). Second, teachers make judgments about the adequacy of their pupils' performances based on the results of the measurements and on what they know of the individuals personally.

The several major approaches teachers use to determine how well a given child has done fall into two broad categories of assessment approaches: norm-referenced and criterion-referenced.

In *norm-referenced assessment*, a given pupil's performance is compared against the average performance of other similar pupils. Low grades or ratings are given to individuals whose scores fall below the group average. Norm-referenced assessments, however, have limitations. Suppose, for example, that a teacher computed a group average score for a group of academically talented third graders. It would be possible to award a low grade to a pupil in this class who would have ranked among the highest of the general population of third graders. When using norm-referenced assessments, the teacher must make certain that the average is based on a truly representative group.

In *criterion-referenced assessment*, the grade or rating results from comparing a given pupil's performance with a predetermined standard. For example, if letter grades were used, the teacher would decide in advance on the specific level of performance that would qualify a pupil for each letter grade. Theoretically, every pupil in the class has the potential to earn any grade. If every pupil performs at the level established for a grade of "A," each would be awarded this grade.

The major difficulty with criterion-referenced grading is identifying appropriate standards of achievement. If standards are set too low, pupils will do less than they might be capable of doing. If they are set too high, they may become frustrated and give up. If standards are set with care, however, criterion-referenced grading provides a defensible basis for making judgments about learners' performances.

Some people espouse evaluating pupils based on their individual improvement. According to proponents of this approach, grades should be based only on how much each child has improved personally. There should be no reference either to group averages or to absolute standards of performance. Arguments for and against this approach are introduced in Box 17–1.

All assessment approaches require the teacher to gather information about a pupil before making any judgment about his or her performance. Sections that follow introduce both informal and informal techniques for obtaining this information.

BOX 17–1   Kids Should Be Measured Only Against Themselves!

Recently, two teachers engaged in an argument about the grading of pupils. The following is part of what each had to say.

Teacher A   Kids should not be graded against a standard. Kids should not be graded against a class average. They should just be graded against themselves. I like to know where a youngster is when he or she comes to my class. Then I can figure out how much progress he or she has made. That's how I award grades. If a youngster shows lots of improvement, then I give an "A."

Teacher B   It is a terrible mistake to grade a youngster against himself or herself. This makes it almost impossible for a bright child to show progress. Suppose that on a pretest a bright student received a grade of 90. He or she would be limited to an improvement of only 10 points on a posttest. A much less able youngster might improve by 50 or 60 points. Does this mean we should give the less able child the better grade and "punish" the other youngster for "knowing too much too soon"?

Think About This
1. How "fair" is grading based on individual improvement?
2. How do you feel about the logic of Teacher A?
3. How do you feel about the logic of Teacher B?
4. What is your own position on grading based on individual improvement? How would you respond to others who might criticize your view?

INFORMAL EVALUATION

Informal evaluation techniques feature teacher observation of a variety of pupil performances. Results are data on behavior patterns that suggest whether a child has mastered a given skill or cognitive understanding. Sometimes these pupil responses cannot easily be graded "right" or "wrong." Sometimes, too, informal evaluation sheds light on pupils' attitudes.

Informal evaluation often can be accomplished quickly. For example, if a teacher wants to know whether a given pupil can get along with others (an important social skill), casual observation of the pupil's behavior in class and on the playground is usually sufficient. There is no need for the teacher to develop a sophisticated test. A simple, dated notation can record the information (e.g., "Marta played well at recess and got along well with others in class today—10/18/91").

Informal evaluation is nonthreatening, and provides information about pupils' "natural" behavior patterns. This is true because much of it takes place without pupils being aware that it is happening. This is a far different situation from that facing learners confronted with a formal test. Though informal evaluation is used throughout the elementary social studies program, it is used more frequently by teachers of younger elementary school pupils than by teachers of fourth, fifth, and sixth graders. One reason for this is that very young pupils lack the reading and writing skills needed to take formal tests, so their teachers must rely heavily on informal procedures. Additionally,

Informally evaluating pupils' progress through observing their work is an important element of an evaluation plan.

the social studies program in the early grades is heavily oriented toward developing basic skills and helping pupils to get along well with others. These skills and behaviors are often more easily assessed informally.

Certain cautions must be observed when using informal evaluation techniques. Because these techniques require the teacher to make inferences about pupils based on observing their "natural" behaviors, sufficient observations must be made to provide a sound basis for judgment. Additionally, there needs to be a systematic scheme for recording information. Because classes often include large numbers of pupils and because many different kinds of things happen each day, teachers sometimes find it hard to recall important behaviors of individual pupils. A record-keeping scheme that prompts the teacher to take notes about individual behavior patterns close to the time of their occurrence is essential. When the teacher keeps careful records and takes multiple observations, informal evaluation can generate much useful information about each pupil's progress. (See Box 17–2.) The subsections that follow introduce several common informal evaluation procedures.

Teacher Observation

Teacher observation of pupils is an important informal evaluation tool. Some aims of the elementary social studies program can be assessed in no other way, such as those related to general attitudes and to interpersonal relations skills. For example, "work cooperatively with others" is an objective for kindergarten pupils found in many school districts' social studies curriculum. Obviously, a written test cannot determine how well children have mastered this objective. The teacher must observe children directly to effectively evaluate how well they get along with each other.

BOX 17–2   **I Don't Think *Good* Kindergarten Teachers Need Records.**

Recently, a prospective kindergarten teacher made the following comments.

> All the kindergarten teachers I've talked to say they spend too much time keeping records. They say they feel they must write down "everything" about every youngster. It seems to me that this is a big waste of time. It *has* to take valuable time away from working with children. Also, I think a really *good* kindergarten teacher should know the children so well as individuals that he or she ought not to need a formal written record. I mean, if a youngster is slow to learn colors or something else, the teacher should know that. I can't understand why so many kindergarten teachers waste so much time on recordkeeping.

Think About This

1. If many kindergarten teachers do spend a great deal of time on recordkeeping, why do they do so?
2. Is time spent on recordkeeping "wasted"? Explain your position.
3. How might a kindergarten teacher react to this person's comments?
4. If you were to argue with this person, what points would you want to make?
5. What is your personal reaction to this statement?

Informal evaluation often prompts the teacher to give specific directions to an individual pupil about an attitude, a skill, a desired interpersonal relations behavior, or an item of academic content. Good teacher observation looks for specific behaviors (being polite when others are speaking, sharing, and so forth). Teachers often maintain a brief written record of pupils who are experiencing specific problems, for the purpose of noting both progress and continuing areas of difficulty.

Teacher-Pupil Discussion

Personal discussions with individual pupils often provide teachers with insights. These conversations may reveal much about their attitudes, interests, and understandings. Teachers may test the accuracy of their perceptions about how individual learners are feeling and about how well they are mastering social studies content.

There are obvious problems with this approach. Time constraints make it difficult for teachers to have long discussions with each pupil (Ebel and Frisbie 1986). Hence, it is not possible to sample individual pupils' learning in this way with a great deal of frequency. Because of this limitation, teachers must supplement this approach with other procedures.

Pupil-Produced Tests

This technique is applicable primarily to learners in grades four, five, and six. By the time pupils have progressed this far in school, they typically have taken dozens of teacher-prepared tests and are quite familiar with the common formats of basic test types, such as true/false and multiple-choice.

Many teachers have found that having pupils develop their own test items over studied content provides useful information about what they have learned. Typically, learners focus on what they perceive to have been most important. From this focus teachers can determine what pupils have learned from a particular body of content, and can identify individuals who have developed mistaken impressions and who need additional work with the material. To make the exercise credible, many teachers incorporate a few pupil-generated items on a subsequent scheduled examination.

My Favorite Idea

A space on the chalkboard or a large sheet of butcher paper is needed for this exercise. The teacher invites pupils to write their "favorite social studies idea" in this space once or twice each week. To get started, the teacher needs to provide examples of the kinds of things that pupils might write. ("I would *hate* to have my feet bound like they used to do to girls in China." "I think men here should be forced to wear pigtails like they used to wear in China.") Children should be encouraged to write about whatever has engaged their interest. Every child should be encouraged to write something, though some may need help. To personalize the activity, the teacher may ask children to sign their names after their comments.

This exercise yields insights for the teacher about the kinds of information and attitudes pupils are taking away from social studies lessons. Teachers often learn things that they will want to include in the records kept on individual class members. The technique also provides benefits for learners. It motivates pupils to think more seriously about their social studies lessons, knowing they will be asked to contribute a "favorite idea."

Headlines

One measure of learning is the ability to summarize accurately. If summaries are accurate, the teacher has grounds for concluding that pupils grasp essential features of the material on which the summary is based. The teacher may test pupils' abilities to summarize by asking them to write or state orally possible headlines for newspaper articles about current study topics. Written headlines can be displayed on butcher paper, a bulletin board, or a chalkboard.

Pupil-produced headlines give the teacher basic information about how each learner grasps a subject's essential features. Comments derived from examining each child's headline can be noted in a grade book, on a progress chart, or in some other appropriate manner. Additionally, a teacher's review of all of the headlines produced by a class can pinpoint any widespread misconceptions. These can be addressed in followup work.

Newspaper Articles

With learners in grades four, five, and six, teachers may expand the headline activity to include actually writing a short, related newspaper article. To prepare for this activity, the teacher introduces pupils to basic formats for newspaper articles, and gives them guidelines concerning length and kinds of information to include. The content of the articles provide the teacher with a great deal of evidence about levels of understanding of each pupil, and lets them identify learners who need additional help. Where large numbers of children appear confused about certain issues, the class as a whole can be involved in a clarifying discussion.

Some teachers find it useful to "publish" some of the best articles, distributing them to all class members (and perhaps to other classes), to the principal, and to parents. Copies may be displayed on a bulletin board in the class or in a display area in the hall. The possibility of becoming a "published journalist" is an incentive that motivates many pupils to do good work.

Word Pairs

In a word-pairs assessment activity, the teacher presents pupils with a set of cards on which single words have been written, and asks them to find pairs of cards that go together. The teacher checks each learner's work and asks why the child thinks cards in each selected pair are associated. The teacher provides help to individuals who are having difficulty and keeps records of each pupil's performance. If many learners are making a similar mistake, the teacher deals with the issue with the whole class. The activity always concludes with a discussion to reinforce appropriate relationships between words in each correct pair.

As an example, a word-pairs activity focusing on naming leaders and what they lead might use cards containing these words:

PRESIDENT   STATE   CLASSROOM   TEACHER

UNITED STATES   CITY   MAYOR   GOVERNOR

Each card contains one of these words. The teacher gives each learner a complete set of eight cards and asks them to make appropriate pairs. The completed pairs should look like this:

- PRESIDENT—UNITED STATES
- GOVERNOR—STATE
- MAYOR—CITY
- TEACHER—CLASSROOM

Alphabet Review Game

The alphabet review game can be used to assess either individuals or groups of learners. This simple exercise provides pupils with a review of basic alphabetizing skills and at the same time reviews currently studied material.

The teacher leads a class discussion to decide what information from the current lesson is the most important. Then, the teacher asks learners to find as many important terms as they can that begin with each letter of the alphabet. Pupils are instructed to skip letters if they cannot find any important terms that begin with them. (For example, relatively few important terms begin with "X.") The teacher sets a limit to the time spent on each letter, usually three or four minutes.

This exercise can be done by pupils working alone or in groups. When in groups, each group works together to find terms beginning with each letter. The teacher walks around the room to monitor each pupil or group. The teacher may wish to keep records of each learner's progress. As a followup activity, lists for each letter can be shared, and pupils can review the meanings of the terms.

Mystery Word Scramble

The mystery word scramble takes advantage of children's love of puzzles. Typically, the exercise focuses on previously introduced key terms. Letters in these terms are scrambled. A definition of the unscrambled term is provided. Pupils look at the definition and try to decide what the word is. As an added feature, the teacher may circle one space in those provided for pupils to copy the correct term. When all terms have been properly unscrambled, the circled letters will spell out a "mystery word," usually another important social studies term.

Pupils like mystery word scrambles. The exercise provides a means for teachers to learn about pupils' understanding in a way that minimizes student anxiety. If many learners have problems identifying the same terms, these can be featured in a followup class discussion. Teachers can easily keep track of each learner's success in identifying the appropriate terms. A sample format for a mystery word scramble is provided in Figure 17–1.

Anagrams

Anagrams are words created by rearranging letters of other words. For example, the word *opus* can be made by using all of the letters of the word *soup*. Anagrams can be used as a means of informal assessment. Teachers typically present the

---

Directions (Answers are provided in parentheses)

The words at the left are real words, but the letters have been mixed up. Arrange the letters to form the correct word. Write the word in the spaces provided. The definition at the right of each mixed-up word will help you decide what the correct word should be.

Mixed-up Word	Definition	Correct Word
tedolingu	Imaginary lines on a globe used to measure distances east and west.	– – –Ⓞ– – – – (longitude)
uteltaid	Imaginary lines on a globe used to measure distances north and south.	Ⓞ– – – – – – – (latitude)
reqtuoa	An imaginary line around the globe that separates the northern and southern hemisphere.	– – – – – –Ⓞ (equator)
mabroteer	A device for measuring air pressure on the earth's surface.	Ⓞ– – – – – – – (barometer)
hehepsimer	A term that means "one half of the earth's surface."	– – – – – – –Ⓞ– – (hemisphere)

Mystery Word Directions

One letter in each of the above words is circled. Together, these letters form the mystery word. Write the letters in the blanks provided below. The mystery word is defined just to the right of the blanks.

_ _ _ _ _: A term used to describe a model of the earth. (globe)

FIGURE 17–1
Sample mystery word scramble exercise

exercise to pupils as a puzzle game. Many pupils will participate in the game completely unaware that the teacher is observing their performance.

In setting up an anagram exercise, teachers usually provide the original term plus a definition of another term that can be made using the letters of the original term. The teacher encourages pupils to look at the definition and to think of a word that fits it that uses all of the letters of the original term. The new terms should relate to content that has been recently studied. Pupil performance on the anagram exercise gives the teacher some indication of how well individual learners have mastered basic terminology.

An example of an anagram exercise for pupils who have recently studied bodies of water and marine life is provided in Figure 17–2.

Other Informal Techniques

These informal observation techniques are only a sample of the many that teachers use. Among other techniques are sorting activities of all kinds, which help pupils recognize major category labels and items that belong within each category. Some teachers may ask groups of learners to debate issues. The positions introduced during the debates reveal the depth of understanding of individual participants. Crossword puzzles, hidden-word puzzles (puzzles where words are disguised in a random-seeming array of letters), and other puzzles and games are widely used. "What I Learned" diaries are favored by some teachers. The list of possibilities goes on and on.

Oral Directions (Answers are provided in parentheses)

Look at the word in capital letters. Then look at the definition. The definition describes a different word from the one at the left, but this new word uses all the letters in the word to the left. Write this new word in the blanks provided at the end of the definition.

LEAK   1. A large body of fresh water completely surrounded by land. _ _ _ _ (lake)

MASTER   2. A body of running water, such as a river or a brook. _ _ _ _ _ _ (stream)

FURS   3. The name given to the waves of the sea as they crash on the shore. _ _ _ _ (surf)

DIET   4. The twice-a-day rising and falling of the level of the ocean. _ _ _ _ (tide)

SALE   5. A sea animal with flippers that lives along rocky coastlines. _ _ _ _ (seal)

LOOP   6. A small and rather deep body of water. _ _ _ _ (pool)

ALIENS   7. This refers to something, such as sea water, that contains salt. _ _ _ _ _ _ (saline)

FIGURE 17–2
Sample anagrams exercise

A teacher's decision to use a given procedure should depend on whether, for the specific classroom and circumstances, the answer to this question is "yes": "Will this procedure provide sufficient information for me to make a reasoned judgment about any given pupil's performance?" When teachers use informal evaluation techniques, it is essential for them to have an effective system of recording information about individual pupil performance.

RECORDKEEPING AND INFORMAL EVALUATION

Informal evaluation techniques generate much useful information. Good record-keeping helps teachers make maximum use of this information. There are many ways to record data on pupil performance.

Secondary school teachers often rely exclusively on a grade book to record information about learners' progress. This scheme does not work as well in elementary classrooms. The informal evaluation procedures that are widely used with younger learners do not lend themselves well to a record reflecting either a numerical score or a letter grade. Instead, much information about pupils is of a "can" or "cannot" or a "yes" or "no" nature. For example, one aim of many

Kindergarten—Mr. Bianca:
Daily Performance Progress Checklist

Today's Date: _____

FOCUS SKILLS

Member of the Class	Identifies Relative Location (near, far)	Cites the Pledge of Allegiance	Names the Days of the Week
Brenda	+	+	+
Erik	+	−	W
Gretchen	−	−	W
Howard	−	W	+
Juan	+	+	+
Karen	+	W	−
Lawrence	W	W	W
Adela	+	+	+
Paul	+	W	W

(This same pattern follows for the rest of the class.)

FIGURE 17–3

Sample daily performance progress checklist

Key: + = the pupil has mastered this competency; W = the pupil has partially mastered this competency, but more work is needed; − = the pupil has not even partially mastered this competency yet.

Because youngsters in the early elementary grades do not take as many formal examinations (multiple choice, true/false, and so forth) as do older pupils, it is not practical to keep records in a grade book where little provision is made except for noting numerical scores and letter grades. Though grades will have to be given to youngsters (at least in most districts), the documentation of youngsters' work is often accomplished more conveniently using a cumulative record form of some kind.

A separate cumulative record form is kept for each pupil. Often, these are kept in individual file folders. Periodically, the teacher will review the information taken from less formal observations of daily performance. (See the daily performance record referenced in the material on "Recordkeeping and Informal Evaluation.") The teacher typically notes on the cumulative record form those competencies a youngster has mastered. These forms provide data that can be used to compile information to share with parents during parent-teacher conferences and during formal progress reports from the school.

Cumulative record forms vary greatly from district to district. The following one is an example of what you might expect to find in a form designed to reflect the progress of a youngster in the social studies component of the kindergarten program.

Cumulative Record: Social Studies—Kindergarten

Name of Pupil: _____

Directions

Place a checkmark in the blank before each competency the pupil has mastered. Also note the date the checkmark was entered.

Area I: History–Social Science—Knowledge, Skills, Values

_____ 1. Understands term "basic needs."
_____ 2. Tells how families meet basic needs.
_____ 3. Identifies property as his/hers/mine/ours/yours.
_____ 4. Defines work and play.
_____ 5. Names self, school, community.
_____ 6. Identifies basic time concepts (minute, hour, day).
_____ 7. Names days of the week.

FIGURE 17–4
Sample social studies cumulative record form for kindergarten.

kindergarten programs is for pupils to know the name of their school and town. The child either does or does not know these facts.

To keep track of pupils' progress in elementary social studies classrooms, many teachers use *daily performance progress checklists.* (Despite the name, teachers do not always update these records daily. Depending on individual circumstances, several times a week may suffice.) These easy-to-use sheets allow the teacher to note quickly how each learner is faring on a limited number of focus competencies. These checklists can be tailored to fit content; specific notations can be modified to accommodate the needs of the teacher. To record such information, the procedures must allow for frequent observation of small increments of learning that cannot necessarily be described in terms of numerical scores or letter grades. Some teachers find it convenient simply to note whether a pupil (1) has mastered

_____ 8. Identifies relative locations (near, far).

_____ 9. Identifies relative size (large, small).

_____ 10. Identifies basic directions (right, left; up, down).

_____ 11. Identifies safety symbols.

_____ 12. Identifies simple road signs.

_____ 13. Explains what is meant by "change" and cites examples.

_____ 14. Identifies contents of photographs and paintings.

_____ 15. Makes inferences from pictures.

_____ 16. Notes sequences in multipart events (first, second, and so forth).

_____ 17. Accepts others' rights to their own opinions.

_____ 18. Identifies major national and state holidays.

_____ 19. Recognizes flags of the nation and state.

_____ 20. Describes alternative solutions to problems.

Area II: Citizenship–Personal Education–Knowledge, Skills, Values

_____ 1. Identifies and states reasons for classroom and school rules.

_____ 2. Explains consequences of breaking rules.

_____ 3. Begins tasks promptly and stays on tasks until they are completed.

_____ 4. Volunteers to participate in discussions.

_____ 5. Behaves in a way reflecting an understanding of right and wrong behavior.

_____ 6. Recites Pledge of Allegiance.

_____ 7. Works cooperatively with others.

_____ 8. Participates in group decision making.

_____ 9. Helps others to learn.

_____ 10. Demonstrates courteous behavior.

_____ 11. Accepts leadership of others when asked to do so.

_____ 12. Accepts responsibility to assume leadership when asked.

_____ 13. Accepts basic idea of accepting decisions of the majority.

_____ 14. Listens when others are talking.

_____ 15. Takes turns willingly.

the competency, (2) has partially mastered the competency, or (3) has not mastered even a part of the competency. Figure 17–3 illustrates an example of such a daily performance progress checklist.

A daily performance record such as shown in Figure 17.3 is easy to use. It can provide the teacher with a frequent measure of each learner's performance on every area emphasized during a day's lesson. Collectively, this information can indicate areas of strength and weakness as they exist within the class as a whole.

Periodically, the teacher may enter this daily information into a cumulative record. A cumulative record form typically includes all grade-level competencies. It summarizes what has been observed about an individual child over time. An example of a social studies cumulative record form for kindergarten is provided in Figure 17–4.

FORMAL EVALUATION

Formal evaluation procedures include tests prepared by teachers and standardized tests prepared by commercial firms. When informal assessment techniques are used, pupils often do not know they are being evaluated. With formal evaluation techniques, learners almost always are aware they are being tested. As a result, pupils' anxiety levels often are higher during formal evaluations.

Many kinds of tests qualify as formal assessment instruments. Subsections that follow introduce several that are commonly prepared by elementary social studies teachers.

Rating Scales

Teachers need to assess learning outcomes beyond those that can be tested using forced-choice examinations such as multiple-choice or true/false tests. For example, some of their learning objectives may call on pupils to give brief oral summaries of positions, to build models, or to increase their frequency of participation in class discussions. A rating scale can provide information about learners' proficiencies in these areas.

Rating scale preparation begins with identifying a set of focus characteristics. The rater makes judgments about a given pupil's relative proficiency by circling or otherwise marking a point on the scale. The points on a good rating scale refer to specifically defined pupil behaviors. Some rating scales are deficient in this regard. Consider this example: Suppose a teacher were interested in the degree to which individual pupils volunteered information during class discussion. A poorly-designed rating scale to gather this information is depicted in Figure 17–5.

The rating scale in Figure 17.5 provides an illusion of specificity, but it fails to indicate exactly what each rating point means. As a result, two raters who ob-

---

Directions

Circle the appropriate number for each item. The numbers represent the following:

5 = Outstanding
4 = Above average
3 = Average
2 = Below average
1 = Unsatisfactory

How would you assess this youngster's willingness to volunteer to speak during classroom discussions?

5   4   3   2   1

FIGURE 17–5
Rating scale with poorly defined rating points

served a given pupil might award the learner quite different ratings. In the language of test-design specialists, this rating scale lacks *reliability* (the ability to produce consistent results when applied to similar situations). A better, more reliable rating scale would be one that more specifically identified meanings of each rating point. Note the improved rating scale shown in Figure 17–6.

The ratings in Figure 17.6 are scaled in such a way that two or more raters observing the same pupil behavior would be quite likely to award the learner a common rating. A reliable rating scale can contribute much good information about important categories of pupil behavior.

Learning Checklists

Checklists share with rating scales the characteristic of measuring behaviors that are not easily assessed through written tests. Learning checklists depend on the teacher's ability to see and record information about behaviors of interest.

Checklists are not as flexible as rating scales, which may offer a continuum that includes many rating points. For instance, the examples in Figures 17.5 and 17.6 allow a teacher to select one of five rating points. Most checklists, on the other hand, are designed only to note the presence or absence of a given behavior. This is not necessarily a limitation; sometimes "yes" or "no" or "present" or "absent" judgments are all a teacher needs. When this is true, a teacher who has decided to use a checklist has made a wise choice.

Measurement specialists Gronlund and Linn (1990, p. 393) have described checklist guidelines. The following list draws upon their work:

1. Identify and describe each desired pupil behavior as specifically as possible.
2. Add to this list the most common incorrect, or error, behaviors.
3. Arrange the list of desired behaviors and incorrect, or error, behaviors in the approximate order one might expect to see them.
4. Develop a simple procedure for checking each action as it occurs.

Directions

Circle the appropriate number for each item. The numbers represent the values indicated.

5 = volunteers on 80–100 percent of opportunities to do so.
4 = volunteers on 60–79 percent of opportunities to do so.
3 = volunteers on 40–59 percent of opportunities to do so.
2 = volunteers on 20–39 percent of opportunities to do so.
1 = volunteers on 0–19 percent of opportunities to do so.

How often does the youngster volunteer to participate in classroom discussions?

5   4   3   2   1

FIGURE 17–6
Rating scale with clearly defined rating points

Suppose a teacher were interested in how individual pupils were grasping the distinctions among the terms "county," "country," and "continent." (Many learners confuse these concepts.) By listening to pupils' oral comments or by short interviews with several class members, the teacher could determine how learners were faring with this task, and could record this information about each pupil on a checklist. A sample checklist is shown in Figure 17–7.

All of the checklists, when completed, would provide information not only about each child but also about any misunderstandings that may be widespread throughout the class. This information would cue the teacher to highlight certain points during class discussions.

Attitude Inventories

Not all assessment is directed at obtaining measures of pupils' cognitive achievement. There are times when teachers are interested in learners' attitudes. Attitude inventories often are used to provide this information.

Attitude inventories call on learners to rate their relative interest in subjects or topics. They are presented a list of alternatives. Directions tell them to indicate their preferences in rank order. If there are six items, they will indicate their first through sixth-place preference.

Suppose at the beginning of the school year a sixth-grade teacher finds that learners do not particularly look forward to their social studies lessons. The teacher might try to develop more positive reactions to this part of the school

Name of Pupil: _____	Yes	No
Distinguishes between "county" and "country."		
Distinguishes between "county" and "continent."		
Distinguishes between "country" and "continent."		
Confuses "country" and "county," but not "country" and "continent."		
Confuses "country" and "continent," but not "country" and "county."		

FIGURE 17–7
Learning checklist
To use this checklist, the teacher simply places a checkmark in the appropriate box or boxes.

Individual assessments of pupil growth such as this teacher is conducting are extremely useful in identifying pupil strengths and weaknesses.

program by involving children in interesting learning activities throughout the year. To test the success of this effort, the teacher might give the same attitude inventory on different occasions. Pupils would take it first at the beginning of the year and then again some months later, after they had been exposed to lessons designed to enhance their interest in the social studies. A sample attitude inventory is depicted in Figure 17–8.

If the teacher's suspicions are correct, many pupils would rank their interest in the social studies program relatively low when the attitude inventory is first given. The teacher's hope is that learners will rank it higher relative to other subjects later in the year after lessons designed to prompt their interest. A higher average rating for the social studies on the second inventory would tell the teacher that the plan to improve learners' attitudes is succeeding.

Essay Tests

Essay tests are much more common in the upper grades than in the middle and lower grades. In fact, few essay tests are used at all with primary-grade learners, for primary-grade pupils lack the writing skills needed to respond properly. These skills are quite rudimentary even in middle-grade pupils.

Though not appropriate for all elementary learners, essay tests do have a place in the overall school social studies program. Quite apart from their function as an

---

Topic: Interest in School Subjects
Directions: Listed below are some of the subjects you will be studying this year. Look at each one. Place a number "1" in the blank in front of the subject in which you have the greatest interest. Place a number "2" in the blank in front of your next favorite subject. Continue this pattern until you conclude with a number "5" in the blank in front of the subject you like least.

_____ mathematics

_____ reading

_____ science

_____ social studies

_____ physical education

FIGURE 17–8
Sample attitude inventory

indicator of pupils' academic learning, they contribute to fluency with the written language. With respect to content, essay tests allow learners to assemble bits of information into meaningful wholes. (See Box 17–3.)

Essay tests are well suited for such purposes as determining pupils' abilities to interpret, compare and contrast, and generalize about given information. Essays help teachers to test more sophisticated kinds of pupil thinking. On the other hand, when assessment focuses on less sophisticated thinking skills (recall of specific names and places, for example), other kinds of tests, including true/false, multiple-choice, and matching, are more appropriate.

Guidelines for preparing good essay items are as follows:

1. Write a question that focuses on a specific and somewhat limited content area. Essays take time to compose. Not too much content can be covered in the time available for pupils to respond.
2. Write questions that encourage pupils to include examples and specific details. Note the differences between items (a) and (b):
   (a) What are differences between the northern and southern hemispheres?
   (b) Discuss the weather and seasons in the northern and southern hemispheres. State the differences in (1) the months of the year when summer occurs, (2) the months of the year when winter occurs. Also, (3) tell what the relative position of the earth and sun have to do with these differences.
3. Give pupils specific instruction about how much they are expected to write. Usually length expectations are best explained in terms of numbers of paragraphs desired. Even upper-grade learners may have trouble writing a full page on a given question.

Correcting essay items poses problems for teachers. More is involved than simply comparing a pupil's response to answers on a key, as with multiple-choice

---

BOX 17–3   Needed: More Essay Tests in Schools.

The following comments appeared on the editorial page of a local newspaper.

Youngsters are poorer writers today than they were fifty years ago. Why has this happened? It surely cannot be that our children are not as smart. It surely *can* be said that something is terribly wrong with the school program. That "wrong" is simply this: Youngsters are no longer compelled to write essays.

Today, we have schools filled with mechanical grading machines that quickly score multiple-choice and true/false tests. These devices doubtless save time. However, they have also invited teacher irresponsibility. Because of easy mechanical grading, too few elementary teachers give essay tests. Since children are not asked to write, many of them never master the skill.

Mastery of the written word is a hallmark of the truly educated adult. We support the adoption of a school policy requiring elementary teachers to give only essay examinations after grade three. The step may be a radical one. However, given the lamentable decline in writing skills, a serious response is warranted.

Think
About
This

1. What problems for teachers would you see if this proposal were adopted by the school board?
2. What other "causes" for a decline in writing proficiency might you suggest, other than the increasing use of objective tests in the schools?
3. Would teachers at some grade levels find implementing this proposal more difficult than teachers at other grade levels?
4. Suppose that you were to respond to the writer of this editorial. What would you say?

---

or true/false tests. While it is more difficult to score essays reliably, certain procedures can make such grading more consistent.

First, the teacher may prepare a sample response to each essay question. This procedure often will reveal potential problems with the language used in the question itself. The completed teacher response will also identify major points the teacher may look for while grading pupil responses. Sometimes teachers list these points separately after they have written their sample responses.

Inexperienced teachers often read one pupil's answers to all questions before going on to the next learner's paper. It is better to read every learner's response to one question at a time. This is desirable because different standards tend to be applied to different questions. If all answers to a given question are read together, there is a better chance that the teacher will apply the same grading standard to each pupil.

Sometimes, the order in which a teacher reads essays will make a difference in how he or she grades them. For example, a teacher may become frustrated when the same mistake appears on paper after paper. Unconsciously, the teacher may grade the papers read later more harshly than those graded earlier. To guard against this possibility, it is wise to read responses several times (when this is practical) and to shuffle the papers so the order is changed with each reading.

Teachers sometimes find that they have expected too much from their pupils. If a review of all answers reveals that many pupils have missed critical material, this may indicate that pupils need more instructional time. Grading criteria occasionally have to be adjusted so learners are not punished for not knowing material that the whole class needs to work on.

True/False Tests

True/false tests are widely used in elementary schools. Individual questions can be prepared quickly. Pupils have little difficulty learning how to take them. Because learners can respond to a large number of questions in a limited time, a single true/false test can cover much content. The tests can be corrected quickly. Many schools have machines that electronically score them, provided that learners mark responses on special answer sheets.

Because true/false tests depend on absolute judgments (that is, the answer must actually be "true" or "false" and not something in between), teachers must take care not to inadvertently oversimplify complex issues.

For example, suppose a teacher asks pupils to respond "true" or "false" to this statement: *The sun set yesterday.* The teacher probably expects learners to respond "true." However, the statement really represents an irresponsible distortion of a more complex issue. True, the sun did *appear* to set yesterday, but it did not actually move at all. What happened was that the earth turned, and, to someone on the earth, the sun seemed to set.

True/false tests also have been accused of encouraging guessing rather than learning. Critics argue that pupils will sometimes get a higher score than they deserve as a result. Measurement specialists doubt that this is terribly serious, stating that pupils are as likely to guess wrong as to guess right. Overall, guessing is unlikely to raise the score of a pupil who does not know the content.

The following are guidelines for preparing true/false tests.

1. Avoid giving unintentional clues. These include use of words such as *all, no, never,* and so forth, which tend to prompt an answer of "false."
2. Approximately half of the questions should be false. True statements are easier to construct. Learners who guess tend to mark "true" more frequently than "false."
3. Every statement should be clearly true or false. "The Yankees are the best baseball team" and similar subjective statements are not appropriate for a true/false test.
4. Avoid double negatives in statements. "It is never undesirable to drink milk for breakfast" is a confusing double-negative statement. "Drinking milk for breakfast is recommended by a majority of health authorities" is much less confusing.

When learners answers are not recorded on electronic scoring sheets, several options are available. Some teachers provide blanks in front of each statement.

When this is done, the teacher should not allow pupils to enter "T" for "true" or "F" for "false." The printing of these letters sometimes results in a hybrid form halfway between "T" and "F." The teacher may not know whether the pupil really means to indicate "true" or "false," and may suspect that the pupil does not know, either.

To remedy this situation, some teachers require pupils to write out the words "true" and "false." Others tell pupils to use a "+" sign for "true" and a "0" for "false." An even better solution is to print the words "true" and "false" to the left of each statement, then direct learners to simply circle their choice.

Better true/false tests probe for understanding. Some of the best require pupils to look at several pieces of information at the same time and to answer related questions. For example, true/false tests can be used to assess pupils' abilities to grasp information presented in graphs, tables, and charts. An example of a true/false test that directs learners' attention to a table of information is presented in Figure 17–9.

Multiple-Choice Tests

Multiple-choice tests have several advantages. Unlike true/false tests, which give learners only two answer choices, multiple-choice tests provide three, four, or even five options. As a result, they can test pupils' abilities to recognize degrees of "correctness." Though the length of individual questions is typically longer than in true/false tests, multiple-choice questions still do not require a great deal of time to complete. Consequently, a given multiple-choice test can cover a fairly large body of content.

Multiple-choice tests reduce chances that a learner will get a high score as a result of guessing. This is true because there are many more answer options than in true/false tests. As is true of true/false tests, multiple-choice tests can be scored quickly. Systems are available to score such tests electronically.

There are difficulties associated with preparing and using multiple-choice tests. A good one takes time to prepare. It is not easy for teachers to think of good *distractors* (plausible incorrect answers). Also, older learners are often inclined to argue that several options may be correct. Most problems associated with multiple-choice tests can be avoided if teachers take care when preparing individual questions.

The part of the multiple-choice question that introduces the item is called the *stem*. The alternative answers are called the *options*. In a properly prepared multiple-choice item, the stem should provide learners with a context for answering, and should serve a focusing function. Consider these two examples:

1. Washington

    (a) is a common family name in France.

    (b) is the capital of the United States.

Name: _____

**Ages at Which the Average American Man and Woman
Married at Different Historical Times***

Year	Age of Average Man When He Married	Age of Average Woman When She Married
1890	26	24
1910	25	21
1930	24	21
1950	23	20
1970	23	21

Directions

This is a true/false test. Each statement refers to the table above. Look at the table before you decide on your answer. Circle "true" for true statements; circle "false" for false statements.

true   false   1. In 1890, the average man was older than the average woman at the time of marriage.

true   false   2. The smallest difference between the age of the average man and the average woman at the time of marriage was in the year 1950.

true   false   3. In 1970, the average man was younger at the time of his marriage than the average man in 1910.

true   false   4. The greatest difference between the age of the average man and the average woman at the time of marriage occurred in the years 1930 and 1970.

true   false   5. This chart tells us that men married in 1890 at younger average ages than in 1970.

FIGURE 17–9
Sample true/false test.

*Data are adapted from the U.S. Bureau of the Census. *Historical Statistics of the United States, Colonial Times to 1970,* Bicentennial ed., Part I. Washington, DC: U.S. Government Printing Office, 1975, p. 19.

(c)   is a province of Canada.

(d)   is a state on the Mississippi River.

2.   The capital city of the United States is called

(a)   Ottawa.

(b)   Washington.

(c)   New York.

(d)   Richmond.

The first example provides the pupil with no clues about the kind of information the teacher is seeking. Is the purpose to identify a name, a capital, a province, or a state? The second example indicates clearly that the task is to identify a capital city. It is a much better item.

The options provided should be plausible. When some options make no logical sense, pupils will respond to the correct answer as much because of the nonsensical options as because of their knowledge of the content. For example, few pupils would have difficulty responding correctly to this item:

What is the softest?

(a) cotton candy

(b) brick

(c) steel

(d) window glass

Stems and options are stated positively in good multiple-choice items. Negatives can be very confusing. Note this example:

Which is not a statement correctly describing the duties of a governor?

(a) The job of a governor cannot be said to include the supervision of his or her

staff.

(b) The governor does not serve as a member of the state supreme court.

(c) The governor is not uninvolved in the affairs of a political party.

(d) The governor is not absent from ceremonial events.

When preparing multiple-choice items, the teacher should take care to assure that each stem has a single correct answer. The correct answer should not be a matter of opinion or judgment. Consider this example:

The very best chili peppers are grown in the state of

(a) Arizona.

"I've spent years in a school, but I still don't do well on standardized tests."

(b) Texas.

(c) New Mexico.

(d) California.

Obviously, the question of which state has the best chili peppers is a matter of opinion. It is not something that can be adequately tested by a forced-choice test. Matters of opinion and debate are much better handled in essays, which allow pupils to support their claims with logic and evidence.

Finally, when preparing multiple-choice questions, teachers need to exercise care in locating the correct answer. Placement of this answer should vary. There is a tendency for some teachers to have either option (b) or (c) be the correct answer in a four-option multiple-choice item. Evidence suggests that pupils who are guessing tend to answer (b) or (c). If too many correct answers are in those two places, these learners may receive higher scores than they deserve.

Matching Tests

Matching tests are especially useful when the teacher wants to test pupils' understandings of new terms. They are easy to construct and correct. They can focus learners' attention on important vocabulary terms they will need to know as they continue to work in a given unit of study. Matching tests cannot assess as broad a range of content as either true/false or multiple-choice tests. A matching test focuses exclusively on terms associated with a limited topic area.

Matching tests consist of two columns of information, one containing the definitions, the other containing the terms. Pupils match the definition with the term it describes. Blanks occur before each numbered definition, and letters of the alphabet precede each term. The teacher instructs learners to place the letter of the correct term in the blank before its definition.

Measurement specialists prefer to set up matching tests so that definitions are on the left and terms are on the right. This practice encourages the learner to read the definition first and then to look for the term. The definition provides specific clues and makes the search for an appropriate term a relatively focused activity. The alternative arrangement causes pupils to look at individual terms and then to look through all of the definitions. This is less efficient than the preferred format.

It is essential that there be at least 25 percent more terms in the right column than there are definitions in the left. If there are *exactly* the same number of items in each column, then a pupil who misses one item is forced to miss two. [If the answer for item 1 is (a) and item 2 is (b), and a pupil selects (b) for item 1, he or she has by default also missed item 2.] Adding choices makes it possible for the student to miss only one item if one of the additional distractors is chosen.

The entire matching test should be printed on a single page. Teachers sometimes prepare a matching test in which the right-hand column of terms is so much longer than the left-hand column of definitions that the right-hand column goes over to a second page. When this happens, some pupils invariably fail to notice the terms on the second page and consequently their scores suffer. If length of the terms column is a problem, it is better to split the matching quiz into two separate tests, each of which contains all items on a single page.

A properly formatted matching test is shown in Figure 17–10.

Completion Tests

Completion tests are easy to construct. They eliminate guessing, and can sample a variety of content. However, an individual completion test does not usually cover as much content as either a true/false test or a multiple-choice test. Pupils must write responses in their own handwriting, which is a slower process than noting choices on true/false or multiple-choice forms.

Teachers must prepare completion items carefully. Unless an item is formatted properly, more than one answer may be logically defensible. Attention to the wording of the items can greatly diminish this problem. Consider these two versions of a completion item:

1. The navigator sailing for Spain who many consider to be the discoverer of America was _____ .
2. The name by which we know the navigator who sometimes is called the discover of America is _____ .

The first version has many logical answers. For example, pupils who answered "a man," "a native of Italy," "A Genoan," or even "a sailor" might make a case for the

---

Name: _____

Topic: Resources

Directions

This is a matching test. Look at the definitions on the left. Then look at the words on the
right. Find the word on the right that matches each definition. Place the letter before the
word in the blank before its definition. There is only one correct answer for each definition.

_____ 1. Materials people take from the earth to
meet needs and wants.

_____ 2. Resources that cannot be replaced.

_____ 3. The source of fuels such as gasoline and
oil

_____ 4. Special skills, knowledge, and tools people
use to create things to make life better.

_____ 5. Resources that can be replaced.

_____ 6. Known supplies of a resource that are
available for use.

a. human resources

b. coal

c. natural resources

d. technology

e. petroleum

f. geology

g. renewable resources

h. nonrenewable resources

i. reserves

FIGURE 17–10
A sample matching test.

correctness of their answer. The second version provides a better focus. It limits
the range of probable answers, as a well-written completion item should do.

There are other correction problems associated with completion items. Para-
mount among these is the issue of spelling. Some teachers claim that since the
major concern is mastery of content, then logically little attention need be paid to
spelling. However, elementary social studies teachers are charged with teaching
spelling as well as social studies. They often find themselves in a quandary when
dealing with completion-test responses. To take too much off for spelling tends to
turn the exercise into a spelling test. To take nothing off for misspelled words may
convey to pupils that spelling is only important during the spelling period. The
teacher may resolve this in part by fixing the amount to be deducted for spelling
errors and informing pupils beforehand.

Another dilemma facing the teacher who corrects completion tests is synonyms.
If the correct word for a blank is *hat*, should the word *cap* be accepted? What
about *chapeau* or *bandanna?* Teachers agonize over how far they should go in
accepting deviations from the word they have in their correction key. The issue is
important because doubts as to what constitutes a correct answer can undermine
a test's reliability.

Some teachers resolve these problems by using a modified form of the basic
completion test. This version provides learners with the usual sentences and
blanks to be filled in, and in addition provides a list of words at the bottom of the
page. This list includes both answers and distractors. Pupils are told to find the
correct word at the bottom of the page and to write it in the blank where it

Name: _____

Test Topic: Climate

Directions

This is a completion test. You are to fill in each blank. Read the words at the bottom of the page, select the word that belongs in each blank, and write it there. You will not use all of the words at the bottom of the page. Every blank has a different correct word; no word at the bottom of the page will be used more than one time.

The four basic elements of climate are temperature, precipitation, air pressure, and ___1___ . The amount of direct sunlight a place receives depends on its ___2___ . Little direct sunlight is received in ___3___ latitudes. Places in high latitudes are generally colder than places in ___4___ latitudes. Most of the United States is located in the ___5___ latitudes. Land surfaces cool more ___6___ than water surfaces. Air temperatures are ___7___ at high elevations than at low elevations. Temperatures are too low for the air to hold much ___8___ in high latitudes.

Choose answers from this list.

wind	latitude	low	cooler	dusts
snow	longitude	hotter	slowly	rapidly
moisture	high	middle	clouds	

FIGURE 17–11
A Sample completion test.

belongs. Since the words are there for pupils to see, they can be held accountable for spelling (simply a matter of correct copying). No synonyms are accepted because learners are directed to use only the words at the bottom of the page. See Figure 17–11 for an example of such a test.

General guidelines for preparing a completion test are as follows:

1. Use only *one* blank per item.
2. Place the blank at or near the end of the item. This provides pupils with context clues.
3. Avoid using *a* or *an* before the blank. These words will cue pupils to look either for a word beginning with a vowel or for a word beginning with a consonant.
4. Avoid placing blanks in statements that have been extracted verbatim from the textbook. Such a practice encourages pupils to focus on textbook wording rather than on textbook content.

USING EVALUATION RESULTS TO IMPROVE INSTRUCTION

Evaluation results have uses beyond the assessment of individual pupil progress. They also help teachers to evaluate the quality of their own instruction. When evaluation results are used for this purpose, scores of all learners are viewed collectively.

Suppose a grade-five teacher gives pupils a test over the general topic of the regions of the United States. The test includes twenty-eight items. Seven items focus on each of these subtopics: (1) climate, (2) topography, (3) natural resources, and (4) population characteristics. After analyzing pupils' scores, the teacher finds that the following percentages of learners had missed three or more questions in each subtopic area:

- climate — 10 percent
- topography — 12 percent
- natural resources — 25 percent
- population characteristics — 55 percent

These figures indicate that class members experienced the most difficulty with content related to population characteristics. Many also missed items associated with natural resources. These results might lead the teacher to provide additional instruction to clear up misunderstandings related to both these topics. Additionally, the next time this teacher teaches this content (perhaps the following year to a new class), he or she may reorganize and improve the material.

Teachers who make systematic use of their evaluation results are in a position to refine their instructional plans rationally. These results tell them what they are doing well and what areas might be presented more effectively another time. Over a period of several years, weak spots in the instructional program can be converted to areas of strength.

KEY IDEAS IN SUMMARY

1. Informal evaluation depends on teachers' observations of many different kinds of pupil performances. Often learners do not even know they are being evaluated. Informal evaluation occurs at all grade levels. Since informal techniques do not require learners to have well-developed reading and writing skills, they are particularly favored by primary-grades teachers.

2. There are many kinds of informal evaluation techniques. Among these are teacher observations, teacher-pupil discussions, pupil-produced tests, My Favorite Idea displays, learner-produced headlines and newspaper articles, word pairs, alphabet review games, mystery word scrambles, and anagrams.

3. Good recordkeeping is essential if teachers are to derive maximum benefit from informal evaluation procedures. Daily performance checklists keep track of pupils' progress. The teacher may later transfer relevant information to a social studies cumulative record form.

4. Formal evaluation includes tests by teachers and standardized tests prepared by commercial firms. Formal evaluation techniques are more common in the

middle and upper grades than in the primary grades because most such procedures require learners to have mastered basic reading and writing skills.

5. Rating scales and checklists provide information about very specific pupil behaviors. Rating scales may be used to make judgments about several levels of performance quality. Most checklists only indicate whether a pupil can or cannot do something.

6. Attitude inventories can be used to provide information about learners' reactions to various school subjects and to various parts of the social studies program. They require pupils to rate their relative interest in provided alternative selections.

7. Essay tests are most common in the upper grades. They require well-developed writing skills and provide learners with opportunities to put together isolated pieces of information in a meaningful way.

8. True/false tests can cover a broad range of content. Some critics say they encourage guessing. Their use is limited to testing content that can be described in terms of absolutes (something must be clearly true or false).

9. Multiple-choice tests help eliminate pupil guessing while allowing the teacher to sample a wide selection of content. Writing good multiple-choice items, however, is a difficult task that requires considerable time and composing skill.

10. Matching tests are useful for testing pupils' grasp of associations. All material for a given matching test should be printed on a single sheet of paper. Care must be exercised to design these tests in such a way that a pupil who misses one item does not automatically miss two.

11. Completion tests pose correction problems for teachers. To what extent should synonyms be accepted? How many misspellings should be tolerated? Some teachers prefer a test type that includes a list of words from which pupils are to select their answers. This reduces correction problems.

12. The evaluation of learning has two important functions. First, it provides a basis for assessing the progress of individual learners. Second, analysis of score patterns of a class can indicate to the teacher areas where instruction was not effective, suggesting areas to cover in a class discussion that reviews content covered in the test. It can also suggest needed modifications in the teacher's instructional plan when the same content is taught again to other pupils.

POSTTEST

Answer each of the following true/false questions.

1. An essay test is a wise choice when the teacher wishes to test less sophisticated thinking abilities, for example recall of specific place names.

2. It is possible for the teacher to use results of the same test to judge the effectiveness of parts of the instructional program as well as to judge the levels of performance of individual pupils.

3. It would be possible to design an attitude inventory that would gather information about pupils' relative interest in studying about (a) Brazil, (b) Mexico, (c) Australia, (d) France, and (e) Kenya.

4. A good multiple-choice item stem gives pupils a general idea of the category of information they should be looking for as they examine the listed choices.

5. A true/false test gives pupils better opportunities to recognize degrees of correctness than does a multiple-choice test.

QUESTIONS

1. What differentiates formal evaluation from informal evaluation?

2. What are three examples of informal evaluation techniques?

3. What kind of record might a teacher keep of information derived through informal evaluation?

4. What are three examples of formal evaluation techniques?

5. How can evaluation results help a teacher improve instructional practices?

6. Defend the use of informal evaluation in the upper grades as part of a total evaluation scheme involving both informal and formal techniques.

7. When taking a formal evaluation test, pupils know they are being assessed. Often they are not aware of being judged when the teacher uses informal techniques. Is this fair?

8. Describe how evaluation procedures might differ in a kindergarten class, a third-grade class, and a sixth-grade class.

9. If someone were to argue against the use of essay tests on the grounds that teachers correct the quality of the handwriting rather than the quality of the content, how would you respond?

10. You are asked to prepare a total evaluation program for a single grade level of your choice. What will be your mix of informal and formal evaluation techniques? How will you defend your selection?

EXTENDING UNDERSTANDING AND SKILL

1. Interview several teachers at a grade level you wish to teach about their recordkeeping procedures. Find out how they keep track of information about

pupils' performance when using informal evaluation techniques. If possible, make copies of some of their forms. Share these with your instructor and class members.

2. Read a textbook on the evaluation of learning. Prepare note cards on three or four formal evaluation techniques not mentioned in this chapter. Orally present these to the class.

3. Review several school social studies textbooks prepared for a grade level you would like to teach. Look at the ends of the chapters. What kinds of tests are provided? Are there other suggestions relating to evaluation? Summarize your findings on a chart. Present it to your instructor for review.

4. Visit someone who teaches a grade level you would like to teach. Ask about the tests used in the social studies program. If possible, bring back samples of formal tests. Present an oral report to the class, and share copies with other students who may have an interest in the same grade level. Take care to point out the numbers of items on the tests and the tests' several levels of difficulty.

5. Begin a resource file of informal assessment techniques. Gather information from interviews of teachers and professors of education, from professional journals, from evaluation textbooks, and from other sources. Do not include any of the informal techniques mentioned in this chapter. Try to find at least ten techniques appropriate for assessing pupils' social studies learning at a grade level you would like to teach. Share this material with your instructor.

REFERENCES

EBEL, R. L., AND D. A. FRISBIE. *Essentials of Educational Measurement*, 4th ed. Englewood Cliffs, NJ: Prentice-Hall, 1986.

GRONLUND, N. E., AND R. L. LINN. *Measurement and Evaluation in Teaching*, 6th ed. New York: Macmillan, 1990.

UNITED STATES BUREAU OF THE CENSUS. *Historical Statistics of the United States, Colonial Times to 1970*, Bicentennial ed., Part 1. Washington, DC: U.S. Government Printing Office, 1975.

SUPPLEMENTAL READING

ALLEN, W. H., AND R. L. VAN SICKLE. "Learning Teams and Low Achievers." *Social Education* (January 1984), pp. 60–64.

ANDERSON, L. W. *Assessing Affective Characteristics in the School*. Boston: Allyn & Bacon, 1981.

ARMSTRONG, D. G. "Evaluation: Conscience of the Social Studies." *The Social Studies* (March/April 1977), pp. 62–64.

Blackey, R. "Bull's Eye: A Teacher's Guide for Developing Student Skill in Responding to Essay Items." *Social Education* (October 1988), pp. 464–66.

Muir, S., and C. Wells. "Informal Evaluation." *The Social Studies* (May/June 1983), pp. 95–97.

Toppino, T. C., and H. A. Brochin. "Learning from Tests: The Case of the True-False Examination." *Journal of Educational Research* (November/December 1989), pp. 119–24.

SUBJECT INDEX

Absolute location, 359
Activity cards, 135, 139
Aesthetic values, 222, 197, 198
Affective domain, 92
Affective learning, 94
Aims, 87
Alcohol fuels, 305
Alphabet Review Game, 448
Alphabetizing, 400
Ambience, 414, 415
American Civil Liberties Union, 247
American economic system, 49
American Forum for Global Education, 257
American Memory: A Report on the Humanities in American Schools, 170
Anagram, 449, 450
Analemma, 349
Annie and the Old One, 74
Anthropology, 71–78, 82
Appleworks, 332
Aquarius, 333
Archaelogy and prehistory, 72
Ashanti to Zulu: African Traditions, 74
Assigned roles group, 148, 164
Attention span, 110
Attitude inventories, 456, 469
Attorney, 242
Audiodiscs, 337

Balch Institute for Ethnic Studies, 293

Basic legal concepts, 233
Beginning class, 419
Better Business Bureau, 247
Bill of Rights, 231, 233
Biodegradable, 310–12
Bradley Commission on History in Schools, 35, 40, 58
Brainstorming, 181
    rules, 181, 182
Broderbund Software, 334
Bulletin board, 417
Bureau of Census, 7
Buzz session, 152

Capital resources, 53
Case studies, 237–42, 248, 260
    debriefing, 242
    preparation, 239
    presentation, 241
    selection, 238
Cases: A Resource Guide for Teaching About the Law, 237
Categories of economic systems, 49
CD ROM, 338, 339
CD ROM Review, 338
Center for Migration Studies, 293
Center for the Study of Ethnic Publications, 293
Characteristics of book chapters, 400
Checklists, 469
Children's games, 263

Children's literature, 74, 286, 309
Children's Software, 333
Chlorofluorocarbons, 303
Citizen participation, 25
Citizenship education, 6–8
　knowledge, 10
　skills, 10
　values, 11
Clarifying values, 200
Clarity, 431
Classroom control difficulties, 412
Classroom debate, 154–56, 165
　sequence, 155
Classroom discipline
　basic principles, 425–27, 437
　causes of misbehavior, 426
　consequences of misbehavior, 427
　consistency, 427
　frequency, 423
　private correction, 425
　problems, 437
　purpose, 422
　serious problems, 427
　teacher responses, 437
Classroom management, 436
Cloze procedure, 392–95, 407
　directions, 392, 393
　guidelines, 394
Cognitive domain, 92
Command economies, 49–50
Communication process, 277
Community resources, 246
Comparative political systems, 62
Completion tests, 465–67
　guidelines, 467
Computers, 324–36
　arguments for use, 326
　aspects of use, 328
　cautionary arguments, 326, 327
　databases, 331
　electronic spreadsheets, 331
　finding software, 333, 334
　increasing instructional options, 324–30
　integration with instruction, 335, 339
　limitations, 327
　teaching specific content, 332
　word processing, 330
Concept attainment, 121, 137
Concept attributes, 137

Concept formation/diagnosis, 123, 138
Concepts, 120–24, 137
　conjunctive, 121
　disjunctive, 121
　relational, 121
Conformal maps, 350–53
Constitutional Rights Foundation, 236
Consumer economics, 49
Consumer law, 234
Consumer Law Resource Kit, 236
Content of learning, 128
Content sources, 30
Controversial issues, 155, 242–43
Cooperative learning, 160–64, 165
　computing team scores, 162
Creative thinking, 181, 190
Criminal law, 233
Criterion-referenced assessment, 442, 443
Critical thinking, 182, 190,
Cross Country USA, 333
Cultural bias, 282
Cultural change, 74
Cultural contact, 280
Cultural deficit, 277
Cultural heritage, 281
Cultural perspectives, 290
Cultural respect, 279
Culture, 73
Cumulative records, 451
Curriculum Task Force of the National Commission
　on Social Studies in the Schools, 58
Curriculum
　kindergarten, 18
　grade 1, 18
　grade 2, 19
　grade 3, 19
　grade 4, 19
　grade 5, 19
　grade 6, 19
　grade 7, 20
　grade 8, 21

Daily performance progress checklists, 451
Daily schedule, 417
Data retrieval chart, 74, 75, 178, 190, 262
Decision making, 86, 186
Deforestation, 302, 316
Discrepant event, 179
Dogsong, 74

Domains of learning, 114
Drug and alcohol abuse, 78
During reading stage, 373, 406
During reading techniques, 376–81

Earth-sun relationships, 368
Economics, 48–55
Educating for global competence, 256, 270
Education Index, 292
Educational activities, 334
Elementary globes, 348
Energy issues, 304–07
Energy sources, 316
Environmental education goals, 307
Environmental and energy awareness, 307–15
Environmental and energy goals, 316
Environmental issues, 300, 315
Equal areas maps, 353–54
Equal roles group, 146, 164
Equipment storage, 417
Equity, 275
Essay tests, 457, 458, 469
    guidelines, 458
Ethnic Cultures of America Calendar, 293
Ethnocentric, 71
Evaluation functions, 468
Evaluation results usage, 467, 468
Expanding horizons, 16
External validity, 40, 55

Family law, 234
Field trip, 247
Firmness, 431
Floor space, 415, 416
Focus questions, 23
Formal evaluation, 454–68
Frustration reading level, 394
Fry Readability Graph, 388–90, 395, 407
    directions, 391

Gender discrimination, 278
Generalizations, 137
Genetic deficit, 277
Geographic Alliance Network, 48
Geography, 41–48
Gifted and talented pupils, 101
Girl Who Loved Wild Horses, The, 286
Global education
    contributions emphasis, 261, 268

Global education, continued
    emphases, 256, 267
    experience emphasis, 260, 261, 268
    intercultural emphasis, 261, 268
    integration, 258
    issues, 268
    monocultural emphasis, 258–60, 268
    personal emphasis, 264–66, 268
Global warming, 301, 315
Globes, 346–49, 366
    disadvantages, 366
    limitations, 347
    parts, 349
    types, 366
Goals, 88
Goals of learning, 129
Golden Spike, The: Building America's First
        Transcontinental Railroad, 333
Government, 60
Government and governmental processes, 62
Graphic post-organizers, 381
Greenhouse effect, 301
Grolier Electronic Publishing, 334
Group instruction, 164
Group learning
    advantages, 144
    difficulties, 145
Guidelines for Geographic Education: Elementary
        and Secondary Schools, 57

Handicapped pupils, 100
Headlines, 447
Heuristic function, 404
Historical events, 217
History, 34–35
History and social science education, 8
    knowledge, 12
    skills, 12
    values, 12
History Matters, 40, 41
Horizon ring, 349
Human brain, 372
Human evolution, 72
Human resources, 53
Human-environmental interactions, 42
Hydropower, 304

Identifying major ideas, 381, 382
Imaginative function, 406

Immigration History Research Center, 293
In-class isolation, 433
Independent reading level, 398
Index, 400
Individualization, 120
Individualized instruction, 128, 138
Inducing a generalization, 124–26, 138
Informal evaluation, 444–51, 468
    cautions, 445
Inquiry, 175
Inquiry approaches, 190
Institute of Texan Cultures, 293
Institutions, 66
Instructional objectives, 88–92, 113
    audience, 89
    behavior, 90
    conditions, 91
    degree, 91
Instructional planning, 112
Instructional planning decisions, 99
Instructional reading level, 394
Instructional units, 114
Instrumental function, 401
Interaction frames, 383
Interactional function, 403
Interactive videodisc, 337
Intermediate globes, 348, 349
Internal validity, 40, 55
Interpreting information on maps and globes,
    364
Interrelationships among learning domains, 97
Interviews with history, 333
Involving others, 434
ISIS—Women's International Information and
    Communication Services, 294
Issues, values, and consequences analysis, 214

Jigsaw, 160
    expert groups, 161
Joint Committee on Geographic Education, 48
Joint Council on Economic Education, 54
Judges, 233
Jury, 233

Knowledge about content, 101
Knowledge about learners, 100
Knowledge about resource materials, 102
Knowledge about teaching methods, 101
Knowledge production, 175

Language-based vocabulary and reading strategy, 388
Language functions, 401–06
Law in Action units, 237
Law in a Free Society, 236
Law-related education, 231, 247
    goals, 231, 232, 248
    questions, 232
    resources, 248
    sources of information, 235
Laws, 230
Lawyers, 233
Learning activity packages, 129, 132–34, 138
Learning acts, 334
Learning centers, 130–32, 138
Learning checklists, 455, 456
    guidelines, 455
Learning contracts, 135, 139
Learning styles, 100, 282
Learning together, 161
Legal system, 233
Legend of Bluebonnet, The, 286
Lesson pacing, 420
Lesson plans, 108–12, 114
    allocating time, 111
    checking understanding, 110
    determining entry point, 109
    eliciting behaviors, 111
    instructional approaches, 108
    instructional materials, 111
    introducing new content, 110
    lesson objectives, 108, 109
    management of learners, 111,
    motivating learners, 109
Location, 41, 42
Loss of priviledge, 433

Makeup of wasted classroom time, 434
Map and globe skills, 354–66
    absolute location, 359
    direction, 358
    earth-sun relationships, 363
    interpreting information on maps and globes, 364
    relative location, 360
    scale, 355, 356
    sequence, 354
    shapes, 355
    symbols, 356–58
Maps, 350–354
    conformal, 350

Maps, *continued*
  distortion, 352, 353, 366
  limitations, 350
  Mercator projection, 351
Market economies, 50
Matching tests, 464, 465, 469
Materials storage, 417
Metacognition, 171, 190
Method of learning, 129
Micro Ed, 334
Microsoft Works, 332
Milliken, 334
Missouri Department of Conservation, 306
Mock trials, 242, 248
  debriefing, 245
  enactment, 244
  preparation, 243
Montreal Protocol on Substances that Deplete the
    Ozone Layer, 303
Moral action, 199
Moral behavior, 197, 222
Moral decision making, 199, 213, 223
Moral development stages, 208–10, 223
  instructional relativism stage, 209
  interpersonal concordance stage, 209
  law and order stage, 209
  punishment and obedience stage, 208
  social-contract legalistic stage, 209
  universal ethical principle stage, 210
Moral dilemma discussions, 210, 211
  discussing reasoning, 212
  formulating a conclusion, 212
  introduction, 211
  tentative responses, 212
Moral judgment, 198, 208
Moral sensitivity, 198
Moral values, 198, 222
Motivation, 5, 109
  identification motive, 109
  novelty, 109
  success, 109
Movement, 43
Multicultural education, 71
  classroom procedures, 282
  goals, 279–82
  multiple-perspectives approach, 284, 289–91,
    295
  program types, 277
  single-group studies, 284–89, 295

Multicultural education, *continued*
  teacher attitudes, 282
  teacher obligations, 278
Multipass reading, 379, 380
Multiple-choice tests, 461–64, 469
My favorite idea, 446
Mystery word scramble, 448, 449

National Center for Economic Education for
    Children, 54
National Council for Geographic Education, 41, 48
National Council for History Education, 40
National Council for the Social Studies, 6, 41
National Geographic Society, 55, 338
National Institute for Citizen Education in the Law,
    237
National Women's History Project, 294
Natural resources, 53
Nature with children, 312
Newspaper articles, 447
Newspaper Education, 247
Nonrenewable fuels, 304
Nonverbal signals, 429
Norm-referenced assessment, 442

Opposing Viewpoints Series, 236
Oral history, 260
Organization for Equal Education of the Sexes,
    Inc., 293
Out-of-date words, 386, 387
Ozone depletion, 303, 304
Ozone layer, 303, 316

Parent conference, 434, 435
Parental assistance, 432
Participant observer, 73
Parts of the textbook, 395
Perceived labor market deficit, 277
Personal belongings storage, 418
Personal economics, 49
Personal function, 404
Photovoltaic effect, 305
Physical arrangement of the classroom, 414
Place, 42
Planned redundancy, 110
Planning, 86
Planning for instruction, 22–25
Political science, 60–66, 82
Political theory, 62

Population Reference Bureau, 294
Postreading stage, 373, 406
Postreading techniques, 381–385
Prereading stage, 373, 406
Prereading techniques, 374–376
Problem solving, 147, 183, 190
Problem-solving conference, 436
Problem-solving education, 9
    knowledge, 12
    skills, 14
    values, 15
Professor Noah's Spaceship, 309
Prosocial behavior, 196, 222
Providing assistance, 420
Proximity control, 429
Psychology, 78–82
Psychomotor domain, 95, 96
Public Affairs Pamphlet Series, 237
Punishment, 433–35
Pupil conference, 431
Pupil questions, 180
Pupil-produced tests, 446
Puzzles, 450

Quiet word to the individual, 431

Rank ordering, 201
Rate of change, 37
Rate of learning, 128
Rating scales, 454, 469
Readability issues, 385
Readiness globes, 347, 348
Reading study guides
    during-reading stage, 380, 381
    postreading stage, 383, 384
    pre-reading stage, 376
Recordkeeping, 451–54, 468
Redirecting pupil activity, 429
Regions, 43
Regulatory function, 403
Reinforcing productive behavior, 429
Relationships within and among groups, 67
Relative location, 360
Removing pupil from classroom, 431, 434
Renewable plants, 304, 305
Representational function, 404, 405
ReQuest, 375
    steps, 375, 376
Responding to misbehavior, 422–36

Role playing, 156, 165, 204
    debriefing, 158
    discussion and evaluation, 157
    enactment, 157
    reenactment, 157
Routines and procedures, 421, 422
Rule remainder, 431

Scarcity, 48, 55
Scientific method, 175
Self-acceptance, 78
Self-concept, 78
Self-monitoring study behavior, 430
Self-understanding, 30, 204, 214
Sex-equity
    goals, 279–82
    myths, 278
    purposes, 278
    sources of information, 293
Simulation, 158, 159, 165, 245
    activity, 159
    debriefing, 159
    overview, 159
    training, 159
Situational assistance, 430
Small group activities, 381
Social Education, 41, 292, 333
Social problems, 30
Social studies
    curriculum, 16–22
    purposes, 6, 25
Social studies for the young learner, 41
Social Studies School Services, 158, 242
Social Studies, The, 41, 292
Sociology, 66–71, 82
Solar energy, 304
Space management, 413–18, 436
Spatial patterns, 55
Special Commission on Youth Education for
    Citizenship, 236
Special needs students, 100
Specialized vocabulary, 387, 388
Stages of the reading process, 406
Standards of achievement, 443
Stanford Program on International and
    Cross-Cultural Education, 257
Sterotypes, 288, 294
Storytelling, 74
Stratified groups, 67

Structure of knowledge, 31, 55
   concepts, 33
   facts, 32
   generalizations, 33, 34
Structured overview, 374, 375
Supporting information, 382
Supporting self-control, 429, 430
SVE, 334
Systematic management planning, 413

Table of contents, 395
Table of specifications, 92
Task Force on Scope and Sequence, 6, 8, 17, 25, 28
Taxonomy of Educational Objectives: Handbook I: Cognitive Domain, 92
Teacher characteristics, 423, 424
Teacher expectations, 283
Teacher observation, 445
Teacher-pupil discussion, 446
Teacher's desk placement 416
Teaching and Computers, 333
Teams Achievement Divisions, 162
Textbook features, 407
T.H.E. Journal, 333
Thinking abilities, 189
Thinking aloud, 171
Thinking skills, 170
Tiananmen Square, 255
Time and chronology, 37
Time management, 418–21
Timelines, 37
Tom Snyder Productions, 334
Toxic waste, 302, 303, 316
Traditional economies, 49
Traffic patterns, 416
Transitions, 419
True/false tests, 460, 461, 469
   guidelines, 460
Turning on Learning: Five Approaches for Multicultural Teaching-Plans for Race, Class, Gender, and Disability, 293

Tutoring groups, 146, 164

Unicorn Software, 334
Unfamiliar vocabulary, 386
Unit format, 104–08
   describing intended learning outcomes, 104
   identifying prerequisite knowledge, 104
   organizing the unit, 105
   reviewing the new unit, 105
Unit planning, 103
Unit plans
   identifying the grade level, 104
   identifying the title or theme, 104
United States Constitution, 231, 233
United States Prepares for Its Future, The: Global Perspectives in Education, 256, 270
Upper Midwest Women's History Center for Teachers, The, 293
Using planning information, 102
Using pupil's name in lesson, 429

Value conflicts, 207, 281
Value dilemmas, 204
Values, 94, 197
Values clarification, 222
Values situation role playing, 203, 222
Videocassettes, 336, 337, 339
Videodiscs, 337, 339
Visual frameworks, 377–79
Visualizing thinking, 172
Vocabulary difficulties, 385
Voluntary groups, 66

Wall space, 417
WEAL: Women's Equity Action League, 294
Wind power, 305
Word pairs, 447, 448
World's Women, The: A Profile, 294
World Watch Institute, 306
Writing skills, 401

NAME INDEX

Abraham, K., 84n
Ackerman, P., 141n
Alexander, P., 192n
Allen, J., 50, 58n
Allen, J. P., 297n
Allen, W., 471n
Anderson, L., 439n, 471n
Armstrong, D., 50, 58n, 96, 116n, 341n, 471n
Aronson, E., 439n
Austin, G., 141n

Baker, C., 409n
Baldwin, D., 84n
Baptiste, H., 297n
Barr, R., 28n,
Barth, J., 28n, 84n
Bash, M., 430, 439n
Berelson, B., 58n
Beyer, B., 141n, 186, 192n, 193n, 396, 401, 402, 409n
Blackey, R., 472n
Bloom, B., 92, 116n
Boehm, R., 58n
Bonar, D., 250n
Borich, G., 87, 116n
Bormuth, J., 409n
Brand, M., 84n
Brochin, H., 472n

Broder, D., 196, 225n
Brophy, J., 283, 297n, 417, 424, 430, 439n
Brown, L., 301, 302, 318n, 319n
Blum, A., 318n
Bruner, J., 32, 141n
Budin, H., 342n

Callahan, R., 116n
Camp, B., 430, 439n
Charles, C., 439n
Cheney, L., 170, 192n
Clark, C., 86, 116n
Cigler, B., 270n
Clements, B., 439n
Clements, D., 328
Cohen, E., 144, 148, 167n
Colman, P., 256, 257, 270n
Costa, A., 193
Craven, J., 396, 402, 409n
Cuban, L., 324, 341n
Culp, W., 168n

Damon, W., 225n
David, D., 369n
DePaola, T., 286
Derrico, P., 193n
Dewey, J., 175, 192n
Doyle, W., 86, 116n, 439n

The "n" following a page number indicates a bibliographic entry.

Drake, C., 271n
Duff, J., 341n
Duke, D., 439n
Dunn, K., 182, 192n
Dunn, R., 182, 192n
Dynneson, T., 84n

Ebel, R., 471n
Eisenberg, N., 225n
Emmer, E., 413, 439n
Englehart, M., 116n
Erickson, F., 277, 297n
Espenshade, E., 368n
Estes, R., 116n
Evans, C., 271n
Evertson, C., 439n

Flavin, C., 301, 304, 318n, 319n
Forsyth, A., 369n
Fraenkel, J., 121, 141n
Francis, A., 250n
Frisbie, D., 471n
Fry, E., 389, 409n
Furlong, M., 251n
Furst, E., 116n

Gael, P., 270n
Gagnon, P., 35, 58n
Garner, R., 192n
Gallup, G., 197, 225n
Gerlach, R., 250n
Gezi, F., 277, 297n
Gilstrip, R., 409n
Glenn, A., 328, 334,
Glaser, R., 141n
Goble, P., 286
Good, T., 283, 297n, 417, 439n
Goodnow, J., 141n
Grant, C., 278, 282, 293, 297n
Greenblatt, C., 168n
Greenhood, D., 369n
Griffin, S., 312, 318n
Gronlund, N., 455, 471n
Gross, R., 84n
Grotta, D., 341n
Grove, G., 270n
Gunter, M., 116n

Halliday, M., 401, 409n

Hamilton, V., 297n
Hardar, R., 116n
Harjo, L., 297n
Harmin, M., 92, 116n, 222, 225n
Hartoonian, H., 28n
Harvey, K., 297n
Hasan, R., 401, 409n
Hass, M., 369n
Hatcher, B., 369n
Heiman, M., 193n
Hendricks, R., 250n
Henriksen, P., 270n
Hentrel, B., 342n
Hess, R., 259n
Hickey, M., 242, 250n
Higgins, A., 225n
Hill, W., 116n
Hirsch, E., 170, 192n
Hoblitt, R., 410n
Hodge, W., 251n
Holubec, E., 167n
Horwitt, S., 8
Howe, L., 225n

Jackson, J., 297n
Jacobson, J., 301, 302, 318n
Jarolimek, J., 84n
Jenness, D., 58n
Johnson, D., 161, 162, 167n
Johnson, E., 84n
Johnson, R., 161, 162, 167n
Johnston, J., 342
Jones, F., 421, 439n
Jones, L., 439n
Jones, K., 168n
Jones, V., 439n
Joyce, B., 157, 167n

Katsh, M., 251n
Kauchak, D., 116n
Keil, F., 141n
Kendall, F., 297n
Kirschenbaum, H., 225n
Kniep, W., 28n
Knowles, M., 141n
Kohlberg, L., 208, 210, 222, 223, 225n
Kounin, J., 413, 439n
Kracht, J., 58n, 225n
Krathwohl, D., 92, 116n

Krogh, S., 251n

Ladouse, G., 168n
Lambert, S., 342n
Lamprech, L., 250n
Lanegran, D., 58n
Larkin, J., 141n
Laughlin, M., 28n
Leacock, E., 298n
Leming, J., 8, 28n
Linglebach, J., 319n
Linn, R., 455, 471n
Lipman, M., 182, 192n

MacArthur, D., 350, 351
Manchester, W., 351, 368n
Manzo, R., 375, 409n
Martin, K., 369n
Masia, B., 116n
May, E., 58n
McFarland, M., 28n, 396, 402, 409n
McGowan, T., 5, 28n
McLean, G., 225n
McMahon, E., 251n
Melahn, D., 369n
Meckel, A., 439n
Merkle, D., 116n
Miles, M., 74, 84n
Monk, J., 58n
Moore, D., 410n
Morrill, R., 58n
Moshman, D., 251n
Muir, S., 472n
Murray, P., 250n
Musgrove, M., 74
Mussen, P., 225n

Natoli, S., 58n
Nickerson, R., 170, 193n
Northup, T., 328, 332, 333, 342

O'Brien, K., 309, 318n
Ochoa, A., 116n
O'Connor, M., 318n
Ogle, L., 409n
Olmstead, J., 144, 167n
Olson, A., 298n
O'Neil, J., 257, 270n
Orlich, D., 116n

Pagnoni, M., 328
Parise, J., 168n
Parker, W., 28n, 170, 193n, 396, 402, 409n
Paulsen, G., 74
Pendergast, R., 116n
Penna, A., 141n
Perkins, D., 170, 181, 193n
Peterson, P., 86, 116n
Pickles, J., 271n
Pogrow, S., 193n
Postel, S., 301, 318n
Poustay, E., 409n
Power, F., 225n
Pugnetti, G., 270n

Raths, L., 92, 116n, 222, 225n
Ravitch, D., 170, 193n
Rawitsch, D., 328, 334
Rest, J., 198, 222, 225n
Riedesel, C., 342n
Rist, R., 282, 297n
Rooze, G., 328, 332, 333, 342
Ropiequest, S., 342n
Roy, P., 167n, 168n
Ruggiero, V., 181, 193n
Ryan, K., 225n

Safa, H., 298n
Sanday, P., 298n
Sanford, J., 439n
Savage, T., 96, 116n, 341n, 439n
Schug, M., 325, 326, 342n
Schuncke, G., 251n
Schwab, J., 116n
Seager, J., 298n
Selen, R., 271n
Shaftel, F., 208, 225n
Shaftel, G., 208, 225n
Sharan, S., 168n
Sharan, Y., 168n
Shea, C., 303, 304, 305, 318n
Shermis, S., 28n
Shuster, S., 116n
Simon, S., 92, 116n, 222, 225n
Sisson, E., 310, 311, 318n
Slavin, R., 162, 167n, 168n
Sleeter, C., 278, 282, 293, 297n
Slomianko, J., 193n
Smith, E., 170, 193n

Smith, P., 5, 28n
Sowards, A., 313, 318n
Stansell, J., 388
Steffens, H., 410n
Steiner, G., 58n
Sterling, D., 298n
Sternberg, R., 141n
Stoner, D., 309, 318n
Strazzella, J., 251n
Suchman, J., 179, 193n
Sunal, C., 263, 270n
Sutton, A., 5, 28n

Taba, H., 32, 58n, 123, 141n
Talbot, B., 410n
Tanck, M., 141n
Taylor, P., 7, 8, 28n
Taylor, W., 392, 409n
Thayer, W., 297n
Thernstrom, S., 298n
Thomas, R., 250n

Toppino, T., 472n
Torney, J., 250n
Turner, E., 297n
Tyre, T., 342n

Van Sickle, R., 471n
Vermette, P., 168n
Vocke, D., 271n

Walton, S., 410n
Warash, B., 369n
Weaver, V., 271n
Weil, M., 157, 167n
Weinstein, C., 414, 439n
Wells, C., 472n
White, J., 141n
Wildsmith, B., 309
Worsham, M., 439n

Zabrucky, K., 410n